1991

Jefferson and Nature

JEFFERSON
and NATURE

An Interpretation

CHARLES A. MILLER

THE JOHNS HOPKINS UNIVERSITY PRESS

Baltimore and London

The Johns Hopkins University Press
701 West 40th Street
Baltimore, Maryland 21211
The Johns Hopkins Press Ltd., London

∞
The paper used in this publication meets
the minimum requirements of American
National Standard for Information Sciences—
Permanence of Paper for Printed Library
Materials, ANSI Z39.48-1984.

LIBRARY OF CONGRESS CATALOGING-IN-PUBLICATION DATA
Miller, Charles A. (Charles Allen), 1937–
  Jefferson and nature.
  Bibliography: p.
  Includes index.
  1. Jefferson, Thomas, 1743–1826—Views on nature.
2. Nature. I. Title.
E332.2.M53   1988   973.4'6'0924   87-29842
ISBN 0-8018-3593-3 (alk. paper)

Frontispiece: Jefferson at the Natural Bridge

Caleb Boyle, the obscure painter of this picture (1801), did not draw Jefferson from life, and it is not known whether he ever visited the Natural Bridge. Composing his painting from the works of others, Boyle nevertheless proclaimed the true character of his subject at the outset of Jefferson's presidency. The portrait shows Jefferson as both a man of the world and a publicist for the Natural Bridge, that "most sublime of Nature's works" in America. The small pile near the walking stick, if not rocks from the bridge, is perhaps the bones of a mammoth. The outsized portrait measures 96″ × 62″.

Courtesy Kirby Collection of Historical Paintings, Lafayette College, Easton, Pennsylvania. Quotation from NVa.24.

To my sister and brothers
ANN, JOHN, AND TOM

CONTENTS

ILLUSTRATIONS

Frontispiece: Jefferson at the Natural Bridge

PLATES

x · ILLUSTRATIONS

Abbreviations

BB   Edwin Morris Betts and James Adam Bear, Jr., eds., *The Family Letters of Thomas Jefferson*. Columbia, Mo., 1966.

BC   Julian P. Boyd and Charles T. Cullen, eds. *The Papers of Thomas Jefferson*. 21 vols. to date. Vols. 1–20 edited by Boyd; vol. 21 edited by Cullen. Princeton, 1950–. The Boyd-Cullen edition is used in this study wherever possible. After August 1791 (BC.XX) Jefferson's writings are cited to other sources.

C   Lester J. Cappon, ed. *The Adams-Jefferson Letters: The Complete Correspondence between Thomas Jefferson and Abigail and John Adams*. 2 vols. Chapel Hill, 1959.

CB   Gilbert Chinard, ed. *The Commonplace Book of Thomas Jefferson: A Repertory of His Ideas on Government*. Baltimore, 1926.

F   Paul Leicester Ford, ed. *The Writings of Thomas Jefferson*. 10 vols. New York, 1892–99. This edition of Ford should be distinguished from the reissue of the text in twelve volumes under the title *The Works of Thomas Jefferson* (Federal Edition) in 1904–5.

FB   Edwin M. Betts, ed. *Thomas Jefferson's Farm Book*. Charlottesville, 1976 (orig. 1953).

FBx   Washington Chauncey Ford, ed. *Thomas Jefferson Correspondence, Printed from the Originals in the Collections of William K. Bixby*. Boston, 1916.

GB   Edwin M. Betts, ed. *Thomas Jefferson's Garden Book, 1766–1824*. Philadelphia, 1944.

KP   Adrienne Koch and William Peden, eds. *The Life and Selected Writings of Thomas Jefferson*. New York, 1944.

LB   Andrew A. Lipscomb and Albert Ellery Bergh, eds. *The Writ-

ings of Thomas Jefferson. Memorial Edition. 20 vols. Washington, D.C., 1904.

LBi — Gilbert Chinard, ed. *The Literary Bible of Thomas Jefferson: His Commonplace Book of Philosophers and Poets.* Baltimore, 1928.

LC — Donald Jackson, ed. *Letters of the Lewis and Clark Expedition with Related Documents, 1783–1854.* 2d ed. 2 vols. Urbana, 1978.

LJ — Gilbert Chinard, ed. *The Letters of Lafayette and Jefferson.* Baltimore, 1929.

M — Dumas Malone. *Jefferson and His Time.* 6 vols. Boston, 1948–81.

NVa — Thomas Jefferson. *Notes on the State of Virginia.* Edited by William Peden. Chapel Hill, 1954.

Pdvr — Saul K. Padover, ed. *The Complete Jefferson; Containing His major Writings, Published and Unpublished, Except His Letters.* New York, 1943.

PJ — Merrill D. Peterson, ed. *The Portable Thomas Jefferson.* New York, 1975.

S — E. Millicent Sowerby, comp. *Catalogue of the Library of Thomas Jefferson.* 5 vols. Washington, D.C., 1952–59. Jefferson's books have Sowerby numbers, e.g., S.1057; references to quotations from Sowerby are to volume and page, e.g., S.IV.215.

JEFFERSON AND NATURE

Chapter I

JEFFERSON, NATURE, AND THE ENLIGHTENMENT

T O READ WIDELY in the papers of Thomas Jefferson is to be struck by a remarkable fact: the words "nature" and "natural" appear with great frequency, in countless contexts, and with many meanings. This study takes Jefferson at his words, his favorite words. It is an attempt to understand how he uses "nature" and "natural" and why he uses the two words so often.

"Nature" flourishes in Jefferson's writings from the earliest letters that have been preserved, in the 1760s, to his final statements in the 1820s. He was always the farmer, always the natural historian, always interested in natural theology and natural morality, always ready to base the political order on natural law and natural right. But as an avowed experimenter and a person outspoken against the constraints of "system"; as an exceptionally long-lived man with myriad interests, a man whose public consciousness began before the French and Indian War and ended after the Missouri Compromise; and as the author of tens of thousands of letters but of no papers that seemed to require a consistent use of the term, Jefferson deployed "nature" not as a bright thread that led through his intellectual universe but as an unpatterned fabric that enveloped it.

Although he was typical of his time and place in using "nature" in his writings, Jefferson uses the word more often, more variously, and more seriously than do other Americans of his era. The published papers of his contemporaries show that Jefferson wrote on nature when John Adams wrote on history and religion; that Jefferson wrote about natural law, while Madison seemed deliberately to avoid it; that Jefferson wrote on the natural sciences but Hamilton did not; and that Jefferson took nature far beyond George Washington's interests in farming and the western territories. Jefferson's only competitor in the use of "nature" was Benjamin Franklin, more than a generation older. Because Franklin's orientation was urban and Jefferson's was rural, Franklin explored natural philosophy, which could be studied in the city, and Jefferson explored natural history, which had to be studied in the field. Franklin's emblem is thus universal nature—lightning—while Jefferson's is particular nature—the Natural Bridge of Virginia.[1]

Jefferson and others of his age regarded nature as an active presence in the world, recalling the earliest nature in the Western tradition, the Roman goddess Natura, who "gave birth" (*natus*). "Nature" was also active in their language. Where a later era uses neutral words or the passive voice, Jefferson's "nature" is alive and animated. During the Revolution he recognized that no fort could be constructed at a site "if Nature has rendered it unfit." Nearly thirty years later, speculating on why the mammoth had vanished from the earth, he wrote: "Nature seems not to have provided other food sufficient for him." Late in life he exhorted a friend in the state legislature not to give up the campaign for a University of Virginia because "Nature will not give you a second life wherein to atone for the omissions of this."[2]

---

1. An experimental, systematic examination of the use of "nature" in the standard editions of the writings of the six men confirms Jefferson as the most active and wide-ranging writer on nature. A one-volume selection of the writings of all of them (except Washington), Adrienne Koch's *The American Enlightenment,* also confirms it. In Koch's *Power, Morals, and the Founding Fathers,* in which a chapter is devoted to each of the figures, the essay on Jefferson is the one most about nature. The same conclusion is reached by a reading of Lester J. Cappon, ed., *The Adams-Jefferson Letters;* Merrill D. Peterson, *John Adams and Thomas Jefferson;* and Adrienne Koch, *Jefferson and Madison.* Complete information on works cited in the footnotes by title only may be found in the select bibliography.

Two examples from Jefferson's *Notes on the State of Virginia* illustrate how compulsive he was and how relatively casual his correspondents were with the word: (1) The Virginia Declaration of Rights, drawn up in the spring of 1776 by George Mason, uses neither "nature" nor "natural" in the clause on religion. But Jefferson, describing the clause, says that the provision "declared [religion] to be a truth and a natural right." NVa.158. (2) Jefferson says that American Indians "lived principally on the spontaneous productions of nature." Speaking to the identical issue, his correspondent Charles Thomson writes that the Indians "depended for subsistence on . . . the spontaneous fruits of the earth." NVa.96, 202.

2. TJ to George Rogers Clark, 19 April 1780, BC.III.354; TJ to William Clark, 10 September 1809, LB.XII.320–22; TJ to Joseph C. Cabell, 31 January 1821, LB.XV.312. As to orthography—"nature" or "Nature"—it was common in the eighteenth century to capitalize nouns in English. It was equally common to be unpredictable in the practice. But since "Nature" was a quasi divinity in the Enlightenment, it was among the nouns most likely to be upper-cased in a world of otherwise almost random capitalization. Jefferson, who was remarkably consistent in his orthography, was also very sparing with upper-case letters, but he normally made an exception for "Nature." Typical is this juxtaposition: "There are places at which . . . the *laws* have said there shall be towns; but *Nature* has said there shall not." NVa.109 (emphasis in the original). Since the present study is based almost entirely on printed sources, and not all of these are trustworthy about original orthography, "nature" as it appears in this essay may not be the way

It is not only Jefferson's vast papers that are filled with nature. His library of sixty-five hundred volumes, the best map to the man's intellect, is filled with nature, too. This is the consequence both of a great interest in the sciences and of having amassed an unrivaled collection of Americana, which at the time had to do, inevitably, largely with nature. But the library is also evidence of how common nature was to Jefferson's world generally and, therefore, of how simple it was for him to adopt its language.[3]

Jefferson's use of the word "nature" is not only extensive in itself but, in an important way, different from "nature" as used by Europeans of the Enlightenment. Jefferson came to "know" nature in America in the way that Thoreau said he came to "know" beans at Walden Pond, by working with it day after day. Further, insofar as nature symbolized America in its entirety, nature *was* America for Jefferson. His interest in nature and his use of the word are therefore a form of nationalism. In Europe national sentiment was expressed through a common history, a royal family, a culture, or a literature. In America and for Jefferson it was expressed through, and as, nature.[4]

These initial observations suggest how the present essay differs from other studies of Jefferson. Most notably, it is grounded in irreducible data that Jefferson himself produced, his uses of a particular word. It is not controlled by an idea, either one of his own or one proposed by someone else. This is not to say that Jefferson's "nature" does not imply any ideas; it certainly does, a great many of them. But since these ideas emanate from or are drawn back to a single word, a study of Jefferson may legitimately be organized according to how he uses that word.[5]

A study of Jefferson and nature is not only an examination of language, however. It is also a study that consciously alters the angles of vision from which Jefferson is traditionally viewed. To see Jefferson through the lens of nature is to see a different man from the one examined under democracy, or reason, or as an "apostle of Americanism," or in connection with "the new nation," or in a biography styled "an intimate history."[6] These broad themes are of course valid ones around

---

Jefferson originally wrote it. Most quotations in the text have been modernized in spelling and, when needed, clarified in punctuation.

3. See E. Millicent Sowerby, comp., *Catalogue of the Library of Thomas Jefferson*.

4. Among the general works that elaborate this theme are Leo Marx, *The Machine in the Garden;* and Roderick Nash, *Wilderness and the American Mind.* See also John C. Greene, *American Science in the Age of Jefferson.* Of special interest among shorter pieces are Ralph N. Miller, "American Nationalism as a Theory of Nature"; and J. R. Pole, "Enlightenment and the Politics of American Nature."

5. "Nature" is not used here as an "idea unit" of the sort advanced by Arthur O. Lovejoy in *The Great Chain of Being.*

6. The biographies referred to are Max Beloff, *Thomas Jefferson and American Democ-*

which to construct Jefferson's life and thought. Nature is an addition to them, not a replacement. To study Jefferson under "nature" does not require uncovering new facts about a man who has been thoroughly investigated. But "nature" enables one to see different relations between the parts of Jefferson and the whole, and different relations between Jefferson and his era.

Nature may also be tied to the other approaches. In his authoritative biography, Merrill Peterson focuses on three elements of Jefferson's life and thought that provide an instructive comparison with the theme of the current work: democracy, nationality, and enlightenment. Jefferson's democracy is based on natural law and natural right. His understanding of American nationality is molded by American nature—the nature of an uncultivated continent contrasted to the culture of the Old World. His Enlightenment represents nature as useful knowledge.

Freedom is an equally successful organizing principle for Jefferson studies, drawing together a wide range of his concerns. In the first volume of his six-volume biography, Dumas Malone writes that "Jefferson's chief concern was for the attainment and maintenance of liberty, and this provides the best single clue, not only to his motives in the Revolution but also to his entire career."[7] In the words of another scholar: "The order of nature, the institutions of society, the conduct of the individual, have but one end and one means: Freedom. For Jefferson, Freedom is the going and the goal. Even happiness is not so elemental."[8] The centrality of freedom to Jefferson is undeniable, but how he came to that position and how he argued for it requires a recognition of his debt to nature.

Yet another approach to Jefferson, also allied with nature, is that of reason. Jefferson held that reason is implanted in both physical nature and human nature. The reason of physical nature is its order. The reason of human nature is our ability to understand a fair portion of that order. Because of that, Jefferson's "nature" is sometimes identified with reason. Like nature, reason is presumed to be always and everywhere the same. But this identification is thrown in doubt when reason is understood, as it often is with Jefferson, in conjunction with abstract thinking only. Jefferson considered abstract thinking to be metaphysics or scholasticism, and to him that meant artificial, that is, unnatural, modes of

---

racy (New York, 1949); Noble E. Cunningham, *In Pursuit of Reason: The Life of Thomas Jefferson* (Baton Rouge, 1987); Gilbert Chinard, *Thomas Jefferson, the Apostle of Americanism;* Merrill D. Peterson, *Thomas Jefferson and the New Nation;* and Fawn Brodie, *Thomas Jefferson, an Intimate History.*

7. M.I.179. Malone also writes that "no influence upon [Jefferson] was more abiding than that of Nature." M.I.4.

8. Horace Kallen, "The Arts and Thomas Jefferson," 278.

proof and demonstration. Artificial reason was not part of his under-standing of reality. To him, most chapters of the book of nature were not chapters of reason: the book of nature was primarily the book of experience.

A final alternative to nature is history. As will be seen throughout this study, Jefferson found many occasions to rely on the past. Yet on these occasions, especially regarding the Whig version of British histo-ry, the past served only to confirm, not to challenge, the lessons of nature. The same is true with respect to classical antiquity. Sometimes, indeed, Jefferson treated the legacy of Greece and Rome as if it were itself a natural object. At the same time, he found that the classics validated the teaching of universal natural principles.[9]

The contrast of nature with these other approaches to studying Jefferson—democracy, nationalism, enlightenment, liberty, reason, and history—reveals both the complexity of the man and the ease of establishing a relationship between each of them and nature. But while all of these concepts, nature included, are artifices for the purposes of understanding Jefferson, nature has a special advantage: it is central not only in Jefferson's language but to the Enlightenment generally.

In the Western tradition "nature" is "the most potent, pervasive, and persistent of all catchwords," and in the Enlightenment, according to one of that era's greatest scholars, it is "the sacred word."[10] That Jeffer-son uses "nature" often is therefore not in itself surprising. It demon-strates that he is like his culture, not different from it. It also marks him as an excellent representative of the European Enlightenment in America.

But there is a risk to using "nature" to understand Jefferson. It is that he may be so captured by the catchword of his age that it becomes difficult to sort out his meanings. According to Arthur O. Lovejoy, "nature"

> is probably the most equivocal [word] in the vocabulary of the European peoples; . . . the range of connotation of the single term covers concep-tions not only distinct but often absolutely antithetic to one another in their implications; . . . the writers who have used it have usually been

9. See, generally, H. Trevor Colbourn, *The Lamp of Experience: Whig History and the Intellectual Origins of the American Revolution*, 158–84; and Karl Lehmann, *Thomas Jefferson: American Humanist*.

10. Arthur O. Lovejoy, *Essays in the History of Ideas*, xiii, 80. A pertinent treatment is Basil Willey, *The Eighteenth-Century Background: Studies on the Idea of Nature in the Thought of the Period*. Other authors, such as Peter Gay, emphasize reason or freedom rather than nature as more central to the Enlightenment. Peter Gay, *The Science of Freedom* (New York, 1969). But in the writings of Enlightenment figures themselves neither "reason" nor "freedom" appears to the extent that "nature" does—or so one gathers from Gay, ed., *The Enlightenment: A Comprehensive Anthology;* hereafter cited as *Enlightenment Anthology.*

little aware of its equivocality and have at all times tended to slip unconsciously from one of its senses to another.[11]

Or as Carl Becker remarks, agreeing that "nature" is the first word
"without which no enlightened person could reach a restful conclusion" in the eighteenth century: "If we would discover the little back-
stairs door that for any age serves as the secret entranceway to knowledge, we will do well to look for certain unobtrusive words with
uncertain meanings that are permitted to slip off the tongue or the pen
without fear and without research."[12] Lovejoy and Becker do not have
Americans in mind in making these assertions, but Jefferson's writings
could easily have been their source. Little aware of the equivocality of
"nature," Jefferson slipped unconsciously from one of its senses, including its antithetic senses, to another. It was an unobtrusive, though
common, word, and often its meaning was uncertain.

The risk of studying Jefferson through his use of the word "nature"
may be diminished by attending to lessons from studies of the Enlightenment and of the word itself. Two essays on language, by Lovejoy
and others and by C. S. Lewis, while showing how typical Jefferson's
use of "nature" is, supply useful lines of distinction. Lovejoy imposes
some order on the many meanings of "nature" that he has abstracted
from Western thought. It is his principal demarcation, between "nature
as being" and "nature as value," that has influenced the organization of
the present study.[13] C. S. Lewis is more discursive than Lovejoy but just
as fruitful. Instead of a catalogue of the positive uses of the word, Lewis
propounds a negative rule: "Ask oneself in each instance what is the
implied opposite to *nature*."[14] The rule is readily applicable to Jefferson.
Jefferson's "nature" is typically a category of argument in which an
implied contrast to concepts such as history, art, or the supernatural
indicates his meaning perfectly.[15]

11. Lovejoy et al., eds., *Documentary History of Primitivism and Related Ideas*, 12.

12. Carl L. Becker, *The Heavenly City of the Eighteenth-Century Philosophers* (New
Haven, 1932), 47. See also John C. Greene, "Objectives and Methods in Intellectual
History." Asking intellectual historians to look for "telltale words and phrases," Greene
takes nature in the eighteenth century as his theme, refers to Jefferson, and remarks
generally—and it is true of Jefferson—that several modes of thought "often coexisted in
the mind of a single individual even when they were not entirely compatible with each
other." P. 60.

13. Lovejoy et al., *Documentary History*, appendix, listing sixty-six meanings of
"nature." In an earlier essay, Lovejoy had charted a "map of the meanings of 'nature'" in
additional territory. "'Nature' as Aesthetic Norm" (1927), in *Essays in the History of Ideas*,
69–77.

14. C. S. Lewis, *Studies in Words*, 43.

15. Lovejoy and Lewis may be supplemented by an early discussion of the linguistic
problem in John Stuart Mill, "Nature"; and by Raymond Williams, who devotes several
pages to the word "nature" in *Keywords*. For a rich discussion of "nature" from outside the
Western tradition see Joseph Needham, "Human Law and the Laws of Nature," in *The*

A final guide to understanding the use of "nature" in Jefferson is Rousseau:

> I have noticed again and again that it is impossible in writing a lengthy work to use the same words always in the same sense. There is no language rich enough to supply terms and expressions sufficient for the modifications of our ideas. . . . In spite of this I am convinced that even in our poor language we can make our meaning clear, not by always using words in the same sense but by taking care that every time we use a word the sense in which we use it is sufficiently indicated by the sense of the context, so that each sentence in which the word occurs acts as a sort of definition.[16]

If one allows each of Jefferson's "nature" sentences to act as a "sort of definition," his meanings in fact normally become clear. In the end, of course, analysis requires that the meanings from different sentences be brought together, and at this point tensions in his thought that are not evident earlier become visible.

Jefferson was no Lovejoy or C. S. Lewis and certainly no Rousseau. He seems never to have noticed the various roles that the word "nature" played in his writings. The verbal changes that appear in drafts of his papers are primarily changes in emphasis and style, seldom hinting at any reflection on the multiple meanings of words. Since he had a considerable vocabulary in English, knew half a dozen ancient and modern languages, wrote essays on language, and was a consummate stylist, this failure ever to talk about the word "nature" may seem odd. But as Lovejoy's enterprise demonstrates, a person is often unconscious of his most ingrained linguistic habits, as well as of the intellectual conflicts they may raise.

However varied its uses, nature in the Enlightenment had a principal purpose: as an engine of attack on the authority of tradition. In opposing tradition, nature came in two varieties: reason and experience. As mentioned earlier, reason was nature in its orderly and universal character; it also enabled human beings to understand the orderly universe. Experience, on the other hand, was nature in its disorderly and particularistic character. Like reason, experience could see through the fog of tradition to truth—but on the basis of one's senses. In epistemology these two branches of nature were represented by the theories of Descartes, who grounded knowledge in the mind and asked us to look within, and of Locke, who relied on the senses and insisted that we look outside. Both methods of knowing were presumed "natural," and

---

Shorter Science and Civilization in China, ed. Colin A. Ronan, vol. I (Cambridge, 1978), 276–306.

16. Rousseau, *Émile,* quoted in Gay, *Enlightenment Anthology,* 308.

both, therefore, stood in contrast to socially determined tradition. Jefferson, though Lockean rather than Cartesian, recognized the value of both means of understanding.

Supported by both reason and experience, nature became its own authority. The challenges it posed to the authority of tradition covered a wide field. It challenged the legacy of medieval science, the power of organized religion, and the feudal, class-based institutions of state and society. But nature in the Enlightenment was effective against these traditions not only because it was backed by reason and experience: it had collected so many affirmative meanings in the history of European thought that it was available to be enrolled in nearly any campaign at hand. What is more, the eighteenth century was peculiarly suited for nature. It was a concept that took a position against institutions and social conventions that were deteriorating from within and attacked from without.

While many eras may be labeled transitional because they have features in common with either earlier or later times, the appropriateness of nature in the eighteenth century is best understood by concentrating on the significance of transition itself. But instead of asking the standard question about transitional eras, that is, What does the Enlightenment share with the time that precedes or follows it? the question to ask is, What do the two outer eras share with each other? If those eras have in common something important, then what falls between them is what makes the Enlightenment different. That difference is nature.

To speak very generally, if the ages preceding and following the Enlightenment are viewed with respect to their dominating social institutions, then what stand out are the church and feudalism on one side and large corporate enterprise and (eventually) the state on the other side. It is in the middle period, the Enlightenment, in the space between the eras of dominating social institutions, that nature has room to breathe.

Social bonds and social control did not, of course, disappear in the Enlightenment. But they had far less force in European and much of colonial society than in the eras that came before and later. In the late eighteenth century the institutions of feudalism and the church did not compel practices with the intensity they had in earlier times. Nor, on the other side, did industry or the state regiment life with the strength they acquired later. Thus, the argument from, or to, nature was adapted to an age when certain modes of social authority were breaking down and others had not yet built up. Nature was a valley between two ranges of social control.

Exceptions and qualifications to these propositions certainly exist. But from the perspective of Jefferson and eighteenth-century America they make special sense. They help define what Jefferson was fighting against on both sides of his era. In America, except in enclaves from which one might escape, there were no overbearing religious institutions. In America, except for plantation slavery, powerful economic institutions had not yet developed, and most government was weak government.

In this setting Jefferson came to believe that nature had blessed what he himself cherished: individual, family, self-sufficient farming, the small community. On the one side, with a success that came easily because the institutions were about to topple, Jefferson worked to end feudal and religious controls in Virginia. On the other side, however, he was unable to ward off the dominating institutions of the future. Despite his efforts, central government authority and large-scale capitalism and banking came to America. In the gap in Western history during the decline of one set of oppressive social institutions and before the rise of another, both Jefferson and nature were successful.

Some of the effectiveness of Jefferson's arguments from nature is explained by the difference between European and American social institutions. But underlying that difference is a more important distinction: against Europe's monuments of history and civilization, America put forward raw, and often grand, nature. Nature in the New World was a special truth that Americans intended to convert into a special virtue. "Europe is a first idea, a crude production, before the maker knew his trade, or had made up his mind as to what he wanted," Jefferson light-heartedly wrote to a woman with whom he hoped to tour the scenic wonders of America.[17] At the same time, nature allowed Americans to prosper because the nation was unencumbered by the traditions of Europe. As the leading nature patriot of America, Jefferson told the nation at his First Inaugural that the United States possessed a "chosen country . . . kindly separated by nature and a wide ocean from the exterminating havoc of one quarter of the globe." With regard to nature, as Henry Steele Commager has said about the Enlightenment generally, Europe imagined it and America realized it. Jefferson realized it more than anyone else of his time.[18]

17. TJ to Angelica Schuyler Church, 17 February 1788, BC.XII.601.

18. Commager, *The Empire of Reason: How Europe Imagined and America Realized the Enlightenment*. Despite its title, Commager's book is more about Nature (always capitalized) than about Reason. Jefferson is the most extensively indexed person in the volume. See also Commager, *Jefferson, Nationalism, and the Enlightenment*, 3. A study of the view from France, referring often to Jefferson, confirms Commager's characterization: Durand Echeverria, *Mirage in the West: A History of the French Image of American Society to 1815* (Princeton, 1957).

The American Enlightenment, like Jefferson, is profitably traversed by routes other than nature. Religion is the route taken by Henry F. May in *The Enlightenment in America*.

American nature was not the "nature of everywhere," the universal nature of the physical sciences and natural philosophy. It was the nature of place, the subject of botany and zoology, of natural history.[19] America had "real nature"—primitive, untouched by Europeans and European history, evidently limitless. From the wilderness of America hundreds of new species of plants were sent back to Europe for its gardens, herbariums, and laboratories. Europeans who traveled to America in the last quarter of the eighteenth century, particularly those interested in botany and those who became acquainted with Jefferson, reflected nature in their writings in a way that few Europeans who stayed at home could do.[20]

While the New World had more, and evidently more interesting, physical nature than Europe, America was also more "natural" than Europe socially and so in a position to revise and implement European political ideas on nature. At the time of colonization and later, at independence and the framing of new constitutions, Americans seemed to be in, or at least not far from, the state of nature that Europeans had only imagined. By this account, America was less affected, and therefore less corrupted, by traditional social and political institutions. It could more conveniently transform the principles of natural law into the statutes of civil law.

As much as anyone of his generation, whether in America or Europe, Jefferson was devoted to both the scientific and the social concerns of nature. In America he was the most European-minded man of nature. When in Europe he was the most nature-minded American. No other American statesman matched his interests in natural history.

But one who goes to May with an eye towards either nature or Jefferson comes away with a dimmed vision. Donald H. Meyer, *Democratic Enlightenment,* has more room for Jefferson.

19. In England in 1755, according to Johnson's *Dictionary,* a naturalist was "a student in natural philosophy." In the United States in 1828, according to the first edition of Webster's *American Dictionary of the English Language,* "naturalist" was a term "more generally applied to one that is versed in natural history." It is true that as nature receded from Newton and approached Darwin, the shift in meaning for "naturalist" took place in both England and America, but it was a shift with a shove from the New World. Jefferson, whose life was roughly bounded by the publication dates of the two dictionaries, would have preferred Webster's definition to Johnson's from the beginning.

20. Among these were the French botanist André Michaux and two members of the French nobility who visited Monticello and left vivid accounts. At the end of his stay at Monticello, the marquis de Chastellux wrote, "I must now take leave of the Friend of Nature." 17 April 1782, in Chastellux, *Travels in North America, 1780, 1781, and 1782,* II.396. For the duc de La Rochefoucauld-Liancourt's visit to Monticello see GB.241–45. Others included Phillip Mazzei, from Italy; Hector St. Jean de Crèvecoeur, whose *Letters from an American Farmer* reads like a Jeffersonian idyll; Joseph Priestley, an exile from England and the greatest polymath among Jefferson's acquaintances; and Albert Gallatin, from Switzerland.

None other matched his reliance on natural law and natural right in politics. In his time and place it would now seem remarkable, contrary to the first sentence of this chapter, if Jefferson had not used "nature" to the extent that he did. Nature and talk of nature were all around him. Considering his wide reading and transatlantic experience and friendships, moreover, it is unnecessary, indeed misguided, to ask who led him there. With a mind of his own, Jefferson absorbed many sources and, in Enlightenment fashion, thought eclectically. He adapted the European understanding of nature to American circumstances and American nature to European thought.

Without attempting to trace pure lines of his intellectual descent, one may fill out the role of nature for both Jefferson and the Enlightenment by a brief look at his three heroes—Bacon, Newton, and Locke.[21] If Jefferson could have composed a sustained argument on behalf of his reasons and methods for understanding nature, its model would have been Francis Bacon's *The Great Instauration* (1620). Bacon's ideas led ultimately to the incorporation in 1662 of the Royal Society of London for Improving Natural Knowledge, which was in turn the model for the American Philosophical Society, founded in Philadelphia in 1743, the year of Jefferson's birth. Jefferson, who became president of the society a few years before he became president of the United States, played Bacon's role in America—more important for the encouragement he gave to others to study nature than for his own contributions. Jefferson used Bacon's organization of nature itself as an intellectual touchstone, organizing his library according to the divisions into which Bacon classified all knowledge: memory, reason, and imagination. As will be seen in chapter II, Jefferson devised further subdivisions in this scheme and heavily impressed them with relations presumed to derive from nature.

Bacon's vision with respect to nature was carried out near the end of the seventeenth century by Newton and Locke, whom Jefferson recognized as incontestably greater intellectuals. Newton, by discovering natural laws in the physical world, seemed to vindicate the Baconian strategy of reasoning from natural facts. Although there was no immediate usefulness for much of his theoretical work, Jefferson's respect for Newton's genius was complete. But in the New World Newton needed to be put to work. Nature's laws by themselves were not enough. The American Philosophical Society had therefore been founded "for pro-

21. These men, Jefferson recalled in old age, "were my trinity of the three greatest men the world had ever produced." TJ to Benjamin Rush, 16 January 1811, KP.609. Jefferson's heroes were also "the trinity adored by Voltaire, d'Alembert, Hume, Lichtenberg, and Kant." Peter Gay, "The Enlightenment," in *The Comparative Approach to American History*, ed. C. Vann Woodward (New York, 1968), 39.

moting useful knowledge," and not, as had been the case with the Royal Society a century earlier, only "for improving natural knowledge."

The contribution of Locke to Jefferson's thinking on nature may be divided into two branches. The first is his theory of knowledge, that we know things about external, material nature through our senses only and that this, rather than any possible innate ideas, is the sole reliable test for truth. The second is Locke's construction of civil society on the basis of natural law and natural right. (Jefferson's indebtedness to Locke in these realms is taken up further on in this study.)

Jefferson was born some years after the last of his three English heroes had died. When he absorbed their ideas, therefore, he was able not only to read them directly but also to learn of them through an intellectual movement of which they were the indirect founding fathers. That movement was the Scottish Enlightenment. Of the several con-stellations of eighteenth-century thought about nature that appealed to Jefferson, the Scottish school made the deepest impression on him. He was attracted to it, first, because the larger mission of the Scots was the mission of many colonial Americans: the conscious development of a national culture distinct from that of England. Second, the Scots were dedicated empiricists. Following Bacon, they were most secure in the presence of facts, not speculation. Third, and most important to Jeffer-son, the Scots founded and explained their ideas in the language of nature. Among the Scottish thinkers, Jefferson preferred the move-ment's leading popularizer, Lord Kames (Henry Home), whose writ-ings are as dense with "nature" as are Jefferson's. The parallels between the lives and thought of the two men are considerable and will emerge several times in the chapters to follow. [22]

While many of Jefferson's views on nature stemmed from the three Englishmen and the Scottish Enlightenment, for the concrete applica-tion of nature to public affairs Jefferson looked to continental Europe. There he found writers on the law of nature and nations—international law—who also claimed their principles derived from nature. When charged with responsibilities in American foreign policy as minister to France and secretary of state, Jefferson was especially attentive to these thinkers.

Finally, Jefferson was affected by environmentalism. More a mood than a theory, eighteenth-century environmentalism asked how habitat and climate influenced living beings, both animals and humans. A pronounced feature in the writing of Montesquieu, whose arguments on this subject (though not on others) Jefferson on the whole accepted,

22. See Gladys Bryson, *Man and Society;* William Christian Lehmann, *Henry Home, Lord Kames, and the Scottish Enlightenment* (The Hague, 1971); and John Clive and Bernard Bailyn, "England's Cultural Provinces."

environmentalism necessarily underlay what was special about America.[23] But an environmental or particularistic approach to nature conflicted with the dominant mood of the Enlightenment, nature in its universal meaning. Montesquieu, in other words, challenged Newton. Though seldom explicitly, Jefferson often struggled with the tension between the universal and particular senses of nature. It was a tension at the core of defining America's place in the world.

The background for appreciating Jefferson's attachment to nature having been sketched, some foreground of the man's life with nature is also necessary before embarking on the central discussion. At the outset it is useful to recall how physically bound to nature Jefferson was and how far Americans have moved away from it two centuries later. Like most of the 95 percent of Americans who, according to the census of 1790, lived in "rural territory," Jefferson depended directly on the land for his livelihood. He could never afford to be indifferent to the weather or to his crops. His correspondence is thick with the comments of a farmer. When he traveled, he was also in contact with nature in a way virtually unimaginable today. This was true whether the trip was a delight, as when he enjoyed southern France from a glass-enclosed carriage set on a barge that was drawn along a canal; or a torment, as when on the way from Monticello to Washington during his presidency he was out in a "constant heavy drizzle through the whole day, sufficient to soak my outer great coat twice."[24]

While association with nature through agriculture and in travel was typical in his time, Jefferson's attachment to a particular spot in nature, to Albemarle County and to Monticello especially, was nearly obsessive. Born not far from the Blue Ridge Mountains in what is today western Virginia, Jefferson was in love with the Albemarle area—"my country"—his entire life. He depicted the region as the physical, moral, and intellectual center of his state—and hence, it sometimes appeared, of all America. His descriptions of the region were often accompanied by engaging, exaggerated accounts of its natural fertility. In an indulgence of unscientific method he claimed that Monticello's central position in the state endowed it with "the best average of the temperature of our climate."[25] As he sanguinely informed a New England acquaintance whom he hoped to attract to the faculty of the University of Virginia, "There is not a healthier or more genial climate in the

23. Extracts from Montesquieu take up more of Jefferson's commonplace book than do the writings of any other author except for Lord Kames. CB.257–96. A discussion of Jefferson's changing attitude towards Montesquieu appears in the introduction by Gilbert Chinard. CB.31–39.
24. TJ to William Short, 21 May 1787, BC.XI.372; TJ to Martha Jefferson Randolph, 14 May 1802, in Edward Dumbauld, *Thomas Jefferson, American Tourist*, 190.
25. NVa.76. He made the identical claim three decades later. GB.622.

world."[26] Those who have visited Monticello in midsummer may doubt the accuracy of such a statement.

In colonial Virginia Jefferson's formal education was pursued as assiduously as the intellectual resources permitted. It, too, was devoted to nature. Jefferson's early training came from a minister with a strong bent towards geography. At the College of William and Mary, where he went in 1760, he found a mentor in Dr. William Small. Small, who had absorbed the Scottish Enlightenment at first hand, taught him what it meant to study nature. From Small, Jefferson said, "I got my first views of the expansion of science, and of the system of things in which we are placed."[27] Continuing his education with George Wythe, the leading legal scholar of Virginia, Jefferson prepared for a professional life with the study of natural law.

In the late 1760s, now engaged in the practice of law, Jefferson began planning Monticello—the farm, the hill, and the mansion.[28] He had inherited the land from his father, Peter Jefferson, who had died when the boy was fourteen. The father was fixed in the son's mind as a man who relished nature while he respected civilization. Monticello was a monument to such an outlook.

At his estate, apart from the general management of the farm and nearby properties, Jefferson worked on leveling the top of the hill, carving out the roads that wound through the woods up to it, and on landscaping, orchards, a vegetable garden, flower gardens, a forest grove, and vineyards. The view from the summit was an impressive one, and Jefferson was its greatest publicist. In the language of a eulogist who knew it well:

> On the west, stretching away to the north and the south, [Monticello] commands a view of the Blue Ridge for a hundred and fifty miles, and brings under the eye one of the boldest and most beautiful horizons in the world; while on the east, it presents an extent of prospect, bounded only by the spherical form of the earth, in which nature seems to sleep in eternal repose, as if to form one of her finest contrasts with the rude and rolling grandeur of the west. In the wide prospect, and scattered to the

26. TJ to Nathaniel Bowditch, 26 October 1818, quoted in Nathan Reingold, ed., *Science in Nineteenth-Century America: A Documentary History* (New York, 1964), 22. A full description of the natural conditions near Monticello appears in a letter to the French scientist Jean Baptiste Say, who was interested in settling in America. TJ to Say, 2 March 1815, LB.XIV.260–67. (Neither Bowditch nor Say moved to Virginia.)

27. TJ to L. H. Girardin, 15 January 1815, LB.XVI.231; TJ, Autobiography (1821), KP.4. On Small see Herbert L. Ganter, "William Small, Jefferson's Beloved Teacher."

28. A succinct description is Frederick D. Nichols and James A. Bear, Jr., *Monticello*. Generally, see William Howard Adams, *Jefferson's Monticello*. Jefferson evidently made up the Italian word "Monticello," meaning "little mountain." See GB.17. There are towns named Monticello in at least a dozen states, most of them not known for mountains, even little ones.

north and south, are several detached mountains, which contribute to animate and diversify this enchanting landscape. . . . From this summit the philosopher was wont to enjoy that spectacle, among the sublimest of Nature's operations, the looming of the distant mountains; and to watch the motions of the planets, and the greater revolution of the celestial sphere.[29]

From the beginning, Monticello was both in nature and the home of a naturalist. As an early visitor recorded, "Nature has so contrived it, that a Sage and a man of taste should find on his own estate the spot where he might best study and enjoy Her."[30] Although the house itself was carefully planned (and often replanned) for the site, it was classical in design and unrelated to local nature. But once one was inside the building, nature took over again. The first impression was of a museum of natural history—"a vast collection of specimens of Indian art . . . an array of fossil productions . . . [a wall] covered with curiosities which Lewis and Clark found in their wild and perilous expedition."[31]

For many years Monticello lay further west than the residence of any other prominent American statesman or scientist, symbolizing Jefferson's projects to explore and acquire new territory, his political vision, and his expectation that the western land would soon be settled by farmers who disdained the commerce and industry of coastal cities. Despite, perhaps because of, the location of Monticello, however, Jefferson himself traveled west of the Shenandoah Valley only once, and only by a very few miles. He did not travel as far to the west as did his father or his compatriots Washington, Madison, and Monroe. He was neither frontiersman nor wanderer in the wilderness.[32]

Monticello and Jefferson's early years provide the frame for a life

29. William Wirt, "Eulogy on Jefferson," LB.XIII.xlv–xlvi. For Jefferson's own depiction of the scene, see TJ to Maria Cosway, 12 October 1786, BC.X.447 (quoted and analyzed below, in chap. IV). John Adams, who was never there, described Monticello similarly in recounting the report of a recent visitor. John Adams to TJ, 10 February 1823, C.II.587. Like much else in Jefferson's life, the view from Monticello was the butt of satire by political opponents, as from Josiah Quincy in 1804: "From the top of Monticello, by the side of the great Jefferson, I have watched its wild uproar, while we philosophized together on its sublime horrors." Quoted in Linda K. Kerber, *Federalists in Dissent: Imagery and Ideology in Jeffersonian America* (Ithaca, 1980), 177.

30. Chastellux, *Travels in North America,* II.390 (entry of 13 April 1782, Jefferson's birthday).

31. Wirt's eulogy, LB.XIII.xlvii (Indian art and fossils); George Ticknor, 7 February 1815, quoted in Howard C. Rice, Jr., "Jefferson's Gift of Fossils to the Museum of Natural History in Paris," 610.

32. Jefferson hoped to visit the "western waters" but missed his chance by being appointed minister to France in the spring of 1784. See BC.VII.83. He received reports about the region from his friends, however: James Monroe, James Madison, Rev. James Madison (of William and Mary), and Francis Hopkinson (reporting on David Rittenhouse). Late in life Jefferson went to take the cure at Warm Springs, Virginia, seventy-five miles from Monticello and the furthest west he ever traveled; the cure did not take.

with nature. The picture is largely filled in during two decades beginning in the early 1770s, when his interests in nature blossomed in both public and private activities. In 1774 he wrote *A Summary View of the Rights of British America,* a pamphlet that argued that the colonists possessed natural rights, among others, in their dispute with Great Britain. Two years later he drafted the Declaration that announced American independence under Nature and Nature's God. As a member of the Continental Congress in 1783–84 he dealt with nature directly, proposing legislation for surveying and governing the western territories. In the next years, as diplomat and secretary of state he prepared detailed reports that either investigated some aspect of nature in commerce or discussed natural law and rights: whale oil trade with France (1788), cod and whale fisheries (1791), Spain's rights over Mississippi navigation (1792), and neutral shipping (1793).

At the same time, Jefferson's private activities concerning nature were no less significant. His residence in Europe itself constituted an encounter with nature, partly through the opportunity to develop comparisons with America, partly through the springtime tours that he took from Paris. The notes he kept of these excursions amount to nature journals. On the first, in 1786, he visited British estate gardens with John Adams. A year later he journeyed to southern France and a portion of northern Italy. The next year he traveled from Amsterdam up the Rhine to Strasbourg and back to Paris, all the while making jottings on soil, climate, and agriculture. (After his return to America he went on the last journey of this sort, visiting upstate New York and New England with James Madison in the spring of 1791.)

In Paris Jefferson was an active member of intellectual circles that discussed natural history and debated natural rights. He acted as a scout in the natural sciences, corresponding with the presidents of Harvard, Yale, and William and Mary and members of the American Philosophical Society. With the aging naturalist Buffon he disputed the theory that animals degenerated on contact with the New World. In the company of Lafayette at the beginning of the French Revolution he advanced an American view of natural rights.

In the middle of his two nature decades Jefferson composed his remarkable *Notes on the State of Virginia.*[33] Begun in the fall of 1780, the

33. For background material and commentary on the *Notes on Virginia,* see S.IV.301–30; the introduction and notes in the William Peden edition (1954); Marie Kimball, *Jefferson: War and Peace, 1776 to 1784* (New York, 1947), 259–305; and Merrill D. Peterson, "Thomas Jefferson's *Notes on the State of Virginia.*" Peterson's summarizing sentence reads: "Jefferson's philosophy first conscripted man in the cause of nature and then—this was the trick—conscripted nature in the cause of mankind." P. 58. David Tucker, "Jefferson's *Notes on the State of Virginia,*" is largely about nature: regarding the structure of the *Notes* (the book proceeds from natural order to human nature to nature and law) and

book was not complete until the summer of 1787, when an authoritative edition was published in London. In form, *Notes on the State of Virginia* consists of answers to a questionnaire circulated by a French diplomat for what might best be termed intelligence gathering during the Revolution. The questionnaire, given to a delegate from each state in the Continental Congress, was sent to Jefferson, who was then governor and the acknowledged authority on Virginia. He eventually replied with an entire book.[34]

Notes on the State of Virginia might as accurately have been titled "Notes on American Nature" or, as Charles Thomson, one of Jefferson's Philadelphia friends proposed, "A Natural History of Virginia," for it is certainly a book about nature.[35] The book is very much mistitled insofar as "notes" implies a relatively brief or ill-considered compilation of material. Yet it is not a systematic and unified treatise, nor is it written with a sense of literary proportion. It veers wildly, from tables of Indian populations, names of plants, and weather data to hymns to the Natural Bridge and the independent farmer. One of the queries ("query" is the name for chapter, which Jefferson retained from the original questionnaire) is only seventeen words long. Another, the principal one on natural history, is approximately a thousand times that length. Although the arrangement of the queries as published is some improvement over the arrangement of the list he was given, Jefferson did not take the liberty that would have been necessary to fashion a greater work.

The words "State of Virginia" in the title are not so simple as they seem. Jefferson normally used "state" only in legal contexts. When he spoke of Virginia, he regularly called it, as he did Albemarle County, his "country." He quite possibly believed, therefore, that "State of Virginia" referred to the condition of Virginia, not to a juridical entity, though he could hardly have thought most readers would take it that way.[36] "Virginia" is open to question, too. Charles Thomson told

---

Jefferson's thought as manifested in the *Notes* (through contrasts in the book between universal and particular nature and between violent nature and nature as the basis for republican government).

34. The questionnaire was apparently answered at length by a representative of only one other state, Gen. John Sullivan, governor of New Hampshire and a friend of Jefferson's. Three other New Englanders published books analogous to *Notes on the State of Virginia* and in part modeled on Jefferson's work: Jeremy Belknap, *The History of New-Hampshire*, 3 vols. (1784–92); Jedidiah Morse, *The American Geography* (1789); and Samuel Williams, *The Natural and Civil History of Vermont* (1794).

35. Charles Thomson to TJ, 6 March 1785, BC.VIII.17n2. For John Adams's title, "History of Virginia," see plate 3.

36. He once called his book "Notes on our country." TJ to George Wythe, 13 August 1786, BC.X.243. At another time he said he had written the book in answer to enquiries

Jefferson that the book was "a most excellent Natural history not merely of Virginia but of No. America."[37] He was right. But there was justification for this broad coverage other than native pride and the likelihood that no one else would reply so thoroughly to the original questionnaire. In 1787 Virginia included what later became Kentucky and West Virginia and was by far the largest state in the union—"one third larger than the islands of Great Britain and Ireland," as Jefferson pointedly told his readers. When he began work on the book, Virginia was far larger still, not yet having ceded the Northwest Territory to the United States.

But Jefferson ranged beyond even these limits and took nature rather than boundary lines to determine his province. He tells the reader about the Missouri and Mississippi rivers and about routes to New Orleans, Santa Fe, and Mexico City. He candidly says that he is writing about Indians "within and circumjacent to the United States." The breadth of the book is best exemplified by the feature of which Jefferson was most proud, its insert "map of the country between Albemarle Sound and Lake Erie."[38] If the book sometimes reads as though it should be titled "Notes on the Vicinity of Monticello," it is almost as unconfined geographically as it is intellectually.

That *Notes on Virginia* is about nature in many of the meanings of that word is manifest from inspection. For most of the first half of the book (queries I–VII and XI), physical nature is the principal subject: "Boundaries of Virginia"; "Rivers"; "Sea-Ports"; "Mountains"; "Cascades"; "Productions Mineral, Vegetable and Animal"; "Climate"; "Aborigines." The second half of the book (and query VIII) appear to be about society. But as table 1 shows, nature occurs in some form in all these queries as well.[39]

After the publication of the *Notes,* the high point of Jefferson's life with nature was the Louisiana Purchase (1803) and the mounting of the

---

"as to the Natural and Political state of Virginia." TJ to Thomas Mann Randolph, Jr., 6 July 1787, BC.XI.558.

37. Charles Thomson to TJ, 6 March 1785, BC.VIII.16. A portion of Thomson's letter is reproduced in plate 4.

38. The map included Virginia, Pennsylvania, Maryland, Delaware, portions of New Jersey, New York, North Carolina, the "states" of Franklin and Kentucky, and three areas simply marked "New State." See, generally, Coolie Verner, "Mr. Jefferson Makes a Map," 14 Imago Mundi 96–108 (1959), reprinted in Cohen, *Thomas Jefferson and the Sciences.* The map itself, in its original 24" × 26" size, is most easily accessible in Merrill D. Peterson, ed., *Thomas Jefferson: Writings.* A portion of the map is reproduced in plate 2.

39. The queries mentioned in the text plus those listed in the table cover more than 95 percent of the *Notes* (only queries IX and X, on the army and navy, are omitted). A complete survey of the vocabulary of the first eleven queries proves conclusively that nature is a principal subject of the book. Seaford William Eubanks, "A Vocabulary Study of Thomas Jefferson's *Notes on Virginia.*"

TABLE 1
References to Nature in Some Queries in *Notes on the State of Virginia*

Query	Reference to Nature
Population (VIII)	Natural right and natural reason in the constitution of Virginia
Counties and Towns (XII)	Nature inhibits the founding of towns in certain places
Constitution (XIII)	Natural rights
Laws (XIV)	Racial distinctions by nature
Colleges, Buildings, and Roads (XV)	Natural philosophy and law of nature at the College of William and Mary
Proceedings as to Tories (XVI)	Forfeiture of lands
Religion (XVII)	A natural right
Manners (XVIII)	Nature and natural means may contribute to a slave rebellion
Manufactures (XIX)	"Those who labour in the earth are the chosen people of God."
Subjects of Commerce (XX)	Profitable tobacco production is beyond the powers of nature
Weights, Measures, and Money (XXI)	Natural properties of Greek and Roman systems of measurement [note by TJ in his copy of the 1787 edition]
Public Revenue and Expense (XXII)	"Generative force of nature"

Lewis and Clark Expedition. During his presidency, too, his interest in natural rights was revived by the struggle for control of the lower Mississippi (resolved by the Louisiana Purchase), in the dispute over British impressment of American seamen, and on behalf of the rights of neutral nations.[40]

40. As president, Jefferson was also drawn to nature in Washington, D.C. Arriving there before his inauguration, he lived in a boarding house said to have been chosen "partly from [his] love of nature . . . being there able to enjoy the beautiful and extensive prospect." Margaret Bayard Smith, *The First Forty Years of Washington Society* (New York, 1906), 12. He rode horseback through the largely forested city and regularly visited its vegetable markets. At the White House his favorite room contained maps, scientific instruments, gardening tools, plants, and (in a cage) a mockingbird. Peterson, *Thomas Jefferson and the New Nation*, 735.

As president of the American Philosophical Society for many years, Jefferson promoted natural science for the nation, even though he seldom attended the society's meetings. From the time he was in France until the end of his life, he actively exchanged or promoted the exchange of seeds, plants, and even animals between the United States and Europe. During retirement he spent a portion of each year at his second home, Poplar Forest, about seventy-five miles southwest of Monticello. From there it was a convenient ride to the Natural Bridge which he owned and showed off with unrestrained pride.

The last years of his life were devoted to the establishment of the University of Virginia. Attending to everything from its gardens to the recruitment of its faculty, he planned a curriculum that championed the causes of nature. Two of the university's eight schools were Natural History and Natural Philosophy. In the others were taught geography; navigation; physiology; the law of nature and nations; and "the principles of government," for which he drew up a reading list emphasizing natural rights. In one of the last letters of his life he outlined plans for the study of botany at the university, which he presumed would be taught advantageously in April and May, "when nature is in general bloom."[41] On July 4, 1826, he died, committing himself in death, as he had in the Declaration of Independence fifty years earlier, to Nature and to Nature's God.

41. TJ to Dr. John P. Emmett, 27 April 1826, LB.XVI.164.

Part One · BEING

Chapter II

PHYSICAL NATURE: "THE SYSTEM OF THINGS IN WHICH WE ARE PLACED"

I N *DE RERUM NATURA* the philosopher-poet Lucretius repeats one passage four times. In a crucial phrase he holds that ignorance and fear can be banished only by the study of "Nature, her outward aspect and inner laws." This is a chorus not only for Lucretius but also for Jefferson.[1]

According to Lucretius and Jefferson, the world is nature alone. The "unnatural" and the "supernatural" do not and cannot exist. All that is not nature is void, empty, nonexistent. Nature itself consists of matter, and only matter. Nothing else—soul, spirit, or thought—has primary existence or a reality independent of a stuff of nature. Ignorance and fear need not exist. Everything has a natural, material explanation. Jefferson is a Lucretian materialist.

The relation of Jefferson to Lucretius is no accident. Jefferson and his age were deeply interested in the philosophy of Lucretius—Epicureanism as it was commonly called—and Jefferson spoke explicitly of his own agreement with much of the Lucretian doctrine. He owned at least five Latin editions of *De Rerum Natura* as well as translations into English, French, and Italian. He advised others to read Lucretius, and his own writing about physical nature reflects a remarkable adherence to the ideas of *De Rerum Natura*.[2]

1. The Latin is *naturae species ratioque*. *De Rerum Natura* I.148; II.61; III.93; VI.41. The usual translation of the title of Lucretius' work is "On the nature of things." Since the sweep of the poem is nature in its entirety, however, a literal translation, "on the things of nature," conveys the meaning better. Better still might be "On the Naturalness of Things," suggested by Jacob Klein in "On the Nature of Nature," 102.

2. S.IV.499–501. Lucretius, a Roman who lived in the first century B.C., claimed to be

Lucretius reduced the world to the tiniest bits of matter, which, though infinitely combinable, in fact combined into a finite number of types or species. (Lucretius called the irreducible bits *semina,* the Latin for "seeds," which must have appealed to the natural historian in Jefferson. Usually the particles have been thought of as atoms, from the Greek for "uncuttable," which may have appealed more to natural philosophers.) The bits of matter move through a void. We know they are there because we sense them—it is not a matter of reasoning.

The parallels between Jefferson and Lucretius are remarkable. The two need only be read together. First Lucretius:

> . . . nature, as it is, consists
> Of two components: bodies, and the void
> In which they are, through which they move diversely.
> Sensation is the universal standard
> For affirming the existence of matter;
> Unless sensation has validity
> And rests on it, we shall be quite unable
> By any stretch of reason, to confirm.

Next, Jefferson:

> I [am] obliged to recur ultimately to my habitual anodyne, "I feel: therefore I exist." I feel bodies which are not myself: there are other existencies then. I call them *matter.* I feel them changing place. This gives me *motion.* Where there is an absence of matter, I call it *void,* or *nothing,* or *immaterial space.* On the basis of sensation, of matter and motion, we may erect the fabric of all the certainties we can have or need.[3]

The same materialism that explains existence explains nonexistence, or death. In the words of Lucretius:

---

recounting the doctrines of Epicurus, a Greek who had lived 250 years earlier. Since the only ancient evidence of Epicurus for Jefferson was *De Rerum Natura,* it is fair to call Jefferson a Lucretian, although he seldom did so himself. But see the diary entry of John Quincy Adams, 3 November 1807, in Francis Coleman Rosenberger, ed., *Jefferson Reader,* 60. Jefferson's most considered profession of Epicureanism appears in TJ to William Short, 31 October 1819, F.X.143–46, to which is appended a "Syllabus of the doctrines of Epicurus," listing first the physical doctrines and then the moral. The brunt of the discussion here refutes the assertion of Karl Lehmann that although Jefferson "professed to be an Epicurean, he failed to appreciate . . . *De Rerum Natura." Thomas Jefferson,* 84. The influence of Lucretius in the eighteenth century is summarized in Wolfgang Bernard Fleischmann, "The Debt of the Enlightenment to Lucretius," 25 *Studies on Voltaire and the Eighteenth Century* 631–43 (1963). Jefferson recommended Lucretius to his nephew as part of a course of study. TJ to Peter Carr, 10 August 1787, BC.XII.18.

3. *De Rerum Natura* I.419–25 (this and the following translations are from Lucretius, *Lucretius: On the Nature of Things,* trans. Palmer Bovie); TJ to John Adams, 15 August 1820, C.II.567–68.

When Nature takes a thing apart, resolving it
Into its basic bodies once again,
She does not change created things to nothing.

. . . .

. . . Nature remakes
One thing from another: and something born
Is aided by the death of something else.

In Jefferson's words: "The dead are not even things. The particles of matter which composed their bodies, make part now of the bodies of other animals, vegetables, or minerals, of a thousand forms."[4]

Materialism generally and a materialist doctrine of death in particular went counter to orthodox Christianity. Although not disturbed by this on intellectual grounds, Jefferson was sensitive both personally and politically to the views of others and was therefore normally reticent in expressing his convictions. Nevertheless, from his student days until the end of his life he doubted the existence of an immaterial soul or spirit. Consequently he did not accept divinity in Jesus. "It is not to be understood that I am with [Jesus] in all of his doctrines," he once wrote. "I am a Materialist; he takes the side of Spiritualism."[5] Jefferson recognized that Jesus "taught emphatically, the doctrines of a future state," which meant a nonmaterial existence. But this was the last and evidently the least of the leading features of Christian dogma. It was the only one he did not directly praise and the only one he described as strictly instrumental.[6] When Jefferson sometimes speaks about a soul, the contexts show that he is speaking of the griefs of life and not from philosophical conviction.[7]

4. *De Rerum Natura* I.216–18, 262–64; TJ to Maj. John Cartwright, 5 June 1824, LB.XVI.48.

5. TJ to William Short, 13 April 1820, LB.XV.244. A few years later, however, Jefferson convinced himself that even Jesus was a good Lucretian. TJ to Thomas Cooper, 11 December 1823, F.X.285. Jefferson's early sympathy with Lucretius is reflected in a passage from Cicero entered into his commonplace book: "The soul, being corporeal, must perish with the rest of the body." CB.73.

6. TJ to Benjamin Rush, 21 April 1803, LB.X.385.

7. In old age, Jefferson's references to a soul are as pagan as they are Christian. TJ to Alexander von Humboldt, 6 December 1813, F.IX.431 (Elysian fields); TJ to Robert Walsh, 6 February 1820, F.X.156 (the river Styx). Jefferson's Calvinist correspondent John Adams once pressed him to explain himself: "You have . . . concluded, there is no human Soul. Will you please to inform me, what matter is? and what Spirit is?" Adams to TJ, 22 July 1813, C.II.363. Jefferson's response begged the question. TJ to Adams, 22 August 1813, C.II.367. When Adams's wife lay dying and he cried out that "human life is . . . as I firmly believe an immortal Existence," Jefferson's moving reply was words of sympathy, not theology. Adams to TJ, 20 October 1818, C.II.529; TJ to Adams, 13 November 1818, C.II.529. In writing to practicing Christians he carefully chose his phrases: "The laws of nature have withheld from us the means of physical knowledge of the country of the spirits." TJ to Rev. Isaac Story, 5 December 1801, F.VIII.107. "The

The Virginian planter and the Roman poet agreed not only on the doctrine of materialism to explain life and death. Both men held that the earth was created in time.[8] Both held that nature's principles act on their own, without the intervention of divinity.[9] Both offered alternative natural explanations for phenomena in order to avoid explanations not derived from nature.[10] Both engaged in meteorological investigation and speculation, assuming, for instance, that optical illusions had natural causes.[11] Both believed in studying nature for utilitarian purposes and in following nature in order to live a good life.[12] Down to the praise of olives the Roman and the Virginian are similar.[13]

Because the Lucretian philosophy was both ancient and comprehensive, however, and because Jefferson was eclectic if not at times inconsistent in his philosophy, it is not surprising that the thoughts of the two men are not identical. Three areas of divergence may be mentioned. First, while the naturalism of Lucretius made him the most sympathetic thinker to Jefferson among the ancients, some of his doctrines were sufficiently pagan as to require modification in order to be acceptable to a Christian epoch. The particular needs of a Christianized Epicureanism were a creator, a purpose, and a system for the universe. All of these Lucretius had either denied or neglected. An orthodox (though challenged) updating had been accomplished by Pierre Gassendi, a seventeenth-century French scientist and philosopher on whom Jefferson relied heavily.[14] Nevertheless, for Jefferson himself a century later, deism largely sufficed, and "Nature's God" accommodated the godless Lucretius to the Christian era.

Second, as a scientist, Lucretius is both more confident and more

---

religion you so sincerely profess tells us we shall meet again." TJ to Maria Cosway, 27 December 1820, LB.XVIII.310. For claims that Jefferson in fact believed in an afterlife, however, see M.VI.491; and Dickinson W. Adams, ed., *Jefferson's Extracts from the Gospels* (Princeton, 1983), 40–41.

8. Cf. *De Rerum Natura* V.325 with TJ to Charles Thomson, 17 December 1786, BC.X.608.

9. Cf. *De Rerum Natura* II.1190 with TJ to Robert Patterson, 27 December 1812, LB.XIII.192.

10. Cf. *De Rerum Natura* VI.712–38 (four explanations for the flooding of the Nile) with NVa.31–33 (three explanations for the appearance of fossil shells on mountain tops).

11. Cf. *De Rerum Natura* II.432–43 (optical illusions) and VI (thunder, lightning, rain, rainbows, earthquakes) with NVa.77, 80–81 (pockets of warm air, terrestrial looming); and TJ to Rev. James Madison, 19 July 1788, BC.XIII.380 (rainbows).

12. See *De Rerum Natura* IV.25 ("Learn the nature of all things and understand their utility") and V.1361 ("Creative Nature was herself the first to give us models of sowing and grafting").

13. Cf. *De Rerum Natura* V.1361–78 with TJ to William Drayton, 30 July 1787, BC.XI.648–49.

14. Jefferson retained Gassendi's three-volume *La Philosophie d'Epicure* for himself when he sold the bulk of his library to Congress in 1815. S.II.88.

speculative than Jefferson. Jefferson did not write about the ultimate stuff of nature with the detail that Lucretius did. Either he lacked the imagination or he had enough understanding to realize how little he actually knew. He was therefore cautious in his scientific claims.

Finally the two differed over extinction. According to Lucretius (and in this Jefferson concurred), each biological species is fixed and has its own natural laws. But a species, Lucretius went on to assert, could become extinct. With less information than Jefferson but also fewer presuppositions about nature itself, Lucretius thus combined observation (that species do not intermix) with observational logic (that some species become rarer, and therefore some may have died out) in a way that Jefferson never did. As will be seen, Jefferson's judgment on extinction ran in another direction.[15]

Inseparable from the assertion and explication of materialism is some test that the doctrine is true. How do we come to know about the things of nature? For a theory of knowledge Jefferson drew principally on John Locke, also an admirer of Lucretius, whose epistemology it was that it is sense experience that leads to knowledge.[16] "I feel, therefore I exist" was how Jefferson summed up both Locke's and his own opposition to Descartes's doctrine of innate ideas. "When once we quit the basis of sensation," he continued, "all is in the wind."[17]

Appealing as this view sounds, however, the sensationist doctrine is not without its deficiencies. The principal one is the hubris of setting human apperception as the sole judge of reality. But there are practical liabilities as well. On the basis of Lockean epistemology, Jefferson often distrusted or was willing to ignore what he could not sense. This in turn set boundaries to his curiosity and therefore to his knowledge. Had he been less wedded to a sensationist theory of knowing, he would have accepted a role for reason independent of its aid to the senses. His receptivity to geology and to new ideas in biology might have been greater. His interest in mathematics, physics, and astronomy might have extended beyond their practical applications. Instead he followed his epistemology in emphasizing "useful" over theoretical knowledge and favoring natural history, which to him meant the nature received by the unmediated senses, over natural philosophy.[18]

Under the doctrine of sensationism, the function of the mind was to

15. See *De Rerum Natura* II.664–68, 706–10; V.855, 877, 920.

16. Jefferson recommended Locke's *Essay Concerning Human Understanding* (1690) for a basic library under the title "Locke's conduct of the mind in search of truth." TJ to Robert Skipwith, 3 August 1771, BC.I.79. Half a century later he was still referring favorably to Locke's theory. TJ to Francis W. Eppes, 27 June 1821, BB.440.

17. TJ to John Adams, 15 August 1820, C.II.567. Lucretius said it, too: "What can be more relied on than the senses?" *De Rerum Natura* IV.483.

18. Even when he praised mathematics, Jefferson's view was not especially informed:

coordinate the sense impressions of nature. Jefferson's doctrine of knowing thus corresponded to his doctrine of being. Both were materialistic. The opportunity for Jefferson to assert a concrete relationship between the two doctrines came through the work of a group of intellectuals whom he met in France and who gave themselves the label Ideologues. Developing a physiological complement to Locke's psychology of knowledge, the Ideologues treated knowledge as the product of internal as well as external physical nature and analyzed the mechanisms of perception, particularly the sense of touch and the nervous system. Jefferson, whose attachment to the Ideologues was as much political as scientific, became an advocate of their theories in America.

Among the Ideologues, one who broadly held the views that Jefferson did in materialism, sensationism, ethics, economics, education, and medicine was a physician, Pierre Jean Georges Cabanis (1757–1808). On its publication in 1802 Cabanis sent Jefferson a copy of his *Rapports du physique et du moral de l'homme,* which, as its title suggests, proposed a material connection between man's physical and moral faculties. In thanking Cabanis for the volumes, which he had not yet read, Jefferson expressed a skepticism, in a way an unconcern, about the likelihood of actually proving the connections between a finding about nature itself (that the mind is matter) and our experience of nature (how the mind senses the external world). What was important was to elaborate the conviction that matter was the ground of thinking:

> That thought may be a faculty of our material organization, has been believed in the gross; and though the modus operandi of nature in this, as in most other cases, can never be developed and demonstrated to beings limited as we are, yet I feel confident you will have conducted us as far on the road as we can go, and have lodged us within reconnoitering distance of the citadel itself. [19]

Near the end of his life Jefferson became excited once more by the possibility that a science of thinking could be established on a materialistic basis. Lafayette had sent him "the most extraordinary of all works," a treatise by a French physiologist on experiments with the nervous systems of vertebrate animals finally proving that "the cerebrum is the thinking organ." "I wish to see," Jefferson wrote tri-

---

"It was ever my favorite [subject]," he wrote with regard to having his grandson tutored in it. "We have no theories there, no uncertainties remain on the mind; all is demonstration and satisfaction." TJ to Benjamin Rush, 17 August 1811, F.IX.328.

19. TJ to Georges Cabanis, 12 July 1803, LB.X.404. See also TJ to Thomas Cooper, 10 July 1812, LB.XIII.177. Generally, see Martin S. Staum, *Cabanis.*

umphantly to John Adams, "what the spiritualists will say to this."[20]

The characteristics of the world and how we know them having been established by Lucretian materialism and Lockean sensationism, and a link between the two established by the Ideologues, Jefferson could now turn to the study of nature itself. Here he was faced with a common problem: how to steer between belief and disbelief, how to know which evidence to accept because it was natural and which to reject because it was reported by people whose senses were not reliable. On the initial determination of what counted as evidence one could not afford to make a mistake, for error at this stage meant working with what was false or overlooking what was true.

Within his framework Jefferson offered an alluring if inadequate view of the road to truth. Faced with "equally unsatisfactory" hypotheses to account for a natural phenomenon (in this case fossil shells on the tops of mountains), he wrote: "He is less remote from the truth who believes nothing than he who believes what is wrong." He added a useful corollary in pointing out that the disproof of a false hypothesis leaves us "wiser than we were, by having an error the less in our catalogue." But at the same time, he phrased his original proposition in a less credible form: "It is always better to have no ideas, than false ones."[21]

Jefferson's assertions need to be examined. It is a mark of psychological and scientific naivete to imagine that one can investigate nature believing nothing, having at hand "only the facts." Jefferson certainly did not proceed this way himself. Further, he missed the point that for the advancement of science it is often positively fruitful that a position be argued that is later shown to be wrong. Late in life he seemed to recognize this: "By the collisions of different hypotheses," he acknowledged, "truth may be elicited and science advanced in the end."[22] But was there not a moral problem in advocating a scientific method that condoned false hypotheses? How could it be "right" actively to encourage what might be wrong? Even when he finally conceded that science could advance only if some people took the risk of error, Jefferson was not inclined to take such risks himself. Although theory of some kind was necessary for progress in knowledge, he feared that scientists would become captive to false theory and so retard the discovery of knowledge.[23]

20. TJ to John Adams, 8 January 1825, C.II.606. The spiritualist Adams was not impressed. "A mere game at push-pin," he replied. Adams to TJ, 22 January 1825, C.II.607. See also TJ to Francis Adrian Van der Kemp, 11 January 1825, F.X.338 ("The materialist [has been] fortified with . . . new proofs of his own creed").

21. NVa.33; TJ to Rev. James Madison, 19 July 1788, BC.XIII.380–81.

22. TJ to George F. Hopkins, 5 September 1822, LB.V.395.

23. Experience with intellectual fashions in Paris in the 1780s contributed to this

In deciding which proposed evidence was beyond nature and therefore not to be believed, Jefferson, like scientists before and since, depended in his judgments very much on the intensity of his initial views and the credentials of those making or disputing the claim. These considerations combined in different ways to test claims in religion and history as well as in science.

When he encountered the supernatural doctrines of Christianity, he rejected them outright on the premises of both materialism and sensationism. From the materialist perspective, the supernatural was untrue in itself for being outside of nature. From the sensationist perspective, the supernatural, such as miracles, abused proper epistemology by persuading the senses to believe something that was simply not the case. Belief in the supernatural also led to forfeiting intellectual freedom, since people came to trust the word of religious authorities rather than nature and their own senses.

Jefferson's careful instructions to his nephew about reading the Bible exemplify this:

> The facts which are within the ordinary course of nature you will believe on the authority of the writer [which] weigh in their favor in one scale, and their not being against the laws of nature does not weigh against them. But those facts of the bible which contradict the laws of nature, must be examined with care. . . . Examine upon what evidence [the] pretensions are founded, and whether that evidence is so strong as that its falsehood would be more improbable than a change of the laws of nature in the case.[24]

Although the writers of the Bible claim divine inspiration, Jefferson continued, and they are believed by millions, their narratives must still be checked against nature. In the Old Testament the account that the sun stood still must be examined in light of the knowledge "how contrary it is to the law of nature that a body revolving on its axis, as the earth does, should have stopped." From the New Testament he posed two "lives of Jesus." In one, Jesus "suspended and reversed the laws of nature at will." In the other he came to believe "pretensions of divinity" and was punished under Roman law for it. Under such presumably open-minded guidance, Jefferson's nephew was expected to select natural religion over supernatural Christianity.

---

outlook. Jefferson found a model, however, in H. B. de Saussure, the Swiss physicist and geologist: "Cautious in not letting his assent run before his evidence, he possesses the wisdom which so few possess in preferring ignorance to error. The contrary disposition in those who call themselves philosophers in [France] classes them in fact with the writers of romance." TJ to John Rutledge, Jr., 9 September 1788, BC.XIII.594.

24. TJ to Peter Carr, 10 August 1787, BC.XII.15–17. Further quotations in the paragraph also come from this source.

When it came to instructing the public in religion, Jefferson was far less open-minded. Discussing an acquaintance's proposed "Life of Jesus," he suggested censorship, which in his view was simply telling the truth. From the incidents of the New Testament, he said, only those should be selected that "are within the physical laws of nature, offending none by a denial or even a mention of what is not."[25]

On historical reports that he considered untrustworthy, Jefferson wasted no time: "When Livy and Siculus . . . tell us things which coincide with our experience of the order of nature, we credit them on their word and place their narrations among the records of credible history. But when they tell us of calves speaking, of statues sweating blood, and other things against the course of nature, we reject these as fables."[26]

With regard to scientific claims, the important question was not how to distinguish between the realms of the natural and the supernatural— it was already settled that only nature existed. Nor were the observed facts themselves much in dispute. The question was what to make of the facts. Which explanation was truly nature's explanation? The problem was especially pointed when scientific claims challenged Jefferson's cosmology, his view of how the world was created and what its order was. Indeed, the nearer science approached the core of his cosmological views, the more easily bent were his standards of what to accept and what to reject. Thus, when he received a report that a thirty-seven-pound stone had fallen from the sky onto a field in Connecticut and that the falling was attested by many reputable observers, he was not convinced: "Where facts are suggested, bearing no analogy with the law of nature as yet known to us, their verity needs proof proportioned to their difficulty."[27] On the other side, he was willing to accept "traditionary testimony" as fact if it certified the existence, somewhere in North America, of the mammoth, a creature that in his eyes could not be

25. TJ to Francis Adrian Van der Kemp, 25 April 1816, LB.XV.3. Jefferson was convinced that "Jesus did not mean to impose himself on mankind as Son of God, physically speaking." TJ to William Short, 4 August 1820, LB.XV.257. He twice prepared his own versions of the Gospels, which included only those events he believed to be within the realm of nature. See Adams, *Jefferson's Extracts from the Gospels*.

26. TJ to William Short, 4 August 1820, LB.XV.257.

27. TJ to Daniel Salmon, 15 February 1808, LB.XI.441. Jefferson's caution is also illustrated in a letter from Paris in which he expressed doubt about William Herschel's theories of volcanos on the moon and Jan Ingenhousz's theory that light promotes vegetation. That Ingenhousz was a scrupulous scientist, and Herschel a genius, Jefferson seems not to have recognized. TJ to Rev. James Madison, 19 July 1788, BC.XIII.379. The Reverend James Madison, obviously without success, had warned Jefferson against disparaging the conclusions of careful scientists: "It is not the Part of a Philosopher to deny the Possibility of certain Dispositions in Nature, when the Phenomena seem to indicate them, merely because he cannot fully comprehend the manner in which they act." Rev. James Madison to TJ, 27 March 1786, BC.IX.355–56.

extinct. He added that he did not need such testimony, however, for it would only "be adding the light of a taper to that of the meridian sun."[28]

At the center of Jefferson's view of the world lies the doctrine of the perfection of nature. Perfection means that the universe had, and still has, a harmonious design; that in this design all species that could be created have been created; that none have died out and no new ones can arise; and that all of this has taken place "in time," that is, at a particular beginning of creation. Jefferson presented these doctrines elegantly at the age of eighty in a letter to John Adams:

> I hold (without appeal to revelation) that when we take a view of the universe, in its parts general or particular, it is impossible for the human mind not to perceive and feel a conviction of design, consummate skill, and indefinite power in every atom of its composition. The movement of the heavenly bodies, so exactly held in their course by the balance of centrifugal and centripetal forces, the structure of our earth itself, with its distribution of lands, waters and atmosphere, animal and vegetable bodies, examined in all their minutest particles, insects mere atoms of life, yet as perfectly organised as man or mammoth, the mineral substances, their generation and uses, it is impossible, I say, for the human mind not to believe that there is, in all this, design, cause and effect, up to an ultimate cause, a fabricator of all things from matter and motion, their preserver and regulator while permitted to exist in their present forms, and their regenerator into new and other forms.[29]

In this statement Jefferson has added to the Lucretian premises of matter and motion an ultimate cause, or maker—God, but without the name—as well as that maker's perfect design of nature. This is scientific deism, or deistic science.

With a faith in a perfected nature, but in the face of the discovery of new plants and animals in America and elsewhere, eighteenth-century intellectuals encountered the challenge of accommodating the facts to their faith. The incentive was to develop a system of classifying nature that would be comprehensive and widely accepted and would reflect, insofar as it could, the design of the creator. Such a taxonomy was the apparent accomplishment of the Swedish naturalist Carolus Linnaeus (1707–78). For his taxonomic system Linnaeus was viewed by much of

28. NVa.54.
29. TJ to John Adams, 11 April 1823, C.II.592. The classic study of Jeffersonian cosmology is Daniel J. Boorstin, *The Lost World of Thomas Jefferson*. Although the world view Boorstin describes is certainly Jefferson's, the book is not so much about Jefferson as about "Jeffersonians," Boorstin's rather inexact name for several members of the American Philosophical Society who, except for Jefferson and Thomas Paine, lived in Philadelphia. A puzzling omission from the study is Charles Thomson, a pillar of the society and Jefferson's most enduring friend among its leaders.

the Enlightenment, including Jefferson (but with reservations), as only slightly less remarkable than Newton.[30]

A standardized system of naming nature, beginning with orders and kingdoms and concluding with genera and species, raised the question whether the categories, particularly the categories of the species, really existed in nature or were instead only categories devised by humans. Linnaeus was not, after all, the Creator. This problem of what was "true to nature" is traditionally understood in the language of particulars and universals. By most accounts, we directly experience only particulars (an olive tree, a court case, Thomas Jefferson). We nevertheless admit to thinking in universals (an olive grove, a legal system, Virginians). What is the status of universals in nature? Are they real, or do we make them up? If we make them up, is this because we cannot help it (it is our nature to do so), or is it because it is convenient for us? On the other hand, if the universals are real, how can we in principle know them, since in Lockean epistemology knowledge springs only from the sensation of the particulars? These were questions in the philosophy of nature in which Jefferson, unlike many others, was genuinely interested.

The activity of devising universals does indeed seem natural to human beings. But since different people, certainly different cultures, devise different universals, it appears that it is the devising that is natural to us, and not the universals themselves. Several aspects of this problem were of obvious importance to those who thought about taxonomy and classification in the eighteenth century, and Jefferson took positions on them. As a materialist and sensationist, he claimed that only the particulars were real; only they could be directly and certainly sensed. Universals, in contrast, were unreal abstractions, the consequence of thinking rather than perceiving. They could not constitute real knowledge. As Locke put it: "All things that exist [are] particulars. . . . [G]*eneral* and *universal* belong not to the real existence of things; but are the inventions and creatures of the understanding."[31]

---

30. Much of the admiration of Linnaeus is owing to his finally impressing a binomial system of names on plants, and not to his larger scheme of organizing the natural world. Jefferson once said, for instance, that "he who attempts to reduce [the productions of nature] into departments, is left to do it by the lines of his own fancy." TJ to Dr. John Manners, 22 February 1814, LB.XIV.99. But as an example of what Linnaean nomenclature replaced, consider Jefferson's own communication about the pecan, or Illinois nut, which had not yet been entered in the Linnaean system: "Juglans alba, foliolis lanceolatis, acuminatis, seratis, tomentosis, fructu minore, ovato, compresso, vix insculpto, dulci, putamine, tenerrimo." NVa.39. (The pecan is today classed with the hickories as *Carya illinoensis* or *Carya pecan*.) See, generally, James L. Larson, *Reason and Experience: The Representation of Natural Order in the Work of Carl von Linné* (Berkeley, 1971). An exhilarating discussion of the meaning of classifying nature in the eighteenth century is Michel Foucault, *The Order of Things*, esp. 125–45.

31. *Essay Concerning Human Understanding*, III.iii.1, 11.

In standard philosophical vocabulary, Locke's was a doctrine of nominalism, the view that universals are things that are named only. The opposite doctrine, that universals are inherent in nature, was called realism. Jefferson was a nominalist, believing that universals were nothing but names, even if they were names that were convenient and necessary. As he explained it: "Nature has, in truth, produced units only through all her works. Classes, orders, genera, species, are not of her work. Her creation is of individuals. No two animals are exactly alike, no two plants, nor even two leaves or blades of grass; no two crystallizations."[32] Nominalism is difficult to maintain without some qualification, however, and Jefferson conceded that while nature creates only individuals, people nevertheless act, perceive, and think as if the individuals were members of families. We do this, Jefferson said, as an aid to our memory. Since memory is not capable of retaining separately all the facts of nature that we sense, we arrange the facts into groups, selecting "such characteristic resemblances and differences as seem to us prominent and invariable."[33]

The key phrase here is the unpretentious "seem to us." It concedes that the resemblances and differences may not be true to nature. Yet if we fail to arrange the facts intelligently, Jefferson says, we might not be able to understand at all. Therefore, since we do understand, we are enabled to do so either because our memory requires, by its own constitution, an intelligent arrangement of nature or because our memory works only when the pattern that it makes corresponds to the pattern of nature. Whichever of these is true, we must make a pattern; we cannot work from particulars only. "By analyzing too minutely," as Jefferson said, "we often reduce our subject to atoms, of which the mind loses hold."[34] Thus, starting as an unqualified nominalist who believed that atoms were in fact the only true stuff of nature, Jefferson became what might be called a realist of convenience. The universals are not themselves real, but it is necessary that we make them up. They then appear real to us.[35]

Even if no system could be proven to be the true system, however, Jefferson was conscious of the need to be practical in the study of nature,

32. TJ to Dr. John Manners, 22 February 1814, LB.XIV.97 (but if species are "not of [nature's] work," how could Jefferson have believed in a chain of being? See below, p. 52). See also TJ to John Adams, 27 May 1813, C.II.323 (on classification in language).

33. TJ to Dr. John Manners, 22 February 1814, LB.XIV.98.

34. TJ to Edward Everett, 24 February 1823, LB.XV.414.

35. Without realizing it, Jefferson had adopted the medieval doctrine of conceptualism, a middle way out of the realism-nominalism debate. Under conceptualism, "universals are neither realities nor mere names but the concepts formed by the intellect when abstracting the similarities between perceived individual things." Betty Radice, *The Letters of Abelard and Heloise* (Baltimore, 1974), 14.

and he laid down criteria for a desirable system of nomenclature. Most important, the system should be easy to fix in the memory. This would happen, Jefferson said, when classifications were based upon the most "prominent and invariable" similarities and differences among groups of individuals. By "prominent" was meant "such exterior and visible characteristics as every traveller is competent to observe."[36] With this, an anticipation of modern field guides, Jefferson democratized the study of nature. Second, a classification system must admit "supplementary insertions as new productions are discovered." In an era of scientific exploration, the need for this standard is obvious. If anything other than an open framework had been adopted, the discoveries of new species by Lewis and Clark and Alexander von Humboldt, to name the most prominent explorers among Jefferson's acquaintances, would have distorted, if not toppled, an existing system. Finally, a system must be widely accepted. Without that, even the best arrangement of nature is worthless, for scientists would be unable to communicate with one another. It was largely by "rallying all to the same names for the same objects," as Jefferson put it, that Linnaeus had achieved what his predecessors had been unable to achieve.

Over his lifetime Jefferson found several occasions to develop his own systems for classifying nature, in these cases nature considered abstractly and as the whole of knowledge. The opportunities came in two practical areas: in arranging a library and in organizing school curriculums. Jefferson's large library, one of the finest in the nation, clearly required a system to make it usable. His instinct for order and his concern about classification ensured that the system would be carefully thought out. But the role of nature can be appreciated only as part of Jefferson's constant urge to understand the productions of the human intellect as a reflection of an external system of nature. In his library classifications nature may be seen first in the basic division of all knowledge into three areas derived from Bacon and then under selected subdivisions of those areas.[37]

Bacon had designated Memory, Reason, and Imagination as the "faculties of the mind" that, together, constituted all human understanding. Jefferson first made use of this division for purposes of organizing his library in 1783, and with only slight changes he used it thereafter, employing it not only for his own library but also for the library of the University of Virginia, which he planned in the 1820s. For his library arrangement Jefferson transformed, if necessarily inexactly, Bacon's

36. TJ to Dr. John Manners, 22 February 1814, LB.XIV.101. The remaining quotations in this paragraph are also from the letter to Manners.

37. See, generally, Charles B. Sanford, *Thomas Jefferson and His Library* (Hamden, Conn., 1977).

categories into the broad subject areas of History, Philosophy, and Fine Arts. Although this plan was an obvious improvement over the typical library organization at the time—by size of book, date of acquisition, or author's name—in retrospect it appears quite awkward. The main reason is that faculties of the mind do not correspond, even in theory, to the external nature that the system as a whole was designed to represent. The plan is also awkward because the three categories substantially underutilize the capacity of the mind to retain distinctions, thereby ignoring a criterion that Jefferson himself had insisted on for scientific classification.[38]

As appears from table 2, nature is intimately bound up with the first two divisions of the plan but is conspicuously absent in the third. Between memory and reason all the natural sciences are covered, as well as all that concerns natural theology, natural morality, natural law, and natural rights. The third division, Fine Arts, is related to nature only by negation: art is precisely what nature is not. (Gardening within Fine Arts refers to landscape gardening—vegetable gardening is under agriculture—which Jefferson considered not a science but an exercise of the imagination.)

Within this outline an obvious logical problem is that half of History is Natural History but none of Philosophy is called Natural Philosophy. Instead, Natural Philosophy quite illogically forms a category within History. A second problem is the plan's ill-considered terminology, as in the forced distinction between Natural History and Natural History Proper. Yet the system has convincing, if obscured, formal properties. Both History and Philosophy have two principal subdivisions, and once "civil" and "moral" are translated as "human," and insofar as "mathematical philosophy" may be transformed into "natural philosophy," the plan may be seen as both elegant and cleanly related to nature:

History: Human history
              Natural history
Philosophy: Human philosophy
              Natural philosophy

In the 1820s, when Jefferson prepared a catalogue of book purchases proposed for the University of Virginia library, he took the occasion to improve the system in table 2. At the same time he made it even more "natural." He accomplished this in part by reducing the number of

38. Several years after Jefferson adopted the threefold Baconian division, James Madison, who always saw a more complex world than did Jefferson, enumerated seven faculties of the mind. His listing, which includes memory and imagination but not reason, was compiled for purposes other than the organization of knowledge, but it illustrates both the arbitrariness and the inconvenience of using faculties of the mind to establish library classes. *Federalist* No. 37 (Wright ed.), 268.

TABLE 2
Jefferson's Library Classification, Adapted to Show Leading Features about Nature

I. History [memory]	Civil History (ancient; foreign; British; American; ecclesiastical)
	Natural History Physics (natural philosophy; agriculture; chemistry; surgery)
	Natural History Proper Animals (anatomy; zoology) Vegetables (botany) Minerals (mineralogy) Occupations of Man (technical arts)
II. Philosophy [reason]	Moral Philosophy (law of nature and nations; religion; law; politics; economics)
	Mathematical Philosophy (engineering; mathematics; astronomy; geography)
III. Fine Arts [imagination]	[Twenty subjects in literature, languages, and the arts, including gardening]

Source: Adapted from the classification Jefferson prepared for the Library of Congress.

subdivisions and in part, paradoxically, by eliminating the word "nature" itself. The large division History remained, but it was now divided into Civil History and Physical History, which included all the sciences. The large division Philosophy likewise remained, but under Mathematical philosophy only arithmetic and geometry were retained. Nothing at all in the revised scheme was called either "natural history" or "natural philosophy."[39]

Jefferson's final words on the place of nature in library classification appear in a garrulous and rather strange letter of 1824.[40] First he accedes to the realities of libraries—and nature—by agreeing with his correspondent that the sciences, not the faculties of the mind, should be the basis of the divisions. But then, inspired by recent contact with the Ideologues, he wished to show that a new "science of the mind" might be incorporated into the library classification. He was uncertain whether such a science should be parallel to zoology, botany, and mineralogy (all under natural history) or should be a subdivision of zoology. And if zoology were to be subdivided, should not one of its branches be "moral zoology"? For purposes of a library classification, when a field is named "moral zoology," something is wrong, whatever

39. The classification plan for the University of Virginia library is in Pdvr. 1093.
40. TJ to Augustus B. Woodward, 24 March 1824, LB.XVI.18.

the theoretical justification. With this completely unnatural idea for classifying books, ironically based on an unqualified doctrine of materialistic nature, Jefferson laid down his library pen.

Jefferson was more successful at incorporating nature into the three curricular organizations he worked on over his life: for the College of William and Mary in the late 1770s, for the entire state of Virginia in 1814 (this remained an ideal only), and for the University of Virginia from 1818 into the 1820s. His task in education was perhaps simpler than that for libraries. The number of professors was far less than the number of categories of books. The detail to be kept in mind was less. A curriculum once under way retained a flexibility that a library plan did not. Above all, an educational system had no alternative but to be practical: teachers and students could not be manipulated as easily as books and mental categories.

Jefferson's educational ideas are those of the Scottish Enlightenment: calling for distinct levels of schools, the lowest level to include the entire citizenry; advocating public rather than private education; transforming colleges that trained primarily for the ministry into full-fledged universities; and emphasizing science.[41] Thus, in 1779, for a committee of the state assembly, Jefferson proposed an expansion and rearrangement of the William and Mary curriculum to "enlarge its sphere of science." New professors were to teach natural philosophy, natural history, anatomy, and medicine. Although the proposals did not pass the legislature, pressure from inside the college (including from Jefferson, who was for a time on the Board of Visitors) eventually led to the adoption of all of them except, in name, a professor of natural history.[42]

Three decades later, in retirement from public office, Jefferson prepared a comprehensive educational program for the state. Central to this plan were "general schools," which followed instruction at the elementary level.[43] The divisions of these schools, corresponding roughly and incompletely to those of his library, were history (including languages), mathematics (including all of science), and philosophy (including ethics, law, politics, and economics). They thus mark a development away from a strict Baconian system of classifying knowledge and towards the modern divisions of a liberal arts curriculum into humanities, natural sciences, and social sciences.

Jefferson's culminating work in the classification of learning was for

41. See William Christian Lehmann, *Henry Home, Lord Kames, and the Scottish Enlightenment* (The Hague, 1971), xx–xxi.
42. Bill No. 80, "for Amending the Constitution of the College of William and Mary, 1779," BC.II.535–42; TJ, Autobiography (1821), KP.50; NVa.150–51.
43. TJ to Peter Carr, 7 September 1814, LB.XIX.219–20.

the University of Virginia. In the document drawn up for the founding of the university, the Rockfish Gap Report of 1818, Jefferson and other commissioners proposed ten branches of learning, with a single professor for each.[44] One branch comprised natural philosophy (physics), chemistry (including agriculture), and mineralogy. Another was for botany and zoology. A third, called physico-mathematics, included astronomy and geography.

Six years after the Rockfish Gap Report, when the University of Virginia was about to open, Jefferson had lost two of the professorships, just as he had for William and Mary over fifty years earlier. But he adjusted now, as he had then, issuing a revised list for eight professors by absorbing two fields into a single School of Natural Philosophy and by forming a new School of Natural History, into which he placed chemistry and mineralogy along with botany and zoology. This arrangement made organizational sense, and it also made more prominent than before the underlying role that nature had in the curriculum. Table 3 presents three stages in Jefferson's classification of nature in higher education. As in the case of the library plans, the later proposals are more coherent than the earlier ones. Renamed, rationalized, and rearranged, the subjects of nature now make more sense relative to other subjects. They are more likely to meet human needs and understanding, as well.

As Jefferson's library and curricular plans suggest, he had two levels of meaning for both natural history and natural philosophy, a general meaning and a specific one. Generally, natural history contained the animal, vegetable, and mineral "productions of nature" that were the subject of the longest chapter in *Notes on the State of Virginia*. In the library and schools this meant zoology, botany, and mineralogy (with which Jefferson associated geology). Generally, natural philosophy consisted of physics, astronomy, and chemistry. The specific meanings of the terms are more difficult to discern from the library and school plans, but they can be deduced easily from Jefferson's private correspondence, where they are not part of a conscious and often compromised system. There, natural history reduces to zoology, natural philosophy to physics. A credit to Jefferson's linguistic habits, this consistency nevertheless demonstrates that only in a retreat to the world of letters could he preserve a verbal integrity with nature. At the same time, it suggests that a durable, rational system of nature, the great aim of Enlightenment cosmology, had no accepted public existence.

44. Rockfish Gap Report (Report of the Commissioners for the University of Virginia), August 1818, PJ.337–38.

TABLE 3
Nature in Higher Education (from three plans by Jefferson)

Plan for General Schools (1814)

Department of Mathematics
   Pure mathematics
   Physico-mathematics (including astronomy and geography)
   Physics or Natural Philosophy
   Chemistry
   Natural history, to wit: mineralogy
   Botany
   Zoology
   Anatomy
   Theory of Medicine

Professors Proposed in the Rockfish Gap Report (1818)

Physico-mathematics (including astronomy and geography)
Physics or Natural Philosophy
Chemistry (including agriculture)
Mineralogy (including geology)
Botany
Zoology

University of Virginia Professorships (1824)

School of Natural Philosophy (including applied mathematics, engineering, physics, and astronomy)

School of Natural History
   Botany
   Zoology
   Mineralogy
   Chemistry
   Geology
   Rural Economy

Note: In the plan of 1814 the Department of Mathematics is the second department; the first and third are for languages and philosophy. TJ to Peter Carr, 7 September 1814, LB.XIX.214–20. In the Rockfish Gap Report of 1818 the professorships not listed were for ancient languages, modern languages, pure mathematics, medicine, government, municipal law, and "ideology" (grammar ethics, rhetoric, fine arts). Pdvr.1100–1101. In the University of Virginia plan of 1824 the professorships not listed are those for ancient languages, modern languages, mathematics, anatomy and medicine, moral philosophy, and law. Minutes of the Board of Visitors of the University of Virginia, 7 April 1824, LB.XIX.433–35.

Among the subjects of nature, Jefferson viewed "no science with more partiality than natural history."[45] Of all the fields of nature, indeed none other suited Jefferson's outlook so well. Natural history in its

45. TJ to G. C. de la Coste, 24 May 1807, LB.XI.206. For an illustration of the *Jeffersonia,* a plant honoring Jefferson as a natural historian, see plate 6.

wider understanding was the perfect subject for a materialist because it was always concretely there. It was the perfect subject for a sensationist because it was studied with all of one's senses and, compared with the subjects of natural philosophy, required less use of reason, imagination, mathematics, or scientific apparatus. It was a fit subject for a particularist and nominalist because each of its objects was knowable and potentially important by itself. It was fit for an Enlightenment scientist because it promised to display the perfection of created nature; for a planter, farmer, and country gentleman because a knowledge of it contributed to his livelihood and was always available for his pleasure; and for an American because it symbolized his nation.

In this setting of Jefferson's basic beliefs and language about physical nature, what were his methods and his subordinate assumptions? how did he proceed as a naturalist?[46] In the first place, he often does not define the questions he wants to answer; rather, his initial step was to accumulate data, nearly any data. Unfortunately, the collection of data was also the most important and at times the only step in Jefferson's studies. At this task of collection, however, he was compulsive. His formal record keeping is scarcely to be believed. In 1766 he began a *Garden Book,* on the planting, the blossoming, and, where appropriate, the harvesting of flowers, fruits, and vegetables at Monticello. With the exception of time spent away from his estate, he maintained the book for fifty-eight years. From 1774 until 1826 he kept a *Farm Book,* organized under two dozen topics, such as tobacco, preparation of ground, slaves, fuel and light, and buildings. From 1776 until 1820 he made entries in a weather memorandum book and twice summarized portions of these, with commentary, noting how many thousands of meteorological observations contributed to his conclusions.[47]

Jefferson not only maintained his own records of nature, he encouraged others to do so. In the middle of the Revolution he proposed an exchange of meteorological data with an Italian correspondent.[48] He asked James Madison to "keep a diary" under twelve headings: ther-

---

46. Three studies provide a chronological backdrop: Raymond Phineas Stearns, *Science in the British Colonies of America;* Brooke Hindle, *The Pursuit of Science in Revolutionary America, 1735–1789;* and John C. Greene, *American Science in the Age of Jefferson.* Greene holds that *Notes on the State of Virginia* "set the tone and posed the problems for much of American science in the early national period." P. 409. Good general studies on Jefferson are Charles A. Browne, "Thomas Jefferson and the Scientific Trends of His Time"; and Edwin T. Martin, *Thomas Jefferson.*

47. The first summary, for 1772–77, is under "Climate" in *Notes on Virginia.* Jefferson says that he made 3,698 observations of the weather for it. The second, apparently prepared simply out of curiosity, covers 1810–16 and is based on 3,905 observations. GB.622–28.

48. TJ to Giovanni Fabbroni, 8 June 1778, BC.II.195.

mometer, barometer, wind direction, and weather conditions twice a day; and the beginning and end of seasons for plants and birds.[49] He envisioned statewide, national, and even international schemes for the systematic collection of information on climate and natural history. For Virginia, he "meant to have engaged some person in every county, giving them each a thermometer, to observe that and the winds twice a day . . . and to communicate their observations to me at the end of the year."[50] He intended to summarize these observations in both tabular and cartographic form and to convey them to the American Philosophical Society as a sample of what should be done in every state. To another correspondent he proposed an elaborate meteorological chart for every day of the year to be kept in the coastal states.[51] Near the end of his life, pointing to *Notes on the State of Virginia* as "perhaps the first attempt . . . to bring together the few facts [on climate] then known," he outlined a project more ambitious than has even yet been implemented from a single source in the United States. He called for the elaborate record keeping proposed earlier, but in each state and to be "repeated once or twice a century, to show the effect of clearing and culture towards changes of climate."[52]

Questionnaires and journals supplemented these systems as means for acquiring data in natural history. *Notes on the State of Virginia* was itself a response to a questionnaire, and in writing the book Jefferson circulated his own subquestionnaire in order to secure additional information. The meticulous instructions he prepared for the Lewis and Clark Expedition include an encyclopedic questionnaire that resulted in journals that were mined long afterwards.[53]

Beyond his own observations and those he elicited from others, Jefferson promoted the study of nature through correspondence, which in many ways took the place of modern conferences, periodicals, and the circulation of studies in draft form. It is not possible to say just how many of Jefferson's estimated thirty-five thousand letters contain scientific information, but perhaps two thousand of them. In addition to the accumulation of written records, Jefferson was active in nature study through the exchange of physical objects: seeds, cuttings of plants, animals, fossils, Indian artifacts. He was active, as well, through his curricular proposals and in the scientific societies to which he belonged, notably the American Philosophical Society. Just before he became president of the United States, he suggested a "central society" of state

49. TJ to James Madison, 16 March 1784, BC.VII.31.
50. TJ to C. F. C. deVolney, 8 January 1797, LB.IX.364.
51. TJ to Nicholas King, 21 April 1805, M.V.25.
52. TJ to Lewis E. Beck, 16 July 1824, LB.XVI.71, 72.
53. See PJ.308–15.

agricultural societies, for which, he noted, there was "certainly a much greater abundance of material" than for a philosophical society. Not long after he retired from office he drew up plans for a federation of these organizations.[54]

Jefferson was unquestionably more comfortable collecting and exchanging information than he was working out ideas explaining the data he had acquired. This was a stance well adapted to refuting other men's theories made up from weak data. The most dramatic example of Jefferson's data in action is his exhaustive refutation, in *Notes on the State of Virginia,* of the comte de Buffon's theory that animals of the New World were inferior to those of the Old.[55] Jefferson did not say he had a better country because it produced so many and such large animals— only that his data refuted Buffon's.

When Jefferson attempted his own theory, his drive for facts led him to exalt, at least in principle, inductive over deductive methods of understanding nature. In this he was Baconian to the core. He complained that unless a scientist believed in patient, open-minded work with facts, he could show very much whatever he wished to show. He found Buffon, for instance, claiming in one place that a cold climate produced large animals and in another place that a hot climate produced them. With such disregard for facts, he remarked, Buffon "takes any hypothesis whatever, or its reverse, and furnishes explanations equally specious or persuasive."[56]

Jefferson's own scientific methods are well illustrated by his work with the archeology and, despite some ideological distortions, the anthropology of American Indians. Of an earlier investigator he once remarked: "He selects . . . all the facts, and adopts all the falsehoods which favor his theory, and very gravely retails such absurdities as zeal for a theory alone could swallow."[57] He therefore counseled against building theory concerning the Indians from too few facts or approaching the facts with too firm a theory in mind.[58] In his own studies he was scrupulous in describing the facts and archeologically advanced in his respect for the original condition of the sites where artifacts were found.[59] He once thought of reducing to a single convenient orthography his prized collection of vocabularies from Indian tribes, ultimately

---

54. TJ to Robert R. Livingston, 16 February 1801, F.VII.492; TJ, "Scheme for a System of Agricultural Societies" for Virginia, March 1811, LB.XVII.404–11.

55. NVa.47–58.

56. NVa.275n98.

57. TJ to John Adams, 11 June 1812, C.II.305–6 (about Joseph François Lafitau [1681–1746], who resided in Canada for six years and left with the same European ideas about Indians with which he had arrived).

58. See, e.g., TJ to Charles Thomson, 20 September 1787, BC.XII.159.

59. NVa.97–100.

lost; but when he considered that "this would occasion two sources of error instead of one," he decided to keep the records in the language in which they had been transcribed—English, French, or German.[60]

Jefferson's caution in most matters of science derived not only from his concentration on facts and factuality but also from his experience in Paris, where unsupportable theories (especially ones concerning America) abounded. The price of this caution, however, as mentioned above in the discussion of Lucretius, was a scientific imagination of restricted range. For this reason among others, he contributed less to science than did Franklin, Rittenhouse, Priestley, Rush, or Barton, his colleagues in the American Philosophical Society. His confidence in the existence of scientific truth was no less than theirs, but he feared more than they the acceptance of scientific error. Now and then he permitted himself some guesses—about winds or about medicine—but he was clear to label his remarks speculative and acknowledged that we know "too little of the operations of Nature in the physical world to assign causes with any degree of confidence."[61] "A patient pursuit of facts, and cautious combination and comparison of them," he wrote in the margin of his own copy of Notes on the State of Virginia, "is the drudgery to which man is subjected by his Maker, if he wishes to attain sure knowledge."[62]

It was indeed sure knowledge that Jefferson sought. But that came only after acquiring particular knowledge. Knowledge itself, moreover, was worth acquiring only if it might lead to the establishment or improvement of a theoretical system that would elaborate the design of nature or if it were useful to mankind. These standards of system and utility, and especially their limitations, may be seen at work in Jefferson's cramped attitude towards chemistry and his confrontation with geology.

Jefferson's early primitiveness regarding chemistry is indicated by a reference in Notes on Virginia to "the elements of earth, air, water, and fire."[63] When he reached France, therefore, his mind was suddenly opened to a new field of science. "The researches of the Natural philosophers of Europe," he wrote to a scientific acquaintance, "seem mostly in the field of chemistry," and he followed the experiments closely.[64] When Buffon, his flawed hero, "affected to consider chemistry but as cookery," he held out a nobler prospect for the science: "I think it, on the contrary, among the most useful of sciences, and big with future

60. TJ to William Dunbar, 12 January 1801, LB.X.193; NVa.101.

61. TJ to Jean Baptiste Le Roy, 17 November 1786, BC.X.525 (the subject was breezes).

62. NVa.277n104.

63. NVa.48.

64. TJ to Ezra Stiles, 17 July 1785, BC.VIII.299.

discoveries for the utility and safety of the human race."[65] But he at once qualified this judgment. He thought that the techniques of analysis were not yet sufficiently refined to be certain of the results. And he felt that Lavoisier's efforts towards a standardized nomenclature were premature, possibly leading to a distorted understanding of relationships in the field and the consequent retarding of "the progress of the science by a jargon."[66]

Jefferson did not maintain his faith in chemistry. On the one hand, order did not come quickly to the science. (The periodic table was not devised until eighty years after Jefferson's initial enthusiasm for the subject.) On the other hand, and perhaps partly because there was no adequate system, he unwittingly found that he was himself reduced to seeing chemistry as cookery. He claimed only to have utilitarian aims in mind and to be chafing over the failure of practicing chemists to be very practical. But in fact he turned against the science. As he wrote a correspondent in 1805: "The chemists have filled volumes on the composition of a thousand substances of no sort of importance to the purposes of life; while the arts of making bread, butter, cheese, vinegar, soap, beer, cider, etc., remain totally unexplained."[67]

In the absence of either theoretical elegance or domestic applications, Jefferson was willing to excuse his grandson from the formal study of chemistry completely:

> It is the least useful and the least amusing to a country gentleman of all the ordinary branches of science. In the exercises of the country and progress over our farms, every step presents some object of botany, natural history, comparative anatomy, etc. But for chemistry you must shut yourself up in your laboratory and neglect the care of your affairs and of your health which calls you out of doors.[68]

Since Jefferson would never wish to be shut up in a laboratory himself, he did not wish it on his grandson. More telling in his comment, and more unfortunate from a later perspective, is his suggestion that a farmer has no use for chemistry. The grandson may have been raised to be a country gentleman, but he also became manager of the family farms. Yet the grandfather deliberately steered him away from an important element of scientific agriculture.

65. TJ to Rev. James Madison, 19 July 1788, BC.XIII.381.

66. Ibid. See, generally, Maurice P. Crosland, *Historical Studies in the Language of Chemistry* (London, 1962), 133–224.

67. TJ to Thomas Ewell, 30 August 1805, S.I.380. For a nearly identical complaint several years later, see TJ to Thomas Cooper, 10 July 1812, LB.XIII.176.

68. TJ to Thomas Jefferson Randolph, 3 January 1809, BB.377. For similar sentiments about the delights of botany over the tedium of mineralogy (for a "country gentleman"), see TJ to Thomas Cooper, 7 October 1814, LB.XIV.201.

The reason why Jefferson ignored the uses of chemistry in agriculture was not that such uses were unknown, although they were not highly developed.[69] Rather, his failure to appreciate chemistry on the farm may have stemmed from his failure to appreciate geology, a failure that was conspicuous.

Anyone contemplating "every step" taken on a farm in western Virginia, as Jefferson does in the letter quoted above, would recall the rocks in its fields and on its hillsides. But Jefferson omits geology from the realms of nature encountered on the walks of a country gentleman. Why? First, geology did not pass his standards for studying nature. It had no discernible system and, so far as he could tell, was not much use either. If ordinary rocks broke down by geochemical process to supply nutrients for the soil, Jefferson neither knew this nor had a niche for it in his organization of nature.[70] Second and more important, geology only confused Jefferson's cosmology of a perfected nature. Geology asked about the interior of the earth, which no naturalist could explore. It asked about time so old that no one could properly reckon it. It seemed to be a nearly imaginary science, unobservable in its processes and unverifiable as to most of its operations.

Jefferson's disrespect for geology, like his indifference to chemistry, developed over a number of years. In *Notes on Virginia* he discussed useful minerals at length and was not without curiosity in geology. He wondered, if not deeply, about the formation of mountain ranges, the declination of limestone veins in rocks, the origin of the Natural Bridge, and whether America once contained inland seas. Most important from the viewpoint of his methods of studying nature, he probed and rejected three theories that had been put forward to explain the presence of shells in fossil form.

The first theory, that a universal deluge had reached the ridge of the North Mountains of Virginia, he considered "out of the laws of nature." The second, that "some great convulsion of nature" might have thrown shells to the peaks of the Andes, he found improbable. "No fact has taken place . . . in the thousands of years of recorded

69   ̲rson publicized the success of gypsum as a fertilizer, though he found the pamp̲let that proved its virtues "bunglingly composed." TJ to John W. Eppes, 19 June 1803, S.I.337. See also TJ to Sir John Sinclair, 23 March 1798, S.I.351 (praising the "application of the new chemistry to the subject of manures"); and, generally, FB.195–200.

70. Jefferson's library catalogue contains no reference to the most significant early study in American geology, which by its title alone would be of interest to a scientific farmer: William Maclure, *Observations on the geology of the United States of America; with some remarks on the effect produced on the nature and fertility of soils by the decomposition of the different classes of rocks; and an application to the fertility of every state in the Union in reference to the accompanying geological map.* The book was published in 1809, the same year Jefferson wrote his grandson that there was no need for a future agriculturalist to study chemistry.

history," he wrote, "which proves the existence of any natural agents" that might have accomplished such a feat. A third theory, also "not established," was that the shells grew where they were found, as if organically. This he likewise rejected. "Nature may," he admitted, "have provided an equivalent operation [besides the usual process for generating shells in animals] by passing the same materials through the pores of calcerous earths and stones." But this hypothesis of an organic geology should be doubted all the more because it violated the principle of the "economy of nature"—that one effect (shells) must have only one cause (they must all have been parts of animals).[71]

The mystery of the shells began a series of encounters between Jefferson and geology in which Nature defeated the naturalist. Only weeks after publication of *Notes on Virginia* in the summer of 1787, he was puzzled once more, this time on the origin and placement of rocks generally, not of fossil rocks alone. Discussing the origin of the inclination of strata of rocks, he rejected the following four theories: (1) subsidence (presumably cooling after being molten, which, he said, should have led to strata in concentric circles); (2) the earth's rotation (which should have resulted in strata parallel to the earth's axis, a position he basically held in *Notes on Virginia*); (3) explosions (widespread volcanic action, for which there was no proof); and (4) convulsions (earthquakes; but it was improbable that such convulsions had "deformed every spot of the earth").[72]

Considering the thoughtfulness of the correspondent to whom he was writing, Jefferson's rejection of all four theories was rather out of hand. But he had recently been persuaded of evidence for a fifth possibility, namely, that rocks, and possibly shells, actually grew. On the basis of speculation and hearsay evidence, with which he normally had no sympathy, this new idea seized his mind, and he accepted for rocks the amazing theory that his just-published book had doubted for shells: "It is now generally agreed that rock grows, and it seems that it grows in layers in every direction, as the branches of trees grow in all directions. Why seek further the solution of this phenomenon? Everything in

71. NVa.32–33. See also TJ to David Rittenhouse, 25 January 1786, BC.IX.216 (arguing against some "throw of nature" that could force up parts of the seabed to the heights of the mountains); and TJ to Rittenhouse, 18 September 1787, BC.XII.144 ("so unlike the processes of nature to produce the same effect in two different ways, that I can only bring myself to agree [that the growth of shells] is not impossible"). Jefferson had leaned one way and then the other concerning the plausibility of the theory from 1785 to 1787. See also the 1785 (Paris) edition of *Notes on Virginia*, 51–55 (F.III.118–19); NVa.265–66n9; Rev. James Madison to TJ, 28 December 1786, BC.X.643; TJ, "Notes of a Tour into the Southern Parts of France, 1787," BC.XI.460–62; and TJ to Rev. James Madison, 13 August 1787, BC.XII.30.

72. TJ to Charles Thomson, 20 September 1787, BC.XII.160 (part of a continuing correspondence set off by NVa.29–33).

nature decays. If it were not reproduced then by growth, there would be a chasm."[73]

The muddle of error that Jefferson waded into by favorably entertaining the growth-of-rocks theory is remarkable. It can be explained only partly by the influence of French scientists, whose fads he ordinarily guarded against. It arises mainly from his need for an explanation, consistent with his cosmology, of a harmoniously created, living world. The potential of what he called a chasm in nature threatened his assumption of a perfect or near-perfect creation of the world. Since everything in nature decayed, and since everything that could be created had been created, growth was necessary for the regeneration of nature. If other natural objects grew, why not rocks? Thus Jefferson succumbed, at least temporarily, to a model of the material earth as a living being. In this he was perhaps supported in the back of his mind by the seeds that Lucretius had held to be the ultimate particles in nature. The view was also confirmed by his classification systems, which, by grouping together animals, vegetables, and minerals under natural history, implied that geology was a kind of history and, like any history, should be about growth and decay. Jefferson had in effect become an organic geologist.

Several points are striking in Jefferson's uninformed, impatient, and ultimately confusing discussion. First, the growth-and-decay solution to the problem of the rocks is supported by no more evidence than are other suggested answers. Indeed, regarding the creation of fossil shells by the same method, where at least some visible "evidence" existed, he had frankly stated that the theory was "not established." Second, especially given the meager evidence, his abrupt foreclosing of investigation ("Why seek further the solution of this phenomenon?") reveals an unexpected antiscientific streak. Finally, the passage is an extreme example of faith in the "economy of nature," the doctrine that everything that happens in nature has only one explanation.

The economy of nature deserves attention on its own. It is a doctrine of monocausality. In Jefferson's words, "According to the rules of philosophizing, when one sufficient cause for an effect is known, it is not within the economy of nature to employ two."[74] In the case of the growth of shells, Jefferson had used the doctrine to suggest that the growth theory was implausible, since another explanation was widely

---

73. Ibid.
74. TJ to John Page, 16 August 1804, F.VIII.316. See also TJ to Charles Thomson, 17 December 1786, BC.X.608 ("Is it reasonable to suppose [the Creator] made two jobs of his creation?"); NVa.56 (a "rule of philosophy . . . teaches us to ascribe like effects to like causes," so that we find "uniformity in the operations of nature"); and TJ to John Adams, 11 April 1823, C.II.592 ("never . . . employ two principles to solve a difficulty when one will suffice").

accepted. But in the seemingly analogous case of the growth of rocks, the doctrine was applied quite differently. The notion that rocks grew was not a theory inherently any more likely than the competing theories. But it was a distinctive theory, while the other three were sufficiently similar to one another that it was difficult to choose among them. Yet if one could not choose from among three theories, then the economy-of-nature doctrine argued against accepting any of them. Thus did monocausality lead to error. By adhering to nature's economy, Jefferson cast aside all the explanations for the origin and placement of rocks eventually proven correct and chose in their place the single available incorrect theory.

For a while Jefferson may have believed this least likely of geological theories. But no single theory of the earth's formation was widely accepted by scientists of the time. A debate over the origin of the earth was then being waged between two schools—the Neptunists, who postulated a universal deluge, after which rocks were formed by sedimentation; and the Vulcanists, who held, or added, that the earth's crust was created by eruptions of molten rock from within. In the large, Jefferson leaned towards the Vulcanists, who seemed to him the more empirical of the two schools and whose story of creation contained appropriate drama and did not have the biblical overtones of the Neptunists. But in his view geology was incapable of being empirical enough, and so he escaped the intellectual warfare by adopting, at least temporarily, the growth hypothesis. "Our researches into the texture of our globe," he said, "could be but so superficial, compared with its vast interior constitution"; in such a situation "we must guard against drawing our conclusions deeper than we dig."[75]

Jefferson was frustrated by geology in the 1780s, and the subject continued to pass his understanding and therefore his interest. Just weeks before he died he chose a timebound deistic image of creation over the two unspecifiably long ones named for pagan gods. Writing about the curriculum for the University of Virginia, he mounted his final attack:

> To [geology] I would give the least possible time. To learn, as far as observation has informed us, the ordinary arrangement of the different strata of minerals in the earth . . . is useful. But the dreams about the modes of creation, inquiries whether our globe has been formed by the agency of fire or water, how many years it cost Vulcan or Neptune to

75. TJ to Thomas Cooper, 10 August 1810, LB.XII.401; TJ to Henry R. Schoolcraft, 26 January 1822, FBx.268. See, generally, Charles Coulston Gillispie, *Genesis and Geology, a Study in the Relations of Scientific Thought, Natural Theology, and Social Opinion in Great Britain, 1790–1850*, 41–97; and Mott T. Greene, *Geology in the Nineteenth Century: Changing Views of a Changing World* (Ithaca, 1982), 19–68.

produce what the fiat of the Creator would effect by a single act of will, is too idle to be worth a single hour of any man's life.[76]

With not many hours left in his own life and certain of his own cosmology, Jefferson could not recommend dreams about the modes of creation.

To go only "as far as observation has informed us" was indeed Jefferson's most constant rule in studying nature. But as his meandering in geological theory shows, it was a rule of selective application. The greatest test of this rule concerns the extinction of animals. Jefferson was an avid paleontologist. At work on *Notes on Virginia,* he asked George Rogers Clark for "the most desirable object in Natural history," namely, specimens of bones. A number of years later he corresponded about fossil remains that had been found in a cave in Greenbriar County, in the western part of the state (now in West Virginia). Shortly after he was elected president he inquired of Robert Livingston about the discovery in New York "of some large bones, supposed to be of the mammoth." During his presidency he arranged for William Clark, recently returned from the expedition up the Missouri, to secure several hundred bones from Big Bone Lick, Kentucky, a portion of which he sent to France for research and exhibit.[77]

Jefferson's paleontological interests sprang not only from scientific curiosity but also from a zeal to prove that his cosmology was correct. Since the earth had been created complete and it remains complete, nothing could become extinct. Paleontology—Jefferson did not use the word—was simply the zoology of the deceased. The guiding axiom was that if the bones exist, the beast exists. Any bones that came from an

76. TJ to John P. Emmet, 2 May 1826, LB.XVI.171. In the Rockfish Gap Report Jefferson had already laid down the guideline in education: "Mineralogy . . . is here understood to embrace what is real in geology." PJ.339. See also Jefferson's "Explanation" accompanying his catalogue of books for the library of the University of Virginia. Pdvr.1092.

77. TJ to George Rogers Clark, 26 November 1782, BC.VI.204; TJ to John Stuart, 10 November 1796, LB.IX.350; TJ to Robert R. Livingston, 14 December 1800, F.VII.463; TJ to William Clark, 19 December 1807, LB.XI.405. The American Philosophical Society circulated a request for "one or more entire skeletons of the Mammoth, so called, or such other unknown animals as either have been, or hereafter may be discovered in America." 4 Trans. Am. Phil. Soc. xxxvii (1799).

The recovery of the great American "*incognitum*" was the project of Jefferson's friend Charles Willson Peale, the natural-history impresario of Philadelphia. See Charles Coleman Sellers, *Mr. Peale's Museum,* 123–58. Peale's painting, *The Exhumation of the Mastodon,* is reproduced in plate 5. On Jefferson as a paleontologist see Silvio A. Bedini's pamphlet, *Thomas Jefferson and American Vertebrate Paleontology* (Charlottesville: Virginia Division of Mineral Resources, 1985); George Gaylord Simpson, "The Beginnings of Vertebrate Paleontology in North America," 86 Proc. Am. Phil. Soc. 130–88 (1958); and Howard C. Rice, Jr., "Jefferson's Gift of Fossils to the Museum of Natural History in Paris."

animal not yet known to be alive must therefore come from an animal that could be found alive somewhere. Further, if the bones came from a large animal, they were a source of national pride—particularly in the face of Buffon's remarks on New World degeneracy. Paleontology thus took on a patriotic dimension and spurred an especial interest in two animals: the mammoth (also called the mastodon in Jefferson's day), a hulking North American precursor of the elephant; and the megalonyx, an outsized sloth which Jefferson believed (or hoped) to be a massive lion. Jefferson's only formal writings on nature, *Notes on the State of Virginia* and a paper read to the American Philosophical Society in 1797, raise the issue of the extinction of these two animals.[78]

Jefferson assumed that "every race of animals seems to have received from their Maker certain laws of extension at the time of their formation," which meant that there had been a moment of creation.[79] But he does not say how long ago this moment occurred or why or how it happened. Nor does he suggest what, if anything, may have taken place since that time. If only he had had an understanding, even a premonition, of geologic time, he would have appreciated the possibility of evolutionary time; and that, in turn, might have allowed the fossil bones he examined to belong to truly extinct species. Instead, this is what he argued about the mammoth:

> It may be asked why I insert the Mammoth [in a list of animals in Virginia] as if it still existed? I ask, in return, why I should omit it, as if it did not exist? Such is the economy of nature, that no instance can be produced of her having permitted any one race of her animals to become extinct; or her having formed any link in her great work so weak as to be broken.[80]

A decade later he claimed the same for the megalonyx:

> the animal species which has once been put into a train of motion is still probably moving in that train. For if one link in nature's chain might be lost, another and another might be lost, till this whole system of things would evanish by piece-meal.[81]

And he tied the two species together:

---

78. For the mammoth, see NVa.43–47, 53–54. For the megalonyx, see TJ, "A Memoir on the Discovery of Certain Bones of a Quadruped of the Clawed Kind in the Western Parts of Virginia," summarized in M.III.341–45.

79. NVa.47. See also TJ to Charles Thomson, 17 December 1786, BC.X.608–9 ("We may as well suppose [a creator] created the earth at once, nearly in the state in which we see it, fit for the preservation of the beings he placed on it"); and, similarly, TJ to John Adams, 11 April 1823, C.II.592.

80. NVa.53–54.

81. TJ, "Memoir on the Discovery of Certain Bones," 255.

I cannot . . . help believing that this animal [the megalonyx], as well as the mammoth, are still existing. The annihilation of any species of existence, is so unexampled in any parts of the economy of nature which we see, that we have a right to conclude, as to the parts we do not see, that the probabilities against such annihilation are stronger than those for it.[82]

What Jefferson has recorded here is that the creator, having set in motion a completely formed earth, established a fixed "chain of being," no link of which could ever be lost. According to this theory, nature may be viewed as an ascending progression of species, from the lowest plant to the highest animal, man. (Above man, in the Christian version of the doctrine, are orders of angels and then God. Jefferson never alluded to this higher part of the chain.) The hierarchical structure is presumed to be so perfectly and delicately created that the absence—the extinction—of any species is conceptually impossible and a horror to contemplate. Reinforced by the unexamined doctrine of the economy of nature, the image of a chain of being supported the conclusion that no species would be created unless it maintained its position in the world. The absence of any species, once created, presaged the downfall of the whole structure. Extinction would be a fatal flaw in the system of things.[83]

Realizing in retrospect that the world of Darwin was closing in on Jefferson, it is important to recall the genuinely scientific reasons for his rejection of possible extinction. A largely fact-minded man, Jefferson was persuaded as much by the paucity of evidence in favor of extinction as by the absence of a convincing theory on its behalf. It is only necessary to note that the Lewis and Clark Expedition, which Jefferson sponsored, fell midway between the voyages of Captain Cook and the voyage of the *Beagle* and that these explorations returned with new species, which were inserted into the Linnaean taxonomy. Why should there be evolution when every discovery could find a niche in a permanent scientific structure? Why should there be extinction when every expedition went to territory where presumptively "lost" species might yet be found? The incentive was to find a creature alive, not to pronounce one permanently dead.

Despite his claims that no creature had really vanished from the

82. TJ to John Stuart, 10 November 1796, LB.IX.350.
83. As Arthur O. Lovejoy, the chronicler of the idea, has said, "Next to the word 'Nature,' the Great Chain of Being was the sacred phrase of the eighteenth century, playing a part somewhat analogous to that of the blessed word 'evolution' in the late nineteenth." *The Great Chain of Being,* 184. Jefferson is not mentioned in Lovejoy's study. He does, however, play a role in the unrivaled presentation of evolution in the history of science and ideas, John C. Greene, *The Death of Adam.* On the "chain" see also Boorstin, *The Lost World of Thomas Jefferson,* 34–40.

earth, Jefferson sensed that he was on uncertain ground. He acknowledged extinction, but in a deliberately qualified fashion, finding refuge in the difference between particular nature, according to which an animal might no longer inhabit an area it had once inhabited, and universal nature, according to which somewhere, somehow, any animal that once existed must still exist. The two meanings of nature were at war with one another, but Jefferson was incapable of recognizing it.

In *Notes on Virginia* Jefferson wrote: "Animals transplanted into unfriendly climates, either change their nature and acquire new fences against the new difficulties in which they are placed, or they multiply poorly and become extinct." Thus, animals might die out in new environments, but they would always exist somewhere on their home territory. Yet if an "unfriendly climate" could lead animals to "change their nature," what was that nature in the first place other than changeable? And if the nature of animals can change, how can there be an unalterable link in the chain of being? Jefferson did not think he had asked this question. He was merely describing an environmentalist outlook that understood nature as varying from place to place. Nevertheless, into this variable nature he sent an invariant species, which was also "nature." He could not give up the particular nature of environmentalism—that was what made America distinctive. But he could not give up a universal nature, for that was fundamental to his cosmological principles and "the system of things" that allowed him to understand the world. Without a credible theory of change, the two understandings of nature could not be reconciled.[84]

Jefferson's adherence to a design of nature, with its economy of expression and chain of being; his pursuit of phantom animals on the ground that none could be extinct; and his temporary acceptance of the growth theory of shells and rocks, all mark a characteristic of his science that he might be reluctant to admit. Yet he himself had said it: "The moment a person forms a theory, his imagination sees, in every object, only the traits which favor that theory."[85] In the end, this is the weakness of Jefferson's approach to physical nature. He forced it to submit to

84. NVa.169. The scrupulousness with which Jefferson used "extinct" to mean "not now here" is remarkable. In addition to the example discussed in the text, see TJ to Philip Nolan, 24 June 1798, LB.X.54; TJ, Instructions to Captain Meriwether Lewis, 20 June 1803, PJ.311; and TJ to Francis Adrian Van der Kemp, 9 February 1818, quoted in Donald Jackson, *Thomas Jefferson and the Stony Mountains,* 39n8. Jefferson had many opportunities to express himself differently on the subject, none of which he accepted. It is therefore ironic but important to note that by sending the bones of a mammoth to France in 1808, he contributed to the establishment of extinction as a scientific fact. See TJ to M. de Lacépède, 14 July 1808, LB.XII.83–108; and Rice, "Jefferson's Gift of Fossils." An unelaborated exception to Jefferson's failure to acknowledge extinction is TJ to John Adams, 11 April 1823, C.II.592.

85. TJ to Charles Thomson, 20 September 1787, BC.XII.159 (on American Indians).

his own system, and where it would not, he preferred to leave the field rather than revise his premises. While he felt obligated to search out the pieces of nature's puzzle and fit them together properly, he did not intend to question the frame.

Conscious of human limitations, certainly his own, Jefferson did not, at the boundaries of knowledge, wish for greater insight or more powerful instruments. Instead he conceded permanent ignorance, though not so much with a sense of awe at nature's ultimate mysteries as with a sigh of defeat. As he claimed about the physiological basis of mental activity, "The modus operandi of nature in this, as in most other cases, can never be developed and demonstrated to beings limited as we are."[86] It is just the modus operandi of nature that most scientists are after. But not Jefferson: whether from a correct appreciation of the limits of human understanding or from a feeling of humility about his own, he candidly declined to press too far into the truths of nature.

Sympathetic contemporaries, like later students, did not always excuse these views or excuse Jefferson as a natural scientist.[87] Jefferson would probably have accepted this criticism. But he might have said that it was valid because fortune had not allowed him to become a student of nature full-time. Instead, as he remarked during his harried second term as president, he was glad for any moment that permitted him "to abstract myself from the dry and dreary waste of politics, into which I have been impressed by the times on which I happened, and to indulge in the rich fields of nature, where alone I should have served as a volunteer, if left to my natural inclinations and partialities."[88]

Yet if Jefferson's inclinations towards nature do seem to have been thwarted, he indulged in the rich fields of nature all his life. He adopted and defended a materialist view of the universe in the tradition of Lucretius, a sensationist view of knowledge on the model of Locke, and a faith in the benefits of exploring and organizing nature on the pattern of Bacon. Although bound by assumptions now overthrown, he respected facts and was determined to keep an open mind. He weighed competing explanations offered for natural phenomena. He adhered to or devel-

86. TJ to Georges Cabanis, 12 July 1803, LB.X.404. See also NVa.48 ("Nature has hidden from us her modus agendi").
87. Jefferson's limitations were recognized, in fact emphasized, in a scholarly eulogy by Samuel L. Mitchill, *A Discourse on the Character and Services of Thomas Jefferson.* Mitchill's reservations may be contrasted with the effusion of a young Virginian whose "Sonnet to Mr. Jefferson" (1822) begins: "To thee all Nature's mysteries are known." Dabney Carr Terrell, quoted in Richard Beale Davis, *Intellectual Life in Jefferson's Virginia, 1790–1830,* xvi.
88. TJ to Caspar Wistar, 21 June 1807, LB.XI.248. See also TJ to Harry Innes, 7 March 1791, BC.XIX.521 (politics was his duty, natural history his passion); and TJ to Wistar, 10 June 1807, S.III.1 (the history of the times drew him into politics; the sciences were his passion).

oped worthy methods of proceeding in scientific work. He admired, in varying degrees, scientists in all fields, though particularly in natural history. The positions he held enabled him to be especially effective in encouraging others to study nature. Through *Notes on Virginia* he set a high standard of public discussion about nature and contributed to identifying nature with American nationalism. When he turned, as this study now does, from physical nature to human nature, he was no less free of cultural predispositions. But here, too, he strove to understand as both a scientist and a member of the human community.

Chapter III

HUMAN NATURE:
VARIATIONS ON EQUALITY

A S A NATURAL HISTORIAN, Jefferson distinguished one species from another by grouping individuals according to their "prominent and invariable" similarities. On this basis, the basis of comparative anatomy, the distinguishing nature of the human species was clear. But the important question was not What are humans physically? but What is human nature itself? What seems most invariable about people is precisely their variability, the great range of individual and social differences among mankind. These variations in temperament and culture unfortunately make it a difficult, perhaps impossible, task to define "human nature" with much assurance or consensus. But such obstacles have seldom hindered pronouncements on the subject, and they did not hinder Jefferson.

As with physical nature, Jefferson never developed his ideas on human nature systematically, and he avoided many of the theoretical difficulties of the ideas that he did consider. His views on humankind have a tenor to them but not a rigor. Entering the discussion on human nature at several points, he wrote on the two most important and intertwined issues of the day, slavery and race. He took positions on human aggression and human affections, on the family, and on the role of women in society. He offered an environmentalist key to human nature in the United States. He explored the ways in which society might improve upon natural human traits through a code of manners to facilitate our conduct and by education to develop our talents and virtues. In considering most of these issues, Jefferson confronted, though at times he notably evaded, the axiom that he himself had penned, the "self-evident truth" that all men are created equal.[1]

1. For the cultural and intellectual context, see Merle Curti, *Human Nature in American Thought*, esp. chap. 3.

Equality is the central theme of Jefferson's view of human nature. As Merrill Peterson has stated, "Jefferson considered all men equals in the order of nature. . . . All men possessed an innate moral sense, the faculty of reason and essentially the same biological needs. Hence the doctrine of equality was grounded in the facts of natural history."[2] But if equality is the theme, it is one that is not always clearly heard. Moreover, Jefferson's other lines of argument are as much counterpoint as variations. His "equality" is continually hedged with qualifications— about race, gender, talents, and the right to political opinions. In the abstract he appreciated at least some human variety:

> Would the world be more beautiful were all our faces alike? were our tempers, our talents, our tastes, our forms, our wishes, our aversions and pursuits cast exactly in the same mould? If no varieties existed in the animal, vegetable, or mineral creation, but all move strictly uniform, catholic, and orthodox, what a world of physical and moral monotony would it be![3]

Avoiding monotony is not the same as welcoming differences, however. "Minor differences of opinion," he wrote, "like differences of face, are a law of our nature, and should be viewed with the same tolerance."[4] But these are only minor differences. When innate differences became major, they could upset social stability. In that case, Jefferson sometimes hoped to blot them out, either by altering the habits of those who practiced them (American Indians), expelling people from the community (emancipated blacks), or denying admission to those who disagreed with the nation's politics (antirepublicans). Even so, equality is the dominant theme, and because humans are the same natural species, there is, in general, a "nature" common to all of us.

Jefferson assumed that central to human nature is that man is a social creature. Man is "formed for society and endowed by nature with those dispositions which fit him for society."[5] Small islands are by nature without human habitation, he once said, because "man, being a gregarious animal, will not remain but where there can be a sufficient herd of his own kind to satisfy his social propensities."[6]

Within society, Jefferson's position was summed up by Robert Burns at the close of the Scottish Enlightenment: "The social, friendly, honest

2. *Thomas Jefferson and the New Nation,* 94.
3. TJ to Charles Thomson, 29 January 1817, F.X.76. See also NVa.160 (uniformity of opinion no more desirable than uniformity of face and stature).
4. TJ to William Duane, 25 July 1811, LB.XIII.67.
5. TJ to William Green Munford, 18 June 1799, in Merrill D. Peterson, ed., *Thomas Jefferson: Writings,* 1064. See also TJ to Dupont de Nemours, 24 April 1816, F.X.22 (society "one of the natural wants with which man has been created"); and TJ to Peter Carr, 10 August 1787, BC.XII.15.
6. TJ to William Plumer, 31 January 1815, LB.XIV.235.

man, / Whate'er he be, / 'Tis he fulfils great Nature's plan, / And none but he!"[7] With the significant exception that blacks and whites would not be able to live harmoniously in America, Jefferson also believed that nature created mankind not merely societal but also sociable. He realized that humans had powerful emotions that could lead to unhappiness or even destruction. But humans were also endowed with reason and moral sense, an innate sense of justice, compassion, generosity—traits more than sufficient to assure our happiness.[8] Such was human nature that Jefferson seldom lacked grounds for optimism. Or such was his optimism that he claimed these traits to be part of human nature.

When human beings acted contrary to this vision, and they did so dismayingly often, Jefferson inclined either to hold the environment responsible—bad habits built up over years by the people or their government—or to treat the delict as an exception, an extreme in the range of human conduct.[9] Nature thus provided a norm, and largely because of the American experience (always excepting slavery and race), the norm was cooperation.

An obvious challenge to this comforting view of human nature was warfare. With Hobbes in mind, Jefferson once noted that "some philosophers, observing [warfare] to be so general in this world, have mistaken it for the natural, instead of the abusive state of man."[10] If war had been the norm, then warfare would be natural, too. But this, despite much evidence, Jefferson could not accept. The "ferociousness of man" was simply among the "perversities of our nature."[11] When war did occur, Jefferson rationalized it by one of two means, both applicable specifically to Europe. Either it had taken place in an environment oppressed by unnatural social institutions or it actually had some benefits. Europe, he once said, was a region "where war seems to be the natural state of man," but in America war could be avoided, because the benevolent environment of the New World would produce social institutions to ameliorate our unnatural dispositions.[12] Or, if environmental differences did not explain war—and Jefferson once wrote that "human nature is the same on every side of the Atlantic and will be alike influenced by the same causes"[13]—perhaps some good could be said for it after all. When war came to Europe, perhaps it offered a Malthusian

7. "Second Epistle to Lapraik" (1786).
8. See, e.g., TJ to Dupont de Nemours, 24 April 1816, F.X.24; and TJ to William Johnson, 12 June 1823, LB.XV.441.
9. For an example of the subnormal, see TJ to James Monroe, 15 July 1802, F.VIII.164 (the ingratitude of a political journalist "presents human nature in a hideous form").
10. TJ to Samuel Kercheval, 12 July 1816, LB.XIII.40.
11. TJ to Noah Worcester, 26 November 1817, LB.XVIII.299.
12. TJ to David Bailey Warden, 26 December 1820, F.X.172 (note the "seems" in the clause).
13. NVa.121.

benefit. Since no animal but man works to destroy his own species, "we must conclude that it is in man alone that nature [in the form of warfare] has been able to find a sufficient barrier against the too great multiplication of other animals and of man himself."[14]

While warfare was the most important unpassed test of Jefferson's sanguine view, it was only an example of a central issue that he was no more successful resolving than others have been. What is the effect of the environment on our presumed innate nature? By which of two kinds of nature, innate or environmental, universal or particular, is mankind either combative or friendly? No one of Jefferson's turn of mind would choose one exclusively and reject the other. Nor was he willing to settle the matter merely by saying that it is innate in humans to be greatly affected by external nature. Rather, he struck one or another balance between the two "natures" as they appeared to fit his facts or his hopes. On the one hand, he was a universalist. Human nature consists of certain characteristics that are the same everywhere. This was the pattern of human nature modeled on Newton and natural philosophy. On the other hand, he was an environmentalist. A pluralist by the evidence of his senses, he believed that humans differ from one another because their environments differ. On this account his guide to human nature was Montesquieu.

A single human nature may have been the greater aim of the Enlightenment and Jefferson, but if only because it takes more space to discuss variety than it does to point out uniformity, Jefferson's writings appear to emphasize environmentalism. With respect to his own "country," for instance, his indefatigable investigations led to the expected conclusion: "When we consider how much climate contributes to the happiness of our condition by the fine sensation it excites and the productions it is the parent of, we have reason to value highly the accident of birth in such a one as that of Virginia."[15] But his environmentalist sensitivity was far wider than his own habitat and personal preference.

For a European friend, Jefferson attempted to correlate human nature according to region of the United States, asserting that the traits he noted were so accurate that in their blending from north to south "an observing traveler . . . may always know his latitude by the character of the people among whom he finds himself."[16] In this field guide to human nature in America (see table 4), Jefferson lists nine parallel traits

14. TJ to James Madison, 1 January 1797, F.VII.100. See also TJ to William Short, 20 August 1814, LB.XVIII.283; and TJ to John Adams, 1 June 1822, C.II.578 ("pugnacious humor of mankind seems to be the law of his nature, one of the obstacles to too great multiplication provided in the mechanism of the Universe").

15. TJ to Martha Jefferson Randolph, 31 May 1791, BB.85.

16. TJ to marquis de Chastellux, 2 September 1785, BC.VIII.468.

TABLE 4
Traits of Americans

Northerners	Southerners
cool	fiery
sober	voluptuary
laborious	indolent
persevering	unsteady
INDEPENDENT	INDEPENDENT
jealous of their own liberties and just to others	zealous for their own liberties, but trampling on those of others
interested	generous
chicaning	candid
superstitious and hypocritical in their religion	without attachment or pretensions to any religion but that of the heart

Source: TJ to marquis de Chastellux, 2 September 1785, BC.VIII.468. The emphasis for "independent" is supplied.

for the northern and southern states. Eight of these traits form pairs of opposites. But the middle one, the peculiarly American and Jeffersonian one, is the same for both regions: independence. The lesson is that since independence does not distinguish one part of the country from another, it is the unifying national characteristic, distinguishing human nature in the United States from human nature in the rest of the world.

Except for independence, Jefferson claims that human nature among (white) Americans varies with predictable regularity according to the environment, in this case the latitude they live in. The eye is drawn at once to two southern characteristics: slavery is treated not among the vices but as a qualification of a virtue; and southern religion is disarmingly presented as Jefferson's own understanding of natural morality. Although he does not explicitly attribute all the differences between North and South to differences in climate, this is a fair inference from the comments with which he qualified the table. He conceded that the warmth of (Tidewater?) Virginia "unnerves and unmans both body and mind." He noted that "peculiar circumstances" have interfered with the character expected for New York on the basis of climate alone. And he remarked that Pennsylvania, while too cold for his own comfort, was nevertheless an optimum environment, because there "the two characters seem to meet and blend to form a people free from the extremes both of vice and virtue."[17]

17. Ibid.

That Jefferson knew his mirrorlike scheme was fanciful when applied with any specificity is evident from observations he prepared only a few months later. Explaining why Rhode Island differed in character from Connecticut, he affirmed that the reason was environmental but that latitude had nothing to do with it. Rhode Island, he said, was a seaport state and therefore dominated by merchants. In Connecticut, a state with a large "interior country," farmers predominated, and farmers are more virtuous than those who live by the sea.[18] This is environmentalism that is both more sophisticated and more true to Jefferson's temperament. It defines environment not by latitude but by expanse. It then ties that to political economy and, finally, derives social character from political economy.[19]

Jefferson's most energetic effort to link environmentalism and human nature was his attempt to justify America against European claims that the New World was inferior to the Old.[20] He was moved to enter this controversy out of a blend of patriotism and scientific curiosity, the former certainly the more significant provocation. Comparisons between the New World and the Old had been made since the earliest European exploration of the Western Hemisphere. The comparisons began with climate, passed through the vegetable and animal kingdoms, and culminated in human beings. Jefferson's advantages in battling his European adversaries were, first, his knowledge, resources, and incentive accurately to depict the true condition of nature in North America and, second, the success of the American Revolution, which inevitably diminished the cogency of European attacks, most of which had preceded the war and implicitly assumed Britain's superiority to the colonies.[21]

Jefferson chose as his chief antagonist the comte de Buffon, not because Buffon's charges against the New World were the most extreme, but because his reputation was the greatest. Jefferson respected Buffon—"the best informed Naturalist who has ever written"—and

18. TJ, "Answers to Démeunier's First Queries," 24 January 1786, BC.X.16.

19. For a speculative discussion of environmentalism in reverse, the potential effect of human activities on physical nature, see TJ to Jean Baptiste Le Roy, 13 November 1786, BC.X.524–30.

20. See, generally, Antonello Gerbi, *The Dispute of the New World;* Henry Steele Commager and Elmo Giordanetti, *Was America a Mistake?* and Gilbert Chinard, "Eighteenth Century Theories of America as a Human Habitat."

21. Jefferson was conscious that he was defending the environment of North America only, and not the entire Western Hemisphere. But this constraint seems to have been based as much on the possibility that allegations of inferiority were in fact justified for Latin America as on his own claim to be inadequately informed about the southern regions. See NVa.59, 273n83, and 276n104. Since the Frenchmen whom Jefferson was disputing had, on the other hand, paid rather little attention to British North America and had used evidence from Latin America to support their theories, the argument between them and Jefferson is to some extent at cross-purposes. By the time *Notes on the State of Virginia*

was therefore willing, indeed gratified, to use Buffon's own figures on European animals to refute the charges of American inferiority in that realm. Defining "inferiority" as "animals of lower weight," Jefferson compiled an extensive list of animals in three tables—animals native to both continents, animals native to only one, and animals domesticated in both. He then demonstrated that on the basis of comparative weights, the American animals were not inferior. They at least held their own against the European.[22]

It is easy to read into Jefferson's discussion a sense of having reversed the argument of the Europeans: that far from being degenerate with respect to fauna, the New World was in fact superior to the Old. But Jefferson does not assert this and wants only to show that the New World was not inferior. Equality was enough. Jefferson's aim is not based solely on modesty or difficulty of proof, however. By aiming only so far as parity between the hemispheres, he leaves the two halves of the globe similar to one another, as if nature had endowed the continents equally—"as if both sides [of the Atlantic] were not warmed by the same genial sun; as if a soil of the same chemical composition was less capable . . . ; as if the fruits and grains from that soil and sun yielded a less rich chyle."[23] He thus permitted a uniform concept of nature to reign even while showing off an environmentalist one.

Parity between the hemispheres was relatively easy to demonstrate if all that was needed was quantitative data about animals. The greater challenge was human beings. Was human nature different and defective in the New World? Jefferson's probes into this subject led him into complexity and controversy that have not yet diminished. Here, too, his knowledge was much greater than that of the European naturalists, though it was far from sufficient (a point he recognized). What was more important, his interpretation of the data had to contend with pronounced personal and cultural predilections.[24]

---

appeared, Jefferson's principal opponents had modified a portion of their views. But both sides were serious about the issue, and the symbolism of Old World versus New was as important as any confrontation on particular facts. A diligent scholar has claimed that Jefferson "set up thirty-one false premises of the French naturalists and meticulously refuted each one." Ruth Henline, "A Study of *Notes on the State of Virginia* as an Evidence of Jefferson's Reaction against the Theories of the French Naturalists," 55 Va. Mag. Hist. & Biog. 233, 245 (1947).

22. NVa. 55; the tables are on pp. 50–52. In support of his claims Jefferson secured the remains of several large American animals and triumphantly, if deferentially, conveyed them to Buffon: "I wish these spoils, Sir, may have the merit of adding any thing new to the treasures of nature." TJ to Buffon, 1 October 1787, BC.XII.195. The reaction of the aging Buffon (he died several months later at eighty-one) is unrecorded. See Anna Clark Jones, "Antlers for Jefferson," 12 New England Qtly. 333–48 (1939).

23. NVa.47 (chyle is a digestive fluid).

24. For the setting of Jefferson's ideas, see John C. Greene, *American Science in the Age of Jefferson,* chap. 12, "The Sciences of Man: Physical Anthropology."

As to his own kind of human beings, white Americans, Jefferson was plain-spoken and confident. European colonists, later citizens of the United States, displayed as much natural genius as could reasonably be expected in a recently settled and sparsely populated land. While a Shakespeare under these circumstances was unlikely, America had produced in George Washington a refutation of "that wretched philosophy . . . which would have arranged him among the degeneracies of nature." And there was Franklin, "than whom no one of the present age has made. . . more ingenious solutions of the phenomena of nature."[25] As he generalized later, there are "seeds of genius which nature sows with even hand through every age and country, and which need only soil and season to germinate."[26] Not only did the United States raise up talent in individuals but the health and growth of the population as a whole matched that of Europe. As the American Philosophical Society under Jefferson hoped to show from the census of 1800, "the duration of human life in this portion of the earth will be found at least equal to what it is in any other, and that its population increases with a rapidity unequalled in all others."[27]

More difficult for Jefferson to treat was the nature of the American Indian.[28] Buffon had written that the Indian was no exception "to the general fact that all living nature has become smaller" in America.[29] Smaller meant inferior, and the Indian's inferiority was complete: he was feeble, insensitive, cowardly, without vivacity or intellectual activity, and—the cause of it all—defective in sexual capacity. "Nature, by refusing him the power of love," Jefferson quoted Buffon, "has treated him worse and lowered him deeper than any animal." "For the honor of human nature"—"for the honor of American nature," he might have added—Jefferson was pleased to tell the world this was not so.[30]

In defending the Indian, Jefferson relied on both universal and en-

---

25. NVa.64.
26. TJ to William Duane, 4 August 1812, F.IX.365.
27. Quoted in Chinard, "America as a Human Habitat," 49–50, from *Early Proceedings of the American Philosophical Society,* 1884, 293–94.
28. Jefferson discusses Indians in several places in *Notes on Virginia,* including an entire query, "Aborigines." NVa.92–107. The argument with Buffon about Indians is in connection with "animal life." NVa.58–64. Charles Thomson, in his commentary on these pages, repeatedly affirms Jefferson's judgment that it is manners and customs, not any "deficiency in nature," that account for the traits of the Indians. NVa.200–201. Early chapters of Bernard W. Sheehan, *Seeds of Extinction,* examine in detail several of the topics mentioned in the text: environmentalism, deficiency, the noble savage. See also Greene, *American Science in the Age of Jefferson,* chap. 14. A gritty discussion is Robert F. Berkhofer, Jr., *The White Man's Indian: Images of the American Indian from Columbus to the Present* (New York, 1978).
29. NVa.58.
30. NVa.59.

vironmental conceptions of nature, showing temperaments of both an Enlightenment scientist and an American nationalist. The tangle into which he was led by these mixtures of arguments and temperaments is evident in his explanations of the Indians' bravery and the number of children borne by Indian women.

The idea of bravery among the Indians, Jefferson says, is not, as with the whites, based on valor in the field, with its high risk of injury. Bravery to the Indian means the destruction of an enemy by strategem, which risks no injury to oneself. How did the Indians come by their conception? At first Jefferson says through their education, an environmental supplement to their original nature. But then he confesses that he is not sure: "Or perhaps this [stealth] is nature, while it is education which teaches us to honor force more than finesse."[31]

The same ambivalence appears in his explanation why Indian women bear fewer children than white women. The original explanation, in the first edition of *Notes on Virginia,* left the matter open: "Whether their raising fewer children proceeds from scarcity of food at certain seasons, from the labours and hazards to which their women are exposed, or from a sterility peculiar to their race, seems not well ascertained."[32] Not many months later, however, he had made up his mind and chose environmentalism: "They raise fewer children than we do. The causes of this are to be found, not in a difference of nature, but of circumstance."[33] Here as elsewhere (but far less so with Afro-Americans), Jefferson posited human equality by nature. But he was pressed by either evidence or cultural assumptions to cope with either difference or inequality. Which was truly natural, the theme or the variations? How does one know?

When he was not ambivalent, Jefferson adopted either of two strategies regarding differences between Indians and whites. The first was to deny the initial European claim, for instance, on the Indians' affection towards children, their friendship, or their "vivacity and activity of mind."[34] The second was to explain the differences as a concomitant of the Indians' stage of civilization. That all societies pass through the same stages of development depending on their mode of subsistence was an accepted doctrine in eighteenth-century thinking. Skirting the dispute between environmental and innate nature, it also makes some anthropological sense. Jefferson accepted a form of it, particularly in his public policy of urging the Indians to give up one stage—hunting—and

31. Ibid.
32. NVa.274n86 (from the 1785 edition).
33. NVa.60.
34. NVa.58.

move quickly, willingly or not, to the next stage—farming.[35] At the end of his remarks against Buffon, however, Jefferson merely noted that it had taken northern Europe sixteen centuries after the introduction of the alphabet "before a Newton could be formed," so we must not yet condemn the Indians "as wanting genius." There are indeed "varieties in the race of man," he said, but the species itself is the same everywhere. One may doubt, he concluded, "whether nature has enlisted herself as a Cis or Trans-Atlantic partisan."[36]

Like the animals, the Indians illustrated the excellence of nature on the American continent. And since nature was no partisan between continents, and human nature was everywhere the same, the amalgamating of the white and red races in America was perfectly acceptable. It was not central to this argument that amalgamation also satisfied the needs of Jeffersonian farmers eager to make use of Indian hunting lands or that it led to the destruction of Indian culture: "The ultimate point of rest and happiness for them is to let our settlements and theirs meet and blend together, to intermix, and become one people. . . . [T]his is what the natural progress of things will . . . bring on, and it will be better to promote than to retard it."[37] In speeches to Indians (whom he always called "my children") Jefferson assured his listeners that white Americans had become like themselves, "grown out of this land," and were thus "united in one family with our red brethren." "You will mix with us by marriage," he said. "Your blood will run in our veins, and will spread with us over this great island."[38]

Jefferson's presumptions about Indians—that they and the whites were by nature the same, that any apparent deficiencies of the Indians were offset by superior traits or could be accounted for by the environment or stage of development—and his hope that the two branches of the human race would eventually become one people contrast starkly with his views on Afro-Americans. No greater flaw has been found in Jefferson's character, in his statements, and in his actions or in his failure to act than with regard to blacks and slavery. Since he owned slaves all

35. A four-stage theory of human development drawn mainly from what was known or believed about American Indians is the subject of Ronald L. Meek, *Social Science and the Ignoble Savage.* Among the proponents of the theory discussed in the study are Lucretius, Locke, Montesquieu, and Kames. No Americans are mentioned, despite the Europeans' purported reliance on data from the New World.

36. NVa.63.

37. TJ to Benjamin Hawkins, 18 February 1803, LB.X.363.

38. TJ to the people of the Mandan Nation, 30 December 1806, LB.XVI.413; TJ to a group of Delawares, Mohicans, and Muncies, 21 December 1808, LB.XVI.452. Despite his regard and sympathy, Jefferson's actual policy towards Indians when he was president was the unyielding acquisition of Indian land for white settlement. See esp. TJ to William Henry Harrison, 27 February 1803, LB.369–73.

his life, one may either charge him with a hypocrisy unmatched among American moralists or accept his anguish over slavery as real. Even in the latter case, because of what he so eloquently wrote about equality, more has been expected of him than of any other American of his time. If so, the disappointment in Jefferson felt by abolitionists in the nineteenth century and students today is a measure as much of their hopes as of their dismay. But the flaws remain, and despite his torment Jefferson was unable to absolve himself or lessen the agonies of later generations.[39]

The overriding issue to be explored is exactly the relation between slavery and race. Had a race been enslaved because it was inferior, or held to be so? or had a race acquired the appearance of inferiority, or become inferior, because it was enslaved? How, in short, did blacks come to be what Jefferson nearly always saw them as, inferior to whites? Was it by nature of the race or by the environment of slavery? And if by environment, was it slavery by itself, or slavery peculiar to the United States?

On a crucial point Jefferson never deviated: slavery violated the natural right of humans to liberty. On this point it is instructive to contrast his views with those of Aristotle, whose writings on society he much admired. Aristotle had seen that slavery was practiced throughout the Mediterranean area, and he therefore assumed that it was a practice natural to mankind. But if slavery is natural to mankind, the uncertain reasoning continued, persons must exist who are "natural slaves." Aristotle recognized that not all slaves in social fact were slaves by nature, but the latter really existed. Slaves by nature were people of unusually diminished rational and moral capacity, not fit for citizenship in the state.[40] Jefferson's contrary position, against slavery by nature, is illuminated by this argument. First, the natural slaves whom Aristotle hypothesized were defective individuals in the mass of mankind, while the social slaves whom Jefferson dealt with were known by the color of their skin. It would have been obvious to Jefferson that since in the United States only African blacks were enslaved, and enslaved without

39. An analytic study of Jefferson, race, and slavery is Winthrop D. Jordan, *White over Black*, 429–81. A chronological account with good contextual information is John Chester Miller, *The Wolf by the Ears*. Two further relevant studies are Robert McColley, *Slavery and Jeffersonian Virginia* (Urbana, 1964); and John P. Diggins, "Slavery, Race, and Equality."

40. Aristotle's discussion of slavery is scattered throughout his *Politics*, but the "naturalness" of slavery is concentrated in 1252b and 1254a. For a quasi-Aristotelian interpretation of Jefferson on slavery see Jack P. Greene, *All Men Are Created Equal: Some Reflections on the Character of the American Revolution* (Oxford, 1976).

having been judged individually as wanting in reason, Aristotle's argument was unrealistic.[41]

Next, three powerful traditions of moral equality had developed since the age of Aristotle, undermining his argument and affecting Jefferson's. The first was that of Roman law, influenced by the Stoics. According to it, slavery might exist by the law of nations and by domestic positive law, but it violated the law of nature. In this tradition, in a court case of 1770 concerning slavery Jefferson invoked a "natural law of liberty," both on its own and as an aid to interpreting the positive law of Virginia.[42] Second, no matter how reticent Jefferson was about religious doctrine, he was affected by the equalitarian ethos of Christianity. Not only deism pronounced that all men were created equal. Third, the emphasis on equality in contemporary natural rights doctrine necessarily applied to the holding of slaves in America. This is what Jefferson alluded to in his list of American traits in asserting that southerners were "zealous for their own liberties, but trampling on those of others."[43]

Finally, unlike Aristotle, Jefferson lived in a world where slavery was not practiced everywhere, including, in his lifetime, in much of the United States. There was, in addition, an active American opposition to slavery, especially among the Quakers, whose social principles he held in esteem.[44] And knowledge of his own slaves provided convincing personal evidence that slavery existed by custom, law, and force, and not by nature. On every count, then, the Aristotelian doctrine that slavery was natural was unthinkable in Jefferson's intellectual universe.

If slavery violated all the imperatives of nature—natural liberty, natural equality, natural law, and natural right—why did Jefferson both maintain slaves himself and not work actively to bring slavery to an end? Several approaches to this central tragedy in Jefferson's moral life

41. Although the Greeks and Romans recognized racial differences, skin color was a far less significant point of distinction to them than it became centuries later, and they identified neither themselves nor their slaves in a modern racial sense. See, generally, Frank M. Snowden, *Blacks in Antiquity: Ethiopians in the Greco-Roman Experience* (Cambridge, Mass., 1970).

42. TJ, "Argument in the Case of Howell vs. Netherland," April 1770, F.I.373–81 (Jefferson lost the case). For a study of how natural law fared generally in cases on slavery, see Robert M. Cover, *Justice Accused: Antislavery and the Judicial Process* (New Haven, 1975).

43. In *American Slavery, American Freedom: The Ordeal of Colonial Virginia* (New York, 1975), Edmund S. Morgan investigates the "central paradox of American history" in the colony where it was most obvious. Morgan's unassertive conclusion is that "Virginians may have had a special appreciation of the freedom dear to republicans, because they saw every day what life without it could be like." Pp. 4, 376. Jefferson plays a role in the study only near the end.

44. See, e.g., TJ to Edward Bancroft, 26 January 1788, BC.XIV.492.

have been proposed. One is that he could not see how to extricate himself from his social and economic setting. This is the argument from environmentalism, personal satisfaction, cultural conservativism, or economic class. Another approach is to recognize that he tried, perhaps through the 1780s, to find "acceptable" ways to end slavery in Virginia, but when he was unsuccessful, he became discouraged and no longer spoke out. A third possibility, to be treated shortly, is that he found African Americans inferior to European Americans and that this racism gave enough support to slavery to retain it, short of emancipation followed by compulsory removal.

When a person leads as manifestly a split life as Jefferson did with regard to slavery, this may well be evident in his use of language. So it is with Jefferson's use of "nature" in writing about slavery. There can be no doubt that by every test of Jeffersonian thinking, slavery violated the requirements of nature. But although he spoke of the institution as a "great political and moral evil," a "moral and political depravity," an "abominable crime," and a "hideous blot," he nearly never stated in simple terms that American chattel slavery was a violation of natural right or natural law.[45] He got only as close as "human nature."

In his *Summary View of the Rights of British America* (1774) he speaks of the "natural right" of the colonists against Britain, but he characterizes the slave trade only as an "infamous practice" that violates the "rights of human nature."[46] In his draft for the Declaration of Independence, in a clause that the Continental Congress deleted, he charged the king with having "waged cruel war against human nature itself, violating its most sacred rights of life and liberty." But these are not the same as natural rights. In *Notes on the State of Virginia* he said he looked forward to the time of a "complete emancipation of human nature" but did not say that slavery violated natural law or right.[47] On the eve of the abolition of the slave trade, when he was president, he still spoke, not of natural rights, but of the "violation of human rights which have been so long continued on the unoffending inhabitants of Africa."[48] Human rights are presumably natural rights, but Jefferson again avoided the precious

45. NVa.87; TJ to Thomas Cooper, 10 September 1814, LB.XIV.184; TJ to Démeunier, 22 June 1786, BC.X.58; TJ to William Short, 8 September 1823, LB.XV.469.

46. TJ, *Summary View* (1774), BC.I.123, 130. The hesitant language in the *Summary View* and the Declaration, even recognizing that both documents were composed for the approval of others, may be compared with the language of James Otis writing in Massachusetts a decade earlier. Otis branded the slave trade "a shocking violation of the law of nature" and said that the colonists were "by the law of nature freeborn, as indeed all men are, white or black." "The Rights of the British Colonies Asserted and Proved" (1764), in *Pamphlets of the American Revolution, 1750–1776,* ed. Bernard Bailyn, vol. I (Cambridge, Mass., 1965), 439.

47. NVa.87.

48. TJ, State of the Union Message, 2 December 1806, Pdvr.424.

term. He edged up to it after he left the presidency, but circuitously and in a parenthetical phrase. Speaking against the impressment of sailors by the British navy, he wrote privately: "And has not the British sea-man, as much as the African, been reduced to this bondage by force, in flagrant violation of his own consent, and of his natural right in his own person?"[49]

What explains this unaccustomed shyness with the language of nature? A likely explanation is that Jefferson found "natural right" and the others so precious that he could not admit that he himself stood in violation of the truths they conveyed. "Nature" had become so sacred to him that "moral depravity" was a comfortable term by comparison. It may be, too, that Jefferson hesitated to denominate slavery a violation of natural law or right because he also recognized natural rights on the side of slave owners, and natural rights should hardly be in conflict with one another.

One possible conflict in this area was that of a natural right to slaves as property. But Jefferson rejected it, if only obliquely. He was not among those who believed that property could be acquired by natural law in the first place and maintained by natural right. Therefore, while acknowledging that a "right of property is founded in our natural wants," it was not to be enjoyed through violating "similar rights of other sensible beings," that is, the natural rights of Africans.[50]

But if a right to property was not a countervailing natural right, what about a right to self-preservation? Here Jefferson did have an argument for retaining slavery, at least an implicit one. He hoped for emancipation, but only if it were gradual and, more telling, only if it were accompanied by the compulsory removal of freedmen from the United States. In the absence of appropriate emancipation, however, he would retain slavery on the basis of a natural law of self-preservation. In blunt language (which still avoided "nature"): "Justice is in one scale, self-preservation in the other."[51] Unfortunately for the slaveholders, the natural law of self-preservation on their side was met by the equal logic of a natural right of rebellion on the other. No one expressed the proba-bility of a slave revolt more unnervingly than Jefferson himself. In a plea containing a variety of uses of "nature," it is the unprecedented evocation of the supernatural that is the best indication of his distress:

> If a slave can have a country in this world, it must be any other in preference to that . . . in which he must lock up the faculties of his

49. TJ to Thomas Cooper, 10 September 1814, LB.XIV.183.
50. TJ to Dupont de Nemours, 24 April 1816, LB.XIV.490.
51. TJ to John Holmes, 22 April 1820, LB.XV.249. See also TJ to Rufus King, 13 July 1802, F.VIII.162 ("safety of society, under actual circumstances, obliges us to treat as a crime [that] which [the slaves'] feelings may represent in a far different shape").

nature. . . . [C]an the liberties of a nation be thought secure when we have removed their only firm basis, a conviction in the minds of the people that these liberties are the gift of God? That they are not to be violated but with his wrath? Indeed I tremble for my country when I reflect that God is just: that his justice cannot sleep forever: that considering numbers, nature and natural means only, a revolution of the wheel of fortune, an exchange of situation, is among possible events: that it may become probable by supernatural interference! The Almighty has no attribute which can take side with us in such a contest. But it is impossible to be temperate and to pursue this subject through the various considerations of policy, of morals, of history natural and civil.[52]

Throughout his life Jefferson offered one argument after another about race or slavery. But to no avail. No matter where he turned, he had to face what his granddaughter wrote after her honeymoon journey to New England. Despite "such great gifts of Nature" as the South's soil and climate, she said, "the canker of slavery . . . diseases the whole body" of the region. In reply, the eighty-two-year-old Jefferson conceded: "One fatal stain deforms what nature had bestowed on us of her fairest gifts."[53]

But was the fatal stain slavery, or was it race? Was the problem of slavery unsolved because of the problem of race? What *was* the problem of race? In handling these questions Jefferson could have looked to two comparative sources he knew well, ancient slavery and contemporary Indians. When he tried the first, he decided that because slaves in antiquity were not black and antiquity had some superior humans in slavery, it was race rather than slavery that accounted for inferior blacks in America. He did not ask how the ancient and modern slave societies differed or how color itself had led to the psychosocial branding of American slaves as inferior. Regarding the Indians, he simply ignored them when it came to understanding Afro-Americans.

To follow Jefferson's thinking about race, it is necessary to understand the eighteenth-century dispute over the origins of mankind. Although he never addressed the controversy directly, his views are not difficult to construct. The dispute was between a monogenetic and a polygenetic origin. It asked whether humans were originally one race (or one species, or one genus) and only afterwards, because of the

---

52. NVa.162–63. Further forebodings emerged at the time of the Missouri Compromise. See TJ to John Holmes, 22 April 1820, LB.XV.249 ("We have the wolf by the ears, and we can neither hold him, nor safely let him go"); and TJ, Autobiography (1821), KP.51 ("Nothing is more certainly written in the book of fate, than that these people are to be free. . . . If [emancipation] is left to force itself on, human nature must shudder at the prospect held up").

53. Ellen Randolph Coolidge to TJ, 1 August 1825, BB.454; TJ to Ellen Randolph Coolidge, 27 August 1825, BB.457.

environment, came to look and act as different groups or whether mankind was originally created in the racial divisions in which we find ourselves today. In short, what is meant by saying that separate races exist by nature?

The answer to this question, if it could be found, was of great moment in Jefferson's age. It would affect the validity of a portion of Christian belief, as well as the orderliness of the natural world and the details of the doctrine of a chain of being.[54] Jefferson was not interested in the theory of a single creation of mankind from the point of view of Christian doctrine. But because his own Creator and the single act of creation for all nature were also theological ideas, he presumably supported monogenesis on theological grounds. The scientific justification for monogenesis likewise appealed to him. A degree of imagination was required to overcome what the senses saw—a variety of races. But the effort was worthwhile because a single-species origin of man retained an order in universal nature and left to particular nature the accident of racial diversity. Monogenesis also accorded with the economy of nature. Why posit multiple creation when no facts are contradicted by a single creation?

The idea of a chain of being raised two problems with respect to the races of man. First, what defined a link in the chain? were the races sufficiently separate to be different links rather than simply variations of a single link called Homo sapiens? By the accepted scientific definition, two individuals belonged to the same species if their offspring were fertile. Since the races of mankind could intermix for reproductive purposes, they were by this account only varieties of the same species and therefore a single link in the chain. Second, one link or more, the very idea of the chain of being contributed to thinking about differences between races. Against this, however, the hierarchical ordering of the chain was ill-suited to an equalitarian America, and Jefferson did say that if blacks should be found intellectually inferior to whites, no matter what the source, whether innate nature or the environment of slavery, such inferiority should be "no measure of their rights."[55]

But accepting the monogenetic origins of race did less to ameliorate Jefferson's racialism than might be supposed. He simply transferred the issue and its problems from species to "varieties in the race of man, distinguished by their powers both of body and mind" and let different races be different varieties.[56] At the level of varieties, it is still helpful,

54. This discussion draws on Jordan, *White over Black,* 482–511 ("The Negro Bound by the Chain of Being"); and John C. Greene, "The American Debate on the Negro's Place in Nature, 1780–1815."

55. TJ to Henri Gregoire, 25 February 1809, F.IX.246.

56. NVa.63.

however, to contrast the views of Jefferson with the views of two northerners who also maintained the monogenetic doctrine, Benjamin Rush, Jefferson's scientific and humanitarian friend in Philadelphia, and Samuel Stanhope Smith, a political opponent but a respected scientist and theologian.[57]

The northerners were far more disposed than the Virginian to explain racial variations by external rather than internal nature. All three men faced what Smith called "the apparent dullness of the negro," but the northerners had some distance from a slave society and knew free Negroes, while Jefferson largely inhabited the world of plantation slavery. It was as if the environment itself had determined whether a person held an environmentalist theory.

In 1787 Smith declared that an "atrocious despotism" first in Africa and then in the American South condemned Negroes "to perpetual sterility of genius."[58] In the same year, in *Notes on Virginia*, Jefferson argued the opposite course. Though he left formally undecided the ultimate source of racial difference—"whether originally a distinct race, or made distinct by time and circumstance"—he nearly always claimed that differences between the two varieties of the human species were differences "by nature."[59]

Jefferson never suggested about blacks, or in the context of slavery, as Smith did, that "genius . . . requires freedom" to flourish. Rather than focus on the environment of blacks under slavery in America, he asserted universal characteristics. He wrote about the "real distinctions which nature has made," "the difference [in color] fixed in nature," "physical distinctions proving a difference of race," "inferiority . . . not the effect merely of their condition of life," "nature . . . which has produced the distinction," and the need to keep the races "as distinct as nature has formed them."[60] After language such as this, few differences between the races were left to be attributed to the environment.

Jefferson's recital of natural racial characteristics, it should be said, carried with it no intention to justify slavery. Its place and purpose in the *Notes* was to support legislation that would emancipate slaves contingent on their being colonized outside the United States. Since forci-

---

57. Rush was a Quaker with an abolitionist incentive to demonstrate intellectual equality among the races. Smith's purpose was to refute the polygenetic theory of Lord Kames by pointing to the scientific chaos that the adoption of such a theory would cause. It is possible that Jefferson's Kamesianism helped to mute his participation in the origins-of-mankind debate. At the same time, Smith upheld monogenesis through the story of Adam and Eve, a position Jefferson would not have taken. Jefferson's Virginia colleague in natural rights theory, George Mason, also argued on behalf of monogenesis.
58. Quoted in Jordan, *White over Black*, 443.
59. NVa.143.
60. NVa.138–43.

ble, even induced, expatriation would normally be unthinkable to Jefferson, his argument understandably emphasized natural rather than environmental differences between the races: people who were different from one another by nature ought to be, and should want to be, in different homelands.[61]

Jefferson pronounced on the particular traits of blacks in no well-ordered fashion, but it appears that he meant to cover characteristics of the race under two triparte schemes: first, under body, heart, and mind; second, as a subset of mind. Of these categories the body was the most obvious, and to Jefferson it was also the most obviously defective. Blacks simply lacked beauty. Their countenance, he claimed, was one of "eternal monotony." Jefferson was certain that blacks had a high degree of sexual ardor, which was a matter of the body, but this was not accompanied by the proper disposition of the heart, "a tender delicate mixture of sentiment and sensation."[62]

When he turned to the heart directly, by which he meant morality, Jefferson found Negroes generally to rank high. The reason was that blacks, like all human beings—even unbeautiful and unintelligent ones—were endowed with a natural moral sense. Praising the blacks' integrity, benevolence, gratitude, and "unshaken fidelity" (presumably to their masters), Jefferson excused any disposition on their part to act immorally (for instance by stealing) as the predictable consequence of enslavement.[63] Since morality was a natural characteristic, environmental influences might affect how it was realized in action, but they could never eradicate it. Why the environment could account for deviations in the effects of human nature with regard to morality yet not with regard to the mind or the body Jefferson did not say.

Jefferson next assessed the intelligence of blacks according to the Baconian faculties of memory, reason, and imagination. He held that the memory of blacks was as good as that of whites; that their imagination, except in music, was deplorable; and that they were "in reason much inferior." Since reason for Jefferson was the highest distinguish-

---

61. After a slave rebellion in Virginia, Jefferson, then president, suggested to James Monroe, then governor, that blacks might best be removed to the West Indies, where there was a climate "congenial with their natural constitution." TJ to James Monroe, 24 November 1801, F.VIII.105.

62. NVa.138. He pointed to albinos as "an anomaly of nature," but he found no beauty in "white Negroes," either. NVa.70. Jefferson did not consider that slaves might have reasons other than race for appearing "monotonous," such as shielding their emotions from their masters. Nor, when writing of the "immoveable veil of black," did he pay attention to the existence of mulattoes, despite their presence at Monticello and his own interest in the mathematics of racial intermixture. TJ to Francis C. Gray, 4 March 1815, LB.XIV.267.

63. NVa.142. See also TJ to Edward Bancroft, 26 January 1788, BC.XIV.492 ("a man's moral sense must be unusually strong, if slavery does not make him a thief").

ing quality of intelligence, and intelligence the highest trait of human beings, the low grade that the blacks made in it tended to push them near the outer edge of the circle of the human species. Indeed, Jefferson was sometimes so concerned to confirm his judgment that blacks were inferior in intelligence that he attacked evidence of black talent as spurious and the undeniable productions of black writers as mediocre.[64]

Even though Jefferson clearly believed that blacks were intellectually inferior to whites at the time, he sometimes held out the possibilities that he had not gathered enough data or that improved circumstances would result in higher-quality reasoning. Acknowledging the receipt of Benjamin Banneker's almanac, he replied to the black surveyor: "Nobody wishes more than I do to see such proofs as you exhibit, that nature has given to our black brethren talents equal to those of the other colors of men, and that the appearance of a want of them is owing merely to the degraded condition of their existence, both in Africa and America."[65] Yet in the face of his detailed and flat statements about natural differences between races, neither such a note, which would hardly have been sent if it had not praised, nor the caution with which Jefferson concluded his discussion in *Notes on Virginia*—"the opinion that [blacks] are inferior in the faculties of reason and imagination, must be hazarded with great diffidence"—is unlikely to impress many readers.[66]

What, then, can be made of Jefferson's views on nature, slavery, and race? First, slavery in any form violated man's rights by nature, rights based on the equal moral creation of all human beings. Second, blacks did not seem to be equally endowed with whites in body and mind. This condition could be explained according to either of two understandings of nature. Between them Jefferson strongly tended towards the view of internal nature, which held that blacks were inherently inferior. But he acknowledged that external nature might account for it.

---

64. He called the poetry of Phyllis Wheatley "compositions published under her name" and the writing of Ignatius Sancho "letters published under his name." NVa.140, 141. Compared with the literature of whites, Wheatley's poetry was "below the dignity of criticism," and Sancho's letters were "at the bottom of the column." He privately dismissed a volume of the "literature of Negroes" even though he sent a cordial note to the French bishop who had compiled the anthology. TJ to Joel Barlow, 8 October 1809, LB.XII.322; TJ to Henri Gregoire, 25 February 1809, F.IX.246.

65. TJ to Benjamin Banneker, 30 August 1791, LB.VIII.241. See also TJ to Condorcet, 30 August 1791, F.V.379 (hoping "that the want of talents observed in [blacks] is merely the effect of their degraded condition"); and TJ to Henri Gregoire, 25 February 1809, F.IX.246 (expressing his wish to see a "complete refutation of the doubts I have myself entertained and expressed on the grade of understanding alloted to [Negroes] by nature"). It should be noted that these comments were sent to intellectuals in France, where Jefferson's reputation was principally as a figure of the American Enlightenment. To Americans active in politics he spoke differently.

66. NVa.143.

External nature in this case did not include the natural environment of America, but it did include the African background, about which Jefferson knew nothing; the consequences on blacks of the attitudes of whites; and above all, slavery, of whose effects Jefferson was by turns acutely conscious and incomprehensibly neglectful. Not choosing between the two ideas of nature, however, his inquiry into what human nature was for blacks remained unanswered.

The contrast is so great between Jefferson's distaste for Negroes and his affection for American Indians, who by any anthropological guideline were culturally no more like whites than the Africans were, that a final word needs to be said on the comparison.[67] The two races were distinguishable to Jefferson by three important characteristics: enslavement, indigenousness, and skin color. While Jefferson never blamed slavery on the slaves, he often seemed more concerned with the impact of slavery on the whites than with a life of enslavement for the blacks. His loathing of slavery was genuine, but it rested more on philosophy than on empathy. In the case of the Indians, however, he overflowed with empathy, and the trait he most admired was the opposite of enslavement, the Indians' sense of freedom (as he understood it). Second, the Indians were natives of America. They had original possession of the land and therefore certain rights regarding it that Afro-Americans could never attain. Further, Jefferson identified the human nature of America with its natural history, thus establishing a bond with the Indians that was inconceivable with the Africans.

But it was skin color, the physical emblem of the difference between the two nonwhite races, that concerned Jefferson most. He recognized color as a natural, not accidental, difference between blacks and Indians. But because of the largely uncomplimentary views of blacks built up through Western history; perhaps an ordinary human disposition to be uneasy about what appears the opposite of one's own condition; the impossibility of disentangling race from slavery in his own experience and therefore the possible transference of the degrading results of slavery to the color of the enslaved race; and his personal penchant to simplify reality into two positions, Jefferson was a ready carrier of racialism, if not of racism. To all of this the Indians stood in stark contrast. Often ennobled in both Enlightenment and Romantic thought, they were not enslaved, not aliens, and—crucially—not black. With respect to the Indians, Jefferson saw "fine mixtures of red and white," and he took literally, or thought white Americans should make literal, the idea of "red brothers"—under a great white father.[68]

---

67. For a stimulating discussion of the three races in Jefferson's thought see Jordan, *White over Black,* 475–81 ("A Dichotomous View of Triracial America").
68. NVa.138.

But as to blacks, "Their amalgamation with the other color produces a degradation to which no lover of his country, no lover of excellence in the human character can innocently consent."[69]

Thus with regard to human nature and race, as also with regard to much of physical nature, Jefferson had only the most limited success in looking beyond his own horizon. He failed seriously to consider the comparative situations of Indians and blacks, scarcely undertaking to contrast the freedom of the one to the slavery of the other, the indigenous habitation of the one to the uprooted life of the other, the social cohesion of the one to the deliberate social fragmenting of the other, the independent government of the one to the absence of any civic bonds of the other. Unfortunately, such undisputed differences did not impress themselves on his mind, and his inadequate use of particular nature to understand race never matched his liberal use of universal nature to understand slavery.

Skin color is one of the two large, recognizable, and permanent kinds of distinctions that exist among humans. The other is gender. Jefferson devoted far more thought to the matter of race than he did to the possible separate natures of men and women, and he was even more a creature of his time and place on the subject of gender than he was on race. His views on gender differences must be drawn as much from the facts of his biography as from the scattered comments in his writing.[70] The death of his wife when she was thirty-three and of his younger daughter at age twenty-five were the great sorrows of his life, strengthening his sense of the importance of family and his own responsibility for the proper upbringing of children. He raised his two daughters and

69. TJ to Edward Coles, 25 August 1814, F.IX.478. Three decades earlier Jefferson had held a more tempered outlook, at least in writing to a French acquaintance: "I believe the Indian to be in body and mind equal to the whiteman. I have suspected the blackman, in his present state, might not be so. But it would be hazardous to affirm that, equally cultivated for a few generations, he would not become so." TJ to marquis de Chastellux, 7 June 1785, BC.VIII.186.

70. Much has been made of Jefferson and women. Fawn Brodie places the speculation, of which there is a great deal, in scholarly order and accepts most of it. *Thomas Jefferson, an Intimate History.* An imagined account is Barbara Chase-Riboud, *Sally Hemings: A Novel* (New York, 1979). Virginius Dabney, in *The Jefferson Scandals* (New York, 1981), rejects ideas of any liaisons. Winthrop Jordan offers a sophisticated view in *White over Black,* 461–75. The long intellectual tradition in which Jefferson formed his views is the subject of Jean Bethke Elshtain, *Public Man, Private Woman: Women in Social and Political Thought* (Princeton, 1981), esp. 114–27 (on Locke). The "two sphere" doctrine reflected in the title of Elshtain's book was held by the Ideologues, Jefferson's closest French associates. Merle Curti notes that Benjamin Franklin, "in holding that the female sex was no weaker than the male in reasoning ability," disagreed with Jefferson. *Human Nature in American Thought,* 103. Jefferson's cultural milieu with respect to women is discussed in Isaac Rhys, *The Transformation of Virginia, 1740–1790* (Chapel Hill, 1982), a study based on "the great cultural metaphor of patriarchy"; and in Jan Lewis, *The Pursuit of Happiness: Family and Values in Jefferson's Virginia* (New York, 1984).

presided over the raising of most of his grandchildren. To judge from his letters, there were few women whose intelligence commanded his respect. These included his elder daughter Martha, Abigail Adams, and Madame de Tessé, a relative of Lafayette's, with whom he shared a love of botany.[71] For the most part it can be said of Jefferson that he was affectionate towards female relatives, flirtatious with Maria Cosway, whom he met with her husband in Paris, and cordial with all others.

Jefferson kept company with his class in Virginia in holding that human society was divided into two realms, public and private; that men were the inhabitants of the public realm, and women of the private; and that nature had ordained it this way. About women and the family, in contrast to the races of mankind, Jefferson found no moral puzzles and engaged in no intellectual disputes. About the family certainly it was not possible to dispute Locke, who wrote that parents were "wisely ordained by nature to love their children."[72] For Jefferson, the domestic sphere posed no challenges. "By a law of our nature," he wrote, "we cannot be happy without the endearing connections of a family."[73] And once a family existed, it was best characterized by the vow that he and his daughter Martha regularly exchanged with one another, that of "natural affection."[74]

Jefferson remarked on natural affection in a number of contexts. He noted that the precivilized practices of infanticide or selling a child into slavery violated the law under which parents show natural affection for their children.[75] He recommended *King Lear,* a play surely about natu-

71. Jefferson's daughter evidently did not insist on intellectual respect, however. See Martha Jefferson Randolph to TJ, 31 March 1797, BB.143 ("a mother's heart [is] of all things in nature the least subject to reason"). In addition to the women mentioned, Jefferson claimed to be impressed with the works of Mercy Otis Warren and an "unassuming lady" in England who wrote on chemistry. TJ to Mrs. Warren, 25 November 1790, BC.XVIII.78; TJ to William Short, 4 August 1820, LB.XV.258. Jefferson also respected the contribution of women to the economy, so long as it was at home. See TJ to John Thomson Mason, 18 August 1814, FB.489.

72. John Locke, *Some Thoughts Concerning Education* (1693), sec. 28.

73. TJ to William Clark, 10 September 1809, LB.XII.311.

74. In the marriage settlement for his daughter, Jefferson refers to "the natural love and affection which he, the said Thos. bears to his daughter." 21 February 1790, BB.49. Martha assured her father some years later that her marriage of over seven years, which she still called "new ties," would never "weaken the first and best of nature." Martha Jefferson Randolph to TJ, received 1 July 1798, BB.166. To Martha and her family Jefferson wrote from Washington a month before his first inauguration: "kiss the dear little objects of our natural love, and be assured of the constance and tenderness of mine to you." TJ to Martha Jefferson Randolph, 5 February 1801, BB.196. Greater distance of blood relationship and even taking the British side in the Revolution did not modify Jefferson's bonds. He wrote to his mother's brother, who had been living in England for some years: "Tho' most heartily engaged in the quarrel . . . I retain the same affection for individuals which nature . . . calls for." TJ to William Randolph, ca. June 1776, BC.I.410.

75. TJ to John W. Eppes, 11 September 1813, LB.XIII.357; TJ to David Williams, 14 November 1803, LB.X.430.

ral affection and the play by Shakespeare that uses the word "nature" more than any other, as impressing "a lively and lasting sense of filial duty . . . on the mind of a son or daughter."[76] In calling for an end to primogeniture, he wrote that the subdivision of property among one's children should "go hand in hand with the natural affections of the human mind."[77] On his return to Monticello after the presidency, Jefferson told his neighbors that he had come home to enjoy "the endearments of family love, which nature has given us all."[78]

Within the family, Jefferson expected the woman to bear and raise children, educate them, superintend the household, and provide comfort for her husband. The first of these roles was poetically put by Jefferson the botanist to his granddaughter: "The flowers come forth like the belles of the day, have their short reign of beauty and splendor, and retire like them to the more interesting office of reproducing their like."[79]

Jefferson's stay in France prompted comments, often quite strong, on a natural place for men and women in the economy. When he saw men taking on tasks he considered assigned by nature to women (shoemaking, upholstering, housecleaning) and the reverse (women becoming porters, sailors, and farmers), he called it "a great derangement in the order of things," words he might have used to describe a river that had reversed its normal direction of flow.[80] In politics it was the same. It was nature, Jefferson claimed, that "marked infants and the weaker sex for the protection, rather than the direction of government."[81] Because of their natural weakness in both body and mind, Jefferson presumed that women would neither vote nor hold public office. He therefore criticized the influence of women in French politics, satisfied that in Virginia such influence did not "extend beyond the domestic line."[82] As he candidly noted once to his secretary of the treasury, "The appointment of a woman to public office is an innovation for which the public is not prepared, nor am I."[83]

76. TJ to Robert Skipwith, 3 August 1771, BC.I.77.
77. TJ to James Madison, 28 October 1785, BC.VIII.682.
78. TJ to the Inhabitants of Albemarle County, 3 April 1809, Pdvr.447.
79. TJ to Anne Randolph Bankhead, 26 May 1811, BB.400.
80. TJ, "Notes of a Tour into the Southern Parts of France," 15 May 1787, BC.XI.446. See also TJ, "Memorandums on a Tour from Paris," 19 April 1788, BC.XIII.27–28 (women "formed by nature for attentions, not for labor").
81. TJ to John Hambden Pleasants, 19 April 1824, LB.XVI.28.
82. TJ to George Washington, 4 December 1788, BC.XIV.330. Jefferson was sharply challenged on such views by a leader of Philadelphia society, Mrs. Anne Willing Bingham. Mrs. Bingham to TJ, 1 June 1787, BC.XI.392–93.
83. TJ to Albert Gallatin, 13 January 1807, F.IX.7. For the provisions of Jefferson's draft constitutions for Virginia enfranchising men only, see BC.I.358 and BC.VI.296. For

Jefferson's ill-digested observations about women paralleled his confusion about both Indians and blacks regarding which "nature" one should give credence to, an original nature or a developed one, a universal nature or a particular one. Condemning "barbarous people" for submitting their women to drudgery, Jefferson held that "civilization . . . replaces women in the enjoyment of their natural equality."[84] But, one asks, why should people wish to escape their "natural equality"? Perhaps the answer is that there exist universal natural goals that, attainable through the stages of civilization, are more basic than particular natural conditions. It is the goal rather than the condition that is more true to the meaning of nature. Nature as environment is an obstacle in the way of realizing innate human nature, and some features of original human nature must be revised if we are to reach our potential.

Not only for women but for society, civilization becomes responsible for the institutions that enable the best in human nature to prosper. It was on this ground that Jefferson, the champion of what was natural, argued on behalf of social manners, which he knew to be artificial. Despite appreciating diversity and some unevenness in human nature, his higher value here was social harmony. To preserve and foster this harmony, our uneven natures must be smoothed out, at least on the surface. This can be accomplished by attention to the shared habits of social intercourse. By temperament, by the traditions of the Virginia aristocracy, by his experience in French society, and, when he was a diplomat, by profession, Jefferson was a master of social convention. Politeness, Jefferson explained to his grandson, who was having difficulty adjusting to Philadelphia, where he had been sent to study, "is artificial good humor, it covers the natural want of it, and ends by rendering a substitute nearly equivalent to the real virtue."[85]

If politeness was necessary inside of society, it was even more necessary between societies, where there were no shared rules of decorum by nature. Attempting to soothe the feelings of the French minister to the United States, Jefferson wrote about a special class of artificial good

---

an explicit argument excluding women in a later state constitution, see TJ to Samuel Kercheval, 5 September 1816, LB.XV.72 (exclusion prevents "depravation of morals and ambiguity of issue").

84. NVa.60; see, similarly, TJ, "Memorandums on a Tour from Paris," 19 April 1788, BC.XIII.36n29 ("barbarous perversion of the natural destination of the two sexes" for Indian women to be obliged to perform certain physical labor).

85. TJ to Thomas Jefferson Randolph, 24 November 1808, BB.363. Jefferson may have been inspired to lecture his grandson by his daughter, the boy's mother, who had just been convinced by a French author that the rules of etiquette "derived from the most amiable and virtuous feelings of the heart." Martha Jefferson Randolph to TJ, 18 November 1808, BB.360. But this reverses Jefferson's reasoning, for the daughter is claiming that etiquette is natural (from the heart), while he insists that it is artificial.

humor, diplomatic behavior. Disputes over protocol, he acknowledged, could not be absolutely determined, for "they have no foundation in reason." They were "arbitrary and senseless in their
nature, . . . decided by every nation for itself." He offered a theoretical
suggestion for avoiding such disputes. If there must be diplomatic
protocol at all in a new country like the United States, it should be made
to depend "on some circumstance founded in nature, such as the age or
stature of the parties."[86]

A second and more serious improvement on human nature that
Jefferson attended to was education. His plans for several institutions of
learning, from primary school to the university, have been treated earlier with regard to the place of nature in the curriculum. But education
was also founded in qualities of human nature, and one of its chief
purposes was to train a "natural aristocracy."

Jefferson's mature and most public statement on the educability of
man appears in the Rockfish Gap Report of 1818, issued by the Commission for the University of Virginia, of which he was chairman. In
justifying the educational system proposed for the state, the commission declared:

> We should be far . . . from the discouraging persuasion that man is
> fixed, by the law of his nature, at a given point; that his improvement is a
> chimera, and the hope delusive of rendering ourselves wiser, happier or
> better than our forefathers were. As well might it be urged that the wild
> and uncultivated tree, hitherto yielding sour and bitter fruit only, can
> never be made to yield better; yet we know that the grafting art implants
> a new tree on the savage stock, producing what is most estimable both in
> kind and degree. Education, in like manner, engrafts a new man on the
> native stock, and improves what in his nature was vicious and perverse
> into qualities of virtue and social worth.[87]

How should one understand the extended simile that Jefferson the
horticulturalist employs? Jefferson had compared human and physical
nature before, as when he wrote his granddaughter that young women
are like "flowers [which] come forth as the belles of the day." But that
example may be taken as a literary flourish. In the Rockfish Gap Report
he had in mind something more substantial. Since humans are as much
nature as plants are, there are principles that, if carefully formulated,
apply equally to both. Simile and analogy are not mere decorations of

---

86. TJ to comte de Moustier, 17 May 1788, BC.XIII.173. Although age and height are
natural characteristics, they may not be randomly distributed among nations. Jefferson
himself told an anecdote of Benjamin Franklin's about a group of tall Americans and short
Frenchmen. LB.XVIII.170–71.

87. TJ, Report of the Commissioners for the University of Virginia (Rockfish Gap
Report), August 1818, PJ.335–36. A facsimile of Jefferson's draft is reproduced in plate 10.

argument here. They are vehicles that convey truths about the intercon-
nectedness of nature. Just as grafting in horticulture improves on physical nature, so, "in a like manner," does education on human nature. Just
as an untended tree is neither good on its own nor productive for others,
so is an untrained intellect incomplete both for oneself and for society.[88]
A related feature of the passage is its unkind and seemingly un-Jeffersonian view of human nature—"vicious and perverse." But perhaps the
degree to which we are vicious ordinarily is not so significant if the
prospects for our improvement are quite substantial.[89]

At heart, Jefferson's educational plans were designed to ensure not
that individuals would be improved but that society would be well
governed. For this purpose, he proposed that persons of talent, a natural
aristocracy, be elevated to positions of leadership through publicly supported education. Without such education, people of lesser worth
would come to political power by a combination of their own mis-
directed drives and the ignorance of the remainder of the populace.

Jefferson's ideas on education in Virginia went back at least to the
Revolution. At that time, as part of his work towards revising the state's
laws generally, he brought bills before the legislature that as a group
were intended to finish off the "pseudoaristocracy" in Virginia. Among
these was the "Bill for the More General Diffusion of Knowledge"
(1779). This bill proposed a plan to educate the general population so
that they would "know ambition under all its shapes" and thereby be
able to protect themselves from the subversion of their natural rights;
and so that they would at the same time educate as governors and
guardians of their natural rights "those persons, whom nature hath
endowed with genius and virtue . . . without regard to wealth, birth or
other accidental condition or circumstance."[90] It is better, Jefferson said
in the bill (which was not enacted), that "children whom nature hath
fitly formed and disposed to become useful instruments for the pub-

---

88. The model horticultural metaphor of an "art which does mend nature" is *The
Winter's Tale* IV.iv. For Jefferson's acquaintances, education was as conveniently based on
agriculture as on horticulture. See Benjamin Franklin, "Proposals Relating to the Education of Youth in Pensilvania" (1751), in *Classics in Education,* ed. Wade Baskin (New York,
1966), 237 (the best capacities must be "well tilled and sowed with profitable seed"); and
Martin S. Staum, *Cabanis,* 127 (Georges Cabanis held that the educational terrain must be
"planted and cultivated carefully to improve the 'wise dispositions' of nature").

89. Jefferson may also have written in this fashion out of regard for other members of
the commission (James Madison, for instance), whose views of human nature were less
favorable than his own.

90. TJ, A Bill for the More General Diffusion of Knowledge (drafted 1776; introduced
into the legislature 1779), BC.II.526–27. See also NVa.148 (educational plan of 1779
would select "youths of genius from among the poor . . . to avail the state of those talents
which nature has sown as liberally among the poor as the rich, but which perish without
use"); TJ to William Duane, 4 August 1812, LB.XIII.180; and TJ, Act for Establishing
Elementary Schools (sec. 41), sent to Joseph C. Cabell, 9 September 1817, LB.XVII.440.

lic . . . should be sought for and educated at the common expense of all, than that the happiness of all should be confided to the weak or the wicked."

Thus, Jefferson wished to maintain a republican government by aristocratic means. But both, he claimed, complied with the principles of nature. What was natural about the educational system was that it reflected the random distribution of innate talent and virtue in society. If this seems undemocratic because it picks only the best, Jefferson would reply that it is nature that is undemocratic in producing differences in human talent and virtue. More important, in practice the system is based on an initial equal chance for all, has no socially imposed barriers to admission, is universal in its coverage in the elementary years, is financed by the public, and, above all, intends to ensure the long-term happiness of the whole people. Almost half a century after drafting the bill, he still referred to a "natural aristocracy of talents and virtue [to be prepared by education] at the public expense, for the care of the public concerns."[91]

Although the idea of a natural aristocracy was, when he first used it, associated with leadership in a republican society, and although the system of education he proposed in connection with the idea was a practicable one, Jefferson eventually allowed the idea to escape its educational mooring, and when it did, it met several difficulties. As a branch of his thinking on human nature, the idea of a natural aristocracy is displayed in a single burst of intellectual energy in a letter to John Adams of October 1813, the longest he ever wrote to his friend in Massachusetts.[92]

The concept of a natural aristocracy, with no reference to education, was common in eighteenth-century Britain, but hardly with the meaning that Jefferson ultimately gave it. British society, based on orders and ranks, gave currency to the idea of a natural aristocracy, which was akin to the idea of a chain of being. Jefferson must have found the idea in the literature he read when young, and in his own early uses of the term outside education he echoed this Augustan heritage.[93] In a letter to

91. TJ to Joseph C. Cabell, 5 January 1825, F.IX.501.

92. TJ to John Adams, 28 October 1813, C.II.387–92. The quotations from Jefferson in the next paragraphs of the text are, unless otherwise stated, from this letter. The proximate cause of Jefferson's devising his theory was a barrage of comments on aristocracy in recent letters from Adams. Adams to TJ, 9 and 13 July, 14 August, 2 and 15 September 1813, C.II.352, 355, 365–66, 371–72, 376–77. See also Adams to TJ, 1 March 1787, C.I.177.

93. For instance, from Pope's *Essay on Man* (1734): "Order is Heav'ns first law, and this confest, / Some are, and must be, greater than the rest, / More rich, more wise." IV.49–51. And from James Thomson's *Coriolanus* (1749): "Who'er amidst the Sons / Of Reason, Valour, Liberty, and Virtue, / Displays distinguish'd Merit, is a Noble / Of Nature's own creating." III.iii.

James Madison, for instance, he used the term "natural aristocrats," apparently without irony, in a way exactly opposite to his later meaning.[94] John Adams, on the other hand, appeared in print in the 1780s with the well-considered conservative meaning of the term that he maintained in his later correspondence with Jefferson.[95] When the two men finally contested the idea, therefore, Jefferson had given less thought to it than Adams, and it is probably this as much as any problems inherent in the idea of a natural aristocracy that accounts for the weakness in his argument.

Jefferson opens his discussion with interpretations of two classical writers who justified sexual union either to achieve immortality for the human species or, by selective interbreeding, to improve the species. As to the first, he responds: "But nature, not trusting to this moral and abstract motive, seems to have provided more securely for the perpetuation of the species by making it the effect of the oestrum [i.e., sexual heat] implanted in the constitution of both sexes." As to the second, neither the oestrum (an "unhallowed impulse") nor wealth and ambition (other unedifying impulses mentioned by the ancients) leads to the interbreeding needed to produce a genuine natural aristocracy. Nor, Jefferson continues, has mankind made any deliberate attempt by intermarriage to improve the beauty, health, understanding, or virtue of the species. Of course it could do this, he says (affirming a patriarchal society and displaying an ignorance of genetics), "for experience proves that the moral and physical qualities of man, whether good or evil, are transmissible in a certain degree from father to son." But because "the equal rights of man" will not permit a "privileged Solomon" to determine mating among humans, the theory is an impractical one and must be discarded.

Jefferson therefore accepts the idea of an "accidental aristoi," still natural but the result of "the fortuitous concourse of breeders," that is, husband and wife as they come together according to the conventions of society. It is their children, the accidental aristocrats, rather than any deliberately produced offspring, who will form the natural aristocracy of society. There was a time, Jefferson asserts, when the characteristics of such an aristocracy included strength, beauty, "good humor, politeness and other accomplishments." But now the leading traits are simply virtue and talents, moral and intellectual worth. A natural aristocracy thus stands in opposition to an artificial aristocracy founded on

94. TJ to James Madison, 12 May 1792, F.VI.251 ("the fashionable circles" of several cities consist of "natural aristocrats").

95. John Adams, *A Defence of the Constitutions of Government of the United States of America* (1787–88), in *The American Enlightenment,* ed. Adrienne Koch, 260–63 ("Equality and Natural Aristocracy").

wealth and birth. Jefferson then explains how to diminish the power of wealth and birth and increase the influence of the "veritable aristoi."[96]

Jefferson's theory raises issues about both nature and aristocracy. Most important is the need to explain how there can be both natural aristocracy and natural equality. Natural equality cannot mean that people are born with equal capabilities, for that would contradict the idea of a natural aristocracy at the start and violate ordinary observation as well. Rather, the best understanding of natural equality is that all persons are born with equal moral rights. But if people have equal moral rights, what aspect of us nevertheless permits the formation of a natural aristocracy? Perhaps it lies in our possession of virtues and talents or, more accurately, in our potential to develop them. The moral sense (to be treated more fully in the next chapter) is common to everyone. But like eyesight, or perhaps a sense for music, people are randomly endowed with better or worse versions of it. Virtues are like talents in forming an aristocracy. Just as society should want to develop musical or inventive capabilities where they exist, or make the best use of people with excellent vision, so it should want to develop the virtue of those people whose potential for public integrity is especially high.

A natural equality in virtue, however, is a minimum that everyone shares. Or perhaps instead of a minimum it is a norm, and those who exceed the natural norm are members of the natural aristocracy. It is to society's advantage to discover these people, to give them the chance to develop their capacity, and to place them in public office. If this is the meaning of Jefferson's argument, then he seems to have turned Aristotle upside down. While there are no natural slaves, there are natural aristocrats. At the same time, Jefferson seems to adopt a modified version of Plato (a connection he would not have appreciated): society should be governed by its naturally best people and should devise a way of ensuring that this will happen.

A second approach to reconciling natural equality with natural aristocracy is to hold that the initial equality refers not to moral rights but to opportunity. Jefferson never speaks of equality of opportunity, but that is what his educational system would provide. Is there, then, a natural right to it? Jefferson never claimed there was, and it could hardly be the necessary consequence of naturally unequal endowments. Yet he may have believed that the right existed, because he was Aristotelian enough to assume that every creature ought, by nature, to fulfill its distinctive, inherent capabilities. If some people, by their potential talents or vir-

---

96. Jefferson also caricatures an artificial aristocracy as "tinsel-aristocracy," "pseudo-aristocracy," and finally simply as "Pseudalists." For an example of his sarcasm about the British, see NVa.119 (reliance on the House of Lords would be "rational . . . if wisdom were hereditary").

tues, were more able than others to benefit from education, then they deserved by nature the chance to develop them.

A final cluster of issues focuses on the meaning of "natural" in natural aristocracy. Adams had looked around and seen aristocracies throughout the world and throughout history. Like Aristotle on slavery, he therefore concluded that no matter how they were defined, aristocracies were natural.[97] On other matters Jefferson surely would have agreed with this method of describing and defining a natural object. It was the method of natural history applied to society. But in this case he took refuge in a different procedure in the study of natural history and separated what he thought to be the essence of natural aristocracies—talent (carefully defined) and virtue—from what he considered accidental or false about them. Since his purpose in identifying a natural aristocracy was strictly functional, namely, to serve society and provide republican government, the qualities he selected were perhaps appropriate. But they were far from complete, and Adams, at once recognizing this, found the theory inadequate. Noticing that people everywhere had talents, height, social class, and other traits, he wrote his friend: "Your distinction between natural and artificial aristocracy does not appear to me well founded. Birth and wealth are conferred on some men, as imperiously by nature, as genius, strength or beauty."[98]

Adams probed Jefferson's terminology further. What are talents, he asked. Isn't the notion of them conditioned by culture? "Fashion," he wrote,

> has introduced an indeterminate use of the word "talents." Education, wealth, strength, beauty, stature, birth, marriage, graceful attitudes and motions, gait, air, complexion, physiognomy, are talents, as well as genius and science and learning. Any one of these talents, that in fact commands or influences true votes in society, gives to the man who possesses it, the character of an aristocrat, in my sense of the word.[99]

Doubtless aware of what he was doing, Adams had completely scrambled the debate, for among his "talents" were items that Jefferson considered variously natural and important (genius), natural but unimportant (strength), artificial (wealth), and indispensable to the use of

---

97. Adams's views were forcefully, if not tauntingly, put: "I say [the idea of the wellborn] is the ordinance of God Almighty, in the constitution of human nature, and wrought into the fabric of the universe. Philosophers and politicians may nibble and quibble, but they never will get rid of it." John Adams to TJ, 14 August 1813, C.II.365.

98. John Adams to TJ, 15 November 1813, C.II.400. If Jefferson had been willing to discuss birth as a part of aristocracy, he might have acknowledged himself a natural aristocrat on his father's side but an artificial aristocrat on his mother's. See TJ, Autobiography (1821), KP.3, 4 (his father was "of a strong mind, sound judgment . . . and improved himself," while his mother's family could "trace their pedigree far back").

99. John Adams to TJ, 15 November 1813, C.II.400.

others (education). After this outburst, however, Adams calmly offered a compromise definition which greatly narrowed the difference between the correspondents, permitting them to join in opposing an artificial aristocracy. He proposed that such an aristocracy refer to a government under which "wealth and powers are made hereditary by municipal laws and political institutions."[100] Jefferson could hardly disagree. But Adams's definition made plain once more a central difference between the two men. Adams founded social institutions on history and law, while Jefferson, despite conceptual and semantic difficulties, reached out to establish them on a presumed natural standard, even on one attached to an idea—aristocracy—that he normally rejected.

Thus ended Jefferson's formal exercise on natural aristocracy. It remains finally to discover what he actually had in mind under talents and virtues by nature. For this one must bring together several descriptions of men whom he considered "naturally endowed" with one talent or another. In most cases, predictably, he found that the unequal talents sown by nature could not be exercised without deliberate training and application. This was true especially in the arts, the area in which he found that such gifts as existed were the most natural of all. John Trumbull's "natural talents for [portraiture] seem almost unparalleled," he wrote, but despite this "natural bias for the art," it was perfectly reasonable that Trumbull come to Europe "to improve himself."[101] The art of war also had its natural talents, such as bravery, leadership, and endurance, but these, also, required training, or at least experience, in order to be complete.[102] In preparing guidelines for the University of Virginia in the granting of honorary degrees, Jefferson appeared to favor the standard of nature fortified by "attention and application" to nature by itself or to some other measurement.[103]

The great men of America whom Jefferson paraded against the Eu-

100. Ibid. Many years earlier, before he had provoked Jefferson into the field, Adams had written that the influence of birth and wealth was inevitable but that so long as there was a "natural right . . . to an equal status before the laws," no artificial aristocracy existed. *Discourses on Davila* (1790), quoted in Benjamin Fletcher Wright, Jr., *American Interpretations of Natural Law* (Cambridge, Mass., 1931), 253.

101. TJ to Ezra Stiles, 1 September 1786, BC.X.317; TJ to comte Thevenard, 5 May 1786, BC.IX.456. On the decline of a need for hard work to succeed in the professions Jefferson wrote cuttingly: "Now men are born scholars, lawyers, doctors; in our day this was confined to poets." TJ to John Tyler, 26 May 1810, F.IX.227.

102. Jefferson's thoughts on natural military talents arose in connection with the poor performance of the U.S. Army in the War of 1812. See TJ to William Duane, 4 August 1812, LB.XIII.180 ("the seeds of genius which nature sows . . . will develop themselves among our military men"); and TJ to Gen. Henry Dearborn, 17 March 1815, LB.XIV.288 ("officers of natural genius now starting forward from the mass").

103. TJ, Rockfish Gap Report, August 1818, PJ.346. Cf. TJ to George Washington, 6 April 1784, BC.VII.84 (also on "nature and application").

ropean theory of New World degeneracy likewise were specially endowed by nature. But in their cases no special training was suggested, and in the case of the astronomer David Rittenhouse being self-taught was an added merit.[104] Franklin was an "ornament of human nature." Rittenhouse was "one of Nature's best samples of the perfection she can cover under human form." George Mason was "one of those strong, very rare intellects which are created only by a special effort of nature." Of Washington: "never did nature and fortune combine more perfectly to make a man great."[105]

The remark on Washington is a reminder that Jefferson left room for Fortune as well as Nature in human affairs. It was Fortune that accounted for his regularly missing the chance to see a French diplomatic acquaintance. It was the "hand of fortune" that had directed the winds and weather to favor the British at Richmond in 1781. To the man who a few years later married his elder daughter Jefferson wrote: "Nature and fortune have been very liberal to you."[106]

But one can tell far less about humanity by consulting fortune rather than nature, and Jefferson hardly relied on fortune for intellectual nourishment. Instead, human nature, like physical nature, has its order and its rules. By nature, according to Jefferson, humans are social beings, normally disposed to harmony. Environments ordinarily influence the way our nature is acted out, but only a defective environment, especially poor government, will bring out the worst in us. By nature humans are morally equal to one another, although not all people, including entire discrete groups—Indians, blacks, and women—are necessarily equal culturally, physically, or intellectually. In an environment improved by society, through government, manners, or education, we can find the conditions for becoming the best that our human nature permits. Culture completes what nature has begun. Further, it is within culture that we exercise our values. And yet our values, Jefferson thought, are like our very being, comprehensible only by reference to nature itself.

104. NVa.64.
105. TJ to Elias Shipman, 12 July 1801, F.VIII.69 (on Franklin); TJ to the American Philosophical Society, 28 January 1797, quoted in Gilbert Chinard, "Jefferson and the American Philosophical Society," 267 (on Rittenhouse); Francis Coleman Rosenberger, ed., *Virginia Reader* (New York, 1948), 242 (on George Mason; quoted without source); TJ to Walter Jones, 2 January 1814, F.IX.449 (on Washington).
106. TJ to comte de Moustier, 3 December 1790, BC.XVIII.119; TJ to Henry Lee, 15 May 1826, F.X.388; TJ to Thomas Mann Randolph, Jr., 27 August 1786, BC.X.308–9. Congratulating his younger daughter on her engagement a number of years later, one that led to a difficult marriage, Jefferson left nature out: "I deem the composition of my family the most precious of all the kindnesses of fortune." TJ to Maria Jefferson, 14 June 1797, BB.148.

Part Two · VALUE

Chapter IV

THE NATURAL BASIS OF THE GOOD AND THE BEAUTIFUL

JEFFERSON ONCE SPOKE of "moral facts as important as physical ones."[1] He treated the two kinds of "facts" in the same manner: they were both facts of nature. Like the realm of physical phenomena, the realm of values was founded in nature. Indeed, with respect to an understanding of nature, Jefferson did not distinguish the two realms at all. Nor, if he was to be true to the lessons of Newton as they were conveyed in his time, should he have:

> To describe the *phenomena* of nature, to explain their causes . . . and to inquire into the whole constitution of the universe, is the business of natural philosophy. . . . But natural philosophy is subservient to purposes of a higher kind, and is chiefly to be valued as it lays a sure foundation for natural religion and moral philosophy; by leading us, in a satisfactory manner, to the knowledge of the Author and Governor of the universe.[2]

Adhering to this lesson, it is understandable that in religion and ethics, in aesthetics, politics, and economics, in all the regions of value, Jefferson was ignorant of any problems associated with deriving a statement of value from a statement about being. Rather, and without thinking about it, he adhered to a variety of ethical naturalism, according to which nature gives direct and certain guidance on matters of human choice. "First follow Nature," said the arbiter of taste in Augustan England, and Jefferson did.[3]

1. TJ to Richard Rush, 20 October 1820, LB.XV.284.
2. Colin Maclaurin, *An Account of Sir Isaac Newton's Philosophical Discoveries,* 3d ed. (1775), quoted in Carl L. Becker, *The Heavenly City of the Eighteenth-Century Philosophers* (New Haven, 1932), 62. Jefferson owned this edition.
3. Pope, *An Essay on Criticism* (1711), I.68. A contemporary American example of

In following the path of nature to create a realm of values, Jefferson either rejected or subordinated the principal alternative paths, those of theology and culture. In place of a transcendent Christian God he adopted a God of nature. He reduced the moral precepts of Jesus to a natural theology. He excised (literally, with scissors) those parts of the New Testament that seemed to him unnatural.[4] At the same time, he rejected historical experience or social needs as the touchstone of values. He assessed both history and society according to their presumed compliance with the standards of nature.

The immediate source of moral standards for Jefferson was an innate moral sense, a sense that nature has set in all human beings and is hence part of human nature. Despite the materialist premise of its existence, the moral sense is unlike other senses in having no elaborated physical location. But Jefferson and his sources usually spoke metaphorically of the moral sense as in—or at least of—the heart. Like other senses under the sensationist view of nature—hearing, sight, touch—the moral sense perceives the things of nature. What most people perceive with their moral sense is the moral choice of the majority, each person presumably acting from an individual recognition of right and wrong. The collective choice becomes the ethical norm. What is normal thus becomes what is normative, the linguistic ambivalence of "norm" mediating between natural fact and natural value. As a corollary, a moral deficiency, like impaired hearing, is merely a minor deviation from the natural norm.[5]

One implication of moral-sense reasoning is that there can be no genuine, or at least no widespread, evil in the world. What appears as evil is just that—apparent only. Nature, or nature's God, has wrought benevolently as much in the realm of value as in the realm of fact. Or so it seemed to Jefferson. Whether Jefferson held this view because he thought that his era, an era of American abundance and independence, was unusually good for mankind; or because he had absorbed so well the learning of the Scottish Enlightenment; or because the landscape and unpuritanical religion of Virginia led him to see good in nature everywhere, he blithely transmuted beneficent natural facts into benefi-

---

ethical naturalism is Johann Daniel Gros, *Natural Principles of Rectitude* (1795). S.1255. An orderly summary of the problems involved is Holmes Rolston III, "Can and Ought We to Follow Nature."

4. See Dickinson W. Adams, ed., *Jefferson's Extracts from the Gospels* (Princeton, 1983).

5. See TJ to Peter Carr, 10 August 1787, BC.XII.15; and TJ to Thomas Law, 13 June 1814, LB.XIV.142. The earliest source of Jefferson's views may be Cicero ("seeds of virtue are natural to our constitutions"). LBi.78. But Jefferson unquestionably adopted the idea of an innate moral sense from members of the Scottish Enlightenment, including Hume and Lord Kames. See, generally, D. D. Raphael, *The Moral Sense* (London, 1947).

cent natural values. If he had recognized much evil in the world, then nature would not be good, and that conclusion Jefferson could never reach.

In a universe so comforting to human needs Jefferson saw no difference between true religion and true morality. The purpose of religion was to inculcate mankind in the use of the moral sense and to ensure that people led an ethical life according to the dictates of nature. For this purpose, received religious ideas and institutions were defective, if not hopeless. When Jefferson looked around him to the sects, ritual, and traditions practiced under the name of Christianity, he was persuaded that natural ethics had been obscured. True religion, rather, consisted in "the moral precepts, innate in man, and made a part of his physical constitution, as necessary for a social being. . . . [T]he sublime doctrines of philanthropism, and deism taught us by Jesus of Nazareth in which all agree constitute true religion."[6] Deism in this use was what was practiced by a teacher who, like everyone else, perceived with a natural moral sense, but with a moral sense far above the norm. While this described Jesus, however, it did not describe a person who was divine. Divinity was reserved for a remote God who had created the natural world—including human beings with their natural senses. It was nature, not Jesus, that was God's only begotten creation.

This collection of ideas, known as natural religion, had a history of several generations when Jefferson came upon his views.[7] The God of natural religion was proven either by the evidence of his creation, the wondrous design of nature, or by the necessity for an original cause of nature. Combining these arguments, Jefferson found it "impossible for the human mind not to perceive and feel a conviction of design" that showed "irresistible . . . evidences of an intelligent and powerful Agent."[8] God had created a nature that was evidence simultaneously for true religion and true science.

The natural religion/morality of Jefferson was also tied to reason, in particular to natural reason. This was the reason that discovered self-evident, natural truths. Natural reason was especially valuable in the discovery of truths that underlay sectarian religion, for beneath them was the religion that could cleanse "artificial systems" from contemporary practices and return religion to its pure, ostensibly original, condi-

6. TJ to John Adams, 5 May 1817, C.II.512.
7. Early works on natural religion that Jefferson owned included Locke's *Letters on Toleration* (1689, 1690, 1692) and *The Reasonableness of Christianity as Delivered in the Scriptures* (1695). The flowering of this view occurred in the next generation, and Jefferson owned several treatises that had in their titles either "religion of nature" or "natural religion." In Jefferson's lifetime, Lord Kames, Joseph Priestley, William Paley, Thomas Paine, and Ethan Allen all published on the subject.
8. TJ to John Adams, 11 April 1823, C.II.592.

tion. Among sectarian artificialities were ideas such as miracles, the trinity, virgin birth, and the resurrection.[9] Once these had been removed, and Christianity enabled to return "to the primitive simplicity of its founder," religion would have neither sects nor dogmas. It would practice instead nothing but natural morality. Jefferson himself was interested only in "the moral branch of religion, which is the same in all religions," though in deference to society he was willing to permit instruction in "religion, [both] natural and sectarian."[10]

Jefferson's most public deistic phrase—a phrase not of his own making—was the one under which American independence was declared, "nature and nature's God." Although one cannot tell from either its grammar or its context whether "nature's God" means that nature created God (as in the parent's child) or that nature is beholden to God (as in the child's parent), Jefferson in fact understood that God was the author of nature. It was not the other way around. Yet he might almost have declared independence under the laws of "nature and nature," so closely did he identify nature and the divine.[11]

Jefferson's natural religion and its accompanying natural moral sense were tested, and by the Virginia assembly found wanting, in his Bill for Religious Freedom, drafted in 1779. Deletions made from the original text show the limits of public acceptance of Jefferson's reasoning, even though the law did put an end to earlier rules that he called Virginia's "religious slavery."[12]

The draft bill had opened with an affirmation of Lockean sensationism: "The opinions and belief of men . . . follow involuntarily the evidence proposed to their minds." It continued with the declaration that "Almighty God" had made the mind "altogether insusceptible of restraint." In its course it consequently pronounced that "the opinions

9. TJ to William Short, 31 October 1819, LB.XV.221.

10. TJ to John Adams, 12 October 1812, C.II.385; TJ to Thomas Leiper, 21 January 1809, LB.XII.236–37; TJ to John Minor, 30 August 1814, F.IX.481.

11. There is no need to look for a single source for the phrase "Nature's God." It was familiar to eighteenth-century British culture, for instance, in Pope's *Essay on Man* (1734), IV.331–32: "Slave to no sect, who takes no private road / But looks through nature up to nature's God!" Once Jefferson had set the phrase into the mainstream of American political vocabulary, James Madison used it to justify the Constitution. *Federalist* No. 43 (Wright ed.), 316.

Jefferson's preference for God as the source of Nature, rather than the reverse, appears in TJ, argument in Howell v. Netherland, April 1770, F.I.376; and TJ to Benjamin Austin, 9 January 1816, LB.XIV.391 ("author of nature"). Just how sensitive Jefferson was to the religious beliefs of his audience is evident in his converting "laws of nature and nature's God" into "laws of god and nature" when, explaining the Declaration, he urged God-fearing Hessian troops to come over to the American side at the beginning of the Revolution. TJ, Report of a Plan to Invite Foreign Officers in the British Service to Desert, 27 August 1776, BC.I.509.

12. NVa.159. The Bill for Religious Freedom as drafted (1779) and as passed (1786) is in BC.II.545–46.

of men are not the object of civil government, nor under its jurisdiction." All of this language the state assembly deleted except "Almighty God," which was acceptable to both the traditional Christian and the deist. This left three implications: (1) that religious beliefs do not originate in nature; (2) that such beliefs were not held by nature ("involuntarily"); and (3) that the civil government does not act improperly if it interferes with such beliefs.

Despite these disappointments, the law did contain an important provision deriving from nature. When the bill was drafted, Virginia was under a constitution that, to Jefferson's great regret, did not protect the rights of religious liberty. In an attempt to make up for that failure, the bill purports to protect religious rights by emphasizing that what is at stake is a natural right and that the legislative act has the strength of a constitutional provision and cannot be altered by a subsequent simple legislative majority: "The rights hereby asserted are of the natural rights of mankind, and . . . if any act shall be hereafter passed to repeal the present, or to narrow its operation, such act will be an infringement of natural right." Still disturbed at the deletion of the clause maintaining opinions were "not the object of civil government," Jefferson made an additional effort to reinforce this passage. In commenting on the law as passed, he claimed, in effect, that the deleted clause had not been necessary in the first place. Perhaps no law was needed at all. "Our rulers," he proclaimed, "can have authority over such natural rights only as we have submitted to them. The rights of conscience we never submitted, we could not submit."[13]

The principal reason why religious rights are natural rights to Jefferson is that, as has been said, true religion was true morality, and moral rights were natural because morality itself sprang from a sense that people were given by nature. But we have an innate moral sense, Jefferson asserted, not merely because nature has placed it there but because it is an indispensable aid to another natural trait that is even more basic, our instinct for society. In the Aristotelian tradition, Jefferson could not imagine morality except as a relation among people who were living in society. Ethics was thus essentially social ethics: "I consider our relations with others as constituting the boundaries of morality."[14]

Jefferson set out his convictions in a letter to his nephew and ward Peter Carr in 1787:

> He who made us would have been a pitiful bungler if he had made the rules of our moral conduct a matter of science. For one man of science, there are thousands who are not. What would have become of them? Man was destined for society. His morality therefore was to be formed to

13. NVa.159.
14. TJ to Thomas Law, 13 June 1814, LB.XIV.140.

this object. He was endowed with a sense of right and wrong merely relative to this. . . . This sense is submitted indeed in some degree to the guidance of reason; but it is a small stock which is required for this. . . . State a moral case to a ploughman and a professor. The former will decide it as well, and often better than the latter, because he has not been led astray by artificial rules.[15]

What stands out in this passage is that the moral sense is independent of our ability to reason, at least our ability to use artificial reason. The capacity for artificial reason must be trained. It must be developed through education. But this suggests an inadequacy in Jefferson's earlier theory. In the Rockfish Gap Report Jefferson argued that education was needed to ameliorate deficiencies in natural morality. But is education needed, or is it not? Any education moves people away from their original nature, perhaps the professor further away than others. This raises the unfortunate possibility, though, that through education, some people may come to distance themselves from, rather than improve upon, their natural morality. The American Indians seem to support this conclusion in favor of the ploughman over the professor. They possessed neither artificial reason nor formal education. Yet Jefferson admired these people, whose "only controls are their manners, and that moral sense of right and wrong, which . . . in every man makes a part of his nature."[16]

Jefferson's determination somehow to found ethics in an innate moral sense led him to deny not only reason and formal education as its chief sources. He also argued against or reduced to "nature" other bases of moral action proposed in his time. Perhaps the most important of these was "self-love," which to Jefferson contradicted the very idea of morality, since morality entails obligations, and obligations entail at least two people. Self-love, by which Jefferson meant egoism or narrow self-interest, was the "sole antagonist of virtue." He acknowledged that egoism could occasionally be a source of moral action, as when one holds that to help those in distress gives one pleasure. But this is not self-love, Jefferson says. Rather, it is to act on the best grounds possible: "Because nature hath implanted in our breasts a love of others, a sense of duty to them, a moral instinct, in short, which prompts us irresistibly to feel and to succor their distresses."[17]

15. TJ to Peter Carr, 10 August 1787, BC.XII.14–15. See also TJ to James Fishback, 27 September 1809, LB.XII.315 (moral precepts so indelibly impressed "on our hearts that they shall not be effaced by the subtleties of our brain"). For a contemporaneous exposition of the ploughman-professor image and natural morality, see Wordsworth's "The Tables Turned" (1798). Wordsworth's natural morality springs from external nature, however, not from the human heart.

16. NVa.93.

17. TJ to Thomas Law, 13 June 1814, LB.XIV.140–41. One wonders how Jefferson

Another potential source for determining what counts as moral is utility, or, as Jefferson often calls it, calculation. Although this is the language of utilitarianism, Jefferson's use of it is not Benthamite in spirit, for beneath utility lies nature:

> Some have argued against the existence of a moral sense by saying that if nature had given us such a sense, impelling us to virtuous actions, and warning us against those which are vicious, then nature would also have designated, by some particular ear-marks, the two sets of action which are, in themselves, the one virtuous and the other vicious. Whereas, we find, in fact, that the same actions are deemed virtuous in one country and vicious in another. The answer is, that nature has constituted *utility* to man, the standard and test of virtue. Men living in different countries under different circumstances, different habits and regimens, may have different utilities; the same act, therefore, may be useful, and consequently virtuous in one country which is injurious and vicious in another differently circumstanced.[18]

Here Jefferson confounds universal and particular nature in moral theory. If there is a natural moral sense, one might expect that a moral code based on it would be a universal code. But Jefferson does not believe there is such a thing. Instead, and quite realistically, he recognizes the existence of various, indeed conflicting, moral codes in the world, noting that these codes come from different cultures and that the cultures in turn arise from different natural environments. In this way the particular nature of the environment comes to modify the universal nature of a moral sense. Whichever nature it is, however, it is nature that sanctions a utilitarian theory of morality. Utility does not, independent of nature, explain why people act or should act one way or another. It does, on the other hand, provide a more complex understanding of social ethics than does the doctrine of moral sense.

To think about a realm of ethics requires developing a conception of moral responsibility. That normally requires some stance towards the idea of free will. When Jefferson fashioned ethical values from natural sources, however, he overlooked the issue. To understand the problem, it is helpful to reconsider what is meant by a law of physical nature. The great advantage of a physical law is that it is uniform and admits of no

felt about the moral theory of his friend Crèvecoeur: "Here [in America] the rewards of [the farmer's] industry follow with equal steps the progress of his labour; his labour is founded on the basis of nature, *self-interest;* can it want a stronger allurement?" Hector St. John de Crèvecoeur, *Letters from an American Farmer* (New York, 1957; orig. 1782), 40 (emphasis in the original).

18. TJ to Thomas Law, 13 June 1814, LB.XIV.143. See, similarly, TJ to John Adams, 14 October 1816, C.II.492. For other uses of utilitarian calculation, see TJ to Maria Cosway, 12 October 1786, BC.X.448; and TJ to James Monroe, 8 January 1804, F.VIII.288.

variation. If, as Jefferson held, nature is material, and if humans consist of the same material nature and are to be explained in the same way as the rest of nature, what role is there for human choice? And if there is no room for choice, what, then, is morality? By adhering to the authority of nature, Jefferson thus diminished the possibility of human choice and accepted a basically deterministic position. Only if he had claimed that nature shows us what *can* be, rather than what must be, would he have preserved the exercise of free will. But Jefferson's nature was not flexible enough for that.

If Jefferson did not develop a theory of individual responsibility, he perforce did not develop a theory of responsibility for an entire society. But he did insist that to follow the prompting of nature led simultaneously to what was good for the individual and what was good for society. By this he did not mean to adopt a version of the self-love theory. To be happy was to be happy on one's own. To be virtuous was to be virtuous in society. But the two were in fact the same: "The order of nature is that individual happiness shall be inseparable from the practice of virtue." In case we should ever feel impelled to question this rule, the fault would lie in our reasoning, not in the truth of nature.[19] This comfortable coinciding of public benefit and personal happiness applied not only within a society. It was paralleled internationally: "With nations as with individuals, our interests soundly calculated, will ever be found inseparable from our moral duties."[20] As Jefferson uses the terms here, in the private realm happiness is related to interest; in the public realm virtue is related to duty. Succinctly stated by George Washington (who uses "advantage" in place of "interest"): "There is no truth more thoroughly established than that there exists in the economy and course of nature an indissoluble union between virtue and happiness; between duty and advantage."[21]

When Jefferson sought a doctrine of personal ethics, that is, a route to individual happiness, he found it in either of two theories of classical antiquity, Stoicism or Epicureanism. Both systems placed the achievement of pleasure or the avoidance of pain at the center of the definition of happiness. More important, and what distinguished them in Jefferson's mind from their chief competitor, Platonism, both were explicitly founded on the presumed teachings of nature. A special merit of Stoicism and Epicureanism, moreover, was that to follow nature was to

19. TJ to J. Correa de Serra, 19 April 1814, LB.XIX.210; TJ to Jean Baptiste Say, 1 February 1804, LB.XI.3. See also TJ to Caesar A. Rodney, 10 February 1810, F.IX.271 ("the connection which the laws of nature have established between [man's] duties and his interests").

20. TJ, Second Inaugural Address, 4 March 1805, Pdvr.411. See also TJ to Albert Gallatin, 28 March 1803, F.VIII.222.

21. First Inaugural Address, 1789.

become reconciled to the limitations of the freedoms that we think we possess. That is, their doctrines provide an unacknowledged refuge from determinism.

To the Stoics, nature is rigorously held together by and permeated with the vital force of *logos,* or reason. By using our individual capacity to reason, we can apprehend the order of nature generally and so act in accordance with it on particular occasions. A deliberately rational approach to nature, the Stoic morality was also a passionless one. Humans should live primarily ascetic, internal lives and remain unaffected by the surrounding world, where one would find only misery. If we understand the ways of nature, if we accept them and do not try to fight them, we will be as happy as it is possible for us to be—which is concededly not very much. Jefferson admitted that Stoicism verged on "grimace"; but at least it held out the avoidance of pain.[22]

The Epicurean, eventually the Lucretian, vision of nature is quite different. According to its atomism, all events were determined by the coming together of the smallest physical particles. But Epicurus introduced into the theory, in arguments that are still obscure or incompletely preserved, an element of free will: the atoms might acquire an evidently uncaused "swerve." Humans could use this swerve, this degree of freedom, to choose pleasures such as the cultivation of friendship and to develop the practical wisdom needed for achieving a happy life. Epicureanism thus held out a more pleasant prospect than Stoicism, and Jefferson found that it led to "ease of body and tranquility of mind," that is, to positive pleasures.[23]

Jefferson lays out the Stoic and the Epicurean routes to happiness in his remarkable "Dialogue Between my Head and my Heart," composed in the fall of 1786. The Head in the dialogue, the Stoic, claims that "the art of life is the art of avoiding pain."[24] "The most effectual means of being secure against pain," the Head states, "is to retire within ourselves and to suffice for our own happiness." The Head is comforted by being "above the concerns of this mortal world, contemplating truth and nature, matter and motion, the laws which bind up their existence and that eternal being who made and bound them up by these laws." Dispassionate knowledge of universal nature becomes the means of avoiding pain.

The Heart, the Epicurean, replies that the Head "mistake[s] for happiness the mere absence of pain." One should indeed contemplate

22. TJ to William Short, 31 October 1819, LB.XV.219.

23. TJ to John Adams, 27 June 1813, C.II.335.

24. TJ to Maria Cosway, 12 October 1786, BC.X.448. This letter is the source of the quotations in the next several paragraphs of the text. A passage from the dialogue is reproduced in plate 20.

nature, the Heart asserts. But one should advance beyond that to participate actively in the world. The Heart suggests two kinds of such participation, friendship and the direct enjoyment of nature. Friendship (which includes love) is both a balm and a delight, "precious not only in the shade, but in the sunshine of life." Friendships do eventually come to an end and so bring pain, but that is no reason to adopt the Stoic's "mantle of self-sufficiency" and undertake no friendships at all. "We have no rose without its thorn; . . . It is the law of our existence; and we must acquiesce."

It is the very witnessing of nature, however, the being in the midst of nature's wonders, that the Heart holds out as an especial pleasure. "I see things wonderfully contrived sometimes to make us happy," says the Heart about a possible visit of Maria Cosway and her husband to the natural sights of America. Wondering what Maria might paint, the Heart introduces its favorite scene:

> And our own dear Monticello, where has Nature spread so rich a mantle under the eye? Mountains, forests, rocks, rivers. With what majesty do we there ride above the storms! How sublime to look down into the workhouse of nature, to see her clouds, hail, snow, rain, thunder, all fabricated at our feet! And the glorious Sun, when rising as if out of a distant water, just gilding the tops of the mountains, and giving life to all nature.

The contrast is clear. While the Stoical Head is contemplating the laws of nature all alone, the Epicurean Heart is out enjoying nature in the company of a friend. Without rejoinder—it is the last speech in the dialogue—the Heart triumphantly as well as omnisciently proclaims:

> When nature assigned us the same habitation, she gave us over it a divided empire. To you she allotted the field of science; to me that of morals. . . . Morals were too essential to the happiness of man to be risked on the incertain combinations of the head. . . . [N]ature has not organized you for our moral direction.

Although on balance neither Head nor Heart, neither Stoic nor Epicurean, is the manifest victor in the dialogue, the Heart, like Epicureanism in Jefferson's life, holds the edge.

The "Dialogue Between my Head and my Heart" is more than an ethical treatise. It is an aesthetic production as well. It thereby acts as a hinge between Jefferson's natural ethics and his natural aesthetics.[25] A small work of art, the dialogue is Jefferson's only work of literary

25. Relevant general works are Horace Kallen, "The Arts and Thomas Jefferson"; Eleanor Davidson Berman, *Thomas Jefferson among the Arts;* and two books edited by William H. Adams, *The Eye of Thomas Jefferson,* esp. 314–51, and *Jefferson and the Arts.*

imagination. As the setting of the dialogue, nature is artistically balanced in the work's composition in two ways. First, it is the scene where each of the partners separately acts. The Head acts in its realm, "contemplat[ing] truth and nature," which are the universal matter and motion of natural philosophy. The Heart acts in its realm, enjoying "the face of nature," the rivers, forests, and mountains, which are the particular phenomena of natural history. Second, the descriptions of nature alternate between Europe and America, between the scene near Paris where Jefferson and the Cosways have taken their outings and the scenes in Virginia which he hopes the Cosways will visit.

The dialogue displays Jefferson as much in love with nature as he is with Maria Cosway. He assumes that Mrs. Cosway is nature's handmaiden and that she will respond favorably to his descriptions of the natural scene. Sometimes, indeed, it seems that he is unable to tell the difference between his two beloveds.[26] In the passage of the dialogue describing the view from Monticello, "nature" appears three times. Stylistically this is perhaps excessive, but Jefferson could not rid himself of the word, as if through its repetition he was expressing his love. As the Heart implies, he and Maria Cosway will love each other all the more in the proper settings of the New World. The Heart's recollections of the walks near Paris imply the same. On those days, the Heart recalls,

> indeed the sun shone brightly! How gay did the face of nature appear! Hills, valleys, chateaux, gardens, rivers, every object wore its liveliest hue! Whence did they borrow it? From the presence of our charming companion. They were pleasing, because she seemed pleased. Alone, the scene would have been dull and insipid: the participation of it with her gave it relish.

Although this is an attractive description of nature, it is more than that. It is a clear, if unphilosophical, expression of an aesthetic theory of nature. The theory holds that we—at least Mrs. Cosway—are the ones who provide nature with its beauty; that we, therefore, not nature itself, are the source of aesthetic values. Mrs. Cosway gives to nature a life it did not have without her. Nature is pleasing, not on its own, but only as a reflection of a person who is already pleasing.

If Jefferson had considered these assertions apart from his infatuation with Maria Cosway, he presumably would have rejected them, for his confirmed position was that value, moral or aesthetic, lies either in

26. Mrs. Cosway seems unable to tell the difference between her two beloveds, too, and assumes that Jefferson is also the servant of nature. After reading *Notes on Virginia*, she wrote the author "I have been reading with great pleasure your description of America. It is wrote by *you*, but Nature represents all the scenes to me in reality. . . . I must refer to your name to make it the more valuable to me, but she is your rival and you her usurper." Maria Cosway to TJ, 25 February 1787, BC.XI.149.

nature, awaiting us to discover it, or in us, implanted there from birth. We do not, Jefferson would ordinarily claim, make up values ourselves and then impute them to nature. While a critic of Jefferson's ideas might well claim that imputing values to nature, the pathetic fallacy, was his regular practice, Jefferson would admit it only in exceptional circumstances. In the case of love, perhaps this lapse in Jefferson's reasoning should be excused.

A final element of Jefferson's nature aesthetic in the dialogue is his reference to the sublime and the beautiful. In the eighteenth century these were the leading categories of natural scene and hence of the artistic representation of nature.[27] The sublime was a scene or feeling of awe or terror, grandeur and elevation, and often of wildness. The beautiful was a scene that was orderly and calm; it existed on a human scale and was subject to human understanding. In the dialogue, the Heart describes France, with its hills, rainbows, and the gardens at St. Germains, as beautiful. The sublime it reserves for America, particularly for the view from Monticello. In addition, while the Heart discovers the sublime at a particular place, the Head discovers it universally, "above the concerns of this mortal world." Both Heart and Head encounter the sublime as they "ride above" nature, the Heart riding with majesty, the Head with serenity.

With the dialogue as an introduction, we are now prepared to take a grander tour of Jefferson's natural aesthetic, beginning with *Notes on the State of Virginia,* where he continues the juxtaposition of the sublime and the beautiful. "The *Ohio,*" he writes, "is the most beautiful river on earth. Its current gentle, waters clear, and bosom smooth and unbroken by rocks and rapids, a single instance only excepted."[28] "The *Natural Bridge,*" on the other hand, is "the most sublime of Nature's works. . . . It is on the ascent of a hill, which seems to have been cloven through its length by some great convulsion."[29] The same aesthetic language applies to Monticello, where, in the words of a protégé, Jefferson could see both "one of the most beautiful horizons in the

27. The terms were most prominently elaborated by Edmund Burke in *A Philosophical Enquiry into the Origin of Our Ideas of the Sublime and Beautiful* (1757), which Jefferson recommended for a basic library. TJ to Robert Skipwith, 3 August 1771, BC.I.79. There was also a minor, third category, the picturesque. Rather than being innate in nature, however, as the sublime and the beautiful were, the picturesque was a contrivance, a natural scene that was given a man-made structure or interpretation for purposes of aesthetic appreciation. Jefferson used "picturesque" seldom, but when he did, it was in the standard way. See, e.g., TJ, "An Account of Louisiana," 14 November 1803, *American State Papers,* Class X, *Miscellaneous,* I. 346 (heights on the west bank of the Mississippi "exhibit a scene truly picturesque. . . [stone] carved into various shapes and figures by the hand of nature [affording] the appearance of a multitude of antique towers").

28. NVa.10. Jefferson never saw the Ohio River, and when he first wrote the passage, before going to Europe, he had not seen many other great rivers, either.

29. NVa.24.

world" (the Blue Ridge Mountains) and one of "the sublimest of Nature's operations" (the apparent changing shape of the mountains).[30]

It should be evident from this that Jefferson's periodic claim to be uninterested in aesthetic theory is misleading. Even as he makes one of those claims, nature is basic: "I am but a son of nature, loving what I see and feel, without being able to give a reason, nor caring much whether there be one."[31] Jefferson was greatly influenced by contemporary standards of taste, many of which were, as he knew, distinctly artificial. When he could convince himself that they were founded in nature, however, he became very interested in them indeed.

The opportunity to associate artistic standards with nature was not difficult to realize according to Jefferson, because we are formed by nature with an innate aesthetic sense, just as we are formed with an innate moral sense. "We have," he says,

> an innate sense of what we call beautiful . . . exercised chiefly on subjects addressed to the fancy, whether through the eye in visible forms, as landscape, animal figure, dress, drapery, architecture, the composition of colors, etc., or to the imagination directly, as imagery, style, or measure in prose or poetry, or whatever else constitutes the domain of criticism or taste, a faculty entirely distinct from the moral one.[32]

Despite this statement, the relation between the natural senses of ethics and aesthetics is not clear in Jefferson's writings. Although he says here that they are "entirely distinct" from one another, he also believes that the proper use of the aesthetic sense is to promote sound morals. When virtue is presented to our imagination and impresses us with its beauty, his argument runs, that in turn spurs the desire to act ethically. "The spacious field of imagination is . . . laid open to our use, and lessons may be formed to illustrate and carry home to the mind every moral rule of life."[33] Since Jefferson's deeper loyalty was to ethics, perhaps it is best to say that the faculty for the beautiful was, relative to that for the moral, separate in form but supporting in function.

If Jefferson's claim of indifference to art theory did not prevent him from discussing a natural aesthetic sense, neither did it bar his recognition of several direct connections between art and nature. How art and

---

30. William Wirt, "Eulogy on Jefferson," LB.XIII.xlv, xlvi.

31. TJ to Maria Cosway, 24 April 1788, BC.XIII.103–4. See also TJ to William Wirt, 12 November 1816, F.X.61 (despises "artificial canons of criticism"; one should ask about a work of art only "whether it gives . . . pleasure, whether it is animating, interesting, attracting? If it is, it is good for those reasons").

32. TJ to Joseph Priestley, 27 January 1800, LB.X.147. See also TJ, "Thoughts on English Prosody," ca. 1790, Pdvr.849 (anyone incapable of reading Homer without sensing the correct meter "is an unfavored son of nature to whom she has given a faculty fewer than to others of her children").

33. TJ to Robert Skipwith, 3 August 1771, BC.I.76–77.

nature were related was a controverted issue in eighteenth-century Europe, particularly because art criticism was often social criticism as well. Arts associated with social institutions that Jefferson considered unnatural, such as feudalism or medieval religion, were also thought to be unnatural, and hence unartistic.[34] Neither government nor the arts should go to excess, which was artificial, unnatural. Moderation and balance were preferred.

The reigning doctrine on the relation between nature and art in Jefferson's formative years was the approach of universal nature, of classicism. Beauty in art confirmed universal truth in nature. It was a doctrine best stated by Joshua Reynolds:

> The first idea that occurs in the consideration of what is fixed in art, or in taste, is that presiding principle—the general idea of nature. The beginning, the middle, and the end of everything that is valuable in taste, is comprised in the knowledge of what is truely nature. . . . The terms beauty, or nature, which are general ideas, are but different modes of expressing the same thing, whether we apply these terms to statues, poetry, or pictures. . . . [T]hose who have cultivated their taste, can distinguish what is beautiful or deformed, or, in other words, what agrees with or deviates from the general idea of nature. . . . [B]eauty or truth, . . . is formed on the uniform, eternal, and immutable laws of nature, and . . . of necessity can be but *one*.[35]

But the contribution of nature in America to Jefferson's ideas on art, the evidence of his senses, and his living into the age of romanticism all qualified his attachment to Reynolds's neoclassical idea that the keys to beauty and taste were the "immutable laws of nature." Rather, as against art characterized by harmony, balance, and inner laws, there stood an art that was related to the other understanding of nature, wild, dynamic, and following the laws (if there were any) of appearance. It was the old distinction between natural philosophy and natural history, universality versus variety. Jefferson, as usual, chose both.

Despite the possibility of accepting either of the approaches to the natural in art, Jefferson was never in doubt that there existed a fundamental contrast between art and nature. He held the common view that nature is what is untouched by man; art is what man has altered or

34. In Europe Jefferson admired architecture descended from the classical, not the medieval, era and he designed his own buildings without the slightest touch of the Gothic, an age that he said was controlled by bigots. TJ to Joseph Priestley, 27 January 1800, F.VII.415. He did once propose "a small Gothic temple of antique appearance" for the grounds of Monticello. TJ, Account Book, 1771, GB.25. But this was ornamental only and in any case was never constructed.

35. Joshua Reynolds, *Discourse on Art* (1776), in Peter Gay, ed., *Enlightenment Anthology*, 435–39.

improved, whether economically or artistically.[36] The distinction between the two, however, did not lead him to see them as competitors, as John Adams did: "The finest productions of the poet or the painter, the statuary or the architect, when they stand in competition with the great and beautiful operations of nature . . . must be pronounced mean and despicable baubles."[37] To Jefferson, art and nature were complementary means of providing beauty to our innate sense of taste.

In appreciating just how nature entered into Jefferson's aesthetic life, the most important place to accompany him is back to the Natural Bridge. Jefferson, who had very likely heard of the bridge through his father, saw it for the first time in 1767. In 1774 he became its first American owner, purchasing it along with the surrounding 150 acres. His attachment to this "most sublime of Nature's works" is evidenced by the spirited recollections of his French friend the marquis de Chastellux, by remarks scattered through his correspondence, by several attempts to have the bridge painted or drawn for the greater glory of America and American nature, by his visits whenever possible, by his erecting at the site a small cabin for guests, and by his refusal, despite temptations, to part with it.[38]

When Jefferson wrote that the Natural Bridge seemed to have been formed "by some great convulsion," he was giving his usual explanation for unusual natural features. A convulsion gave drama to the act of creation that the bridge was presumed to display. It also did not challenge his assumptions about geologic time. But the special appeal of the Natural Bridge was that it showed that the United States had been blessed with a natural feature worthy of European attention. The prospect from the bridge into the chasm was sublime. Looking up to the arch from below, or through the arch to the distant mountains, the scene was beautiful. Described in the language of the sublime and the

36. See e.g., TJ to William Short, 7 April 1787, BC.XI.281 (near Toulon: "Nothing can be ruder or more savage than the country I am in as it must have come from the hands of nature, and nothing more rich and variegated in the productions with which art has covered it").

37. *Diary and Autobiography of John Adams* (an entry of 1763), quoted in Thomas Bender, *Toward an Urban Vision*, 4.

38. The best sources are BC.XIX.298–301; Garry Wills, *Inventing America*, 259–72; Edmund P. Tompkins and J. Lee Davis, *The Natural Bridge and Its Historical Surroundings;* and Chester A. Reeds, *The Natural Bridge of Virginia and Its Environs* (a geological study). The bridge is depicted in the frontispiece and plate 8.

A cultural history of the Natural Bridge remains to be written. Besides comparing the bridge with Niagara Falls, such a history would take up Jefferson's own role in converting a minor natural phenomenon into a major natural wonder, the competing theories of its formation (the sublime spectacle of convulsion versus the "beautiful" enactment of mere erosion), and its place in literature, such as in Chateaubriand's *Atala* (1803) and *Moby-Dick*.

beautiful, it was American nature become art.[39]

Jefferson's second artistic-natural wonder of Virgina was the confluence of the Shenandoah and Potomac rivers at Harpers Ferry. He visited this spot only once, in October 1783, and recorded it in *Notes on Virginia* very much in the fashion in which he described the Natural Bridge. So perfectly does his description fit his aesthetic that it should be taken in nearly complete:

> The passage of the Potomac through the Blue Ridge is perhaps one of the most stupendous scenes in nature. You stand on a very high point of land. On your right comes up the Shenandoah, having ranged along the foot of the mountain an hundred miles to seek a vent. On your left approaches the Potomac, in quest of a passage also. In the moment of their junction they rush together against the mountain, rend it asunder, and pass off to the sea. . . . The piles of rock on each hand, but particularly the Shenandoah, [are] the evident marks of [the rivers'] disrupture and avulsion from their beds by the most powerful agents of nature. . . . But the most distant finishing which nature has given to the picture is a very different character. It is a true contrast to the foreground. It is as placid and delightful as that is wild and tremendous. For the mountain being cloven asunder, she presents to your eye, through the cleft, a small catch of smooth blue horizon, at an infinite distance in the plain country, inviting you, as it were, from the riot and tumult roaring around, to pass through the breach and participate in the calm below.[40]

Like the description of the Natural Bridge, this one begins with a close-up scene of the sublime and a statement of an origin in convulsion, an origin whose signs are still at hand. It concludes with a faraway scene of the beautiful, where one looks off into the distant calm. The parallel descriptions of Virginia's showplaces endow the state with a convincing aesthetic of nature.

When Jefferson turned to the arts themselves, he assumed, as may be recalled from the discussion of his library organization, that they were outside of nature. Within the arts he distinguished those that were "useful" (architecture) from those that were "elegant" (music).[41] The others—literature, painting, sculpture, and landscape gardening—presumably fell in between. But if Jefferson did not define the arts on the basis of an association with nature, his treatment of them contains innumerable references to it.

In literature he asked for "a tolerable picture of nature" so that the work would achieve an aesthetic impact and ultimately serve its moral

---

39. NVa.25. The view of the distant mountains, Jefferson realized after publishing the *Notes,* was available only from atop the bridge and not from the narrow valley below.
40. NVa.19. The confluence of the two rivers is depicted in plate 7.
41. TJ to Benjamin Rush, 23 September 1800, LB.X.173.

purpose.[42] In the same way, a reproduction of a work of art was quite as satisfactory as the original, because it could convey just as well as the original a moral or patriotic message.[43] Regarding depictions of scenery, moreover, art was at such a remove from the true original in nature that the difference between a painting and its reproduction must have seemed unimportant.[44]

Because the portrayal of American nature served a nationalist as well as an aesthetic end, Jefferson was eager to have the Natural Bridge given its artistic due. He urged John Trumbull, whose natural talent he had advertised to correspondents, to visit the bridge and "take to yourself and your country the honor of presenting to the world this singular landscape."[45] Maria Cosway, whom Jefferson hoped to lure to the United States by Virginia's natural wonders, was several times importuned to draw the bridge. But Trumbull never painted it, Mrs. Cosway never visited, and an attempt by one of Jefferson's acquaintances to induce Charles Willson Peale to paint it also failed. It was not until a quarter-century after Jefferson's death that the bridge found an artist it deserved, the Hudson River school painter Frederick Edwin Church.

The two most minor arts with respect to nature, at least in Jefferson's encounter with them, were sculpture and music.[46] Music, the most abstract of arts, was Jefferson's joy. Evidently a quite passable violinist when young, he was fascinated with the mechanisms of musical instruments, and at Monticello he built up a sizable collection of printed music. Nature entered his understanding of music in two rather modest ways. The first was through lyrics. The only song about which he left any views employs a text of the most gloomy, romanticized nature. Set in the mountains, its story so affected his daughter Maria, Jefferson wrote to his friend Francis Hopkinson, the composer, that she was in tears merely on listening to the melody. The second connection was through music theory. Jefferson presumably read about the natural scale in a standard treatise he owned, discovering that this was a "rational system," because it enabled all music to be made up of "a few primitive

42. TJ to Robert Skipwith, 3 August 1771, BC.I.77.

43. TJ, "Hints to Americans Traveling in Europe," June 1788, BC.XIII.269. Jefferson's own art collection was essentially a collection of copies.

44. Copies of American Indian artifacts, however, would not have appealed to Jefferson, for what he admired about Indian art was that it stood "very near to nature itself." TJ to William Clark, 12 September 1825, in Donald Jackson, *Thomas Jefferson and the Stony Mountains*, 306–7.

45. TJ to John Trumbull, 20 February 1791, BC.XIX.298 (unless Trumbull painted the bridge, "some bungling European will represent it").

46. Regarding sculpture, he once explained the rudiments of art theory with a metaphor from western Virginia: "A statue is not made, like a mountain, to be seen at a distance." TJ to Virginia Delegates in Congress, 12 July 1785, BC.VIII.290. On music see, generally, Helen Cripe, *Thomas Jefferson and Music* (Charlottesville, 1974).

sounds." Perhaps he knew, too, of the dispute between the contemporary German and Italian schools of composition over which of them was the more "natural."[47]

If music theory did not much engage Jefferson's attention, theory of language and literature did, the more so when nature could be made to play a role. Although a monogenist with regard to race, Jefferson never suggested, as a number of Enlightenment theorists did, that there was a single, original, "natural" language for humans. Different cultures, he assumed, inevitably and by nature produced different languages and literatures. The older and more primitive a language was, the more "natural" it seemed to be, and the more it fascinated him. Thus, his most engaged explorations were in Greek and Latin, Anglo-Saxon and Gaelic, and the languages and rhetoric of the American Indians. In the literature of his own times he respected Pope, whose hodgepodge philosophy of nature was phrased in the most artificial forms, but probably felt closer to the preromantic James Thomson.[48]

Jefferson doubtless agreed with Pope that "Nature and Homer were . . . the same."[49] No language compared with ancient Greek, "this most beautiful of all languages," which made Homer "the first of poets."[50] When young, he recorded in his commonplace book one of the great Homeric nature similes, about the clash of arms resounding like the torrent of mountain streams, a sound that he had certainly heard in the Blue Ridge Mountains.[51] At the height of his nature consciousness in France, he pointed to another Homeric simile to claim that since American farmers were the only ones who could read Homer, it was they, rather than the British, who first learned from the *Iliad* how to construct the rims of wagon wheels from bent saplings.[52]

47. TJ to Francis Hopkinson, 13 March 1789, BC.XIV.649. The text of "Whilst thro' the sharp hawthorn blows the cold wind" tells of a winter traveler lost in the wilderness. The composer noted that the words and music "were the work of an hour in the height of a storm." Hopkinson to TJ, 1 December 1788, BC.XIV.324; John Holden, *Rational System of Music* (1807 ed.), 3 (Jefferson owned the original, 1770 edition). The debate on the Continent was represented by Gluck and Vivaldi, both of whose works were in Jefferson's library.

48. For a survey of literature of this sort, see Margaret Mary FitzGerald, *First Follow Nature: Primitivism in English Poetry, 1725–1750* (New York, 1947); a brilliant interpretation is M. H. Abrams, *The Mirror and the Lamp: Romantic Theory and the Critical Tradition* (New York, 1953), chap. 8.

49. Pope, *Essay on Criticism*, I.136. Jefferson said that he enjoyed Homer "in his own language infinitely beyond Pope's translation of him." TJ to Joseph Priestley, 27 January 1800, LB.X.147.

50. TJ to Nathaniel F. Moore, 22 September 1819, LB.XV.218; TJ to John Waldo, 16 August 1813, LB.XIII.341.

51. *Iliad* IV.452–56, in LBi.191. Jefferson wrote out the passage in the original but also supplied the English.

52. TJ to Hector St. Jean de Crèvecoeur, 15 January 1787, BC.XI.44; *Iliad* IV.482–87.

Through his language and many of his images, Homer represented nature wild and primitive. He was the Natural Bridge of literature. But Jefferson was equally attracted to the later ancient poets of nature, the pastoralists. Singing of nature tamed and civilized, they are the literary Monticello. Jefferson's favorites among the pastoralists are predictable: Theocritus, the Greek founder of the genre, and Virgil and Horace among the Romans. In planning Monticello in the early 1770s, Jefferson selected some lines in Latin from Horace that he intended to have inscribed on a marker and set on or near a tree in his park, not far from a spring:

Beneath the ancient oak one loves to lie,
    Or on the matted grass.
While deep waters from the spring rush off,
    Birds chatter in the trees;
And pouring forth, the stream resounds,
    Inviting gentle sleep.[53]

Nature in Greek and Latin literature was matched in Jefferson's artistic consciousness only by nature in the poetry of the legendary Celtic bard Ossian (presumably third century A.D.). Here was a Homer whose purported works challenged the carefully composed poetry of neoclassical England, who seemed to emerge from the researches of the Scottish Enlightenment, and who found a "translator" in James McPherson, a real translator of the *Iliad*. Ossian's writings, the rage of Europe for some years after their publication in the 1760s, presented wild scenes in the grandest imagery, perfect for a man contemplating the acquisition of the Natural Bridge. The refutation of McPherson's Ossian, beginning in the 1770s, made little impact on Jefferson. In old age, when he indirectly acknowledged that the poetry might not be ancient, he still thought it "equal to the best morsels of antiquity."[54]

After Homer, the pastoralists, and Ossian, it was the American Indians who provided Jefferson with languages that seemed close to nature. The Indians also provided a literature—still in its oral form only—that appeared to grow directly from the natural world. Interested in native Americans since childhood, Jefferson was moved by the Indians' eloquence in their own councils and in their meetings with white officials. Since he did not understand what the Indians said in

---

Jefferson, who provided Crèvecoeur with a translation, hoped his friend would publish something to "reclaim the honor" of American farmers on the matter. Crèvecoeur did so.

53. TJ, Account Book, 1771, GB.26, quoting *Epodes* II.23–28. Jefferson owned a number of editions of Theocritus, Virgil, and Horace, in several languages.

54. TJ to Lafayette, 4 November 1823, F.XII.324. In *Notes of an American Lyre* (1813), a

their own tongues, however, he was moved exclusively by translations, the sentiment of the message, and, when he was present, the sight of the declaiming.[55]

Jefferson's great project with Indian languages was a collection of vocabularies from different tribes. Accumulating several dozen comparable lists of words, he intended to determine linguistic relations among the tribes, certain, as his successors also have been, that these would point to historic and ethnic connections and thereby aid in charting eras and patterns of migration and settlement.[56] As explained in *Notes on Virginia*, the project was to gather from each tribe "appellations of the most common objects in nature." The vocabulary form prepared for this project contained about 250 words, other than the words for numbers. Approximately half the words were about nature, including the names for twenty mammals (beginning with the elusive mammoth) and about the same number each for birds and plants. Unfortunately, the vocabularies Jefferson acquired gave only partial access to Indian languages. They were limited in range and gave no hint of such things as gender, number, conjugation, or declension, to say nothing of grammar; but they were prepared for use in the field by persons hardly trained for the task. Despite these liabilities, the idea itself was sound. It met a swift and tragic end, however, when the vocabulary manuscripts were plundered while in transit to Monticello after Jefferson retired from the presidency.

Since "nature" itself is not on the vocabulary list, one is prompted to ask whether Jefferson thought Indian languages contained such a word or concept. Two considerations suggest that he did not. First, while his favorable disposition towards Indians might lead one to believe that he expected their languages to contain a general word of this sort, in fact he felt that the Indians, close as they were to nature-in-fact, "have use but

---

collection of forgettable verse dedicated to Jefferson by a close friend of the family, Judith Lomax heard Ossian tell her in a vision: "I know thee for a votaress of Nature,—tomorrow thou shalt ascend the Mountain's height . . . there I will watch thee, and witness the inspirations of Nature on thy fervent mind." P. 68.

55. The two great episodes of Indian oratory in Jefferson's life were an address of a Cherokee chieftain whom he heard in Williamsburg in 1762 and the lamentation of Logan, whose family had been killed by whites, which he read in 1775. TJ to John Adams, 11 June 1812, C.II.307; NVa.62–63, 226–58.

56. NVa.100–102. A beginning of the project may be seen in Jefferson's bill of 1779 to revise the charter of the College of William and Mary. BC.II.540. A summary of the project appears in Bernard W. Sheehan, *Seeds of Extinction*, 54–58. Oddly, Jefferson once speculated that a few entire Indian languages might be artificial rather than natural, noting that any group of Indians that had broken away from the main body was bound by honor "not to use the language of those with whom they have quarreled." NVa.282 (ms. note by Jefferson). If that had proved the case, linguistic connections among tribes would have been impossible to discover.

for few words and possess but few."[57] He therefore might not have been surprised if a particular word, even the one most important to himself, was not common among the Indians.[58]

Second, one might ask whether Jefferson supposed that his own uses of "nature" were of the sort that Indian languages would also include. The answer to this is almost certainly no. Jefferson was as conscious of the Indians' stage of culture as he was of the Western tradition from which his own ideas about nature came, and he did not think these were the same. What he said when describing the vocabulary project to a scholar of languages was that he had "formed a model expressing such objects in nature as must be familiar to every people, savage or civilized," thereby implying that savage Indians would not have all the words or concepts important to Western culture. The "barren vocabularies" of the Indians, he continued, would require the creation of "new words for . . . new ideas" if the tribes were to be instructed in theology, law, or the sciences, that is, in realms where "nature" was so prominent in Jefferson's own intellectual universe.[59]

A test for this conclusion is Jefferson's own formal speeches to the Indians. These addresses were at the time an art form that was rank with the aroma of cultural superiority: they assumed that Indians could understand nothing subtle, and they often explicitly considered the Indians to be children. In the dozens of addresses that Jefferson wrote out for translation into Indian languages the word "nature" never appears. On one occasion, indeed, he seems deliberately to have avoided it. Obedience to majority rule, a practice that he asserted was a "law of nature" when writing for a white audience, he explained to the Indians merely as a "rule in all countries."[60] It is as if he reserved the word "nature," as he reserved most of its meanings, for his cultural peers.

Of the languages that seemed to Jefferson close to nature, he mastered Greek, studied Anglo-Saxon, was unsuccessful with Gaelic, and, apart from the vocabulary comparisons, never attempted any American Indian languages. Towards all languages, however, he had a linguist's curiosity, studying them for their own sake, for practical use, and in

57. NVa.282 (ms. note by Jefferson).

58. An extensive comparative dictionary of one Algonquian and one Iroquois language compiled (though not published) in Jefferson's time does contains words under "nature." But these apparently refer to the nature or character of a person rather than to the world of nature itself, and Jefferson would surely have been looking for the latter idea. See David Zeisberger, *Indian Dictionary* (1887), 128.

59. TJ to Peter Wilson, 20 January 1816, LB.XIV.402, 403. Even if new words were created for ideas imported from European culture, Jefferson was sensitive enough to both languages and native Americans to wonder whether they would convey the European meanings, a problem that would be considerable with a word like "nature." TJ to John Pickering, 20 February 1825, LB.XVI.108.

60. TJ to the Miamis and Delawares, 8 January 1803, LB.XVI.398.

order to learn about social conventions. But he also wished to determine from languages what was true in nature. He owned an Italian-English-French dictionary that promised in its title that each word was "accented according to its true and natural pronunciation."[61] He aided the founder of a "natural method" for teaching foreign languages, which, avoiding grammar, promised to follow "principles which belong to Nature." "Ignorance and learned presumption," the author continued, "perplex and render every thing complicated; while Nature does the very reverse, as every one of her processes is a sublime model of simplicity."[62]

For his part, Jefferson took up the cause of simplifying English orthography by making spelling more phonetic and hence presumably more natural.[63] Discussing nouns in his "Essay on the Anglo-Saxon Language" (1798), he wrote of "the two real genders which Nature has established," apparently pleased that no more than two were needed in a study of a natural language like Anglo-Saxon, while other languages introduced artificial genders and complicated noun and adjective endings. At the same time, he explained that cases—accusative, dative, and others—"exist in nature" and on that ground was willing to excuse the endings that other languages assigned to nouns following prepositions.[64] He sought a natural basis for literary composition, hoping "to find out the real circumstances which give harmony to English poetry and laws to those who make it."[65]

A student of language all his life, a lover of much literature when young and some literature when old (at the end Homer alone), Jefferson was no imaginative writer himself. "I knew that nature had not formed me for a continuator of Sterne," he once acknowledged, and this self-assessment is certainly correct.[66] The only exception to his claim not to be an imaginative writer is the "Dialogue Between my Head and my Heart," which he probably would have held not to be literature.

As the dialogue demonstrates, however, style is not the exclusive preserve of poetry and fiction, and Jefferson was certainly one of America's greatest stylists. To recall only the most notable instances—the

61. F. Botarelli, *The New Italian, English, and French Pocket-Dictionary* (1777). S.4809.
62. N. G. Dufief, *Nature Displayed in her Mode of Teaching Language to Man*, 8th ed. (1834), 2, 8. (Jefferson owned the first edition, of 1804. S.4819.) The introduction reproduces a brief letter from Jefferson encouraging the author's activities. P. iv.
63. He chose "honor" over "honour" and "tho" over "though." He recognized that his efforts were futile, however, unless sanctioned by Noah Webster, a Federalist whom he only grudgingly respected for his lexicography.
64. "Essay on the Anglo-Saxon Language," LB.XVIII.376–78.
65. TJ to marquis de Chastellux, October 1786, BC.X.498. In this letter Jefferson also spoke of a "law of poetical numbers" in English verse.
66. TJ to Maria Cosway, 24 April 1788, BC.XIII.104. Jefferson once proposed, per-

dialogue in its entirety, "nature and nature's God" in the Declaration of Independence, and the scenic descriptions in *Notes on the State of Virginia*—is to recognize how memorable and enhancing "nature" can be in his writing. As a feature of Jefferson's style, the use of nature as word, as topic, and as image contributes to both the distinctiveness of the writing and the persuasiveness of the argument. With respect to the argument only, by driving his principles back to nature, Jefferson gives his writing a sense of profoundness and impregnability that furthers the acceptance of his meaning, even when, as many examples in this essay have shown, analysis proves—and the use of nature may even cause—the argument to be weak or incomplete.

Nature can also offer relief to Jefferson's usual earnestness. This is true when it is depicted for its own sake, as in scenic descriptions, or in the form of ornament. Indeed, it is as literary embellishment that is Jefferson's most decidedly aesthetic use of nature. Although the writing, like the man himself, has few flourishes, it does employ, repeatedly and certainly deliberately, the nature metaphor, a figure at which Jefferson was both adept and precise. His extended comparison of education to the grafting of a "new tree on the savage stock," discussed earlier, has nearly the proportions of a Homeric simile.[67] Or consider the following analogies for both their literary merit and their aid to the argument:

> Our seventeen States compose a great and growing nation. Their children are as the leaves of the trees, which the winds are spreading over the forest.

> Man, like the fruit he eats, has his period of ripeness. Like that, too, if he continues longer hanging to the stem, it is but an useless and unsightly appendage.

The first comes from a speech to a group of Indian leaders, delivered when Jefferson was president, the second from a letter to a friend when both men were in their seventies.[68]

Among Jefferson's best-known nature images are two responses to Shays' Rebellion, the uprising of debt-burdened farmers in western Massachusetts in 1786. To one correspondent he wrote: "The tree of

---

haps seriously, an environmental theory of literary creation. Asserting that nightingales sang more beautifully in southern France than near Paris, he said this explained "why there never was a poet North of the Alps, and why there never will be one. A poet is as much the creation of climate as an orange or a palm tree." TJ to William Short, 21 May 1787, BC.XI.372. Where northern poets like Shakespeare and Ossian were when these lines were written is a mystery.

67. See above. p. 80.

68. TJ to Brothers of the Choctaw Nation, 17 December 1803, LB.XVI.401; TJ to Gen. Henry Dearborn, 17 August 1821, LB.XV.329.

liberty must be refreshed from time to time with the blood of patriots and tyrants. It is its natural manure." Shifting from natural history to natural philosophy, he wrote another: "A little rebellion, now and then is a good thing, and as necessary in the political world as storms in the physical."[69] One of his most elaborate metaphors in natural philosophy likens the federal system to the solar system:

> I dare say that in time all [the state governments] as well as their central government, like the planets revolving round their common sun, acting and acted upon according to their respective weights and distances, will produce that beautiful equilibrium on which our Constitution is founded, and which I believe it will exhibit to the world in a degree of perfection, unexampled but in the planetary system itself.[70]

As in the case of botany and education, however, the comparison is far more than ornament. It means to show a congruence in theory between science and society.

Remarkably few of Jefferson's nature metaphors come from agriculture, his profession, and few are drawn from natural scenery, in which he delighted. Indeed, the most frequent ones are about seafaring. Jefferson's nautical images are not only frequent but unexpected, for he was proud to come from Piedmont Virginia and was personally uncomfortable aboard ship. Yet scores of maritime images are spread throughout his writings, from the early 1780s until shortly before his death.[71] Most of Jefferson's nautical metaphors refer to politics, and many are cousins of the "ship of state" theme which dates to classical antiquity. As a group, they show a self-conscious and inventive literary mind. A single example may illustrate:

> The storm through which we have passed, has been tremendous indeed. The tough sides of our Argosie have been thoroughly tried. Her strength has stood the waves into which she was steered, with a view to sink her. We shall put her on her republican tack, and she will now show by the beauty of her motion the skill of her builders.[72]

69. TJ to William Stephens Smith, 12 November 1787, BC.XII.356; TJ to James Madison, 30 January 1787, BC.XI.93.

70. TJ to Peregrine Fitzhugh, 23 February 1798, LB.X.3. For an even more involved simile drawn from astronomy, see TJ to John Melish, 10 December 1814, LB.XIV. 220–21.

71. The final recorded one is in his last letter to John Adams. TJ to John Adams, 25 March 1826, C.II.614.

72. TJ to John Dickinson, 6 March 1801, F.VIII.7. Explication: Jefferson's recent election as president was nearly prevented by Federalists and subsequently by certain Republicans (Aaron Burr) in the House of Representatives, which body was constitutionally required to choose a victor after the electoral college was unable to. As a member of the Philadelphia Convention of 1787, Dickinson was a builder of the Argosie, the Constitution.

There is no obvious source for Jefferson's imaginative references to ships and the sea, but some background for them may be suggested other than classical learning. Jefferson had a planter's and a diplomat's interest in oceanic trade, a scientist's interest in navigation, a gentleman's interest in British literature that contained nautical images, and a public official's interest in naval forces. Even so, it is not clear why a man whose favorite view was the Blue Ridge Mountains elaborated his correspondence with nautical metaphors. It is perhaps safest to say, as Jefferson might have, that he had a natural inclination in this direction and leave it as a literary delight.

The arts towards which Jefferson was most attracted, professionally and with regard to theory, were landscaping, which could not avoid nature, and architecture, which he did not permit to escape it. He defined gardening as "the art of embellishing grounds by fancy."[73] It was an art, however, that differed from its sisters in that it alone both was about nature and could be practiced only in nature. For that reason it may be thought of as the nature subclass under fine arts in Jefferson's library classification, while the others—painting, sculpture, music, literature, and architecture—may be thought of as manufactured arts. Jefferson considered landscape gardening akin to landscape painting because they were both "of nature," even though the gardening was "in nature." Accordingly, he remarked, "we generally find the landscape painter the best designer of a garden."[74]

As an art constituted from the materials of natural history, gardening was the only art that lived, and in his pleasure garden Jefferson intended to experience the pleasures of life. In the 1770s he envisioned on the grounds of Monticello a centrally located spring which would be the "scene of every evening's joy. There we should talk over the lessons of the day, or lose them in music, chess, or the merriments of our family companions." Decades later he planned to read Joel Barlow's national epic, *The Columbiad,* at Monticello, where he could "enjoy it in full concert with its kindred scenes, amidst those rural delights which join in chorus with the poet, and give his song all its magic effect."[75]

While the foundation and setting of the landscape garden is neces-

73. TJ to Ellen Wayles Randolph, 10 July 1805, BB.276. *Thomas Jefferson's Garden Book, 1766–1824,* ed. Edwin M. Betts, is a chronological sourcebook. Jefferson's philosophy of landscape gardening, as well as his mature plans for Monticello, is set out in TJ to William Hamilton, July 1806, GB.322–24. The leading study is Frederick D. Nichols and Ralph E. Griswold, *Thomas Jefferson, Landscape Architect.* See also Berman, *Thomas Jefferson among the Arts,* chap. 8; and Edwin M. Betts and Hazlehurst B. Perkins, *Thomas Jefferson's Flower Garden at Monticello.*

74. TJ to Ellen Wayles Randolph, 10 July 1805, BB.276.

75. TJ to Robert Skipwith, 3 August 1771, BC.I.77; TJ to Joel Barlow, 24 January 1808, LB.XI.430.

sarily nature, Jefferson did not think that all landscape gardens were equally natural. Touring the estate gardens of England with John Adams, he found a model in what had been accomplished there. But even in England he found a garden where "art appears too much," and he did not intend to permit that in his own landscape design.[76] At Monticello, instead, he would work with the American advantage, that "the noblest gardens may be made without expense. We have only to cut out the superabundant plants."[77] On the forested slope of Monticello this directive was put into practice, while nearer the house Jefferson adapted the English style, consulting, as always, Lord Kames (in the chapter "Gardening and Architecture" in his *Elements of Criticism,* 1762), as well as the leading British authority, Thomas Whatley (*Observations on Modern Gardening,* 1770).[78]

In landscape design Jefferson especially appreciated a wavy line, a curve, or an oval, the "lovely mixture of concave and convex" that he discovered in a park in England.[79] The line in flux symbolized a dynamic force in nature that he saw in everything, from the creation of the world to the flowering of plants. The justification for an appreciation of this in art theory was the rococo aesthetic of William Hogarth, whose *Analysis of Beauty* (1753) pronounced a curved line in nature to be a mark of the beautiful.[80] Jefferson made such a line visible in the winding walk in his flower garden at Monticello and in the serpentine wall that he designed for the grounds of the University of Virginia. He found a beautiful curve, too, in the horizontal plowing that followed the contours of the Piedmont hills.[81]

If in landscape gardening Jefferson sought a nature that was organic and in flux, in architecture he followed a nature that was stable and ordered. This was evident in his plans for individual buildings, such as Monticello or the state capitol at Richmond; for groups of buildings, such as the University of Virginia; and for entire cities, such as Wash-

76. TJ, "A Tour to some of the Gardens of England," March–April 1786, BC.IX.372 (disapproving of the grounds at Blenheim).

77. TJ, "Hints to Americans Travelling in Europe," June 1788, BC.XIII.269.

78. Jefferson chose the English garden over the more formal French garden on the basis of observation. But he never criticized the French style directly, nor did he comment on the idea popular in the mid-eighteenth century that differences between countries' styles in gardens reflected differences in their styles in governing, the severe French versus the milder British.

79. TJ, "A Tour to some of the Gardens of England," March–April 1786, B.IX.370 (the park was Esher-Place).

80. Jefferson recommended Hogarth for a basic library. TJ to Robert Skipwith, 3 August 1771, BC.I.79. See, generally, Berman, *Thomas Jefferson among the Arts,* chap. 4.

81. Utility played as much a role as did beauty in all these cases. The winding walk in the flower garden permitted more plantings (see plates 15 and 16), the serpentine wall saved on bricks, and contour plowing reduced erosion.

ington, D.C., a place, he said, that "nature has formed on a beautiful scale."[82]

Jefferson read of the universal laws of nature as they applied to architecture in the works of Andrea Palladio (1508–80). The architecture of Palladio, whose studies of Roman architecture and whose own designs influenced British practice from the early seventeenth century on, impressed itself on Americans beginning with Jefferson himself. To Jefferson and many of his time, Palladian architecture followed nature in a rational, even Newtonian, way, a standing rebuke to the artificial "customary" styles of Gothic, baroque, and rococo.[83] As Christopher Wren, the Newton of English architecture, put it: "There are two causes of Beauty—natural and customary. Natural is from Geometry, consisting in Uniformity. . . . Geometrical Figures are naturally more beautiful than any other irregular; in this all consent, as to a Law of Nature."[84] In Virginia, where he found public buildings without proper proportion or symmetry and decorated with the "barbarous elements" of the unnatural styles, Jefferson hoped for an architect whose "natural taste" would produce natural beauty, who would reform the practices of his country along classical lines.[85]

Jefferson was this architect himself, nowhere more than at Monticello. There he created a house in the Palladian tradition, its lines and balance representing nature as the universal rule of reason. It was complemented by the landscaping, with its curves and colors, its sloping lawn, its planned casualness, nature as fidelity to particularistic, dynamic form. "What nature has done for us is sublime and unique," he wrote about the grounds.[86] The estate thus displayed a continuum of Jefferson's aesthetic of nature, from the classic to the romantic, from the creation of man to the creation of God. It began at the mansion, scrupulously composed, universal, and beautiful. It proceeded to the garden, designed for variety; and then to the farm, pastoral and productive. It ended with the view of storms and wild scenery, untouched, particularistic, and sublime.

82. TJ to Joseph Priestley, 9 April 1803, LB.X.376. See, generally, Saul K. Padover, ed., *Thomas Jefferson and the National Capital, 1783–1946* (Washington, D.C., 1946); and on the University of Virginia, the stimulating essay "Jefferson's Charlottesville," in Walter L. Creese, *The Crowning of the American Landscape,* 9–42.

83. Jefferson owned several editions of Palladio's *Four Books of Architecture* (1570). On Jefferson and architecture see, generally, Fiske Kimball, *Thomas Jefferson, Architect* (1916; reprint, New York, 1968); Frederick D. Nichols, "Jefferson: The Making of an Architect," in Adams, *Jefferson and the Arts,* 163–85; Berman, *Thomas Jefferson among the Arts,* chap. 7; and Lewis Mumford, "The Universalism of Thomas Jefferson."

84. Quoted in Arthur O. Lovejoy, *Essays in the History of Ideas,* 99.

85. NVa.153.

86. TJ to Benjamin H. Latrobe, 10 October 1809, GB.416. See, generally, William Howard Adams, *Jefferson's Monticello.*

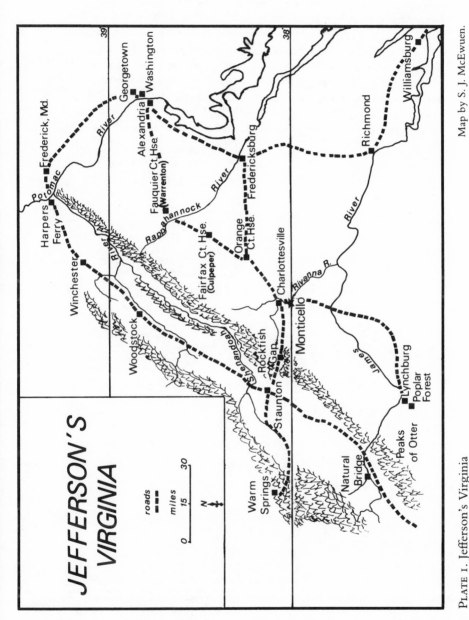

JEFFERSON'S
VIRGINIA

roads

N

miles

0   15   30

39

Frederick, Md.

Harpers
Ferry

Potomac   River

Georgetown

Washington

Alexandria

Fauquier Ct. Hse.
(Warrenton)

Winchester

Shenandoah   River

Rappahannock   River

Fairfax Ct. Hse.
(Culpeper)

Orange
Ct. Hse.

Fredericksburg

38

Woodstock

Rockfish
Gap

Charlottesville

Rivanna R.

River

Richmond

Williamsburg

Staunton

Monticello

James   River

Lynchburg

Poplar
Forest

Warm
Springs

Natural
Bridge

Peaks
of Otter

Map by S. J. McEwuen.

PLATE 1. Jefferson's Virginia

119

PLATE 2. Jefferson's Map for *Notes on the State of Virginia*

To accompany *Notes on Virginia,* Jefferson prepared "a map of the country between Albemarle County and Lake Erie, comprehending the whole of Virginia, Maryland, Delaware and Pennsylvania, with parts of several other of the United States of America." The map was based largely on one published in 1751 by his father and his father's partner from original field work. Jefferson considered it perhaps the most valuable part of his book. Among its features on the detail shown here are Monticello, Poplar Forest, and the Natural Bridge. The confluence of the Shenandoah and Potomac rivers is at the northeast corner.

Map from *Notes on the State of Virginia* (London, 1787), in *Thomas Jefferson, Writings* (New York, 1984), edited by Merrill D. Peterson, reprinted with permission of the publisher, The Library of America, 14 E. 6oth Street, New York, New York 10022.

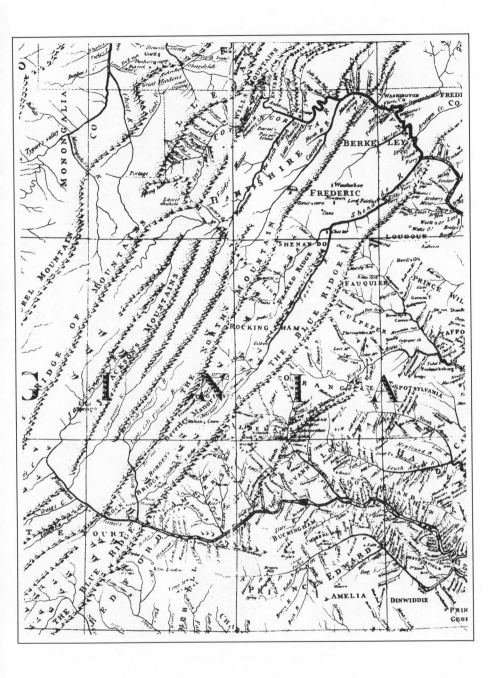

PLATE 4. Charles Thomson Praises Jefferson's "Natural History of No. America"

No one except its author knew as much about *Notes on the State of Virginia* as did Charles Thomson (1729–1824), Secretary to Congress prior to the Constitution and Jefferson's dearest friend in the American Philosophical Society. Thomson read the *Notes* in draft and wrote out extensive commentaries—mostly on Indians—which Jefferson thought so valuable that he published them as an appendix to the book. In a letter that reached Paris too late to have an effect, Thomson suggested that Jefferson find a "more dignified title" for a book that he considered "a most excellent Natural history not merely of Virginia but of No. America." The copy of the letter that Thomson retained proposed the title, "a Natural history of Virginia."

Courtesy Library of Congress. The letter is Charles Thomson to TJ, 6 March 1785, BC.VIII.16, 17n2.

(*opposite page*)
PLATE 3. John Adams with Jefferson's "History of Virginia"

In 1788 Jefferson commissioned Mather Brown, an American artist resident in England, to paint a portrait of his friend John Adams. At Adams's side, symbolizing the friendship, is a volume labeled "Jefferson Hist. of Virginia." The liberty taken with the title of Jefferson's book suggests that Adams may have read *Notes on the State of Virginia* in a spirit different from that in which Jefferson wrote it and in which many of his other friends understood it. Adams was inclined to see the world through the lens of history, not nature.

Courtesy Boston Athenaeum.

123

PLATE 5. C. W. Peale, Exhumation of the Mastodon

Jefferson was as eager to have the skeleton of a mammoth reconstructed as he was determined to prove that the animal had not become extinct. He therefore supported the effort of his enthusiastic friend Charles Willson Peale to exhume bones of the animal from a water-mired pit on a farm in New York State. He authorized the loan of a pump from the navy to drain the pit, but Peale devised instead a revolving drum that drove a conveyor belt of buckets that in turn bailed out the water. The drum was powered by visitors to the site, who gladly took turns walking on its planks while workmen down below unearthed the bones and passed them up to Peale and his assistants. A drawing of one of the bones is displayed at the lower right. The digging took place in the summer of 1801, shortly after Jefferson became president. During the fall, with the aid of Caspar Wistar of the American Philosophical Society, Peale reconstructed the mastodon for display in his natural history museum. In 1806, the mastodon having become the centerpiece of his exhibits, Peale painted the scene of its exhumation.

Courtesy The Peale Museum, Baltimore, Maryland.

PLATE 6. *Jeffersonia diphylla,* The Twinleaf

In 1792 Jefferson's friend, the botanist Benjamin Smith Barton, challenged the Linnaean classification of a plant native to the southern Appalachians. Describing the plant as a distinct genus, Barton designated it *Jeffersonia,* noting pointedly that in honoring Jefferson he intended "no reference . . . to his political character. . . . My business was with his knowledge of natural history." At the same time, speculating that the plant might be among those that are "constantly creating" from the union of others, Barton ironically attached the possibility of evolution to a plant named for a man who believed that all species (certainly animal species) had been created by nature at a single moment. The common name of the plant is twinleaf (a direct translation of *diphylla*), after the divided, butterfly-shaped leaves. The eight-petaled flower blooms in scattered sites in the mountains in April and May. The drawing shown here was prepared by Barton in collaboration with William Bartram.

Courtesy American Philosophical Society. Quotations and illustration from B. S. Barton, "A Botanical Description of the *Podophyllum diphyllum* of Linnaeus," 3 Trans. Am. Phil. Soc. 334, at 342 and 346 (1793). Barton's original name for the plant was *Jeffersonia binata.* This was later revised to *J. diphylla* in order to conform with international standards of botanical nomenclature.

PLATE 7. Rembrandt Peale, Harpers Ferry

Jefferson visited the juncture of the Shenandoah and Potomac rivers at Harpers Ferry in October 1783 and described it as "perhaps one of the most stupendous scenes in nature." Piles of rock became to him "monuments of a war between rivers and mountains," evidence that "the most powerful agents of nature [had] torn the mountain down from its summit to its base." Downstream from this tumult, Jefferson discerned a "distant finishing which nature has given to the picture . . . as placid and delightful, as [the foreground] is wild and tremendous." It is this placid scene that is depicted by Rembrandt Peale, who sketched it in 1810 and painted it in 1811. His view is from a spot not far from Jefferson Rock, where Jefferson is supposed to have witnessed the scene. In the painting one is looking south down the Potomac; the entrance of the Shenandoah is hidden by trees at the lower right. (A substantial extract from Jefferson's description of the scene is printed on p. 106.)

Courtesy Collection Walker Art Center, Minneapolis. Gift of the T. B. Walker Foundation, 1912. Quoted material from NVa.19, 20. Paul R. Lee, Chief of Interpretation, Harpers Ferry National Historical Park, kindly provided information about the view.

PLATE 8. Frederick Edwin Church, Natural Bridge

Jefferson attempted several times to have a competent artist paint the Natural Bridge, that "most sublime of Nature's works," which he himself owned and publicized ceaselessly. But it was only with the brush of the Hudson River school artist Frederick Edwin Church, born the year that Jefferson died, that the bridge received its due. Wedded to scientific fact and influenced by the writings of Jefferson's acquaintance, the German naturalist Alexander von Humboldt, Church combined in his art grandeur with meticulous realism, in this case in a very small compass: the painting is 28″ × 23″. (Contrast the seven-foot figure of Jefferson in the frontispiece with the one-inch figure that provides the scale here.) Church visited the bridge in 1851 and completed the painting the following year.

Courtesy University of Virginia Art Museum.

PLATE 9. A Natural Right to Expatriation

Jefferson derived the right of American independence in part from a natural right of emigration and expatriation. It was a corollary to "a law in the nature of man to pursue his own happiness." First set down in his *Summary View of the Rights of British America* (1774), Jefferson's final expression of a right to expatriation is contained in a letter of June 1817. "Nature" or "natural" appears five times in the lines reproduced here. (The passage is printed on p. 170.)

Courtesy Library of Congress. The letter is TJ to Dr. John Manners, 12 June 1817, F.X.87.

the evidence of this natural right, like that of our right to life, liberty, the use of our faculties, the pursuit of happiness, is not left to the fable and sophistical investigations of reason, but is impressed on the sense of every man. we do not claim these under the Charters of kings or legislators; but under the king of kings. if he has made it a law in the nature of man to pursue his own happiness, he has left him free in the choice of place as well as mode; and we may safely call on the whole body of English jurists to produce the map on which Nature has traced, for each individual, the geographical line which she forbids him to cross in pursuit of happiness. it certainly does not exist in his mind. where then is it? I believe too I might safely affirm that there is not another nation, civilized or savage, which has ever denied this natural right. I doubt if there is another which refuses its exercise. I know it is allowed in some of the most unprepared countries of continental Europe; nor have I ever heard of one in which it was not. how it is among our savage neighbors, who have no law but that of Nature, we all know.

PLATE 10. Education Engrafts a New Man on the Native Stock

In August 1818 Jefferson chaired a commission to plan the University of Virginia. Escaping the heat of the Piedmont, the commission met at Rockfish Gap, twenty-five miles west of Monticello in the Blue Ridge Mountains. In the Rockfish Gap Report, Jefferson compares education to horticulture. For Jefferson, at least, the comparison is not merely analogy; it is argument. Man is not "fixed by a law of his nature," he writes, but, "just as the grafting art implants a new tree on the savage stock, . . . education, in like manner, engrafts a new man on the native stock, and improves what in his nature was vicious and perverse into qualities of virtue and social worth." (The passage is printed on p. 80.)

Courtesy Thomas Jefferson Papers (TB-1567), University of Virginia Library.

the advantages of well directed education; moral, political and economical,
are truly above all estimate. education generates habits of application,
order, and the love of virtue; and corrects, by the force of habit, any innate
obliquities in our moral organization. we should be far too from the doctrine
.ny persuasion that man is fixed by the law of his nature, at a given point;
that his improvement is a chimaera, and the hope to be renovating our-
-selves wiser, happier, or better than our forefathers were. as well might it be urged
that the wild and uncultivated tree, hitherto yielding sour and bitter fruit only,
yet in health
can never be made to yield better, and by the grafting art, implants a new
tree on the savage stock, producing what is most estimable both in kind and degree..
education, in like manner, engrafts a new man on the native stock, & improves
what in his nature was vicious and perverse into qualities of virtue and social
worth.

135

When in the course of human events it becomes necessary for one people to dissolve the political bands which have connected them with another, and to [   ] as -sume among the powers of the earth the separate and equal station to which the laws of nature & of nature's god entitle them, a decent respect to the opinions of mankind requires that they should declare the causes which impel them to the separation.

PLATE 11. The Laws of Nature and of Nature's God

The Declaration of Independence declares the colonies' separation from England under "the Laws of Nature and of Nature's God." Jefferson's draft of this language was written, as was his custom, in lowercase letters. Both the phrase and the philosophy behind it were common to the era. As Jefferson said about the opening paragraphs of the Declaration nearly half a century after the fact, he was aiming not at "originality of principle or sentiment"; rather, he intended the document to be "an expression of the American mind [in] the proper tone and spirit called for by the occasion."

Courtesy Library of Congress. Quotation from TJ to Henry Lee, 8 May 1825, F.X.343.

(opposite page)

PLATE 12. Rembrandt Peale, Portrait of Jefferson

Jefferson was a close friend of Charles Willson Peale and his family, artists and naturalists in Philadelphia. Rembrandt Peale, one of the sons, painted two portraits of Jefferson, the first in 1800, the second, shown here, in early 1805, when Jefferson was at the height of his presidential acclaim. The fox-fur collar provides a touch of American nature to an Enlightenment countenance.

Courtesy The New-York Historical Society, New York.

PLATE 13. Jefferson-Hartley Map of the Western Territory

In the spring of 1784, Jefferson chaired a committee of Congress to prepare a plan of governance for the western territory. Later that year, in Europe, he provided information on the states to be established in the territory to David Hartley, the English official who had helped to draw up the treaty of peace between the United States and Great Britain. Hartley's sketch of the boundaries of fourteen states illustrates the rational order that Jefferson attempted to impose on the new land. It shows the beginnings of the old Northwest: Ohio, Indiana, Illinois, Michigan, and Wisconsin; of Alabama and Mississippi, which ultimately violated the plan to give as many states as possible access to the Mississippi River; and of Kentucky, which eventually upset Jefferson's wish to determine state boundaries by universal nature (lines of latitude) instead of by particular nature (the Ohio River).

Courtesy William L. Clements Library, University of Michigan. A discussion of the map and the state boundaries is in BC. VI. 588–95.

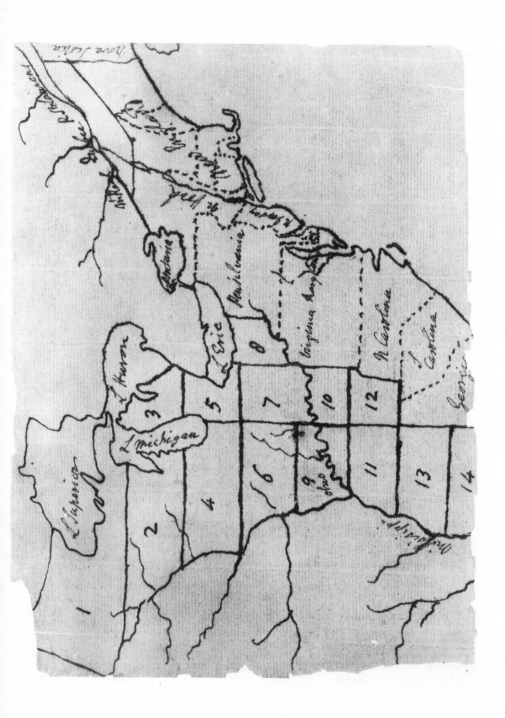

PLATE 14. The Vegetable Garden at Monticello

Not far from the house at Monticello—on the south slope, in order to take advantage of the sun—Jefferson laid out an immense vegetable garden. It was the principal subject of his *Garden Book*, a chronological record that he maintained, with some gaps, from 1766 until 1824. In 1812 the garden was eighty feet wide and one thousand feet long, arranged on three terraces ("platforms") and planted in twenty-four numbered beds ("squares"). Along the "N.W. Border" were planted seedlings. The orderly arrangement of nature shown here, with its three main divisions, several subdivisions, and many specific classes, is reminiscent of Jefferson's library classification. The spelling "tomata" was common at the time.

Courtesy Massachusetts Historical Society; p. 45 of the original *Garden Book*.

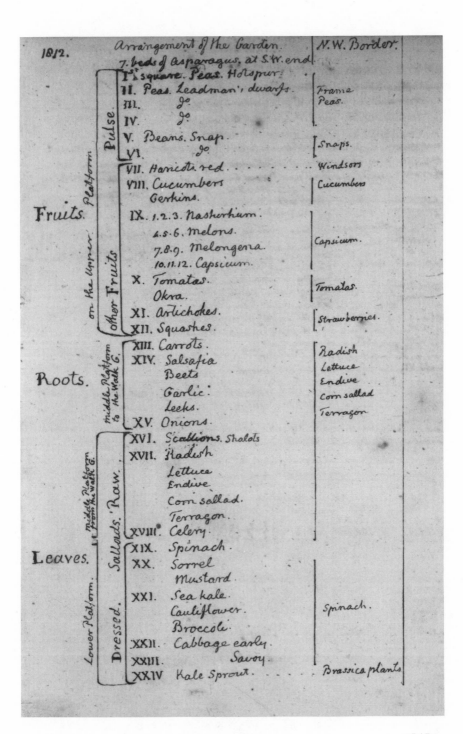

1812.   Arrangement of the Garden.   N. W. Border.
7. beds of Asparagus, at S.W. end.

Fruits. — on the Upper Platform

Pulse:
I. square. Peas. Hotspur.
II. Peas. Leadman's dwarfs.   Frame Peas.
III.   do.
IV.   do.
V. Beans. Snap.   Snaps.
VI.   do.

other Fruits:
VII. Haricots. red . . . .   Windsors
VIII. Cucumbers Gerkins.   Cucumbers
IX. 1.2.3. Nasturtium.
    4.5.6. melons.
    7.8.9. Melongena.
    10.11.12. Capsicum.   Capsicum.
X. Tomatas. Okra.   Tomatas.
XI. Artichokes.   Strawberries.
XII. Squashes.

Roots. — middle Platform to the walk G.
XIII. Carrots.   Radish
XIV. Salsafia   Lettuce
    Beets   Endive
    Garlic.   Corn sallad
    Leeks.   Terragon
XV. Onions.

Leaves. — middle Platform from the walk G. — Lower Platform.

Sallads. Raw.
XVI. Scallions. Shalots
XVII. Radish
    Lettuce
    Endive
    Corn sallad.
    Terragon
XVIII. Celery.

Dressed.
XIX. Spinach.
XX. Sorrel Mustard.
XXI. Sea kale. Cauliflower. Broccoli.   Spinach.
XXII. Cabbage early.
XXIII.   Savoy.
XXIV. Kale Sprout . . . . .   Brassica plants

141

PLATE 15. Flower Beds and the Roundabout Walk at Monticello

Fond of curves in nature and searching for a design that would "not too much restrain the variety of flowers in which we might wish to indulge," Jefferson proposed a Roundabout Walk on the west lawn of Monticello. On the sketch shown here, which Jefferson sent to his granddaughter in the spring of 1807, the dotted lines represent a border of flowers along the walkway. The large ovals indicate beds of flowering shrubs. Among the smaller "shrub circles," the one immediately to the northeast of the house (*upper left*) was reserved for *Jeffersonia diphylla* (see Plate 6).

Courtesy Massachusetts Historical Society. Quotation from TJ to Anne Cary Randolph, 7 June 1807, GB.349.

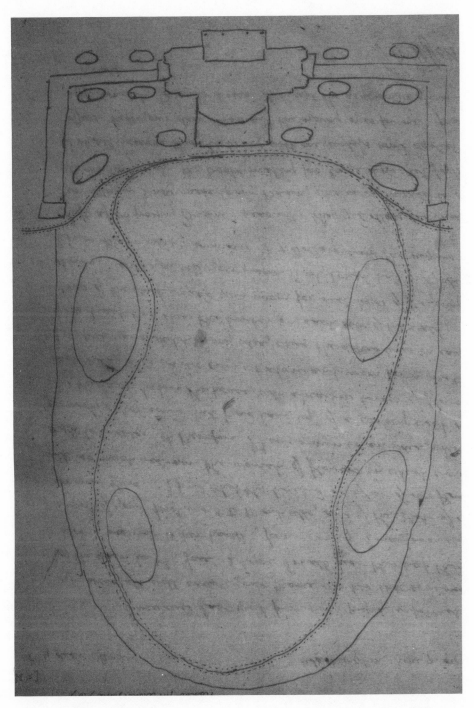

PLATE 16. Monticello from the Southwest

Monticello has two "fronts," east and west. The view here shows the Roundabout Walk on the lawn of the west front (see Plate 14), the reconstructed vegetable garden (see Plate 15), and a portion of the L-shaped southern wing (under which were the smokehouse, the kitchen, and quarters for house slaves). The wing terminates in the South Pavillion, the first portion of the mansion to be completed (1770).

Photograph by C. L. Koral.

PLATE 17. Buffalo Robe from the Lewis and Clark Expedition

In April 1805, before breaking winter camp on the expedition to the Pacific, Meriwether Lewis shipped to Jefferson four boxes, one trunk, and three cages of objects of natural history. (The cages contained live animals, not all of which survived the journey down the Missouri to St. Louis, then down the Mississippi to New Orleans, and then by coastal ship to Baltimore.) The articles did not reach Washington, D.C. until August and Jefferson, who was at Monticello at the time, did not see them until October. Many of the objects he sent to Philadelphia, either for Charles Willson Peale's museum or for the collection of the American Philosophical Society. Among the items was "1 Buffalow robe painted by a Mandan man representing a battle which was fought 8 years since, by the Sioux & Ricaras, against the Mandans, Minitarras & Ahwahharways." Although not absolutely documented, the robe shown here, with its great variety in the depiction of Indians, their horses, and their weapons, has long been considered the robe that Lewis sent.

Courtesy Peabody Museum, Harvard University; photograph by Hillel Burger. Quotation from LC.I.235–36.

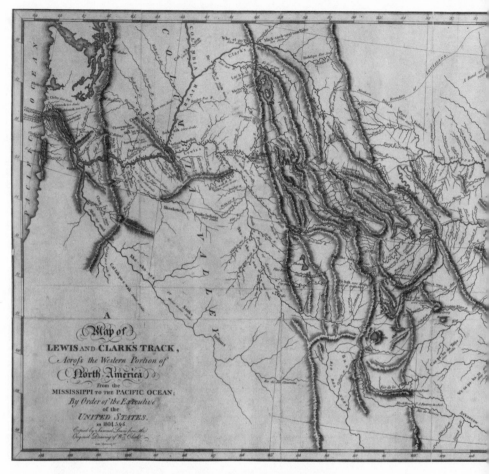

PLATE 18. William Clark's Map of the Expedition to the Pacific

Jefferson's efforts to have the American Northwest explored dated to the mid-1780s and culminated in the Lewis and Clark Expedition of 1804–6. His most fervent hope for the expedition was dashed, however, when the explorers found that a convenient water route to the Pacific, a Northwest Passage, did not exist. In 1810, William Clark prepared a master map of the expedition based primarily on his own field maps. He put to rest the idea of a single, narrow ridge of mountains not far from the Pacific Coast where the navigable headwaters of the Missouri were expected

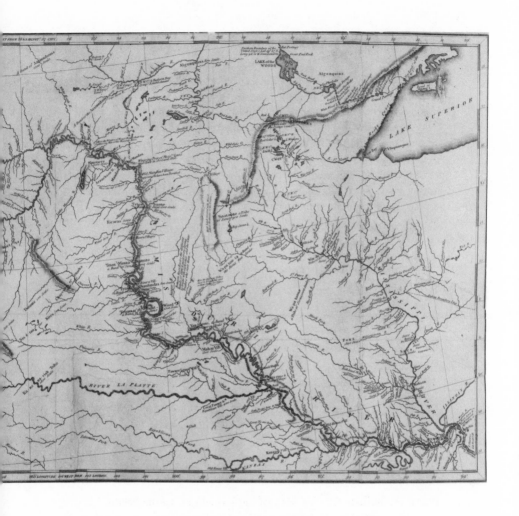

nearly to meet the navigable headwaters of a "River of the West" (the
Columbia). Instead, when Clark's map was published in 1814,
Americans learned definitively about the complexity of the Rockies, the
Cascade Range, and the Great Columbia Plain between them.

Courtesy Library of Congress. From Nicholas Biddle, ed., *History of the Expedition
under the Command of Captains Lewis and Clark, to the sources of the Missouri, Thence across
the Rocky Mountains and down the River Columbia to the Pacific Ocean.* 2 vols.
Philadelphia, 1814.

PLATE 19. *Farm Book,* Diary for 1795

From 1774 until shortly before his death, Jefferson maintained a *Farm Book,* organized according to topics such as plants, slaves, and preparation of ground. During 1795 and 1796, when he stayed at Monticello the entire time and attended to farming more than at any other time in his life, he also entered an annual diary. On the page shown here he names twelve different fields on four farms in Albemarle County (Lego, Monticello, Shadwell, and Tufton), recounts activities from ploughing to fencing, specifies corn, wheat, oats, peas, and clover among his field crops, and records when fruit trees are in bloom and lettuce and strawberries first "come to table."

Courtesy Massachusetts Historical Society; p. 45 of the original *Farm Book.*

Diary for 1795.

The fall of 1794. had been fine, yet little ploughing was done, partly from the want of horses, partly neglect in the overseers, & a three months confinement by sickness in myself, viz from Sep. 1. to the latter end of Nov.

Petit came to Monticello about the middle of Nov. & soon after they began to plough on both sides, first with one plough, then 2. then 3. they did not get the 4th plough each till the 2d week in Mar. in the mean time 8. horses for each had been made up by purchasing 5.

Before Christmas, at Tufton the Highfield of about 35. acres, & at Monticello a part of the River field, to wit about 20. acres, & about 15. acres for an Oatfield were ploughed, say about 70. a.

On the other side about 25. or 30. a. of the Square field were ploughed.

1795. Jan. 7 Not a single ploughing day in either of these months. a degree
Feb. } of cold of extraordinary severity, with many little snows, prevailed through the whole of them.

Petit cut down & grubbed about 8. acres between Franklin & Poggio fields, grubbed the S. Orchard cleaned part of the Hollow & East f.
Alexander grubbed the patches in Square field
    employed his men in Mauling & cart in hauling rails to inclose East f.
    & repair the fences in general.

Mar. 9. at night. John & his 4. companions have turned over the brick-earth.
    have cut for firewood 23. cords, & for coal 50. cords.
    the mule carts have brought in 403½ hampers of coal.
        12. loads of dung from Shadwell to the Lucerne.
19. P.M. John &c. have cut 86. cords of pine & 2 of hiccory, & 28½ of firewood
    Alexander has about 90. a. ploughed.
    Petit about 113 viz Highfield 30. & 8 a. of Hollow f. for corn, 15 a. of the
    River f. 30. of Slate f. for wheat, 20 for oats & about 10. a. of S. orch for pees
Apr. 4. began to plant corn at Lego.
    finished bringing dung to the Lucerne with the Mule carts.
    peaches & cherries in blossom.
    martins came to Charlottesville about the 24th of March.
Apr. 1. began to sow clover. on trial with the box it took 11. gills to the acre. Col°. N. Lewis
    sowed an acre with 12. gills, but not so well done. the sowings are Antient f°.
    and an Oatfield at the head of Slate f°. about 15. a. also about 4. or 5. acres to com-
    plete Poggio.
    at Shadwell began to sow the Upper field about 30. a.
6. the Oatfield has taken 135 gills of clover seed, so at 11. gills to the acre, there must
    be about 12½ acres.
20. finish sowing clover this day. 15. gallons have sowed Oatfield & Infield at Tufton.
May. 6. the fallowing is finished here to about 10. a.
    9. the clover at Poggio in general blossom, begin now only to cut it for
    green food. it has not been high enough till now.
    10. the first lettuce comes to table.
    14. strawberries come to table.

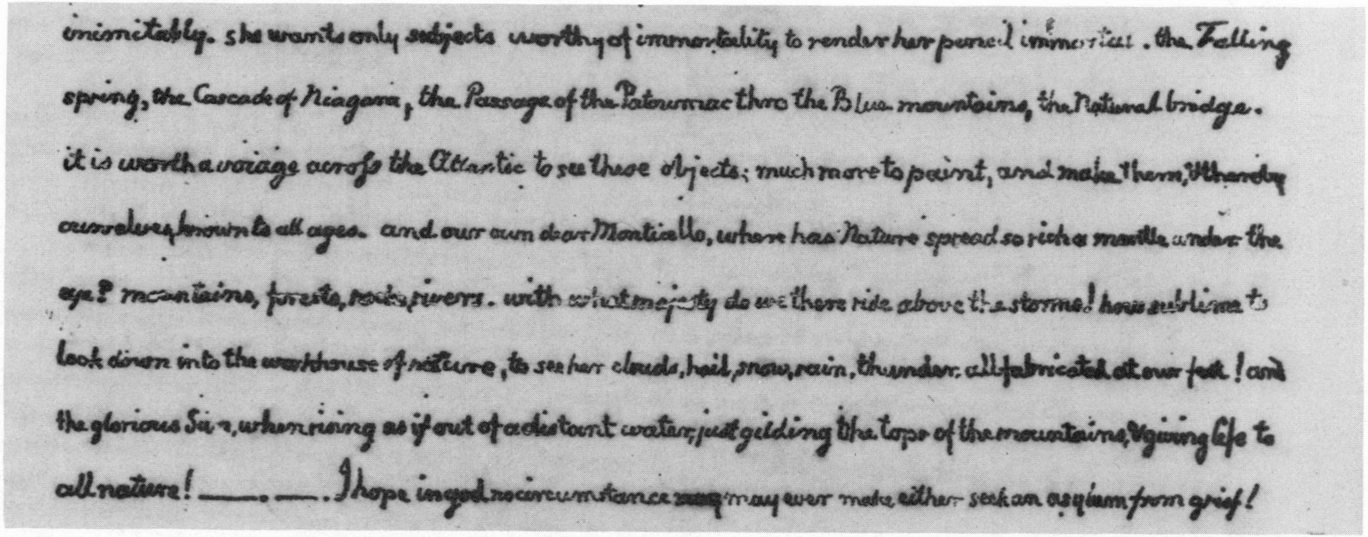

inimitably. she wants only subjects worthy of immortality to render her pencil immortal. the Falling spring, the Cascade of Niagara, the Passage of the Patowmac thro the Blue mountains, the Natural bridge. it is worth a voyage across the Atlantic to see these objects; much more to paint, and make them thereby known to all ages. and our own dear Monticello, where has nature spread so rich a mantle under the eye? mountains, forests, rocks, rivers. with what majesty do we there ride above the storms! how sublime to look down into the workhouse of nature, to see her clouds, hail, snow, rain, thunder, all fabricated at our feet! and the glorious Sun, when rising as if out of a distant water, just gilding the tops of the mountains, & giving life to all nature! ———. I hope in good time a circumstance may ever make either seek an asylum from grief!

PLATE 20. Where has Nature Spread So Rich a Mantle under the Eye?

In his memorable love letter to Maria Cosway in the fall of 1786, the "Dialogue Between my Head and my Heart," Jefferson invited Mrs. Cosway to visit America. There she would paint both natural scenery (the "Falling spring" is a high cascade about seventy-five miles west of Monticello) and "our own dear Monticello," where viewers looked "down into the workhouse of nature" and up towards the rising sun "just gilding the tops of the mountains and giving life to all nature!" Jefferson painstakingly wrote the letter with his left hand, his right wrist having been badly fractured in the company of Mrs. Cosway on an outing near Paris.

Courtesy Library of Congress. The letter is TJ to Maria Cosway, 12 October 1786, BC.X.443–53.

PLATE 21. Monticello from the West   Photograph by C. L. Koral.

Jefferson's home is still surrounded by forest, cultivated fields, and landscaping. The swirls of trees suggest the contours of Monticello, his "little mountain."

THOSE WHO LABOR IN THE EARTH ARE THE CHOSEN PEOPLE OF GOD IF HE EVER HAD A CHOSEN PEOPLE WHOSE BREASTS HE HAS MADE THE PECULIAR DEPOSITS FOR SUBSTANTIAL AND GENUINE VIRTUE · IT IS THE FOCUS IN WHICH HE KEEPS ALIVE THAT SACRED FIRE WHICH OTHERWISE MIGHT ESCAPE FROM THE EARTH.

PLATE 22. Those Who Labor in the Earth are the Chosen People of God

The legacy of Jefferson's views on nature may be seen in the Thomas Jefferson Room at the Library of Congress. Dedicated in December 1941, on the 150th anniversary of the Bill of Rights (which Jefferson had so strenuously urged), the room contains murals designed by Ezra Winter (1886–1949). The four panels form a continuous, six-foot-high frieze around the top. Massed with foliage, and depicting the activities of a pioneer society, each mural contains a quotation from Jefferson's writings. On the panel entitled "Labor," a detail of which is shown here, Jefferson's rhetoric in *Notes on Virginia* is slightly marred by a reversal in the first line. It should read: ". . . if ever he had a chosen people." The second and third lines are also not accurate. See p. 209.

Courtesy Library of Congress. Quotation from NVa.164–65.

Chapter V

THE NATURAL BASIS OF POLITICS AND ECONOMICS

A FTER MORE than a quarter-century in public affairs, but before he became president, Jefferson wrote about his life's work: "Politics is such a torment that I should advise every one I love not to mix with them."[1] By temperament, he claimed, he was suited to be a scientist, but as he saw it, the times had decreed otherwise. For him, Fortune had ousted Nature.

Jefferson's contributions to American politics are plain. His contributions to political theory are more difficult to specify. Politics is certainly the most fertile field of both his thought and rhetoric, but as is the case in other areas, he cannot be called an original thinker. Further, as Merrill Peterson has remarked, Jefferson "never attempted to throw his own [political] thought into a system," so that compared with John Adams, whose "political science is readily identified, Jefferson's remains formless and elusive."[2] But if Jefferson's political science is perceived as one of his explorations in nature, it takes on a coherence and range that other means of comprehending it, such as freedom, independence, democracy, reason, or American nationalism, do not provide.

Jefferson was aware of the difficulty of explaining political ideas founded in nature. He complained about the absence of "a good elementary work on the organization of society into civil government: I mean a work which presents in one full and comprehensive view the system of principles on which such an organization should be founded, according to the rights of nature."[3] He recommended, therefore, two

1. TJ to Martha Jefferson Randolph, 11 February 1800, BB.184.
2. *John Adams and Thomas Jefferson*, 41.
3. TJ to John Norvell, 11 June 1807, LB.XI.222.

works that stated his own principles: Locke's *Second Treatise on Civil Government* (published in 1690 though written a decade earlier) and Algernon Sidney's *Discourses Concerning Government* (1698). Locke and Sidney had written to refute the tradition of divine right, especially as it was justified in Sir Robert Filmer's *Patriarcha* (1680), subtitled *the Natural Power of Kings*. Locke and Sidney, and Jefferson after them, turned Filmer around and gave natural rights to freemen.[4]

Jefferson held that Sidney's treatise was "probably the best elementary book of principles of government, as founded in natural right which has ever been published in any language" and that "Locke's little book on government is perfect as far as it goes."[5] But as may be inferred from the second testimonial, the works of the two men did not go far enough. They were written for another country and another era. Nevertheless, Jefferson always recommended them, and he ensured that the University of Virginia would assign them in teaching the principles of government "according to the rights of nature."[6]

Locke, whose general view on the natural basis of politics Jefferson's most closely resembles, is encapsulated by a modern scholar:

> There is, [Locke] thought, a Natural Law rooted and grounded in the reasonable nature of man; there are Natural Rights, existing in virtue of such law. . . ; and finally there is a natural system of government under which all political power is a trust for the benefit of the people (to ensure their living by natural law, and in the enjoyment of natural rights).[7]

4. A stylistic progression of "nature" can be traced from Filmer to Jefferson. Filmer, despite his use of "nature," writes primarily in a theological mold. Sidney typically relies on "God and nature" together. Locke invokes God and nature separately, for different purposes. Jefferson uses "nature" everywhere and "God" alone almost never.

5. TJ to Mason Locke Weems, 13 December 1804, S.III.13; TJ to Thomas Mann Randolph, Jr., 30 May 1790, BC.XVI.449.

6. Minutes of the Board of Visitors, University of Virginia, 4 March 1825, LB.XIX.460–61. Locke and Sidney appear on Jefferson's two basic reading lists. TJ to Robert Skipwith, 3 August 1771, BC.I.79; TJ to John Minor, 10 August 1814, F.IX.483. They do not appear on the reading list prepared for Peter Carr in 1787, but no books on politics are listed there, the subject having been turned over to George Wythe, a man devoted to "the natural and equal rights of man." TJ to Peter Carr, 10 August 1787, BC.XII.19; TJ to John Saunderson, 31 August 1820, LB.I.169.

Jefferson sometimes added two contemporary works anchored in natural law and rights: Joseph Priestley, *Essay on the First Principles of Government* (1768), and Nathaniel Chipman, *Principles of Government* (1793). He also recommended *The Federalist*. Among the ancients, he was indebted to Aristotle and perhaps to Lucretius. See the suggestive study by James H. Nichols, Jr., *Epicurean Political Philosophy: The "De Rerum Natura" of Lucretius* (Ithaca, 1976). The decline of Jefferson's estimate of Montesquieu as a guide to political theory is indicated by the removal of *The Spirit of the Laws* from first place on his 1771 list and the substitution of a critical commentary on the book in last place on his reading list of 1814.

7. Ernest Barker, Introduction to *Social Contract* (New York, 1960), xvi. A systematic treatment of Jefferson's political thought based principally on natural law and rights is

It is this Lockean natural system of government, updated by a century and removed to America, that Jefferson endorses. It is a rather unsystematic system, but it can be pieced together from Jefferson's writings, for everywhere in his political explanations there lies the evidence of a belief in a natural political order. It is treated below under the following heads: the establishment of political society; principles and institutions of the political order; international relations; and political economy.

THE ESTABLISHMENT OF POLITICAL SOCIETY

Among the leading concepts in the political vocabulary of Jefferson's time were the state of nature and social contract. The state of nature was the hypothesized circumstance of mankind before the establishment of organized civil society. Recognizing the insufficiencies of such a state, individuals eventually came together for their own benefit and voluntarily agreed to a social contract. The contract brought them out of the natural state and established society, which then established government. This theory had been devised not so much in order to understand how civil society had come about as to understand, if not postulate, the existence of natural law and natural rights and why, or whether, people should obey political authority. Jefferson found the state of nature and contract theory constructions only, not descriptions of actual situations and real behavior. He was too much an anthropologist for that. In addition, believing that humans were social by nature, he could not believe in a literal presocial state of human existence. But he did believe—fervently—in the natural law and natural rights commonly associated with the state of nature and contract theory.[8]

Natural law led many lives. Philosophically it was susceptible to the naturalist fallacy, discussed in the previous chapter with respect to ethics and aesthetics. In that discussion the movement from *is* to *ought* was illuminated by the ambivalence of "norm." In politics it is the ambivalence of "law" that aids. Natural law was simultaneously what is, because it is a regularity of nature, and what ought to be, because it is an unfailing guide to right action.[9] It was description and prescription at

---

A. J. Beitzinger, "Political Theorist," in *Thomas Jefferson: A Reference Biography,* ed. Merrill D. Peterson, 81–99.

8. In the late 1780s, when he was in France and a new constitution was under discussion in America, Jefferson apparently entertained an analytic view of the state of nature and the social compact. BC.XIII.4–8. See also TJ, "Opinion on the question whether the United States have a right to renounce their treaties with France," 28 April 1793, LB.III.228 ("moral duties which exist between individual and individual in a state of nature, accompany them into a state of society").

9. Had Jefferson been sympathetic to the philosophy of Bishop Berkeley instead of

the same time. When social and political theory relied on prescriptive natural law or natural rights, the claims were nearly always urged against constituted authority, though as Filmer shows and the "reason of state" doctrine demonstrates (see below), they need not have been. Natural rights were the original, inherent, moral claims of individuals against others—rulers, the state, or even society in general. Since natural rights existed both logically and chronologically prior to the formation of society and government, they were distinguished from, and superior to, civil rights.

The political use that Jefferson made of natural law and natural rights is almost endless. While never defining the terms as general ideas, he was capable of great dexterity with them and often took advantage of their attractive ambiguities. For instance, although there could be no state of nature in the sense of European theorists, he was intently curious about a modified state of nature in the setting of American Indian society. This society was not—because it could not be—presocial, but it was, Jefferson believed, precivil. Indian tribes were collections of families held together by blood ties, a distinctive language, and a set of customs. In this stage of society, Jefferson praised the Indians as having "no law but that of Nature." This meant that they lived without government but nevertheless enjoyed peace, justice, liberty, and equality.[10] When they did acquire law, they moved directly to a republican form of government, confirming Jefferson in his belief that such a government was natural to man.

However well the Indians provided lessons about a life in nature, they could not help meet contemporary issues springing from large, well-established political societies. To understand these, Jefferson devised a typology of societies, fearing (especially after Shays' Rebellion) that Americans might "conclude too hastily that nature has formed man insusceptible of any other government than that of force, a conclusion not founded in truth nor experience." Rather, he said,

> societies exist under three forms, sufficiently distinguishable. 1. Without government as among our Indians. 2. Under governments wherein the

---

that of Locke, he would have been warned about the confusion: "We ought to distinguish between a twofold signification of the term *law of nature;* which words do either denote a rule or a precept for the direction of the voluntary actions of reasonable agents, and in that sense they imply a duty; or else they are used to signify any general rule which we observe to obtain in the works of nature, independent of the wills of men; in which sense no duty is implied." Berkeley, "Passive Obedience" (1712), quoted in Morton White, *The Philosophy of the American Revolution,* 151.

10. TJ to John Manners, 12 June 1817, LB.XV.125. Jefferson did once say that Indians lived in a "state of nature." But he meant only that they had not yet "passed the association of a single family," and the family was the irreducible unit of mankind. TJ to Francis W. Gilmer, 7 June 1816, F.X.32–33.

will of everyone has a just influence; as is the case in England, in a slight degree, and in our States in a great one. 3. Under governments of force; as is the case in all other monarchies, and in most of the other republics.[11]

Since the first of these societies was impossible in Europeanized America and the third was abhorrent, it was Jefferson's lifetime task to erect the second form for the United States, a government "wherein the will of every one has a just influence."

To do this, Jefferson needed to establish three related doctrines: the law of majority rule, the right of the present to govern itself, and the right of revolution. Only then could he take up particular internal and external arrangements of the political order. None of these three doctrines is without serious theoretical problems, and Jefferson did not explore his creed with enough refinement or even open-mindedness to discover them; but he did ground them all in nature.

Majority rule, or the "law of the majority," as he called it, is an example of natural law. It recognizes the equal worth of each person in coming to a decision; but the *lex majoris partis*—Jefferson often used the Latin—did not tell what should be done, only how to determine it. It is an example of what may be termed procedural rather than substantive natural law, or, in effect, a natural law of convenience, ordinarily promoting the peaceful determination of public policy. To Jefferson it was the "fundamental rule of nature, by which alone self-government can be exercised by society."[12]

Jefferson insisted on majority rule precisely to establish republicanism, that form of society which lay between no government and government based on force. He feared disorder so much that the natural law of the majority was to be thought of as virtually divine—a word he seldom used. As he said more than once, it was necessary "to consider the will of the society enounced by the majority of a single vote, as sacred as if unanimous."[13] There are several difficulties with this formulation. First, since Jefferson believed in frequent elections and the right of new majorities to repeal earlier laws, he hardly took a majority vote as necessarily sacred for very long, which is an unusual notion of the word.

Second, since majority rule says nothing about the substance or the quality of decisions made under it, what happens when the rule leads to

11. TJ to James Madison, 30 January 1787, BC.XI.92–93.
12. TJ to John Breckenridge, 29 January 1800, F.X.417.
13. TJ to Alexander von Humboldt, 13 June 1817, F.X.89. Similar language appears in Jefferson's First Inaugural. See also TJ to John Gassaway, 17 February 1809, LB.XVI.337 ("Where the law of the majority ceases to be acknowledged, there government ends, the law of the strongest takes its place, and life and property are his who can take them").

"wrong" results? Jefferson did not believe this would happen often. "The Natural law of every society . . . may sometimes err," he admitted, but "its errors are honest, solitary and short-lived."[14] In addition, to err is to be unreasonable, and people are reasonable by nature. "Our people are in a body wise," Jefferson declared, "because they are under the unrestrained and unperverted operation of their own understanding."[15] This may be a self-validating argument on behalf of republicanism: If by nature we are free and equal, and if we remain that way, then we can exercise our natural understanding and, as a majority, not fall into error. But Jefferson took even further precautions to protect majority rule. He made honesty a condition for its practice and, in times of crisis, strength of conviction a precondition for its exercise.[16] If, in spite of all these qualifications and safeguards, however, the majority was "wrong," Jefferson accepted the sacredness of the rule and was prepared to obey.[17]

Finally, in the doctrine of minority rights Jefferson established a substantive limit to his procedural natural law. Although "the will of the majority, the Natural law of every society, is the only sure guardian of the rights of man," it is the substantive rights that are ultimately to be protected.[18] For this reason Jefferson campaigned for a bill of rights to the Constitution and looked to judicial enforcement of them. In the meantime, he attempted to reduce the likelihood of conflict between the potentially conflicting doctrines of natural law by championing reason in politics and by pressing for a society of such harmony and affection (he uses the two words in the First Inaugural) that a collision between majority rule and minority rights would never take place.

The natural law of the majority having been established and explained, Jefferson now ¡roposed that the law be understood in a way that initially seems obvious but was peculiar to his own bent of political theory. It seems obvious that the law of the majority should apply only

14. TJ, "Response to Address of Citizens of Albemarle," 12 February 1790, BC.XVI.179.

15. TJ to Joseph Priestley, 19 June 1802, F.VIII.158. See also TJ to John Melish, 13 January 1813, S.III.35 (confidence "in the natural integrity and discretion of the people").

16. See TJ, "The Anas," 7 February 1793, Pdvr.1234–35 (the "will of the majority, honestly expressed, should give law"); and the Declaration of Independence ("governments long established should not be changed for light and transient causes").

17. For examples of majority decisions that Jefferson accepted even though he strongly disapproved of them, see TJ to David Humphreys, 18 March 1789, BC.XIV.679 (accepting refusal of the states to request a constitutional amendment limiting the president's term in office); and TJ to John W. Eppes, 6 November 1813, F.IX.406 (Congress having established the first Bank of the United States, "its opponents true to the sacred principle of submission to a majority" did not obstruct its operation).

18. TJ, "Response to Address of Citizens of Albemarle," 12 February 1790, BC.XVI.179.

to people who are alive, and not to the dead. But it was this point that led Jefferson to develop his most distinctive political idea, that "the earth belongs to the living."

In the heady, early days of the French Revolution, Jefferson and his circle in Paris sought a principle of natural law that would irrefutably prove how immoral earlier regimes had been in burdening France with its current debts, the debts that contributed to the collapse of the monarchy. These debts, which the past had handed down to the present and which the present might hand down to the future, Jefferson thought were both avoidable and wrong. In a long letter to Madison, he argued that in accumulating debts that a later generation was to pay, the French monarchs and their advisers had violated natural law.[19]

Jefferson's fundamental question is "whether one generation of men has a right to bind another." He answers this through two analogies about the relation between the individual and society. The first begins with the assertion that "no man can, by *natural right,* oblige [his successors] to the payment of debts contracted by him." Then follows the unelaborated, minor premise: "What is true of every member of the society individually, is true of them all collectively, since the rights of the whole can be no more than the sum of the rights of the individuals." The conclusion is that there exists a "law of nature that succeeding generations are not responsible for the preceding."

The second argument presumes that society, like the individual, has a life span. "Let us suppose," Jefferson begins, "a whole generation of men to be born on the same day, to attain mature age on the same day, and to die on the same day." On this assumption, each successive generation would "come on, and go off the stage at a fixed moment, as individuals do now."[20] From this definition of generation as individual it follows that half a generation will be dead at half an individual's lifetime (considered only during a person's mature years when he is contributing to society). When a majority of the members of such a generation are dead, according to Jefferson, the entire generation may be considered dead, and their right to exercise the natural law of majority rule expires with them.

According to such reasoning, no society may make a promise—a

19. TJ to James Madison, 6 September 1789, BC.XV.392–97. Unless otherwise noted, this letter is the source of the quotations from Jefferson in the next paragraphs. For background, see BC.XV.384–91. See, generally, Adrienne Koch, *Jefferson and Madison,* chap. 4.

20. Jefferson's mode of reasoning may be contrasted with Edmund Burke's observation that it is "the pattern of nature" that society is a "permanent body composed of transitory parts . . . never old, or middle-aged, or young." *Reflections on the Revolution in France* (1790) (New York, 1959), 38, 39.

debt, treaty, constitution, or ordinary legislation—that lasts longer than half the life span of the mature human. That would be to bind a succeeding generation, that is, a future majority. Since the half-life of such a generation, according to contemporary mortality tables, was nineteen years, Jefferson suggested this figure as the natural life span for a country's debts or other agreements. In this way he hoped to ensure that the earth was ruled by the living and that only a live majority exercised the natural right of majority rule.

Any weaknesses in the structure of this reasoning would not have occurred to Jefferson himself. He did not believe that he was making analogies or that he was committing an error in logic, the fallacy of composition. He was simply pointing out a relationship that he supposed existed in nature.[21]

Having established the rule that the earth belongs to the living, and holding that generations must be considered independent of one another, Jefferson next drew conclusions in public policy that show the strength of his theoretical conviction. Public debts must be limited in duration. Societies are forbidden to make "a perpetual constitution, or even a perpetual law," and like the debts, these should be "extinguished . . . in their natural course with those who gave them."

To effectuate his idea, Jefferson suggested that his doctrine become the preamble to the first appropriation bill passed by Congress (it being too late to implant it in the Constitution itself). Although he had developed the principle from the conditions in France, by transferring it to the United States he hoped to "exclude at the threshold of our new government the contagious errors of this quarter of the globe, which have armed despots with means, not sanctioned by nature, for binding in chains their fellow men."

Madison replied to his friend's theory not long after Jefferson returned to the United States. His reply is remarkable for not once mentioning natural rights, the concept that underlies Jefferson's entire argument. Instead, he proposes in a Burkean manner that there is a "foundation in the nature of things" that supports precisely what Jefferson had argued against: the descent of obligations from one generation to the next. He flatly rejects a natural law of the majority, while implying at the same time the existence of what Jefferson denied, a utilitarian social contract: "On what principle does the voice of the majority bind the minority? It does not result I conceive from the law of nature, but

21. The indiscriminate, intermixed subordination of both individual and society to the laws of nature is a common feature in Jefferson's writing. See, e.g., TJ, "Opinion on the Constitutionality of the Residence Bill," 15 July 1790, BC.XVII.195 ("Every man, and every body of men on earth, possesses the right of self-government: they receive it with their being from the hand of nature. Individuals exercise it by their individual will: collections of men by that of their majority").

from compact founded on conveniency."[22] Disregarding or challenging all of Jefferson's arguments from nature, Madison finally responds to the specific proposals by taking up constitutions, public debts, and ordinary legislation in turn. He shows that for each of them it is impractical, indeed harmful, to expect these agreements to go out of force after a generation or to require their positive reenactment if their validity is to be maintained.

Jefferson never again wrote Madison about the earth's belonging to the living. But he did keep the principle alive with other correspondents.[23] His most extended later discussion was with his son-in-law, John Wayles Eppes, who as a member of Congress was faced with financing the War of 1812. In three unusually long letters, Jefferson argued against reestablishing a Bank of the United States, against long-term debt for the government, and against paper money. "What is to hinder [Congress] from creating a perpetual debt?" he asked. "The law of nature, I answer. The earth belongs to the living, not to the dead. . . . [T]he laws of nature impose no obligation" on one generation to pay a debt of the previous one. "And although, like some other natural rights, this has not yet entered into any declaration of rights, it is no less a law, and ought to be acted on by honest governments." He ultimately proposed to Eppes that his natural law principle be enshrined in the Constitution.[24]

For all this, Jefferson must have sensed the weakness of his generation theory when he was president himself one generation after the Constitution had been ratified, for he breathed no hint of the document's lapsing according to natural law. And although later he pressed for a clause in the Virginia constitution requiring that it be revised every generation, he did not use arguments from natural law but rather justified his position with a liberal's faith:

> Laws and institutions must go hand in hand with the progress of the human mind. As that becomes more developed, more enlightened, as new discoveries are made, new truths disclosed, and manners and opin-

22. James Madison to TJ, 4 February 1790, BC.XVI.149.

23. A few years after he had failed to convince Madison, Jefferson tried out a part of his theory on John Adams and failed with him, too. TJ to Adams, 25 April 1794, C.I.254; Adams to TJ, 11 May 1794, C.I.255. With George Washington, however, his idea had some success. In his Farewell Address, Washington admonished the nation to avoid the "accumulation of debt . . . not ungenerously throwing upon posterity the burthen which we ourselves ought to bear."

24. TJ to John W. Eppes, 24 June 1813, LB.XIII.269–70, 272; 11 September 1813, LB.XIII.360; 6 November 1813, LB.XIII.404. There are numerous further expressions of the principle. A visitor to Monticello remarked that Jefferson's opinions on "the natural impossibility that one generation should bind another to pay a public debt" were "curious indicia of an extraordinary character." George Ticknor to Elisha Ticknor, 7 February 1815, in George Ticknor, *Life, Letters, and Journals* (1876), I.37.

ions change with the change of circumstances, institutions must advance also, and keep pace with the times.[25]

Near the end of his life Jefferson implicitly accepted Madison's practical arguments against putting the generation principle into effect. But he acknowledged them reluctantly, avoiding the active voice in his language and qualifying the concession by a restatement of his own early position:

> It is also found more convenient to suffer the laws of our predecessors to stand on our implied assent, as if positively re-enacted, until the existing majority positively repeals them. But this does not lessen the right of that majority to repeal whenever a change of circumstances or of wills calls for it. Habit alone confounds what is civil practice with natural right.[26]

This statement, however clear in some contexts, has a danger to it that Jefferson wished to guard against. What would happen if natural rights themselves were not binding from one generation to the next? One need only recall his efforts to prevent legislative tampering with natural rights in the Virginia Act for Establishing Religious Freedom. Thus, while "a generation may bind itself as long as its majority continues in life," and a successor majority "may change their laws and institutions to suit themselves," something is unchangeable: "the inherent and unalienable rights of man."[27]

Among these unalienable rights is the last of Jefferson's three doctrines needed to establish a political order: the right of revolution in order to secure other natural rights. Because, in the words of the Declaration of Independence, for many years "evils [had been] sufferable," it was also a right that one should delay acting on. It is notable, then, that in his most important political tract prior to the Declaration Jefferson stopped short of pronouncing it. The tract, *A Summary View of the Rights of British America,* was prepared in the summer of 1774 as draft instructions for Virginia's delegation to the Continental Congress.[28] Widely circulated though never officially adopted, it was intemperate in tone (especially against king and Parliament) and misleading in some of its history (for instance, about the Saxon contribution to British constitutionalism). But its significance in preparing for independence two years later lies in the mixture of rights that it claims Britain is denying

---

25. TJ to Samuel Kercheval, 12 July 1816, LB.XV.41.
26. TJ to Thomas Earle, 24 September 1823, LB.XV.470.
27. TJ to Maj. John Cartwright, 5 June 1824, LB.XVI.48.
28. BC.I.121–35.

the colonists: divine, natural, constitutional, and legal.[29] Looking back many years later, Jefferson regretted this mixture. He could now "deride . . . the ordinary doctrine that we brought with us from England the *common law rights*, . . . [a] narrow notion . . . of men who felt their rights before they had thought of their explanation. The truth is, that we brought with us the *rights of men*."[30]

Jefferson's pamphlet might accurately have been titled "A Summary View of the Several Kinds of Rights of British America." At the beginning it holds that Parliament has made "many unwarrantable encroachments . . . upon those rights which God and the laws have given equal and independently to all." But God-given rights are never alluded to again, and Jefferson wanders from the path of rights into a self-constructed thicket of British and colonial history of expatriation, commerce, and the suspension of a colonial legislature. Suddenly, in the last paragraph he reemerges to say that the colonists have all along been "claiming their rights from the laws of nature."[31] The difference between the first and last paragraphs is striking. It is as if they had been written by different people, or the first added as an afterthought, while the ending is authentic Jefferson, championing nature and avoiding God. Perhaps Jefferson proposed these uncoordinated sources for the colonists' rights in order to secure the initial assent of legislators who did not hold his views of natural law and then, having gained that approval, concluded with his own truest beliefs.

Two years after the *Summary View,* when it was manifest what was at stake—revolution and political independence—the rights of nature were in the lead. Constitutions, charters, statutes, and the common law find no place in the opening paragraphs of the Declaration of Independence. Even divine rights have been modified, as the "God" of the *Summary View* is transformed into "nature's God" in the Declaration. The Declaration does list grievances against king and Parliament that are based on other kinds of law, but these are listed only as proof of a

29. During the weeks he was preparing the *Summary View,* Jefferson drafted resolutions for the freeholders of Albemarle County that amount to a summary of the *Summary View.* They likewise point to violations of several kinds of rights: natural (also called "the common rights of mankind"), constitutional, and legal. TJ, "Resolutions of Freeholders of Albemarle County," 26 July 1774, BC.I.119.

30. TJ to Judge John Tyler, 17 June 1812, LB.XIII.165. As a natural rights theorist of the break with England, Jefferson was hardly in the lead. In 1765 James Otis had relied heavily on natural law and right. (A comparison of Otis and Jefferson suggests that the hesitancy of the Virginian on natural rights may be related to slavery. See above, p. 68, n46.) Just a few years later, James Wilson was also more outspoken. And so, too, was the First Continental Congress, to whose deliberations the *Summary View* was designed to contribute.

31. BC.I.121, 134.

"design to reduce [the colonists] under absolute despotism" and in
support of the colonists' exercising a natural right.[32]

The natural law and natural rights language of the Declaration is
memorable.[33] The first paragraph announces that the United States will
"assume among the powers of the earth the separate and equal station to
which the laws of nature and of nature's God entitle them." The second
paragraph explains those laws:

> We hold these truths to be self-evident: [1] that all men are created equal;
> [2] that they are endowed by their Creator with certain inalienable rights;
> [3] that among these are life, liberty, and the pursuit of happiness; [4] that
> to secure these rights, governments are instituted among men, deriving
> their just powers from the consent of the governed; [5] that whenever any
> form of government becomes destructive of these ends, it is the right of
> the people to alter or to abolish it, and to institute new government,
> laying its foundation on such principles, and organizing its powers in
> such form, as to them shall seem most likely to effect their safety and
> happiness.

The Congress made only one change in these lines from Jefferson's
original draft, but that change illustrates Jefferson's greater attachment
to the concept of natural rights. Jefferson had written "endowed by
their Creator with inherent and inalienable rights." The Congress deleted "inherent" and added "certain." Since inherent rights were natural
rights, the deletion by Congress diminishes, and by some interpretations even eliminates, the idea that the rights proclaimed in the Declaration exist by nature. Moreover, the addition of "certain" implies that

32. For an argument that the list of grievances neither exemplifies natural rights that
are violated nor constitutes a justification for exercising one, see Lester H. Cohen, *The
Revolutionary Histories*, 132. After the Revolution, Cohen claims, historians and to some
degree Jefferson himself brought political contingency and immutable principles together
into a single conception of natural law, so that it became defined as a process. Historical
events, instead of independently justifying the Revolution, became the fulfillment of the
law of nature.

33. Among the many attempts to make the philosophical implications of the Declara-
tion as clear as the words themselves seem to be. the most penetrating and encompassing
is White, *The Philosophy of the American Revolution*. See also John H. Hazelton, *The
Declaration of Independence: Its History* (New York, 1906); Carl L. Becker, *The Declaration of
Independence*; Ernest Barker, "Natural Law and the American Revolution"; Paul
Eidelberg, *On the Silence of the Declaration of Independence* (Amherst, Mass., 1976); and
Garry Wills, *Inventing America*. Depending on which of these studies one consults, the
significant background of the Declaration rests with Locke (Becker), Burlamaqui
(White), or the Scottish Enlightenment (Wills). The plainest and most contemporary
source, however, is the Virginia Declaration of Rights. Written by George Mason and
adopted by the state convention on June 12, 1776, the Virginia Declaration reached
Philadelphia while Jefferson was at work on the Declaration of Independence. With the
exception of the implication in the Virginia document that there exists a state of nature, the
two documents contain essentially the same arguments, in the same order, often in the
same language.

whatever inalienable rights do exist, they are not beyond enumerating, thus seeming to confine a circle of rights that Jefferson had left more open.

As presumably well understood as these lines of the Declaration are, the difference between natural laws and natural rights in them is little appreciated. While a consistent and logical distinction between them is necessarily speculative, the attempt to discover one enriches an understanding of the Declaration and of Jefferson's reliance on nature to establish political society.

The difference seems to be this. The laws exist in nature and are about nature, whether physical or human nature. Thus the Declaration refers generally to "laws of nature" and specifies two such laws concerning humans: that all men are created equal and that all men are created with certain inalienable rights. Natural rights exist at two levels. At the primary level they are rights to life, liberty, and the pursuit of happiness. These rights effectuate the natural law of being created equal. At the secondary level they are rights "to secure these [primary] rights": instituting a government with the consent of the governed, and its necessary corollary, the right of abolishing one government and instituting a new one. The argument thus moves from natural law to natural right, and from primary natural rights to secondary ones. It concludes with one of the secondary rights, the right of revolution.

The text of the Declaration does not define these differences, and for good reasons. Definitions, even if they could present the terms unambiguously, not only have no place in a state paper like the Declaration, they might subvert, by exposing, an important function of the language of natural law and rights. This function is to blend what is ordinarily conceived to be immutable, a natural law, with what can be violated, a natural right. The opening of the Declaration achieves a remarkable transition from the descriptive to the prescriptive language of nature. It begins with the laws of nature, none of them specified, and it ends with specified natural rights. They are hinged by "truths," which could be either laws or rights, and with a multiple internal hinge, the repetition of a single word, "that." Since all five clauses of the second paragraph take the identical grammatical form by beginning with this word, the group together can shift from natural law to natural rights, from truth to value, without drawing linguistic attention to the fact. Table 5 shows how tightly these ties bind the opening sentences of the Declaration together. But neither an explanation nor a diagram can replace the effect of the prose itself, artfully joining, if not confusing, natural law and natural right. Reason and rhetoric have combined to found a political order sanctioned by nature.

One ground for invoking nature to justify a revolution is that nature

TABLE 5
Natural Laws and Natural Rights in the Declaration of Independence

Text	Commentary
"laws of nature and of nature's God [entitle the United States to independence]"	A general promise that natural laws justify independence
"We hold these truths to be self-evident"	The promise will be fulfilled by specifying natural laws
"[1] that all men are created equal"	A natural law
"[2] that they are endowed . . . with . . . inalienable rights"	A natural law
"[3] that among these are life, liberty, and the pursuit of happiness"	Primary natural rights that explain [2]
"[4] that to secure these rights, governments are instituted among men"	A secondary natural right to effectuate [3]
"[5] that [when government fails to secure its proper ends] it is the right of the people to alter or to abolish it"	A secondary natural right, related to [4]

offers a source of value at a time when all other sources of value are thrown into doubt—a community's history, its religion, its social ties, and, most particularly, its customary political legitimacy. Since American colonists shared so much with Great Britain, an appeal to British values might under some circumstances have seemed helpful if not unavoidable; this indeed took up much of the pre-Declaration pamphleteering. But by itself such an appeal would never lead to the breaking point. Nature seemed necessary.

But if one calls on nature at a time of revolution, it may be difficult to confine it to only those uses one wishes, as the nascent antislavery movement in America at once recognized, and as happened in France. The theory might extend itself to the state of nature and sanction the dissolution of all society. This Jefferson neither believed in conceptually nor accepted politically. It is true that in the *Summary View* he had challenged: "Shall these governments be dissolved, their property annihilated, and their people reduced to a state of nature, at the imperious breath of a body of men whom they never saw. . . ?"[34] But this was a rebuke to British actions, not an affirmative appeal to the colonists. The Declaration of Independence recognized only that "political bands" were being dissolved, not an entire society.

34. BC.I.126.

Once the Revolution had succeeded, Jefferson strenuously opposed the idea that it had created a state of nature, urging instead that the institutions of society had in most respects crossed the revolutionary terrain intact. Questioning a Virginia law proclaiming that the state had acquired the property of citizens who had fled during the war, he wrote that such legislation was premised on a "doctrine of the most mischievous tendency," namely, "the dissolution of the social contract on a revolutionary government . . . that on changing the form of our government all our laws were dissolved, and ourselves reduced to a state of nature."[35]

Jefferson the lawyer, the social realist, and the conservator of institutional stability justified the Revolution by natural law and natural right. But at the same time, he denied that the Revolution threw Americans back into that state where many theorists assumed the law and rights of nature had originated. His accomplishment was to provide support for independence and revolutionary ends without creating a lasting crisis of legitimacy. From an amalgam of doctrines of nature—majority rule, the generation principle, and the right of revolution—he devised a strategy to justify the establishment of a lasting political society.

PRINCIPLES AND INSTITUTIONS
OF THE POLITICAL ORDER

Once the political order has been established on the basis of primary natural rights, it requires a proper constitution to preserve the founding principles. A well-considered constitution is required, Jefferson once said with unaccustomed pessimism, because "the natural progress of things is for liberty to yield and government to gain."[36] Although not every political arrangement that Jefferson supported was derived immediately from nature, so many of them were that it is not difficult to construct a constitutional and legal order on a natural basis. Government in America, he once said, is a "composition of the freest principles of the English constitution, with others derived from natural right and natural reason."[37]

35. TJ to Edmund Randolph, 15 February 1783, BC.VI.247–48. But compare the following, written at about the same time: "Necessities which dissolve a government . . . throw back, into the hands of the people, the powers they had delegated, and leave them as individuals to shift for themselves." NVa.127. On the subject generally see John Fenton, Jr., *The Theory of the Social Compact and its Influence upon the American Revolution* (1891); and Thad W. Tate, "The Social Contract in America, 1774–1787."
36. TJ to Edward Carrington, 27 May 1788, BC.XIII.208–9.
37. NVa.84. Jefferson also took the principles of the English constitution back to nature. See TJ to George Washington Lewis, 25 October 1825, KP.725 (although the battle of Hastings was lost, "the natural rights of the nation were not staked on the event of a single battle").

The first, the fundamental, matter to be decided in a political system is eligibility for membership. What are the qualifications for joining (i.e., citizenship)? and what are the conditions for leaving (i.e., expatriation)? In the answers to these questions Jefferson's political order departs most strikingly and consistently from the British tradition.[38] That tradition, in accord with Filmer's *Patriarcha,* assumed that nature establishes a hierarchy modeled on the father-child relationship. On that basis a person is by nature, involuntarily, and from birth the subject of a sovereign. The republican theory of Jefferson, largely in accord with Locke, turned this completely around: by nature people are in an equal and independent relationship to one another. They have a natural right to form their own government and voluntarily become members of a political community. They become citizens, not subjects. By the same reasoning, they have the right by nature to leave the community.

It is this natural right of expatriation that lies at the base of Jefferson's version of the settlement of the American colonies. It is the right that is the source of the colonists' subsequent rights, including the right to be independent of England. Jefferson's most theoretical statement of this position was formulated decades after its initial usefulness at the time of independence:

> The evidence of this natural right [of expatriation], like that of our right to life, liberty, the use of our faculties, the pursuit of happiness, is not left to the feeble and sophistical investigations of reason, but is impressed on the sense of every man. We do not claim these under the charters of kings or legislators, but under the King of kings. If he has made it a law in the nature of man to pursue his own happiness, he has left him free in the choice of place as well as mode; and we may safely call on the whole body of English jurists to produce the map on which Nature has traced, for each individual, the geographical line which she forbids him to cross in pursuit of happiness. . . . [T]here is not another nation, civilized or savage, which has ever denied this natural right. I doubt if there is another which refuses its exercise. I know it is allowed in some of the most respectable countries of continental Europe, nor have I heard of one in which it was not. How it is among our savage neighbors, who have no law but that of Nature, we all know.[39]

Bound into this creed of a natural right of expatriation are the doctrine of an innate moral sense, the natural right to pursue happiness, and a

38. See, generally, James H. Kettner, *The Development of American Citizenship, 1608–1870* (Chapel Hill, 1978). Jefferson's ideas are laid out with respect to his uses of history in H. Trevor Colbourn, *The Lamp of Experience,* 158–93.

39. TJ to Dr. John Manners, 12 June 1817, F.X.87. A facsimile of this passage is shown in plate 9.

liberal interpretation of European and native American practices.

Jefferson first set out a natural right of expatriation in the guise of historical facts in the *Summary View*. There he proposed that the Virginia delegates to the Continental Congress remind King George III that the "universal law" of expatriation had been exercised by the Saxons when they migrated to Britain from the European continent. Settlers in America merely carried on the tradition. They "possessed a right, which nature has given to all men, of departing from the country in which chance, not choice has placed them." In the New World, Jefferson continued somewhat disingenuously, they were on their own. In his cadence: "For themselves they fought, for themselves they conquered, and for themselves alone they have right to hold."[40]

From this asserted natural right and supposed initial independence flowed all other arguments needed by the colonists. Jefferson conceded (much later) that early in the struggle many Virginia patriots had granted Parliament some rights over the colonists. "But for this ground," he wrote, "there was no foundation in colonization, nor in reason: expatriation being a natural right, and acted on as such, by all nations, in all ages."[41]

Once started on the path of a natural right of expatriation, Jefferson never left it, although American state and national law did not keep up with him. In June 1776 he charged the king in both the Declaration of Independence and his proposed constitution for Virginia with "obstructing the laws for naturalization of foreigners." The draft constitution contained a prompt corrective for this, essentially citizenship on demand.[42] He explained the right to vote accompanying such citizenship as a "natural right of assisting in [the] preservation" of a country where one intended to live permanently.[43] When the state failed to include any naturalization provision in the new constitution, he drafted a statute to fill the need. It was his most significant attempt to incorporate the natural right of expatriation into the American political system:

> And in order to preserve to the citizens of this commonwealth, that natural right, which all men have of relinquishing the country, in which birth, or other accident may have thrown them, and seeking subsistence and happiness wheresoever they may be able, or may hope to find them . . . it is enacted and declared [that when a citizen relinquishes his

40. TJ, *Summary View*, BC.I.121.

41. TJ, Autobiography (1821), KP.10. See also TJ to Judge John Tyler, 17 June 1812, LB.XIII.165 (the colonists brought not common law rights but the "rights of men; of expatriated men").

42. TJ, First Draft of the Virginia Constitution, June 1776, BC.I.338, 344.

43. TJ to Edmund Pendleton, 26 August 1776, BC.I.504.

citizenship and departs] such person shall be considered as having exercised his natural right of expatriating himself.[44]

The natural right to leave one country and renounce its citizenship may seem to entail the existence of a correlative natural right to enter another country and become a citizen. For theoretical and practical reasons, however, Jefferson did not accept this logic. He came only so close as to agree—but he was persuaded not to say it in public—that "every man has a right to live some where on earth, and if some where, no one society has a greater right than another to exclude him."[45] Although the "right to live somewhere" is not a right to live in a particular place, it may imply that all nations should have similar laws concerning the renunciation and acquisition of citizenship and concerning leaving and entering the country. There is nevertheless a theoretical insufficiency in establishing a natural right to citizenship as the mirror image of a natural right to expatriation. While any single individual can renounce citizenship and leave a society, each society has the right to define itself, which means the right to determine its own law of citizenship.[46]

The right of exclusion from American citizenship also raised intensely practical problems that were as delicate in Jefferson's time as they are today. To what extent should a country founded on the natural right of expatriation, a haven for people from many lands, exercise control over its composition, ideological, ethnic, or otherwise? Like later generations, Jefferson was of a divided mind. First he asked, "Shall we refuse the unhappy fugitives from distress that hospitality which the savages of the wilderness extended to our fathers arriving in this land?"[47] But he also asked:

> Are there no inconveniences . . . against the advantage expected from a multiplication of numbers by the importations of foreigners? . . . Civil government being the sole object of forming societies, its administration must be conducted by common consent. . . . [Emigrants from monarchies] will infuse into [American legislation] their spirit, warp and bias

44. Bill No. 55, "Declaring Who Shall be Deemed Citizens of This Commonwealth," 1779, BC.II.477. Jefferson's pride in this bill is attested by his listing it among eleven "Services to his Country." Ca. 1800, F.VII.476 ("The act . . . establishing the natural right of man to expatriate himself at will"). See, similarly, TJ, Autobiography (1821), KP.42.
45. TJ, ms. note for First Annual Message, 8 December 1801, F.VIII.124.
46. See TJ to William H. Crawford, 20 June 1816, F.X.34–35 ("Every society has a right to fix the fundamental principles of its association"; those not adhering to the principles may be excluded "from our territory, as we do persons infected with disease"). When new members are admitted, however, the majority cannot "subject [a naturalized citizen] to unequal rules, to rules from which they exempt themselves." TJ, ms. note for First Annual Message, 8 December 1801, F.VIII.124.
47. TJ, First Annual Message, 8 December 1801, Pdvr.393.

its direction, and render it a heterogeneous, incoherent, distracted mass.[48]

Although stated with respect to antirepublican ideology, this argument also, if awkwardly, supports Jefferson's view that since the United States could not become a biracial society, freed slaves should be induced or forced to exercise their right of expatriation.

In the face of the strains on pronouncing a natural right to enter a country analogous to the natural right of leaving it, Jefferson simply advocated easy procedures for naturalization. While such liberality normally benefited his own political program, and to that degree may be seen as self-serving, both at its inception in the revolutionary period and at its greatest trial—over British impressment of seamen from American ships—the theory operated relatively neutrally with regard to domestic politics and is evidence of a consistent position in natural rights. It was at this time, when Britain seized sailors from American ships on the ground that they were British subjects, that the common law of England and Jeffersonian natural law came into sharpest conflict. According to Jefferson's theory, even if the sailors did not affirmatively become U.S. citizens, they could still renounce their allegiance to the crown, claim a natural right of expatriation, and hope in that way to avoid forced service on British ships. When the War of 1812 was over, Jefferson was confident that America's victory had "rallied the opinions of mankind to the natural rights of expatriation."[49]

Once the nation's membership had been determined on natural principles, Jefferson could begin to organize the government. The civil society he preferred was of small dimensions, variously called by him ward, hundred, or canton. In this intensely local political unit most public affairs would be handled by the citizens directly. But if this was a natural community, it would not in practice subsist by itself. It joined with others to form a larger, artificial association. When this association was in place, its political doctrines were also to be drawn from nature. In America, at a second remove from the local community, this meant federalism.

In a turnabout of traditional constitutional history, Jefferson held that the national government under the Articles of Confederation was quite strong but that the national government under the Constitution was rather weak. The Confederation Congress, Jefferson said, did not need an express power to enforce its legitimate demands: "they have it

48. NVa.84–85.
49. TJ to P. H. Wendover, 15 March 1815, LB.XIV.279. For a statement during his presidency, see TJ to Albert Gallatin, 26 June 1806, F.VIII.458 (right of expatriation "inherent in every man by the laws of nature and incapable of being taken from him even by the united will of every other person in the nation").

by the law of nature. When two nations make a compact, there results to each a power of compelling the other to execute it."[50] The "two nations" are presumably a recalcitrant state on one side and the remaining states, collectively, on the other. If each of these parties has the natural right to enforce the compact on the other, it must be because the two sides have not agreed upon a common judge. They are in an international state of nature, in which natural law and rights, if they are not recognized voluntarily, may be enforced through self-help. Since self-help was an unlikely step for the Confederation to take, Jefferson's observation suggests that a different political organization might be preferable, bringing the American states out of a state of nature, supplying the union with a judiciary, and clarifying the relation between the federation and its members.

This is what the Constitution did. Yet when Jefferson came to assess the new charter, instead of finding that the general government under the Constitution was stronger relative to the member states than its predecessor had been, he found that it was weaker. In the Kentucky Resolutions, drafted in 1798 to challenge the national Alien and Sedition legislation, he proclaimed (anonymously) that "every State has a natural right in cases not within the compact (*casus non foederis*) to nullify on their own authority all assumptions of power by others within their limits."[51] Understandably, Jefferson's natural rights claims uphold his political position in the two instances. But the claims on their own do not mesh well. The Articles of Confederation created a weak national government, which Jefferson strengthened with natural rights against the states. The Constitution created a stronger national government, which Jefferson weakened with natural rights on behalf of the states.

With the government in place, its republican branch, the legislature, should be organized by looking to nature—for the qualification of its membership, its size, and its internal procedures.[52] All men being created equal and government requiring the consent of the governed, property qualifications for membership in the legislature violated natural right. Eligibility was simply citizenship in the society.[53] As to its

50. TJ to Edward Carrington, 4 August 1787, BC.XI.678.

51. TJ, Kentucky Resolutions, fall 1798, F.VII.301; see also F.VII.306, 307. The Virginia Resolutions, drafted by Madison, do not refer to natural right.

52. The most important structural feature of American government after federalism is separation of powers, which Jefferson accepted unreservedly. But he had nearly nothing to say about it in connection with nature. He did note, on the basis of experience, that the executive power needed a united direction, since it was in "the nature of man" that a multiple executive would not cooperate sufficiently. TJ to Destutt de Tracy, 26 January 1811, F.IX.306–8. See also TJ to Aaron Burr, 17 June 1797, F.X.147 ("natural feelings of the people towards liberty" would restore the constitutional balance between executive and legislative once George Washington retired).

53. See TJ to Maj. John Cartwright, 5 June 1824, LB.XVI.45 ("natural right has been

size, Jefferson no doubt accepted what he entered into his commonplace book: "Nature herself has confined, or limited, the number of men in all societies that meet together to inform and be informed by argument and debate, within the natural powers of hearing and speech."[54] Regarding the internal organization of the legislature, Jefferson maintained that a republican assembly as "a part of the natural right of self-government" could, insofar as its right had not been modified by the constitution, exercise a "natural right of governing itself." In doing this the legislature, predictably, should attend to "the Law of the majority . . . the natural law of every assembly of men, whose numbers are not fixed by any other law."[55]

The text of the original U.S. Constitution contained few explicit limitations on governmental power, a point that led Jefferson to protest. "A bill of rights," he wrote to Madison from Paris, "is what the people are entitled to against every government on earth."[56] With this began his campaign—in four letters to Madison—for the amendments that became the Bill of Rights. In the last, he proposed language to extend the coverage of the amendments beyond the draft that Madison, succumbing to pressure, had prepared.[57] He concentrated on freedoms of religion, speech, and press; jury trial; and limits on standing armies, monopolies, and the suspension of habeas corpus.

Nowhere in his letters does Jefferson refer to the rights he wished for as natural rights. Nor did he on the several public occasions when he considered civil liberties as a group—his draft constitutions for Virginia (1776 and 1783) and his list of "essential principles of our Government" in the First Inaugural Address. What happened to nature in these cases? Why did he not label as natural the rights he considered indispensable to a government founded on natural law and right? One possible reason is

---

mistaken" in permitting property qualifications); and TJ to John Hambden Pleasants, 19 April 1824, F.X.303 (state constitution defective in refusing "to all but freeholders any participation in the natural right of self-government").

54. CB.297 (from an anonymously published *Historical Essay on the English Constitution;* for the probable author see S.V.205).

55. TJ to George Washington, 15 July 1790, BC.XVII.197; NVa.125 (criticizing a quorum figure of less than half of the Virginia Assembly; this follows Locke, *Second Treatise on Civil Government,* sec. 96). Jefferson reported arguments from nature on a right of the Senate to punish allegedly harmful political expression directed at it by a journalist. Should punishment be allowed because "every man, by the law of nature, and every body of men, possesses the right of self-defense"? or should it not, because no governmental body derived its powers from "natural or necessary right," but only from express law, which in this case did not exist? Jefferson took no side in the controversy. TJ, *A Manual of Parliamentary Practice* (U.S. Senate), 1800, LB.II.341, 342.

56. TJ to James Madison, 20 December 1787, BC.XII.440. For a dissent to Jefferson's civil liberties reputation, primarily with respect to implementation rather than theory, see Leonard W. Levy, *Jefferson and Civil Liberties.*

57. The letters, with reference to the relevant passages, are TJ to Madison, 20 De-

that he may not in fact have considered them rights by nature—or not at the time. Except in the case of religious freedom, in the letters to Madison he either qualified the rights or surrounded them with historical discussion. He may also have been sensitive to Madison's disinterest in, if not antipathy towards, natural rights thinking. It is just as likely, however, that strategic reasons account for this failure to call the rights "natural."

First, since a constitution is a fundamental law, there is no need to designate any of its separate provisions as fundamental also. Second, in both the draft constitutions and the inaugural address, as well as in the letters to Madison, Jefferson knew he was mixing natural rights with historically grounded rights. To have called them all natural rights would have overstated the case, while to have distinguished natural rights from other rights might have implied a lesser attachment to the rights not called "natural." It may have seemed best, then, to find all the rights "essential" (the word he used in writing to Madison as well as in the First Inaugural) and leave it at that. Finally, to explain in public that the people were guaranteed the exercise of natural rights by civil institutions might unnecessarily weaken the rights themselves, as if one positively needed the government in order to enjoy them.

On other occasions, and for particular purposes, however, Jefferson did not hesitate to found provisions of the Bill of Rights in nature or to apply them by reference to principles he claimed to find there. At the head of these rights was liberty of conscience, a liberty that embraces not only religious liberty but also liberty of expression—in religion, science, and public affairs.

Limited to conscience, the liberty is natural in itself. One's conscience or thoughts are inherently one's own, the product of one's own physical nature. But a natural right to religious freedom implies more. It implies protection against external, governmental determination of what one must do in religion or of what one is prohibited from doing. These kinds of liberties are guaranteed in both the Virginia Bill for Establishing Religious Freedom and the religion clauses of the First Amendment. In urging the provisions, Jefferson said he had a single aim: "to restore to man all his natural rights."[58]

---

cember 1787, BC.XII.440; 31 July 1788, BC.XIII.442; 15 March 1789, BC.XIV.659–61; and 28 August 1789, BC.XV.367–68. In the first three he speaks of a "bill of rights." In the last phrase is "declaration of rights," the shift in language perhaps influenced by the incipient French Declaration of the Rights of Man and Citizen, in the drafting of which he had a hand.

58. TJ to the Danbury Baptist Association, 1 January 1802, KP.332. Much earlier Jefferson had copied in his commonplace book a passage from Locke's *Letters on Toleration*, holding that a church must be voluntary because "no man is *by nature* bound to any church." CB.379 (emphasis in the original).

The theory embodied in the Virginia bill and inferable from the free speech and press clauses of the First Amendment, however, is that more than expression of religious beliefs is guaranteed. Jefferson's dictum in the bill that "it is time enough for the rightful purposes of civil government for its officers to interfere when principles break out into overt acts against peace and good order" is wide enough to protect political and scientific opinions as well.

Here it is important to recognize the significance of "principles" (or "opinions"—the word appears nine times in the Bill for Religious Freedom) and to understand why they are protected even though they are not truths. Jefferson believed that truths existed in religion, politics, and science. They were to be found in nature: natural religion, natural law and rights, and natural history or philosophy. They were to be discovered by the use of natural, or unimpeded, reason. But he spoke as much of opinion as he did of truth, and among the opinions he would protect were "false opinion" and "error."[59]

Jefferson's concern for opinion reflects two impulses, both leading to tolerance and to the constitutional guarantees of freedom of expression. The first is that of humility. Though truth exists, we may not know it. This is testified by the history of science, as well as the history of politics and religion. The natural equality of humans precludes the infallibility of any one person or of several persons. Therefore, natural law requires that "our first object should be . . . to leave open . . . all avenues to truth."[60] The second approach to tolerance is a pragmatic one: the suppression of opinion tends to produce violence. As Jefferson said in the First Inaugural, religious and political intolerance have led to "bitter and bloody persecution." But in America, those states with no established religions exist in "harmony . . . unparalleled [which can] be ascribed to nothing but their unbounded tolerance."[61] Though truth exists, the controversies that arise in its pursuit are not worth suppressing.

Tolerance, however, should not mean the encouragement of false opinions, only that truth is the more effectively discovered. Nature provides help once more: "Truth is great and will prevail if left to herself; . . . she is the proper and sufficient antagonist to error, and has nothing to fear from the conflict, unless by human interposition disarmed of her natural weapons, free argument and debate, errors ceasing

59. See, e.g., Kentucky Resolutions, October 1798, F.VII.295 ("false religion"); and First Inaugural ("error of opinion" in politics).

60. TJ to John Tyler, 28 June 1804, LB.XI.33. See also TJ to Dr. Hosea Humphrey, 15 June 1816, S.I.297 (advocating "freedom of challenge of every fact and principle which one may suspect to be founded in error. . . . The freer the enquiry, the more favorable to truth").

61. NVa.161.

to be dangerous when it is permitted freely to contradict them."[62] To trace the circle of argument, freedom of expression is sanctioned by the source of the truth it is intended to protect: "Nature has given man no other means [than a free press] of sifting out the truth either in religion, law, or politics."[63]

Once one understands the basis in nature of a right to free expression, it is instructive to note an example of Jefferson's creativity in the field. In what appeared to be a rather narrow political problem, he discovered a principle that enabled him to argue well beyond the initial circumstance. The question was, What are the rights involved in communication between an elected representative and his constituents? Jefferson could have founded a right to such communication in the right to self-government, according to which the electorate must be able to receive whatever their representative sends to them. Instead he set out a natural right for a larger sphere of free communication: "A right of free correspondence between citizen and citizen, on their joint interests, whether public or private . . . is a natural right; it is not the gift of any municipal law . . . but in common with all our other natural rights, is one of the objects for the protection of which society is formed."[64]

Using similarly expansive reasoning, one may imagine how Jefferson would have argued from nature to explain the right of petition. Petition is either a species of public expression, and so justified on the same ground as expression, namely, to discover and convey opinions about politics; or an adjunct to the natural right of self-government, a means of communicating with one's representatives.

Freedom of assembly, the final First Amendment right to be considered, poses a more difficult question. If assembly refers to the mere coming together of people, Jefferson certainly recognized that it would take place either out of natural sociability or in order better to discover truth. But if assembly implied permanent association, he rejected the idea, at least the idea of his own membership: "I never submitted the whole system of my opinions to the creed of any party of men whatever in religion, in philosophy, in politics, or in any thing else where I was capable of thinking for myself. Such an addiction is the last degradation of a free and moral agent."[65] Religious association is nevertheless openly protected by the First Amendment, even if Jefferson would not join. A scientific association, such as the American Philosophical Soci-

62. Act for Establishing Religious Freedom, NVa.224.
63. TJ to George Washington, 9 September 1792, F.VI.108.
64. TJ to James Monroe, 7 September 1797, F.VII.172. Cf. the narrower argument that without an informed citizenry, "it seems to be a law of our general nature" that public officials will become, as they are in Europe, "wolves." TJ to Edward Carrington, 16 January 1787, BC.XI.49.
65. TJ to Francis Hopkinson, 13 March 1789, BC.XIV.650.

ety, he did join; but dedicated to searching out the truths of nature, such a group would never require the submission of a member's "whole system of opinions." However, about political associations, although they certainly appear to be covered by constitutional provisions or even by natural law, Jefferson was equivocal, in effect distinguishing good associations from bad ones and protecting them accordingly. When he spoke of a natural right of the people to assemble, it was for republican or revolutionary purposes. The committees of correspondence of the early 1770s had exercised an "inalienable" right. The Democratic Societies of the 1790s, defending republican principles, exercised "natural and constitutional rights." But an association such as the Society of the Cincinnati, premised on disregard for the "natural equality of man" and the "natural rights of the people," was suspect. Freedom of assembly, one may conclude, depends on the public purpose of the organization and is not itself founded in natural right.[66]

The freedoms of the First Amendment make up one of the two large classes of civil liberties guaranteed by the Constitution. To a considerable degree, Jefferson invoked nature to explain them. But the bulk of civil liberties protect fairness of government conduct towards individuals, and these, with one exception, Jefferson did not base explicitly in natural law or rights. These protections, whether from the legislature, the executive, or the judiciary, may be summed up as the guarantees of due process of law. The list of them is long: prohibitions on ex post facto legislation, bills of attainder, cruel and unusual punishment, excessive bail and fines, compulsory testimony against oneself, suspension of habeas corpus, unreasonable searches and seizures, and double jeopardy; rights to grand jury indictment, counsel, compulsory process for witnesses, and speedy, public, and impartial jury trial.

Jefferson's most important qualification to legislation is the restraint against ex post facto legislation. Such a law, which makes illegal an act that was legal when it was performed, leads to unexpected and therefore unfair criminal punishment. It may also affect, presumably unfairly, the rights of property. In either case it violates the understanding that legislation is about future rather than past conduct. "Nature and reason," Jefferson said, "as well as all our constitutions condemn retrospective conditions as mere acts of power against right."[67] While an argument did exist in favor of some ex post facto legislation with respect to property so that the living generation might be better able to govern itself, that same legislation might subvert the right of individuals to pursue happiness. On balance, Jefferson chose to protect property. He

66. TJ to William Duane, 24 July 1803, F.VIII.256; TJ to James Madison, 28 December 1794, F.VI.517; TJ to George Washington, 16 April 1784, BC.VII.105, 106.
67. TJ to Charles Yancey, 6 January 1816, F.X.2.

may have insisted that property holders had no natural rights of representation because of their property, but he believed that property, once acquired, had strong claims against certain acts of the legislature.

In court, defendants were protected by other provisions of due process, which Jefferson probably held to be the elaboration of a natural right to fair treatment. But he never spoke directly about such a right; instead, like most lawyers, he understood due process guarantees to be culturally relative and to come from the constitutional and judicial traditions of Great Britain rather than from the tradition of natural rights or natural law.[68]

When legislators finally turned to ordinary lawmaking, it was their "true office," Jefferson said, "to declare and enforce only our natural rights and duties, and to take none of them from us." In fulfilling this duty, an assembly was to follow three rules:

> No man has a natural right to commit aggression on the equal rights of another; and this is all from which the laws ought to restrain him; every man is under the natural duty of contributing to the necessities of society; and this is all the laws should enforce on him; and no man having a natural right to be the judge between himself and another, it is his natural duty to submit to the umpirage of an impartial third. When the laws have declared and enforced all this, they have fulfilled their functions, and the idea is quite unfounded, that on entering into society we give up any natural right.[69]

In brief, the subjects of permitted legislation are criminal law, taxation and conscription for purposes of defense, and a judiciary to settle civil disputes. Nothing is said about property, or welfare, or what Madison claimed to be "the principal task of modern legislation," "the regulation of various interests."[70] Jefferson's legislature is strictly limited.

The first of Jefferson's principles, that "no man has a natural right to commit aggression on the equal rights of another," he had considered at length in his Bill for Proportioning Crimes and Punishments of 1779. The opening sentences of the bill, deducing guidelines for a criminal code "from the purposes of society," remind one of the Declaration of Independence. "The secure enjoyment of [lives, liberty, and property] having principally induced men to enter into society," he wrote, "gov-

68. On judicial interpretation of any legitimate ex post facto legislation see TJ to Isaac McPherson, 13 August 1813, LB.XIII.326 (laws "abridging the natural right of the citizen should be restrained by rigorous constructions within their narrowest limits"). Among other guarantees, only the right against self-incrimination did Jefferson discover in nature (assuming that he accepted what he entered into his commonplace book). CB.322.

69. TJ to Francis W. Gilmer, 7 June 1816, F.X.32.

70. *Federalist* No. 10 (Wright ed.), 131.

ernment would be defective in its principal purpose, were it not to restrain [certain] criminal acts."[71]

In formulating a criminal code Jefferson found it useful to have in mind principles of natural law against which positive law could be measured and modified. But he knew that law was tied to both the history of a people and the needs of a living community. He therefore assessed a code of laws according to both universal and particular standards: "their harmony with reason and nature, and their adaptation to the habits and sentiments of those for whom they are prepared."[72]

A model of "harmony with reason and nature" was the legal system of ancient Rome. It was a system, Jefferson said, that was "carried to a degree of conformity with natural reason attained by no other."[73] By no means perfect, the Roman system was based on natural law, even if natural law less well understood than in modern times.[74] Jefferson would not have maintained that natural law itself had changed, only that even a society that had abided by natural law more than any other could be improved upon through greater powers of reason. Law judged by its adaptation to the habits of the people is also connected with nature, but to the particular nature of the environment. Here is Jefferson the relativist, accepting the theme of Montesquieu's *Spirit of the Laws*. "Every people," he wrote, "have their own particular habits, ways of thinking, manners, etc., which have grown up with them from infancy, are become part of their nature."[75] The spirit of environmentalism did not mean the abandonment of judgment, however. He found, for instance, a "superiority of the civil over the common law code, as a system of perfect justice."[76]

However much the Roman and civil law systems might be a model, Jefferson knew he had to deal with the laws of England. He admired, though not uncritically, the form given to the British legal system in

71. TJ, A Bill for Proportioning Crimes and Punishments, 1779, BC.II.492. See also NVa.143–45; and TJ, Autobiography (1821), KP.46–49. Jefferson was influenced by the work of Caesare Beccaria, from whose *Essay on Crimes and Punishments* (1764) he had extracted at length (in Italian) in his commonplace book. CB.298–316.

72. TJ to Edward Livingston, 25 March 1825, LB.XV.112. See also TJ, "Observations on the article Etats-unis prepared for the Encyclopedie," 22 June 1786, BC.X.47 ("In forming a scale of crimes and punishments, two considerations have principal weight. 1. The atrocity of the crime. 2. The peculiar circumstances of a country").

73. TJ, "The Batture at New Orleans," 1812, LB.XVIII.35; similarly, TJ to George Hammond, 29 May 1792, F.VI.38.

74. See TJ to John W. Eppes, 11 September 1813, LB.XIII.357 (criticizing Roman law for permitting a father to sell his child into slavery: "We, in this age, and in this country especially, are advanced beyond those notions of natural law").

75. TJ to William Lee, 16 June 1817, LB.XV.100 (declining to prepare a model government for a group he knew nothing about).

76. TJ to Judge John Tyler, 17 June 1812, LB.XIII.166.

Blackstone's *Commentaries on the Laws of England.* Published in the late 1760s, just as he was beginning his legal practice, the *Commentaries* provided positive law with a firm foundation in nature.[77] Even more than Blackstone, however, it was Lord Kames, a generation older, who supplied him with materials to connect natural with positive law. In his commonplace book, Jefferson excerpted or paraphrased Kames's *Historical Law Tracts* (1758) more than any other work, especially selecting passages on nature. In criminal law he found, for instance: "The dread of punishment is a natural restraint; . . . Revenge . . . belongs to every person by the law of nature. . . . Every heinous transgression of the law of nature raiseth indignation in all. . . . The purposes of human punishment are to add weight to those which nature has provided."[78] In the law of procedure, Kames used nature to overcome the force of tradition, classifying legal evidence according to whether it was "natural," which included proof by witnesses, confession, or documents, or "artificial," which meant the relics of the Middle Ages, trials by fire, water, and battle.[79]

Jefferson was so imbued with a positive law based in nature that he sometimes replaced reflection with reflex in invoking the natural standard. On initial reading, and perhaps in context, his uses of nature in the exposition of legal questions may make sense. But as one of his guidelines for penal law illustrates, his uses may be unrealistic or even dangerous:

> It is not only vain but wicked in a legislator to frame laws in opposition to the laws of nature, and to arm them with the terrors of death. This is truly creating crimes in order to punish them. The law of nature impels everyone to escape from confinement; it should not, therefore, be subjected to punishment. Let the legislator restrain his criminal by walls, not by parchment.[80]

It is understandable that Jefferson should want to remove the terrors of death (capital punishment) in the case of escape from prison. It is also understandable that he should point out the futility of trying to restrain a law of nature. But here he has said flatly that because nature impels our

77. For example, having in mind a universal prohibition against murder, Blackstone had written that "this law of nature . . . is binding over all the globe in all countries, at all times: no human laws are of any validity, if contrary to this." I.41. Jefferson was also in good company with a man who held that humans are made for society, not for a state of nature, and that the pursuit of happiness lies at the foundation of natural law. For a study of Blackstone's jurisprudence organized according to "nature," "reason," and "value," see Daniel J. Boorstin, *The Mysterious Science of the Law.*

78. CB.96, 102.

79. CB.104–5. See also CB.135 (English law of inheritance "deviates from natural justice") and CB.322 (judging harshly a statute that in effect punished a mother for loving her child on the grounds that it waged war "with the natural sentiments of the heart").

80. TJ, A Bill for Proportioning Crimes and Punishments, 1779, BC.II.502.

escape from confinement, the escape should not be punished at all.

A nearly reverse example of Jefferson's easy use of natural law—that is, a broadening rather than a restricting use—also deserves notice. "It is a maxim of our municipal law," he writes, "and, I believe, of universal law, that he who permits the *end,* permits of course the *means,* without which the end cannot be effected." Again, context may explain such a claim, but it cannot justify it. It is as dangerous as it is casual to state baldly that under natural law if an end is permitted, so, too, are the means.[81]

A study of Jefferson's natural law career makes clear how much specific occasions rather than a system of principles marked his use of doctrines presumed to come from nature. In preparing to justify a private bill of divorce in the Virginia Assembly he brought together an entire host of arguments from nature and natural law.[82] When he recalled his accomplishments as a legislator in Williamsburg—repealing entail, abolishing primogeniture, and establishing (he said it was "restoring") the rights of conscience—he claimed that these were "effected without the violation of a single natural right."[83] In a scholarly reply to the demand of the British minister that Americans who owed money to British creditors be imprisoned, he wrote, "It may be safely affirmed that neither natural right nor reason subjects the body of a man for debt."[84] When he defended his presidential order for repossession of a shoal at New Orleans that was, depending on the season of the year, either a beach or submerged beneath the waters, he persistently called on nature for support.[85]

The correctness of these assertions about what natural law and right hold, or what Jefferson's sources say they hold, is not the issue. Arguments against imprisonment for debt or on behalf of the retaking of property seized by force do not challenge one's ingenuity. Rather, the hesitation to accept Jefferson's claims arises from the circumstances in which he pronounced them—always on behalf of a cause, never as part of a system, never in relation to other principles of natural law, and seldom in connection with any limits. He was far more a retailer or a consumer than a philosopher of nature.

81. TJ to Albert Gallatin, 23 March 1808, LB.XII.18 (interpreting a regulation in the commercial war against England). See also TJ, "Spain and the Mississippi," 18 March 1792, Pdvr.247–48 ("the means follow their end. . . . This principle is founded in natural reason").

82. See Frank L. Dewey, *Thomas Jefferson, Lawyer* (Charlottesville, 1986), 57–72.

83. TJ, Autobiography (1821), KP.52.

84. TJ to George Hammond, 29 May 1792, F.VI.38.

85. TJ, "The Batture at New Orleans," 1812, LB.XVIII.103 ("By nature's law, every man has a right to seize, and retake by force, his own property, taken from him by another, by force or fraud"). See also LB.XVIII.106, 107 (reference to the same natural right).

In one instance, however, Jefferson's argument about a law of nature is both strong and detailed. Unfortunately, it stops in the realm of nature because it cannot, by definition, reach the status of positive law. The first of the inalienable rights in the Declaration of Independence is the right to life. To Jefferson, life, or self-preservation, is the primal, the original, and the most natural of all laws. It is the "first principle of nature."[86] It is a case in which fact determines value, in which a biological law, that people nearly always act to save their life, coincides with a social law (or right), that people have the ethical right to act this way. When individuals follow this law of nature, even when they break the positive law of the state in the exercise of their right, no one finds it remarkable. But when self-preservation is acted on by society as a whole, when public officials break positive law in order, they insist, to preserve the life of the state, then there can be alarming political consequences, and people begin to pay attention. Jefferson, already receptive to arguments treating the individual and society alike, had much to say about a natural law and right of social self-preservation.

The doctrine that explains or justifies a public officer's taking action beyond the law in order to preserve the state is the doctrine of "reason of state." Under reason of state, a law of nature temporarily puts out of force some or all of the legislation previously enacted. The same laws or constitutional provisions are to resume their power when the special circumstances—an emergency or an unusual opportunity—have passed. If natural law puts out of force an entire constitution, then the circumstance is one of revolution, in effect a "reason of society." "Should we have ever gained our Revolution," Jefferson asked, "if we had bound our hands by the manacles of the law?"[87] More generally: "A strict observance of the written laws is doubtless *one* of the highest duties of a good citizen, but it is not *the highest*. The laws of necessity, of self-preservation, of saving our country when in danger, are of higher obligation."[88] One senses that mere unelaborated "necessity" is an insufficient justification for exercising reason of state. In a republican state its exercise must serve a republican goal, such as liberty or the welfare of the people. But there is little that is beyond rationalizing under such language, and the circumstances that Jefferson recalled as justifying obedience to natural law over the requirements of positive law covered a very wide range.

---

86. CB.322.

87. TJ to James Brown, 27 October 1808, F.IX.211.

88. TJ to John B. Colvin, 20 September 1810, LB.XII.421 (a letter containing many examples of reason of state). See also TJ to William C. C. Claiborne, 3 February 1807, F.IX.14–15 ("On great occasions every good officer must be ready to risk himself in going beyond the strict line of the law, when public preservation requires it").

In Jefferson's political order not only are the laws, their limitations, and their preservation defined by characteristics given by nature. So, too, are individuals and groups who constitute the government. Government is, or ought to be, controlled by individuals whom nature has endowed with special political talent. And government is run by groups—political parties—which, by a principle of nature, contend in society for the right to administer public affairs.

Jefferson was eager to secure the services of his friends on behalf of the public good. If their political principles were correct, this satisfied one standard of their usefulness. If they were southern aristocrats like himself, then they were meeting their social obligations. But if these people were innately gifted for public service, then their duty to serve depended not on politics or custom but on nature. The reasoning is this. Nature has made men morally equal. They therefore ought to live under a republican government, where all enjoy equal citizenship. But as Jefferson's efforts on behalf of a natural aristocracy demonstrate, nature has not made men equal in their talents. This is as true regarding public service as in science and the arts. A person especially suited for government has the obligation to fulfill his potential.

Jefferson's earliest statement of the idea displays its breadth. Writing to David Rittenhouse in the middle of the Revolution, he complimented the scientist for his work "in the civil government of your country [Pennsylvania]." But, he continued,

> duly impressed with a sense of the arduousness of government, and the obligation those are under who are able to conduct it, yet, I am also satisfied there is an order of geniuses above that obligation, and therefore exempted from it. No body can conceive that nature ever intended to throw away a Newton upon the occupation of a crown. . . . Cooperating with nature in her ordinary economy, we should dispose and employ the geniuses of men according to their several orders and degrees.[89]

Principles that Jefferson accepted for the physical world are at work here in society. Just as nature's "ordinary economy" in the animal kingdom meant that each species had its place, so in society each person has particular characteristics given by nature and to be used in the proper place. A scientific genius like Rittenhouse should stick to science. Someone especially fit for public service should serve the public. (The inegalitarian reference to "several orders and degrees," which seems to be a social analogue of the chain of being, may instead point only to the internal rankings of a natural aristocracy in which scientists, because they study nature, deserve to be on top.)

Jefferson said that his own natural inclinations, if not his natural

89. TJ to David Rittenhouse, 19 July 1778, BC.II.202–3.

talents, were towards science and that he "had naturally no inclination" towards politics and government.[90] But in a republican government the judgments of the people about the talents of individuals count heavily, even replacing the direct judgment of nature itself. Thus, when Jefferson became vice-president but said that he would have preferred to remain in retirement at Monticello, he acknowledged that he had "no right to a will on the subject."[91] He made several attempts to persuade fellow southerners to serve the national administration, beginning with a plea to George Washington to accept a second term as president.[92] He unsuccessfully appealed to Edward Rutledge of South Carolina to join Washington's cabinet: "The present situation of the President, unable to get the offices filled, really calls with uncommon obligation on those whom nature has fitted for them."[93]

Jefferson also used the argument from nature in his most intense effort to recruit a friend to public employment, and this time he succeeded. He believed, correctly, that James Monroe was well suited to be special minister to France to treat with Napoleon for New Orleans. Because Monroe's earlier national career had not been satisfying, Jefferson had to overcome his friend's strong disinclination. He claimed that Monroe's qualifications were unmatched by those of anyone else, that "on the event of this mission depend the future destinies of the republic," and that Monroe's reputation might suffer irreparable damage if he declined. Finally, acknowledging the personal sacrifice the mission would require, he reasoned: "But some men were born for the public. Nature fitting them for the service of the human race on a broad scale, has stamped them with the evidence of her destination and their duty."[94] There is no reason to suppose that he was indulging in rhetoric with such a remark.

Since Monroe's mission resulted in the greatest accomplishment of Jefferson's presidency, the Louisiana Purchase, the stamp of nature's destination and duty on Monroe must have been clear, and the success of the mission must also have convinced Jefferson of the validity of his principle. But the principle is flawed. It is based on questionable assumptions, such as that people have fixed and determinable talents by

90. TJ to Caspar Wistar, 21 June 1807, LB.XI.248; TJ to Wistar, 10 June 1817, S.III.1.

91. TJ to John Langdon, 22 January 1797, LB.IX.371. See also TJ to James Sullivan, 9 February 1797, LB.IX.377 ("free exercise of my fellow-citizens to . . . call into their service [persons] according to their fitness").

92. TJ to George Washington, 23 May 1792, F.VI.5 ("law imposed on you by providence in forming your character"). Cf. William Wirt, "Eulogy on Jefferson," LB.XIII.xxxvi (when Jefferson was nominated for president, "his adversaries publicly objected—'that nature had made him only for a Secretary of State' ").

93. TJ to Edward Rutledge, 30 November 1795, LB.IX.314.

94. TJ to James Monroe, 13 January 1803, F.VIII.191.

nature; or that one can move directly from nature's truths to human values—that if a person is fit for service, he has the obligation to serve. The principle can also be rebutted from nature, as Jefferson himself proved, and against Monroe, of all people. Pressed by Monroe in 1782 to justify his refusal to accept election from Albemarle County to the state assembly, Jefferson said that no man had "less right in himself than one of his neighbors or all of them put together. This would be slavery and not that liberty which the [state] bill of rights has made inviolable. . . . [It would] contradict the giver of life who gave it for happiness and not for wretchedness."[95] Nature was to justify society's claim over the individual to serve and the individual's claim over society not to serve. As had happened before, Jefferson required nature by his side, no matter which side he was on himself.

Jefferson's use of nature to characterize political parties, while of more consequence than using it to characterize individuals, was equally unrefined. He held that in all societies, nature provided two fundamental attitudes towards governing, and two only. Where freedom of expression and political action are permitted, these attitudes are manifested as two political parties. Society gives the parties various names, but it is nature that has imposed the division:

> Men by their constitutions are naturally divided into two parties. 1. Those who fear and distrust the people, and wish to draw all powers from them into the hands of the higher classes. 2ndly those who identify themselves with the people, have confidence in them, cherish and consider them as the most honest and safe, although not the most wise depository of the public interests.[96]

Two parties by nature was not an idea original with Jefferson, but he maintained it in the face of a more complex theory of natural divisions in society advanced by Madison, divisions he sometimes called parties or interests but usually factions.[97] The two men begin with a source in human nature. Madison writes: "The latent causes of faction

95. TJ to James Monroe, 20 May 1782, BC.VI.185–86. See also TJ to James Madison, 7 June 1793, F.VI.290 (everyone owes a service to his country, but not for an entire life, "for that would be to be born a slave").

96. TJ to Henry Lee, 10 August 1824, F.X.317–18. In British history the parties are Tories and Whigs. In Jefferson's own time they are Federalists and Republicans. They may also be independents and anti-independents (before the Revolution), feds and antis (on ratifying the Constitution), honest men and rogues, Ultras and Jacobins. At core the distinction is between democrats and aristocrats, and it goes back to antiquity: "Whether the power of the people, or that of the aristoi should prevail, were questions which kept the states of Greece and Rome in eternal convulsions; . . . [T]he terms whig and tory belong to natural, as well as to civil history." TJ to John Adams, 27 June 1813, C.II.335.

97. The discussion that follows is based on *Federalist* No. 10 and on a letter Madison wrote to Jefferson during the days he was composing that essay. James Madison to TJ, 24 October 1787, BC.XII.277.

are . . . sown in the nature of man." Jefferson concurs: "In every free and deliberating society, there must, from the nature of man, be opposite parties."[98] But the two men disagree as to both the cause of the division and the complexity of the outcome. Madison finds that the underlying, or natural, cause is economic: differing and unequal faculties for the acquisition of property. This cause and other, more artificial ones lead to differing opinions on public affairs. These opinions in turn lead to the growth of a broad range of political factions.[99] Jefferson also recognizes differences in faculties, but he does not derive parties from them. For him, the underlying cause of parties is social attitude—which is not further derived—where the opinions of man, though "as various as their faces," can ultimately be found "reducing themselves to two stations."[100]

With its membership, structure, civil liberties, standards for legislation, and leadership founded in nature, Jefferson's political order was complete. It next needed to treat with other nations. A republican government could thrive only in an international order that recognized the principles of nature. In the next stage of his political thought, therefore, Jefferson attempts to protect New World nature for Americans, while extending the lessons of natural law and right to the rest of the world.

INTERNATIONAL RELATIONS

In international affairs Jefferson called on the law of nature primarily during his few years as the nation's first secretary of state. Invoking nature in the national interest, he gave American foreign policy a moral impress that has characterized it ever since. In doing so he not only acted as an ethical naturalist, believing that a correct reading of nature would yield a correct foreign policy. Among ethical naturalists his reading of nature was contrary to that of most European philosophers and to much of the experience of history. He believed that the law of nature yielded a

98. James Madison, *Federalist* No. 10 (Wright ed.), 131; TJ to John Taylor, 1 June 1798, F. VII.264.

99. Madison lists at least eight distinctions based on property and then adds religious, political, and personal reasons for mankind being further "divided . . . into parties." *Federalist* No. 10, 131.

100. TJ to Wilson Cary Nicholas, 26 March 1805, F. VIII.348. Both Madison and Jefferson made a virtue of the necessity for party divisions. Madison used the existence of factions to justify an "extensive republic" as the best means of controlling their effects. Jefferson rationalized the division of society into parties as healthy—even though republicans outnumbered antirepublicans by five hundred to one—because "mutual jealousies produce mutual security"; or as "necessary to induce each to teach and relate to the people the proceedings of the other"; or in order to avoid "some more dangerous princi-

law of nations whose principles were the principles of benevolent political ethics. By nature, the nations of the world were not at war with one
another, but at peace.

In Europe it was the mitigation of the presumed natural condition of
war that had led Jean Bodin and Thomas Hobbes to develop the concept
and characteristics of sovereignty and Hugo Grotius to found the modern law of nations. As the era of Napoleonic warfare opened, Immanuel
Kant wrote in the same tradition: "The state of peace among men living
side by side is not the natural state; the natural state is one of war. . . . A
state of peace, therefore, must be *established*."[101] But Jefferson, who
never mentioned Bodin, respected Grotius, despised Hobbes, and evidently did not know of Kant, accepted the views of none of them.
Instead, he held about nations what Locke said about individuals, that
there was a "plain difference between the state of nature and the state of
war" and that in the state of nature "natural law . . . enjoins that all men
should live in peace."[102] Whatever "some philosophers" have observed
about the belligerent dispositions of humanity, Jefferson said, referring
to Hobbes, the United States, and presumably any nation, was "in a
state of peace . . . with all [nations] by the law of nature."[103] Moreover,
when nations through their governments were at war, their inhabitants
retained their peaceable dispositions.[104]

Just as Jefferson had argued from the individual to society in explaining why "the earth belongs to the living," so he argued from models of
individual relationships in explaining how societies behave, or should
behave, towards one another. For this he relied on two images, the
family and friendship. The image of the family includes both a mother
country in association with her colonial offspring and a wider broth-
erhood among all nations, the "family of nations." Thus, with respect
to colonies, when they were legitimate at all, Jefferson accepted in the
international order what he rejected within a republic, the parent-child
model of Filmer's *Patriarcha*. But he expected from the family of nations

---

ple of division." TJ, "Notes on Professor Ebling's Letter," late 1795, F.VII.48; TJ, ms.
note for First Inaugural Address, March 1801, F.VIII.1; TJ to John Taylor, 1 June 1798,
F.VII.264; TJ to William Short, 8 January 1825, F.X.35. Cf. Jefferson's rationalization for
the unnatural practice of war, above, p. 58.

101. Kant, *Perpetual Peace* (1795), in Peter Gay, ed., *Enlightenment Anthology*, 789.

102. Locke, *Second Treatise on Civil Government*, sec. 19; idem, *Essays on the Law of
Nature*, ed. Wolfgang von Leyden (New York, 1954), 100. Reginald C. Stuart, *The Half-
way Pacifist*, maintains that Jefferson found war deplorable but nevertheless natural and
that he took a pragmatic rather than a pacifist approach to it.

103. TJ to Samuel Kercheval, 12 July 1816, LB.XV.40; TJ to Gouverneur Morris, 16
August 1793, F.VI.381.

104. See TJ to John Adams, 25 November 1816, C.II.498; and TJ to John Hollins, 19
February 1809, LB.XII.253.

just what he expected from the biological family, namely, natural affection.[105]

According to this reasoning, colonies, as children, should be the "natural allies" of the mother country. When there was still hope of preserving the family bond between Britain and the North American colonies, he altered this to the equality of "fraternal love and harmony." And when the war for independence came, it was predictably called an "unnatural contest."[106] Just how unnatural the contest was is evident in Jefferson's draft of the Declaration of Independence, larded with the language of family ties. Several of his usages were retained by the Continental Congress: "British brethren," "common kindred," "consanguinity." But equally intense language of the sort was deleted: "soldiers of our common blood," "last stab to agonizing affection," "unfeeling brethren," "former love." While the Congress dissolved the "political bands" between Britain and the colonies, it declined to make a further break by dissolving the ties of natural affection within the British family.

Congress did, however, retain Jefferson's famous chiasmus, that the British would be "enemies in war, in peace friends," which introduces the second model in international affairs, friendship. To populate a naturally peaceful world with natural enemies in addition to natural friends seems at first odd. But in its dualistic vision of the world it is familiar Jefferson, similar to the division of domestic society into two parties. It suffers from the same lack of sophistication. Just as in domestic affairs the Madisonian factions reflect society better than do Jefferson's two parties, so in international relations other concepts, such as balance of power, have normally served policy and analysis better than an image of natural friends and enemies. Yet an important difference between the domestic and international dualisms makes more comprehensible the doctrine of natural friends and enemies. Natural friends and enemies do not represent a fundamental position in social or political theory, as the two parties do, but are rather a presumed observation of geopolitics. They are not fixed in universal nature. While ties of blood (with Britain) or ideology (with France) give a durable cast to the idea of a natural friend, these are not necessarily permanent. Only

---

105. For discussions of the breakdown of a family tie between Great Britain and the American colonies see Wills, *Inventing America*, 259–319; and Edwin G. Burrows and Michael Wallace, "The American Revolution: The Ideology and Psychology of National Liberation," 6 Perspectives in Am. Hist. 167–306 (1972). The best-known contemporary attack on the parent-child understanding of the colonial relation was Thomas Paine's *Common Sense* (1776).

106. TJ to Stael de Holstein, 12 June 1786, BC.IX.631; TJ to Luis de Onis, 28 April 1814, LB.XIV.131; TJ, *Summary View* (1774), BC.I.135; TJ to John Randolph, 25 August 1775, BC.I.241.

proximity can contribute to permanence: "There is on the globe one single spot, the possessor of which is our natural and habitual enemy. It is New Orleans."[107] Natural friends and enemies are particularistic, vary according to circumstances, and describe the actual, volatile relations among states.

The Revolution, on this theory, converted England into a natural enemy of the United States. At the same time, it changed France, England's natural enemy, into America's natural friend.[108] But because the international landscape could change, such a situation was subject to reversal with geopolitical fortunes. When France acquired Louisiana from Spain, Jefferson was ready to throw over his natural friend and enter an alliance with Britain.[109] When a year later the United States acquired Louisiana for itself, the impending alliance with Britain was called off. Much later, despite the embargo on British goods and the subsequent War of 1812, Jefferson held out the prospect of eventual reconciliation with England, reviving his earliest feelings:

> [If the present government were thrown off,] I am in hopes a purer nation will result, and a purer government be instituted, one which, instead of endeavoring to make us their natural enemies, will see in us what we really are, their natural friends and brethren, and more interested in a fraternal connection with them than with any other nation on earth.[110]

Outside the models of family and friendship, the most important contribution of nature to Jefferson's view of international relations was the Atlantic Ocean. It is the overarching axiom of the First Inaugural that the United States is "kindly separated by nature and a wide ocean from the exterminating havoc of one quarter of the globe." This is particular nature with a permanent face. It fixed the difference between the Old World and the New and was to be America's protection from Europe. When supplemented by claims of national interest, it was to become the foundation of the Monroe Doctrine: "We should consider any attempt on [the part of European powers] to extend their system to any position of this hemisphere as dangerous to our peace and safety."

---

107. TJ to Robert R. Livingston, 18 April 1802, F.VIII.144. Cf. Hamilton on the "axiom in politics, that vicinity, or nearness of situation, constitutes nations natural enemies." *Federalist* No. 6 (Wright ed.), 113.

108. TJ to William Carmichael, 15 December 1787, BC.XII.424 ("I considered the British as our natural enemies"); TJ to Robert R. Livingston, 18 April 1802, F.VIII.144 ("We have ever looked to [France] as our *natural friend*").

109. TJ to Robert R. Livingston, 18 April 1802, F.VIII.145 ("we must marry ourselves to the British fleet and nation").

110. TJ to John Adams, 25 November 1816, C.II.498. The language of natural enemies and friends may be found throughout Jefferson's correspondence, applying not only to England and France but also to the Caribbean, Latin America, Turkey, and states and regions of the United States.

In his campaign against European domination of the New World Jefferson scouted beyond the ideas of the First Inaugural and the Monroe Doctrine. In doing so he illustrated the difficulty of attempting to combine particular and universal conceptions of nature. The Western Hemisphere, he remarked at the height of the Napoleonic Wars,

> having a different system of interests flowing from different climates, different soils, different productions, different modes of existence, and its own local relations and duties, is made subservient to all the petty interests of [Europe], to *their* laws, *their* regulations, *their* passions and wars, and interdicted from social intercourse, from the exchange of mutual duties and comforts with their neighbors, enjoined on all men by the laws of nature.[111]

But how can it be that universal laws of nature mandate certain relationships that particular facts of nature prevent? One possibility is that enough sordid particular facts can outweigh the purest of universal ideas. Thus, Jefferson once distinguished those nations favoring "unlimited commerce and war" from those "which are for peace and agriculture."[112]

A more startling possibility is that there is a variable natural law: "I strongly suspect that our geographical peculiarities may call for a different code of natural law to govern our relations with other nations from that which the conditions of Europe have given rise to there."[113] But how can a natural law that differs from place to place provide firm guidance for international conduct? Fortunately Jefferson did not pursue the idea.

In a world in which peace was presumed to be the natural state of mankind but conflict was so extensive, was there no durable law of nature to follow? Jefferson promoted one such standard, a procedural rule of natural law that had been emphasized by Hugo Grotius. It was *pacta servanda sunt,* "agreements are to be honored." This doctrine acts as a touchstone for Jefferson's natural/international law in three ways: (1) it shows how the law of nature is the same for nations as for individuals; (2) it is an actual, beneficial rule of conduct that reduces the rigors of warfare; and (3) it exemplifies the authority of treatises on the law of nature and nations, which Jefferson invariably consulted in formulating foreign policy.

Nations must honor their agreements just as individuals do, because society is only the sum of the individuals composing it. Using the

111. TJ to Clement Caine, 16 September 1811, LB.XIII.91.
112. TJ to William H. Crawford, 20 June 1816, LB.XV.29.
113. TJ to Samuel L. Mitchill, 13 June 1800, quoted in Mitchill, *A Discourse on the Character and Services of Thomas Jefferson,* 64.

reasoning that yielded "the earth belongs to the living," whatever holds for people individually also holds for peoples collectively: "Nations, like . . . individuals, stand towards each other only in the relations of natural right."[114] If *pacta servanda sunt* is always right for individuals, it is always right for nations.

Second, not only does warfare not set aside the fundamental rule to keep one's promises, it actually heightens the need to maintain trust and honor between nations. By setting out rules ahead of time for the unhappy circumstances of war and then honoring them when war comes, a rule of natural law can restrain acts of belligerents. Jefferson looked to the doctrine for aid on two occasions concerning treatment of prisoners of war. Required to deal with a notorious prisoner when he was governor of Virginia, he wrote of "the highest idea of the sacredness of those contracts which take place between nation and nation at war."[115] As minister in Europe, he bore in mind *pacta servanda sunt* when he prepared the draft of a treaty with Portugal to secure the humane treatment of prisoners in the event of war. "The state of war," he declared, "is precisely that for which [the treaty articles] are provided, and during which they are to be as sacredly observed as the most acknowledged articles in the laws of nature or nations."[116]

A final lesson of *pacta servanda sunt* is that it derives much of its legitimacy from treatises on the law of nature and of nations. Since nations possessed no innate moral sense or an exemplar such as Jesus, it is the writings of jurists of the seventeenth and eighteenth centuries that constitute Jefferson's main sources for a law of nature in international affairs. In a formal opinion when he was secretary of state he claimed that it was in "the head and heart of every rational and honest man [that] nature has written her moral laws, and [there] every man may read them for himself." But at the same time, he quoted—in parallel columns— the four most prominent authorities on the law of nations.[117] *Pacta*

114. TJ to John Sinclair, 23 March 1798, 4 Trans. Am. Phil. Soc. 321 (1799). See also TJ, "Opinion on the question whether the United States have a right to renounce their treaties with France," 28 April 1793, LB.III.228 ("between society and society, the same moral duties exist as . . . between the individuals composing them"); TJ to the Society of Tammany, 29 February 1808, LB.XVI.302 ("moral obligations . . . constitute a law for nations as well as individuals"); and TJ to Benjamin Austin, 9 January 1816, LB.XIV.391 ("moral laws established by the Author of nature between nation and nation, as between man and man").

115. TJ to George Washington, 17 July 1779, BC.III.41. On this troubling incident see M.I.308–12.

116. TJ, Project of a Treaty, March–April 1786, BC.IX.420.

117. TJ, "Opinion on the treaties with France," 28 April 1793, LB.III.229. The four authorities were Grotius (1583–1645), Samuel Pufendorf (1632–84), Christian Wolff (1679–1754), and Emerich de Vattel (1714–67). LB.III.235–37. The same authorities were cited in TJ, "Report relative to negotiations with Spain to secure the free navigation of the Mississippi, and a port on the same," 18 March 1792, LB.III.179.

servanda sunt may have sprung from the heart for individuals, but for nations it was aided by scholarly explication. International law was conducted by professors, not ploughmen.

The phrase "law of nature and nations" was so familiar to Jefferson that Madison could write him simply about "Books on the Law of N. and N." Many of the volumes in Jefferson's library on the subject had precisely that title.[118] As with other "nature" subjects in the library, Jefferson searched for and sometimes changed his mind about a proper place for the law of nature and nations in his collection and in his curricular schemes as well. It is the moral character of the law of nature and nations that predominates in his library catalogues of 1783 and 1815. There the field is allied with ethics, not law (by which Jefferson meant positive or municipal law only, law that can be enforced).[119] In two of his curricular plans he also linked the law of nature and nations to moral philosophy and not to law.[120]

Near the end of his life, however, a significant change took place in Jefferson's ideas about teaching the law of nature and nations. The evidence is in the plan for the University of Virginia. One cannot tell whether the change was the result of working with others (he had composed the earlier plans himself) or of his own growing sense that the law of nature and nations could be made practical only if it were distinguished from ethics. But of the ten professorships proposed for the university, the last three are these:

VIII.   Government
        Political Economy
        Law of Nature and Nations
        History, being interwoven with Politics and Law
IX.   Law, municipal
X.   Ideology; General Grammar; Ethics; Rhetoric; Belles Lettres, and the fine arts

The law of nature and nations is separated from ethics here. Further— and this is crucial—it has not at the same time joined positive law.

118. James Madison to TJ, 16 March 1784, BC.VII.37. The treatises Jefferson cited in his official opinions are all titled "Law of nature and nations." For secondary studies, see Louis Martin Sears, "Jefferson and the Laws of Nations"; Charles M. Wiltse, "Thomas Jefferson on the Law of Nations;" and Stuart, *The Half-Way Pacifist*.

119. He once attempted to separate a "natural law of nations" from a "conventional law of nations" for his library, but that proved unworkable, and he retreated to the combined name under ethics. S.I.ix; facsimile page before S.I.1; S.II.1. The plan for the University of Virginia library (1820–25) is similar to that in the catalogue of 1815. Pdvr.1093.

120. See TJ, Bill No. 80, 1779, BC.II.541; and TJ to Peter Carr, 7 September 1814, LB.XIX.215, 219.

Instead it has found a home with politics, where, under the name international law, it has largely remained.[121]

In accord with his European authorities, Jefferson held that the law of nations and nature was composed of three branches: nature, usage, and convention.[122] The first and most important of these branches, "natural law proper," or universal nature, supplies a standard for the other two. It was a standard so important to Jefferson that he once went so far as to mistranslate a Latin text as "law of nature" when it plainly said "law of nations" (indeed said so in an adjacent column).[123] But it was usage that constituted the bulk of the available law of nature and nations and therefore the bulk of the treatises. The third branch, "special conventions," consisted of positive law, or treaties.

Jefferson realized that on occasion the three branches of the law of nature and nations might conflict. In particular, a treaty might alter usage or deviate from the standard set by natural law proper. One might assume that in such a conflict Jefferson would uphold the pure natural law principle. But the one time when it mattered, he chose the treaty over nature and devised a special rationale for his choice.

The subject was the rights of neutral shipping when the British conducted forcible searches of American ships carrying goods destined for France. Jefferson presumed that the applicable natural law principle was that "goods follow the owner."[124] According to this principle, if Britain were at war with France, goods owned by French citizens could be seized from any ship at sea, including an American one, and wherever found. But adhering to this principle caused an "inconvenience," namely, the search of neutral ships (in this case American ships) carrying French goods, with the result that neutrals might become belligerents and so enlarge the conflict. An enlarged conflict, however, was an affront to a greater principle of natural law, namely, that nations remain at peace with each other. Some way had to be found to resolve this disagreement in the teachings of nature. The way that most seafaring nations found was through treaties or conventions. But nations that did this consciously followed a principle they did not think was based on nature.

121. TJ, Rockfish Gap Report, August 1818, PJ.338. When the university was actually founded, professorships VIII and IX were combined. This still left the law of nature and nations separated from ethics, however. Minutes of the Board of Visitors of the University of Virginia, 7 April 1824, LB.XIX.434–35.

122. TJ, "Opinion relative to a case of recapture . . . of slaves," 23 December 1792, LB.III.213. See, similarly, TJ, "Opinion on the treaties with France," 28 April 1793, LB.III.228.

123. TJ "The Batture at New Orleans," 1812, LB.XVIII.67 (*jure gentium* mistranslated as "by the law of nature"); see also LB.XVIII.86 ("*jure gentium* [i.e., *gentis humanae*]" misrepresented as "By the law of nations [i.e., of nature]").

124. The quotations in this and the following paragraphs, unless otherwise noted,

The conventional principle adopted by most of Europe (Britain was the chief exception) was that "free ships made free goods." A ship of a neutral (free) nation was immunized from having goods on it seized by belligerents, no matter who owned the goods or where the ship was heading. Since the United States was neutral, since it sailed many ships, and since there were few American goods in French ships that the British might seize, American shipping interests understandably favored this rule. Jefferson consequently argued, successfully, for the adoption of the new rule as American policy, even though the United States had not itself concluded treaties stipulating it and even though it ran against both the law of nature and historical usage.

Yet it was not easy to forgo the law of nature. If, as Jefferson admitted, "we are to consider the [early] practice of nations as the sole and sufficient evidence of the law of nature among nations, we should unquestionably place this principle [that goods follow the owner] among those of the natural laws." But, he continued, the United States had no more control over the development of the conventional law (which had been practiced for more than a century) than over the original law of nature (which had been practiced before that). On this ground America was no more bound to follow one than it was the other. Perhaps, he rationalized, it was the modern rule that was "the genuine principle dictated by natural morality," in which case the United States should of course follow it.

This last proposition Jefferson elaborated with an inventive argument. Since belligerents could not seize the property of one another when that property was on neutral territory, because they did not possess that territory, by analogy no belligerent could subject the ship of a neutral nation to a search at sea, because, "on an element which nature has not subjected to the jurisdiction of any particular nation, but has made common to all," no belligerent possessed it, either. "By what law," he concluded, can a belligerent "enter that ship while in a peaceable and orderly use of the common element? We recognize no natural precept for submission to such a right."

With this argument Jefferson had turned the usual course of reasoning on its head. Instead of nature setting the standard for convention, convention pointed the way towards nature. The earlier natural law evidently had not been well thought out. As he summed it up without restricting the language even to neutral nations: "The sea belongs to no nation. No nation therefore has a natural right to search the ship of

come from TJ, "Explanation of the origin of the principle that 'free bottoms make free goods.'" 20 December 1793, F.VI.485; and TJ to Robert R. Livingston, 9 September 1801, F.VII.88–92.

another on the high seas. The contrary practice has been an abuse, and the abandonment of it is a reformation of that abuse, a re-establishment of natural right."[125]

Jefferson was capable not only of revising the meaning of natural law but also of admitting its practical failure. Protesting wrongs inflicted by the French and the British, he wrote that "the laws of nature and the usages which have hitherto regulated the intercourse of nations and interposed some restraint between power and right [are] now totally disregarded." While the United States was willing "to relax for a time, and in some cases, that strictness of right which the laws of nature . . . entitle us to," the natural lawyer conceded the ineffectiveness of the natural law.[126]

No matter the turnarounds or embarrassments, by what methods were Americans to define the rights to which the laws of nature and nations entitled them? Jefferson developed several answers to this question. Within the executive, whether as minister to France, secretary of state, or president, he provided many of the definitions himself. But he also asked for help from the judiciary, collating for George Washington, for instance, a list of twenty-nine questions to submit to the Supreme Court on "the construction of our treaties, on the laws of nature and nations, and on the laws of the land." At about the same time, he proposed that Congress consider domestic legislation to uphold "the duties of a nation at peace towards those at war, imposed by the law and usages of nature, and nations."[127]

When Congress and the judiciary supplied insufficient aid, he looked to the people, entreating "all our citizens to recover and preserve the rights which nature had given them."[128] And how would the citizens accomplish this? Ultimately by virtue of their numbers, which Jefferson believed for the United States would correspond with the number of their virtues. More accurately, this meant through national power, which was a reflection of numbers. That numbers are necessary to uphold natural rights might suggest one of the definitions of justice in Plato's *Republic:* that it is simply the interest of the stronger. But Jefferson believed that national might could only enforce, not define, natural

125. TJ, "Observations on the Congre-Projet," November 1788, BC.XIV.162.
126. TJ to Republicans of the County of Niagara, 24 February 1809, LB.XVI.343–44; TJ to the Legislature, Council, and House of Representatives of the Territory of Orleans, 18 June 1808, LB.XVI.306. See also TJ to William Short, 28 July 1791, F.V.364 ("circumstances sometimes require, that rights the most unquestionable should be advanced with delicacy").
127. TJ to George Washington (enclosure), 18 July 1792, F.VI.351 (none of the questions, which had been drafted by Hamilton, explicitly referred to the law of nature, and the Supreme Court declined to answer them); TJ, ms. note, spring 1793, F.VI.276.
128. TJ to James Hochie, 2 April 1809, LB.XVI.359.

right.[129] Despite the likelihood of a self-serving quality when invoked, force was to be used to vindicate, not to violate, the directives of natural law.

Jefferson's law of nature and nations was as diverse as were the needs of American foreign policy, but it was perhaps at its most moral when it mirrored the rule of the Good Samaritan. Outspoken on behalf of a natural obligation to come to the aid of persons in distress, Jefferson pled the cause of a Spanish commander who allegedly violated regulations by aiding American vessels: "The generous character of the nation is a security to us that their regulations can in no instance run counter to the laws of nature; and among the first of her laws is that which bids us to succour those in distress."[130] A variant of the rule was "Do no harm to those who have caused no injury." On the basis of this standard, Jefferson was cautious about binding the nation to extradition rules when the alleged criminals had committed no harm against the United States. Although there existed a "natural right of arresting and re-delivering fugitives," he said, this was not the same as a natural obligation to do so. Therefore, while he sanctioned the delivery of fugitives charged with ordinary homicide, other crimes did not warrant extradition.[131] Jefferson also noted an inverse Good Samaritan axiom: that a nation had no natural right to intervene against punishment that was deserved. If the British strike at the Indians, he wrote during the Revolution, "these will have a natural right to punish the aggressors and we none to hinder them."[132]

Shorn of their context and enlarged in their spirit, Jefferson's uses of natural law and right in foreign affairs seem universal and unexceptionable. But as is by now evident, his uses are typically discovered and manipulated so as to serve his definition of the national interest. Jefferson claimed that diplomats, when abroad, are "not bound to an acquaintance with the laws of the land [where they serve]. . . . They are bound by the laws of natural justice only." At home, however, "every nation has of natural right, entirely and exclusively, all the jurisdiction

129. See TJ to William Short, 3 October 1801, LB.X.287 ("We feel ourselves strong, and daily growing stronger. The census now concluded, shows we have added to our population a third of what it was ten years ago. . . . If we can delay but a few years the necessity of vindicating the laws of nature on the ocean, we shall be the more sure of doing it with effect").

130. TJ to William Carmichael, 11 April 1790, BC.XVI.330. See also TJ to Albert Gallatin, 24 January 1807, LB.XI.144 ("laws of humanity make it a duty for nations, as well as individuals, to succour those whom accident and distress have thrown upon them"); and TJ to Alexander, Emperor of Russia, 15 June 1804, LB.XIX.143 (acknowledging aid against "barbarians whose habitual violations of the laws of nature" had left an American ship stranded on the coast of Tripoli).

131. TJ to William Carmichael and William Short, 22 March 1792, LB.VIII.330–31 (enclosure on "mutual delivery of fugitives from justice").

132. TJ to George Rogers Clark, 29 January 1780, BC.III.276.

which may be rightfully exercised in the territory it occupies."[133] In an attempt to steer a neutral's course between France and Britain in the 1790s, he stated (to a British diplomat) that all nations (in this case France) had a right to cruise on the American or any coast. It was "a right not derived from our permission, but from the law of nature." At the same time he argued (to a French diplomat) that America's prohibition against arming the vessels of belligerents (such as France) in the ports of neutrals (the United States) was not "contrary to the law of nature and the usage of nations."[134] Such refined analyses may have strained the law of nature, but to Jefferson they came easily.

At heart Jefferson appeared uncomfortable with international relations altogether. If only other nations would become like the United States and adopt the principles of universal nature for their political systems; or, alternatively, if only the world would leave the United States alone in its superior environment. Although doggedly extracting from nature a number of rules for the behavior of nations premised on his deepest hope that by nature mankind was at peace, Jefferson confronted a reality of international conflict that rebuffed him on nearly every hand. He did hold out an international vision. Just as often he retreated to the pastures of home.

POLITICAL ECONOMY

Like most thinkers of his era, Jefferson did not divorce economics from politics. He also had much to say on the subject known in his era as political economy. He never defined the term himself, but he would have agreed with his Philadelphia friend George Logan that

> by *political economy* is to be understood, that natural order appointed by the Creator of the Universe, for the purpose of promoting the happiness of men in united society. This science is supported by the physical order of cultivation, calculated to render the soil the most productive possible.[135]

Here are Jefferson's beliefs succinctly laid out: political economy is an ordained natural order; it promotes the natural right of mankind to

133. TJ to William Short, 30 September 1790, BC.XVIII.545 (the statement was provoked by a dispute between Jefferson and his former landlord in Paris); TJ to Gouverneur Morris, 16 August 1793, F.VI.382–83 (admitting that a nation might still, by agreement, cede a portion of its natural jurisdiction to judges appointed by another nation).

134. TJ to George Hammond, 9 September 1793, F.VI.423; TJ to Edmond C. Genêt, 17 June 1793, LB.IX.134. For the role of nature and natural law in Jefferson's effort to secure American control of the Mississippi, see the discussion in chapter VI.

135. George Logan, *Letters, addressed to the yeomanry of the United States* (1791), 11, S.3156. On the use of the term "political economy" see Drew R. McCoy, *The Elusive Republic*, 5–7.

pursue happiness; it is best undertaken close to nature. But it is in just this multiple vision—political, economic, and ethical—that trouble lies. It is not easy to impose a coherence on Jefferson's economic views.[136]

As an economist Jefferson has usually been considered inconsistent, naive, or simply wrong. Against the program of Alexander Hamilton in setting national economic policy he was certainly unsuccessful. He explained a change in his views as a consequence of changing circumstances. But however his economic views are assessed, underlying them was always nature. It is this that accounts for both the attractiveness and the inadequacies of his doctrines. Nature pervades his thoughts on property, trade, patents, and a preferred livelihood on the land.

It was through nature that Jefferson rather uncertainly explained how and why property came into existence. It was "a moot point," he claimed, "whether the origin of any kind of property was derived from nature."[137] But he is surely close to Locke, who believed that property was originally formed by the addition of human labor to some portion of nature that was held in common. If one is to engage in farming, as Jefferson expected, then (leaving aside slavery) occupying the land and laboring on it amount to the same thing. Assuming that Jefferson uses the words interchangeably, the equation is that labor or occupancy, plus land, equals property. Keeping the labor-occupancy identity in mind, the argument is, first, that "the spontaneous energies of the earth are a gift of nature, but they require the labor [occupancy] of man to direct their operation"; and second, that "no individual has, of natural right, a separate property in an acre of land," but gains that through occupancy (labor), and if occupation is relinquished, "the property goes with it."[138]

---

136. William D. Grampp shows that much sense can be made of Jefferson's evidently changing economic views by distinguishing them according to three periods: (1) agrarian-based self-sufficiency (the era of *Notes on the State of Virginia*); (2) free trade and laissez faire (from the 1790s into his first term as president); and (3) protectionist (from 1805 on, bowing to the pressures of the Napoleonic Wars). "A Re-examination of Jeffersonian Economics." Other overviews are Joseph Dorfman, "The Economic Philosophy of Thomas Jefferson"; and Richard E. Ellis, "The Political Economy of Thomas Jefferson."

Jefferson's economic doctrines resemble those of John Locke, the French Physiocrats, and Adam Smith without being identical to any of them. The resemblance to the first two is mentioned in the text. Jefferson professed admiration for Adam Smith but did not make much of him. He followed Smith in his antimercantilism, but his heart was in agriculture, not manufacturing and commerce. In addition, his economic arguments were aligned with moral ones, while Smith's explication, despite a moral basis, was that of an economist.

137. TJ to Isaac McPherson, 13 August 1813, LB.XIII.333. Blackstone had said that property "is probably founded in nature" with "modifications entirely derived from society." *Commentaries*, I.137. See, generally, Stanley N. Katz, "Thomas Jefferson and the Right to Property in Revolutionary America," 19 J. Law & Economics 467–88 (1976).

138. TJ to Charles Willson Peale, 17 April 1813, LB.XVIII.277; TJ to Isaac McPherson, 13 August 1813, LB.XIII.333.

If the material origin of property lies in physical nature, the teleological origin of property lies in human nature, and the two are eventually brought together. It is a law of human nature to pursue happiness. It is a natural right to comply with a natural law. The right to pursue happiness means the right to use our faculties, which means the right to labor. Laboring means, primarily, working the land. Possession of land is thereby required to fulfill natural law and right. The only, though important, limitation to this is that possession and laboring take place "without violating the rights of other sensible beings." Such a violation would occur if there were a conjunction of "uncultivated lands and unemployed poor." In that case it would be "clear that the laws of property have been so far extended as to violate natural right."[139]

That Jefferson was conscious of society's right to regulate property, that property rights are not natural rights, is suggested by his adopting the language of pursuit of happiness but not the language of property in composing the Declaration of Independence. A dozen years later, when "life, liberty, and the pursuit of happiness" was modified to "life, liberty, and property" for inclusion in the Fifth Amendment of the national Bill of Rights, this was a modification that was possible in Jeffersonian theory only because ideas about property had left the Declaration's realm of nature and entered the Constitution's realm of society. Although no one could by nature be deprived of the right to pursue happiness, a person could be deprived by society of certain rights to control property (so long as due process were not violated).[140]

The principal characteristic of Jefferson's natural political economy, also flowing from the natural right to the use of one's faculties, is freedom of competition. This means freedom of occupation, freedom of trade, freedom from monopoly, and, generally, freedom from government intervention in the operation of the economic order. Jefferson's comments on freedom of occupation illuminate the right to pursue happiness. One pursues happiness by pursuing a calling; and everyone "has a natural right to choose that which he thinks most likely to give him comfortable subsistence." But this proposition is qualified, as before, by a prohibition against violating the natural rights of others. "No

---

139. TJ to John Manners, 12 June 1817, F.X.87; TJ to Dupont de Nemours, 24 April 1816, LB.XIV.490; TJ to James Madison, 18 October 1785, BC.VIII.682.

140. Jefferson had nothing directly to do with preparing the Fifth Amendment, since he was in Paris at the time. But that he was quite aware of these distinctions is confirmed by his unsuccessful attempt to have the word "property" deleted from the list of inalienable rights in the French Declaration of the Rights of Man and Citizen. TJ to Lafayette, 10 July 1789, BC.XV.230. For the possible natural right to pass property on to one's children, a corollary to the original mixed natural and social right to property, see TJ, "A Note communicated to the Editor" (Joseph Milligan), 6 April 1816, LB.XIV.466; TJ, Second Inaugural Address, 4 March 1805, Pdvr.414; and TJ, Autobiography (1821), KP.51–52.

man," Jefferson remarked, "can have a natural right to enter on a calling by which it is at least ten to one he will ruin many better men than himself."[141]

Freedom of trade, which was closely associated with freedom of occupation, Jefferson surrounded with natural rights, especially in an international setting. As colonists, Americans proposed a "free trade with all parts of the world . . . as of natural right." After the Revolution the same right was enjoyed by an independent United States.[142] The benefits of free trade were realized best by following the doctrine of comparative advantage, according to which each country would produce "that which nature has best fitted it to produce."[143] Unfortunately, because the world did not act on the theory of free trade and its corollary, freedom of the seas, natural rights often suffered. This was true under both the policy of mercantilism and the burdens of war. When war came Jefferson especially pressed for natural rights of occupations and trade, but unsuccessfully. Indeed, it was precisely "in the tyranny of those nations who deprive us of the natural right of trading with our neighbors" that he saw the source of war.[144]

If the world would not conform to the requirements of a natural economy, Jefferson still argued for one inside the United States. He accepted some accommodation—a "proper interference," he called it—in order to promote the growth of new industry, to meet established foreign competition, or to have certain goods available in the face of foreign control of ocean commerce.[145] But his underlying doctrine was simple: "In [political economy], as in medicine, it is best to leave nature

141. TJ, "Thoughts on Lotteries," February 1826, F.X.367; TJ to Nathaniel Tracy, 17 August 1785, BC.VIII.399 (on trading without adequate capital). See also TJ to John W. Eppes, 24 June 1813, LB.XIII.277 ("no one has a natural right to the trade of a money lender, but he who has money to lend").

142. TJ, Summary View (1774), BC.I.123; TJ to William Short, 28 July 1791, LB.VIII.219.

143. TJ, "Report on the Privileges and Restrictions of the Commerce of the United States in Foreign Countries," December 1793, F.VI.479. For another observation in the classical economics of free trade, see TJ, "Observations on the Whale-Fishery," November 1788, BC.XIV.242 (when one good largely useful for the same purposes as another freely competes with the second, the competition "limits its price . . . and becomes, as it were, a law of its nature").

144. TJ to George Washington, 4 December 1788, BC.XIV.328. See also TJ to Thomas Pinckney, 7 September 1793, F.VI.413 ("when two nations go to war, those who choose to live in peace retain their natural right to pursue their agriculture, manufactures, and their ordinary vocations").

145. TJ to John Hancock, 20 February 1791, BC.XIX.237. See also TJ, "Opinion on Proposal for Manufacture of Woolen Textiles in Virginia," 3 December 1790, BC.XVIII.120–21; TJ, Seventh and Eighth Annual Messages, 27 October 1807 and 8 November 1808, Pdvr. 434, 441 (justifying embargo legislation); TJ to Gen. Samuel Smith, 3 May 1823, LB.XV.433 ("foster for a while certain infant manufactures"); and TJ to William A. Burwell, 25 February 1810, LB. XII.364 (outlining three stages of retreat in strictly upholding the nation's natural rights in maritime trade).

to her agency without interruption in cases we do not perfectly understand."[146] In Jeffersonian theory the only significant economic role of the government was to keep it free for producers, merchants, and consumers.

Nothing seemed to Jefferson more economically "unnatural" than monopoly, an institution he thought possible only if it secured the support of the government. His most extended and dispiriting encounter with monopolies was with the Farmers-General of France, the company of influential men to whom the king, by farming out the collection of national revenues, gave a monopoly over tobacco. The experience in France led him to urge a provision against monopolies in the Bill of Rights. Although the attempt did not succeed, he was pleased to assure the French that in the United States "neither our republic nor its ministers meddle with any thing commercial. They leave their commerce free, to their citizens and others, convinced it is never better than when left to itself."[147]

No matter what form monopolies took, Jefferson considered them an affront to the teaching of nature, nowhere more than in the case of monopolies in the form of patent rights. He thought that ideas, formulas, and the physical properties of materials were all part of nature and were therefore no more the legitimate subject of private property than was the sea or unworked land. Although the capacities of physical nature might be discovered, nobody invented them. Most distinctively, ideas are the product of natural understanding, which all humans possess from birth. A socially declared property right in invention, therefore, had to overcome a stiff variety of arguments from nature.

Already cautious about the definition of property rights in things, Jefferson was even more doubtful about rights associated with ideas:

> It would be curious then if an idea, the fugitive fermentation of an individual brain, could, of natural right, be claimed in exclusive and stable property. If nature has made any one thing less susceptible than all others of exclusive property, it is the action of the thinking power called an idea, which an individual may exclusively possess as long as he keeps it to himself, but the moment it is divulged, it forces itself into the possession of everyone, and the receiver cannot dispossess himself of it.

What was wonderful about ideas, Jefferson continued in an access of Enlightenment liberality, was that unlike land or water, or ordinary physical materials, nature had created ideas inherently unlimited:

146. TJ to Littleton Dennis Teackle, 22 June 1824, FBx.286. See also TJ to Thomas Diggs, 19 June 1788, BC.XIII.261 (state policy is to "let things take their natural course without help or impediment, which is generally the best"); TJ to Joseph Priestley, 29 November 1802, F.VIII.180; and TJ to William B. Bibb, 28 July 1808, LB.XII.107.

147. TJ to Cavalier fils, 27 July 1789, BC.XV.311.

He who receives an idea from me receives instruction himself without lessening mine; as he who lights his taper at mine, receives light without darkening me. That ideas should freely spread from one to another over the globe for the moral and mutual instruction of man, and improvement of his condition, seems to have been peculiarly designed by nature, when she made them . . . incapable of confinement or exclusive appropriation. Inventions then cannot, in nature, be a subject of property.[148]

Because inventions could not be property in nature, Jefferson only with the greatest reluctance accepted them as property in society and was willing to give up a considerable measure of technological progress in the service of this conviction. He argued passionately for a constitutional clause severely restricting such rights.[149] When, as secretary of state, he became the equivalent of the first commissioner of patents, he examined the applications of inventors with the strictest scrutiny in order to ensure that the tests of originality and usefulness had been met. He declined to patent his own improvement in the design of the ploughshare, convinced that no monopoly was deserved for a design created merely by applying ordinary laws of nature to easily obtained materials and that no monopoly for himself could outweigh the social benefit to be gained through the free dissemination of the idea.[150] When he did come to agree that limited patent rights could be socially valuable, he still insisted that "natural understanding" would eventually suggest the same devices without the incentive of a monopoly for the original inventor.[151]

If Jefferson failed to distinguish between a patent as a spur to invention and a patent as a spur to production (and production as the prelude to profit), it was understandable. In the rather static economy that he envisioned, production was not an especially important value, while in the intellectual world he inhabited, invention was. Regardless of his own position, however, he encouraged others to proceed with their inventions, for instance with the steam engine and the submarine, keenly aware that a successful invention depended on understanding and conforming to the laws of nature.[152]

148. TJ to Isaac McPherson, 13 August 1813, LB.XIII.333, 334. See also TJ to Henry Dearborn, 21 June 1807, LB.XI.252 ("the field of knowledge is the common property of all mankind").

149. See TJ to James Madison, 31 July 1788, BC.XIII.443; Madison to TJ, 17 October 1788, BC.XIV.21; James Rumsey to TJ, 6 June 1789, BC.XV.171; and TJ to James Madison, 29 August 1789, BC.XV.368.

150. See TJ to Charles Willson Peale, 13 June 1815, LB.VIII.288; and TJ to George Fleming, 2 December 1815, LB.XIV.369.

151. TJ to Oliver Evans, 2 May 1807, LB.XI.201.

152. See TJ to James Sylvester McLean, 25 October 1802, M.IV.181 ("no law of nature forbids us to hope [that the use of steam will benefit man], and the ingenuity of man leaves us to despair of nothing within the laws of nature"); and TJ to Robert Fulton,

Nearest to nature and nearest to Jefferson's heart in political economy lies agriculture.[153] It is in this field that his ethical, political, and
economic theories of nature are completely intertwined. It was on
behalf of agriculture that he waged his greatest struggles over public
policy. Although the candid concessions he eventually made showed
that he would accept a mix of occupations in society, his lifelong preference was expressed in a rigid order: agriculture, manufactures, commerce, and navigation. This primacy can be found in the most diverse
contexts. Agriculture was the first of "four pillars" of national prosperity and the last to benefit from a public debt. It was the first of the
interests that higher education was charged with promoting. It was the
first of several "objects of attention" for Americans traveling in Europe.
It was the first occupation deserving of protection in wartime, because
farmers were exercising a natural right "for the subsistence of mankind."[154]

The economic theory underlying Jefferson's attachment to agriculture is that both the ultimate and the greatest economic value belong
with raw nature. Agriculture is productive, manufacturing is sterile,
and it is nature that makes this so. In typical high rhetoric: "To the labor
of the husbandman, a vast addition is made by the spontaneous energies
of the earth on which it is employed: for one grain of wheat committed
to the earth, she renders twenty, thirty, and even fifty fold, whereas to
the labor of the manufacturer nothing is added."[155]

Jefferson's is the doctrine of the French Physiocrats, who developed
the first complete system of economics. "Physiocracy" itself means the
rule of nature, and the principal collection of writings of the school's
founder, François Quesnay, breathed nature in its title—it was about the
"natural constitution of government."[156] Concentration of land in the

21 July 1812, LB.XIX.193 ("no law of nature opposes" the effectiveness of the submarine). See, similarly, TJ to Matthew Carr, 19 June 1813, LB.XIII.263; and TJ to James
Madison, 13 July 1813, LB.XIX.191.

153. Among the relevant studies are Douglas Greybill Adair, "The Intellectual Origins of Jeffersonian Democracy" (stressing Greek and Roman sources of Jefferson's agrarian ideas); Chester E. Eisinger, "The Influence of Natural Rights and Physiocratic Doctrines on American Agrarian Thought during the Revolutionary Period"; A. Whitney
Griswold, *Farming and Democracy,* chap. 2; McCoy, *The Elusive Republic;* Joyce Appleby,
"Commercial Farming and the 'Agrarian Myth' in the Early Republic"; Richard K.
Matthews, *The Radical Politics of Thomas Jefferson;* and Robert E. Shalhope, "Agriculture,"
in Peterson, *Thomas Jefferson: A Reference Biography,* 385–96.

154. TJ, First Annual Message, 8 December 1801, Pdvr.392; TJ to John W. Eppes, 6
November 1813, F.IX.411; TJ, Rockfish Gap Report, August 1818, PJ.334; TJ, "Hints to
Americans Travelling in Europe," 19 June 1788, BC.XIII.269; TJ, "Reasons in support of
the new proposed articles in the treaties of commerce," 10 November 1784, BC.VII.492.

155. TJ to Benjamin Austin, 9 January 1816, F.X.9. See, similarly, TJ to J. Lithgow, 4
January 1805, LB.XI.56; and TJ to Sir John Sinclair, 24 March 1798, S.I.351.

156. *Physiocratie, ou constitution naturelle du gouvernement le plus avantageux au genre*

hands of a few, the most apparent violation of a physiocratic natural economy, is the subject of Jefferson's affecting observations on land use in Europe, prompted by his conversation with a poor woman he met near Paris: "I asked myself what could be the reason so many should be permitted to beg who are willing to work, in a country where there is a very considerable proportion of uncultivated lands? These lands are undisturbed only for the sake of game." Recognizing "that an equal division of property [was] impracticable," Jefferson poured forth ideas to correct the situation in Virginia as far as feasible.[157]

He asked for legislation leading to the equal division of family property among children so that it would become compatible with the "natural affections of the human mind." He proposed that property of low value be exempt from taxation entirely and that taxable property be subject to progressive rates. He insisted that society find employment for anyone whose land was expropriated for nonagricultural purposes—otherwise "the fundamental right to labor the earth returns to the unemployed." He tentatively suggested that the poor be entitled to cultivate unused lands, "paying a moderate rent to the owners." And he hoped that Virginia would provide "by every possible means that as few as possible shall be without a little portion of land," for as he summed up his creed, "the small landholder is the most precious part of the state."

In its artless transition from economic policy to moral assertion, Jefferson's letter to Madison is typical of his expressions about life as a farmer. The most well known of these declarations appears in *Notes on the State of Virginia,* where in two chapters ostensibly on the topics

---

humain (1768), S.2370. Jefferson's tie to physiocratic doctrine was as much personal as doctrinal. Quesnay's editor and leading disciple was Pierre Samuel Dupont de Nemours, Jefferson's friend, who emigrated to the United States in 1799. Jefferson did not agree with everything the French school held. The Physiocrats were aristocratic in their political views, Dupont, for instance, favoring a landed-property qualification for voting. But basic agreement with the school's doctrines about the primacy of agriculture in a natural economic order mark Jefferson as physiocratic in his sympathies. He nevertheless translated from the French a work in political economy by Destutt de Tracy, who, though in the line of thinkers descending from the Physiocrats, rejected the centrality of agriculture for a correct (and natural) political economy. TJ to Joseph Milligan, 6 April 1816 LB.XIV.459–61.

157. TJ to James Madison, 28 October 1785, BC.VIII.682. (Though the context differs utterly, the argument about lands uncultivated for the sake of game is the same one that was to convert Indians into farmers. See above, p. 65.) Further quotations in the text come from this letter. Jefferson's concrete schemes to increase the number of small landholders appear in his draft constitution for Virginia of 1776, where he would have granted fifty acres to each freeman who did not have that much land; in his draft land office bill for Virginia in 1779, a similar proposal; and in a plan for the Louisiana Territory to grant fifty acres to anyone who settled there immediately and who promised two years of military service. BC.I.362; BC.II.139–40; TJ, "Circular to Cabinet on Defense of New Orleans," 28 February 1806, F.VIII.425.

"Manufactures" and "Public Revenue and Expences" he first proclaims the "substantial and genuine virtue" of the farmers; and then: "I repeat it again, cultivators of the earth are the most virtuous and independent citizens."[158]

The brief chapter "Manufactures" is notable not only for its antagonism to its alleged subject matter and the encomium to agriculture but also for its relation to the preceding chapter, on slavery. By the juxtaposition Jefferson suggests, whether consciously or not, that it is not manufacturing only that stands in the way of independent farming but also plantation slavery.[159]

Portions of the selective argument in the chapter on manufactures also seem at variance with the premises of his discussion of commerce under "Public Revenue" only a few pages later. At first Jefferson claims that "the political economists of Europe have established it as a principle that every state should endeavor to manufacture for itself." But the economists whom he respected—Adam Smith and the Physiocrats—thought no such thing. They thought, as he says a few pages on, that "our interest will be to throw open the doors of commerce, . . . giving a perfect freedom to all persons for the vent of whatever they may choose to bring into our ports, and asking the same in theirs." This doctrine, however, implies that the United States will require manufactures from abroad, an implication that is confirmed when Jefferson notes that "such is our attachment to agriculture" that Americans will forgo manufacturing if at all possible. But manufacturing having been forgone because of an attachment to agriculture, American crops must nevertheless get to Europe, and European manufactures must still get to America. How will this happen? It will happen because, as Jefferson remarks with satisfaction, "the actual habits of our countrymen attach them to commerce."[160]

John Adams sketched a political theory on behalf of small landholding that was at least as persuasive as Jefferson's: "The only possible way . . . of preserving the balance of power on the side of equal liberty and public virtue, is to make the acquisition of land easy to every member of society; to make a division of the land into small quantities, so that the multitude may be possessed of landed estates." John Adams to James Sullivan, 26 May 1776, quoted in White, *The Philosophy of the American Revolution*, 265–66. A radical proposal on landholding is Paine's "Agrarian justice opposed to agrarian law, and to agrarian monopoly. Being a plan for meliorating the condition of man . . ." (1797), S.3187. Forwarding this essay to Madison, Jefferson remarked only that it was "worth notice." TJ to James Madison, 15 June 1797, F.VII.144.

158. NVa.165, 175.

159. An effective analysis of this feature of Jefferson's "pastoral tension" is Lewis P. Simpson, *The Dispossessed Garden: Pastoral and History in Southern Literature* (Athens, Ga., 1975), 24–33.

160. NVa.164, 174, 175. For a discussion stressing the ties rather than the tensions of commerce and agriculture in Jefferson's thought, especially as they are part of his public policy, see Joyce Appleby, "What Is Still American in the Political Philosophy of Thomas Jefferson?"

What should be made of an "attachment" to agriculture but "actual habits" that "attach [Americans] to commerce"? Is the first a wish, and the second reality? The fragile reasoning appears to be this. Commerce takes off the excess crops and gives farmers money with which to buy the manufactured goods they want. Producing these goods in cities is a corrupting activity both because the work is not next to the soil and because the workers cannot be independent of their employers or the vicissitudes of the economy. It is therefore desirable that this work take place in Europe. The goods must then be imported, and that is possible only if international commerce can flourish.

Given a critical reading, this theory is difficult to maintain. If American farmers took seriously the doctrines of independence and self-sufficiency, they would not produce for commerce at all. The problem inherent in Jefferson's political economy is that the political virtues of farming are at odds with the farmers' desire for manufactured goods and therefore for the benefits of commerce.

Jefferson was not oblivious to the problem, but he seldom confronted it directly, only rationalized it away, compromised with necessity, or issued pronouncements of praise and blame. He also leaned on the irrefutable fact of nature in America— "an immensity of land courting the industry of the husbandman."[161] Europe had good soil, but it was not sufficient for its population, which was therefore unlikely to be virtuous. American virtue, on the other hand, was secure so long as farming remained the nation's chief occupation, which would be "as long as there shall be vacant lands in any part of America" and apparently regardless of farmers being in commerce.[162] Jefferson's understanding of vacant lands was necessarily imprecise as to both their extent and their suitability for farming but still correct. With breathtaking hyperbole in the First Inaugural he assured Americans that they already possessed "a chosen country, with room enough for our descendants to the hundredth and thousandth generation." Two years later, with the purchase of Louisiana, America's vastness seemed permanently established.[163]

In his own life Jefferson wanted it both ways. He would be independent by raising everything that the sizable establishment at Monticello needed to eat; at the same time, he planned to sell enough at market to

161. NVa.164.

162. TJ to James Madison, 20 December 1787, BC.XII.442.

163. For Jefferson on population, see Drew R. McCoy, "Jefferson and Madison on Malthus: Population Growth in Jeffersonian Political Economy," 88 Va. Mag. Hist. & Biog. 259–76 (1980). The ideas of Malthus, Jefferson said, were inapplicable to the United States, with its "singular circumstance of the immense extent of rich and uncultivated lands." TJ to Thomas Cooper, 24 February 1804, quoted in McCoy, *The Elusive Republic,* 194.

live according to his highly civilized wishes. Presumably most American farmers wanted to do what he did, even if they could not expect to do so on his scale. Thus, while agricultural virtue required independence from commerce, agricultural practice required dependence on it, and the position of the farmer in Jefferson's economic thought remains a muddle.

In Jefferson's moral thought, however, the farmer has an unambiguous position, and his political economy, which is concededly a confusion with the morality left in, is incomprehensible with the morality left out. The central expression is the paean in *Notes on Virginia:*

> Those who labor in the earth are the chosen people of God, if ever he had a chosen people, whose breasts he has made his peculiar deposit for substantial and genuine virtue. It is the focus in which he keeps alive that sacred fire, which otherwise might escape from the face of the earth. Corruption of morals in the mass of cultivators is a phenomenon of which no age nor nation has furnished an example.[164]

This passage prompts several observations. First, because Jefferson so often worked to avoid the word "God," it is initially unexpected to find that farmers are God's chosen people. Indeed, if he had wished to write his message unadorned, he might have said that farmers are the chosen people of nature, just as a decade earlier he might have declared America independent only under the laws of nature. But for independent farmers, as for independent states, he sought the blended support of nature and God. Independence for both was blessed by nature made divine. Yet what sort of God does Jefferson have in mind for his farmers? It is neither a Christian God nor even the remote God of deism; rather, it is an agricultural divinity, pre-Christian and pagan. The clue lies in the term "sacred fire."

While the sacred fire was generally understood to refer to liberty (George Washington speaks of the "sacred fire of liberty" in his First Inaugural), in the sacred fire of ancient Rome Jefferson calls to mind more. As has been seen, from Lucretius to Horace, Roman culture suffused Jefferson's personal life, and nowhere more than on his farm. The friezes at Monticello portray Roman agriculture. Adapted from ancient temples, they depict the fecundity of the earth, the sacrifice of animals, the instruments of farming. The glow of the sacred fire itself

---

164. NVa.164–65. Jefferson wrote comparably exalted language in several letters when *Notes on Virginia* first appeared, in the mid-1780s. The best-known contemporary exposition of the yeoman idyll was Crèvecoeur's *Letters from an American Farmer* (1782). For a different understanding of the dignity of agriculture in the South at the time, see Robert E. Shalhope, *John Taylor of Caroline: Pastoral Republican* (Columbia, S.C., 1980). Taylor's ideal was a static, uncommercial agricultural society, but his model was plantation slavery.

may be seen in the dome at Monticello, modeled on the temple in Rome dedicated to Vesta, the goddess of the hearth, who brought the sacred fire from Troy and whose priestesses vowed to keep it burning forever. It is pagan antiquity, not physiocratic political economy, that supplies Jefferson's farmers with a household of substantial and genuine virtue.[165]

Jefferson's final claim for agricultural life is that the mass of cultivators cannot be morally corrupted. This claim is difficult to support. What ages or nations he might have had in mind other than an idealized slice of Rome under the republic or an equally imagined view of Saxon England is hard to know. Certainly the agricultural societies about which he knew most, those of feudal and postfeudal Europe, he never understood as especially virtuous; nor was Piedmont Virginia a very good model. What he meant to convey, however, is clear: a faith in rural virtue and an intense suspicion of urban life.

Jefferson's pronounced distaste for cities is the obverse of his love for agriculture. As with the two political parties by nature, he often reduced social life to a Manichean dualism, and cities were the forces of darkness. "The commercial cities," he said, "are as different in sentiment and character from the country people as any two distinct nations."[166] Avarice and corruption were their principal vices. Those who lived in them were likely to be office hunters, stockjobbers, or lazy loungers, witnessing or participating in the mobs that were endemic to urban centers. Life in the city was pestilential to the morals, to the health, and to the liberties of man.[167] Worst of all, those who engaged in commerce did not really care for their homeland. "Merchants have no country," wrote the man who loved Albemarle. "The mere spot

165. For examples of the sacred fire in Virgil, see *Georgics* IV.379 and *Aeneid* VII.71, 704; for Horace, see *Epodes* II.43. Jefferson's most important Roman master on nature, Lucretius, would not have credited divine intervention in farming, but he did write about sacrifice at the altar (sacred hearth), the pleasures of rural society, and the significance of fire. *De Rerum Natura* IV.1237, V.1355–1445, V.1091–1109. An incisive discussion of Monticello and agrarian Rome appears in Karl Lehmann, *Thomas Jefferson*, 178–81. See also Douglas L. Wilson, "The American *agricola*: Jefferson's Agrarianism and the Classical Tradition," 80 So. Atlantic Qtly. 339–54 (1981).

166. TJ to Mr. Pictet, 5 February 1803, LB.X.356. See also TJ to Du pont de Nemours, 18 January 1802, F.VIII.125. Consider the lines from Horace that Jefferson planned to display in the garden at Monticello: "Happy is the man who, like the early race of mankind, is far from the schemes of business, who works his ancestral fields with his own oxen, and is completely free of interest payments." *Epodes* II.1–4. TJ, Account Book, 1771, GB.26 (translation supplied).

167. The several terms come from TJ to Arthur Campbell, 1 September 1797, LB.IX.420; TJ to George Mason, 4 February 1791, BC.XIX.242; TJ, "Observations on Démeunier's Manuscript," 22 June 1786, BC.X.53; NVa.165; TJ to Henry Middleton, 8 January 1813, LB.XIII.203; TJ to Pierre August Adet, 29 June 1806, LB.XIX.154; and TJ to Benjamin Rush, 23 September 1800, F.VII.459.

they stand on does not constitute so strong an attachment as that from which they draw their gains."[168]

Jefferson conceded that cities "nourish some of the elegant arts" and that "particular branches of science" may best be taught there.[169] He also had a constructive, at times avid, interest in urban planning from the standpoints of health, convenience, and aesthetic design. But the final judgment was that to dwell in nature was to dwell in virtue, while to live in the city was to risk living in corrpution. Why the inhabitants of American cities were so often Jeffersonian in politics is inexplicable on the basis of these remarks on rural and urban life. But these people were Jeffersonians because they were republicans—of the party that trusted the people. They were not republicans because they were Jeffersonians—of the people who trusted the land.

No one was more influential than Jefferson in defining and promoting "the order of things established by the agricultural interest."[170] He anticipated that congressional apportionment following the first census would lead to "the augmentation of the numbers in the lower house, so as to get a more agricultural representation."[171] He advocated taxing only the surplus of agricultural production rather than that which sustained the independence and therefore the virtue of the farmer. When that surplus was taxed, he wanted the tax collected from the consumers so that "the farmer would not be sensible that he had paid it." He would not have taxed the land itself, for without labor nature was not property.[172] Jefferson assumed that the government's finances should be "capable of being understood by common farmers"; that import taxes on luxuries (which no virtuous farmer should want) could finance the federal budget so completely that "the farmer will see his government supported, his children educated, and the face of his country made a paradise by the contributions of the rich alone"; and that farmers should be exempt from the uniformity required by the Constitution for federal bankruptcy laws.[173]

---

168. TJ to Horatio G. Spafford, 17 March 1814, LB.XIV.119. See also TJ, "Answers to Démeunier's First Queries," 24 January 1786, BC.X.16 (cultivators of the earth "possess most of the amor patriae. Merchants . . . the least").

169. TJ to Benjamin Rush, 23 September 1800, F.VII.459. See also TJ to Caspar Wistar, 21 June 1807, F.IX.79 (sending his grandson to study in Philadelphia despite the possibility of his acquiring there "habits and partialities which do not contribute to [his later] happiness" as a farmer).

170. TJ to Mr. Pictet, 5 February 1803, LB.X.356.

171. TJ to George Mason, 4 February 1791, BC.XIX.242. See also TJ to Arthur Campbell, 1 September 1797, LB.IX.420 (to return to "the principles of 1776," the people need only elect to Congress "farmers . . . the true representatives of the great American interest").

172. TJ to James Madison, 8 December 1784, BC.VII.558.

173. TJ to James Madison, 6 March 1796, F.VII.61–62; TJ to Dupont de Nemours, 15 April 1811, LB.XIII.39; TJ to James Pleasants, 26 December 1821, F.X.198.

In his dissent from much of Hamilton's early national economic policy Jefferson was especially watchful for the agricultural interest. He did not develop a sustained argument from nature, but his perspective insofar as it was not that of a constitutional lawyer was that of the small farmer. On every ground available—economic, political, and ultimately moral—he opposed Hamilton's programs for a large national debt, for a Bank of the United States, and for the promotion of manufacturing.

The new national debt consolidated earlier state debts with the debt that the general government had contracted under the Articles of Confederation. Since Virginia had no debts to be assumed; since the new bondholders were expected to be urban merchants and bankers; and since the size of the consolidated obligations was so great, Jefferson objected to the Funding Act, even though he gave formal support for it in return for a promise to build the national capital on the Potomac. In the tradition that the "earth belongs to the living," he thought the national debt might carry the new government "beyond the possibility of payment."[174] Any public debt ought to be repaid within one generation, and he feared that the U.S. debt would not be. By good fortune and a Jeffersonian administration, however, the debt was nearly paid off, in large part through revenue taken in by the sale of public lands. The abundance of American nature thus helped rescue the nation from what Jefferson considered to be the violation of natural right.

Jefferson's opposition to the plan for a national bank ran even deeper. Bankers were manipulators of money, credit, and the economy generally. They were unproductive and insensitive to the needs of farmers. In an opinion prepared for the president, Jefferson argued chiefly that the bank's incorporation exceeded the powers of Congress under the Constitution. But before reaching this stage of his argument, he listed eight objections to the bank's establishment. One was that it would be "against the laws of monopoly," and five of the objections directly or indirectly attempted to demonstrate that the bank would acquire unacceptable influence over land.[175]

The most fundamental, but oddly muted, dispute between Jefferson and Hamilton was over the Report on Manufactures, which the secretary of the treasury submitted to Congress in December 1791. This acute and far-seeing report was carefully but disingenuously obeisant to the primacy of agriculture in the American economy:

> It ought readily be conceded that the cultivation of the earth . . . as the immediate and chief source of subsistence to man, as the principal source

174. TJ, "The Anas," 10 July 1792, Pdvr.1226.
175. TJ, "Opinion on the Constitutionality of the Bill for Establishing a National Bank," 15 February 1791, BC.XIX.275–76.

of those materials which constitute the nutriment of other kinds of labor, as including a state more favorable to the freedom and independence of the human mind . . . has intrinsically a strong claim to pre-eminence over every other kind of industry.[176]

But the principal recommendation of the report, that the national budget aid in the establishment of new industries, strikes at the vision of an agrarian nation. Hamilton argues that the real, that is, the economic, interests of agriculture will be advanced only by accepting domestic manufacturing.

He challenges Jefferson's naive economics drawn from the "spontaneous energies of the earth" first by skepticism: more evidence is required to prove that agriculture is the most productive branch of industry. Then he hurls a barrage of propositions, most of which ignore or reject Jefferson's arguments from nature. He proposes a version of comparative advantage, that the division of labor between cultivators and artificers is to the benefit of both. He notes that the "artificial force" of machinery is a helpful supplement to the "natural force of man" (nothing is said about the forces of nature); that in manufacturing, expenses are saved "in maintaining the laborer" (an allusion to slavery); that women and especially children will be able to have household employment at machines (perhaps disrupting the natural affection in the Jeffersonian family); and that large cities employing immigrant labor will permit farmers to stay on the land (thus potentially admitting to the United States persons without a republican disposition).

To these arguments from political economy Hamilton adds one from psychology, one that Madison could have made, too. Since humans have diverse talents and interests, "when all different kinds of industry obtain in a community, each individual can find his proper element, and call into activity the whole vigor of his nature." Jefferson's agriculturalists may have been independent, but they were also uniform. What America needs, says Hamilton, is "the spirit of enterprise [which] must be less in a nation of mere cultivators, than in a nation of cultivators and merchants, less in a nation of cultivators and merchants, than in a nation of cultivators, artificers, and merchants."

Hamilton's arguments are strong. But Jefferson's only rebuttal to the Report on Manufactures was a constitutional one.[177] Indeed, he seems to have agreed with many of its points, though seldom all at one time and not in public. What was most unsettling about the report, however,

176. This and other quotations come from the abridgment of the Report of Manufactures in Adrienne Koch, ed., *The American Enlightenment*, 631–39.

177. A direct Jeffersonian refutation is George Logan, *Five Letters, addressed to the yeomanry of the United States: containing some observations on the dangerous scheme of Governor Duer and Mr. Secretary Hamilton, to establish National Manufactories* (1792). S.3157.

was not its separate arguments but its tone and the political economy that it held out for the United States. It did not discover in farmers the chosen people of God, and it declared, in effect, that a natural economic system was an illusion.

While Jefferson the political philosopher continued to pursue the agricultural dream, Jefferson the political official did not identify his personal preferences with his public responsibilities. As he said of his own view, it was "theory only, and a theory which the servants of America are not at liberty to follow."[178] As his nation's servant, indeed, Jefferson was at least as assiduous as Hamilton in his economic investigations, proposals, and activities—all outside of agriculture. In his diplomatic work in Europe one finds him an outright commercial expansionist. So realistic had he become by the time he left the cabinet that his official economic views were hardly distinguishable from Hamilton's, and they were very far from his own in *Notes on Virginia* of less than a decade earlier.[179]

Although Jefferson maintained his agrarian rhetoric, he adopted techniques that eased the nation's transition to the Hamiltonian order. About some aspects of manufacturing—labor-saving devices, interchangeable parts, production that could be done at home—he became enthusiastic.[180] Inside the United States he separated urban from rural manufacturing and claimed that it was the cities, not the occupation, that corrupted people. He subtly equated a Hamiltonian economic position with his own moral one by saying that manufacturing in the United States enabled America to avoid contact with an imperfect world built on non-American principles, a world in which natural rights were regularly violated. Self-sufficiency would keep the United States virtuous just as it had the farmer.

Jefferson's most measured statement on the American political economy comes in a letter written a month after he left the presidency. At the time, when freedom of the seas appeared an impossible goal, he wrote:

An equilibrium of agriculture, manufactures, and commerce, is certainly become essential to our independence. Manufactures, sufficient

178. TJ to Charles Van Hogendorp, 13 October 1785, BC.VIII.633.
179. On this see an undated note, very likely from the 1790s, in which Jefferson takes a Hamiltonian position and tone about manufacturing that are astonishing. CB.391. The chapter on—i.e., against—manufactures in *Notes on Virginia* is the only significant portion of the book that Jefferson later said he would revise. See TJ to J. Lithgow, 4 January 1805, LB.XI.55; and TJ to Benjamin Austin, 9 January 1816, LB.XIV.387.
180. See, e.g., TJ to William Sampson, 26 January 1817, F.X.73 ("labor-saving machines do as much now for the manufacturer as the earth for the cultivator").

for our own consumption, of what we raise the raw material (and no more). Commerce sufficient to carry the surplus produce of agriculture, beyond our consumption, to a market for exchanging it for articles we cannot raise (and no more). These are the true limits of manufactures and commerce. To go beyond them is to increase our dependence on foreign nations, and our liability to war. These three important branches of human industry will then grow together, and be really handmaids to each other.[181]

In his First Inaugural Jefferson had omitted manufacturing entirely and claimed that commerce was the "handmaid" of agriculture. Now the three vocations come into equilibrium, handmaids to each other. It is a valedictory notable for attaching neither virtue nor vice to any occupation, but written in the plain language of political economy. Jefferson had been obliged to affirm his support for some manufacturing, or there might be no manufactured goods in the United States at all. He had been obliged to affirm his support for commerce, or the surplus agricultural produce that he counted on to increase the happiness of the United States could not be marketed.

However primary agriculture was, the accommodations that Jefferson agreed to, coupled with the protests he made on behalf of agriculture, reflect a permanent difficulty with his—and, as he would say, God's—chosen field. The difficulty has its origin in the natural right to pursue happiness, for this pursuit heads down two quite different roads—an economic road and a moral one—and Jefferson wanted to travel them simultaneously. Along the first road nature was the source of property, and material happiness lay at the end. Along the second road nature determined how and where one ought to live, and moral happiness was the result. The two were not the same. It may well be that happiness cannot be bought by money, but neither, evidently, can it be bought by morality. Yet to the degree that Jefferson integrated economics and ethics it was through agriculture. Agriculture lies next to the source of economic value. It is the way of life most in accord with nature. The farmer has at least as much natural moral sense as those who have been formally educated. He is surrounded by scenes of natural beauty. Although permeated—and therefore often vitiated—by slav-

---

181. TJ to Governor James Jay, 7 April 1809, LB.XII.271. See also TJ to Thomas Leiper, 21 January 1809, F.IX.239 ("greatest prosperity depends on a due balance between agriculture, manufactures and commerce"). Yet see Jefferson's frantic message not many months before his death about corporations "under the guises and cloak of their favored branches of manufactures, commerce and navigation, riding and ruling over the plundered ploughman and beggared yeomanry." TJ to William B. Giles, 26 December 1825, F.X.356.

ery, these were the values Jefferson lived by at Monticello: a natural economy joined to a natural morality, an aesthetics bound to nature, a private life of natural affection, the whole within a natural political order.

Part Three · ACTION

Chapter VI

JEFFERSON'S LIFE WITH NATURE

F OR JEFFERSON, politics was nearly always an interruption of a life
meant to be lived on a farm. Although Dumas Malone has called
one of Jefferson's stays at Monticello between political assignments a
"rural interlude," Jefferson himself might have said it was the other way
around. It was public service that made up the interludes. Monticello
was the main stage on which he played out his truer life.[1]

Jefferson hoped to retire as early as his mid-thirties, shortly after the
Declaration of Independence and before he became governor of Virginia. From France in the 1780s he wrote to a friend in Virginia: "All my
wishes end, where I hope my days will end, at Monticello. Too many
scenes of happiness mingle themselves with all the recollections of my
native woods and fields, to suffer them to be supplanted in my affection
by any other." After three years as secretary of state, nearly desperate to
end his public service, he longed for "the wholesome occupations of
my farm," where he had "an interest or affection in every bud that
opens, in every breath that blows around me." But his retirement from
public office again did not last long, and he was soon back in Philadelphia as vice-president, reminded by his daughter that in the Virginia
springtime "every object in nature invites one into the fields." On being
elected president a few years later, he knew that he would miss above all
the "attractive nature and the country employments" of Monticello.
Each year during his presidency, for a month in the spring and at least
two months beginning in middle or late July, he retreated to Virginia.
After nearly seven years as president, he said once more that it was
among his "most fervent longings to be on my farm." When he finally
retired, he sculpted the lesson entire: "The whole of my life has been at
war with my natural tastes, feelings and wishes. . . . [L]ike a bow long

1. M.III.165.

bent I resume with delight the character and pursuits for which nature designed me."[2]

As a student Jefferson had entered a passage from Lord Kames in his commonplace book that, without much alteration, describes the course of his own life: "A man who has bestowed labor in preparing and improving a field, contracts an affection for a spot, which in a manner is the workmanship of his own hands. After a summer expedition, or years of a foreign war, he returns with avidity to his own house, and his own fields, there to pass his time in ease and plenty."[3] Jefferson's labor (and that of his slaves) certainly led to an affection for Monticello. Whenever he returned from public service, he did so with Kamesian avidity. He passed his time at ease because he was engaged in what he wished to be doing. He passed his time in plenty because the spontaneous energies of the Monticello earth yielded sufficient bounty.

Jefferson's agricultural inclinations were what Virginia society expected of a man who had inherited more than five thousand acres from his father and had acquired that much again through the estate of his wife.[4] His farms were divided between those in Albemarle County, which were predominantly in wheat and grains, and those about seventy-five miles southwest, in three other counties, which were predominantly in tobacco. In Albemarle he owned two estates, each consisting of several farms. Of the six farms on the Rivanna estate, Monticello was the largest. Somewhat more than half of its thousand acres were cultivated, and much of the rest, in the words of a visitor of 1815, was "covered with a noble forest of oaks in all stages of growth and of decay . . . abandoned to nature."[5] Besides the farm and the forest, Monticello included the Palladian house, an elaborate flower garden in which flowers bloomed from March to December, a vegetable garden of over 250 varieties of edible plants, an orchard in which were tested perhaps 150 varieties of fruit, vineyards, two modest nurseries and a greenhouse, and (in plan) a special forest grove.[6] This summary scarce-

2. TJ to George Gilmer, 12 August 1787, BC.XII.26; TJ to James Madison, 9 June 1793, F.VI.291; Martha Jefferson Randolph to TJ, 12 May 1798, GB.264; TJ to Andrew Ellicott, 18 December 1800, LB.XIX.121; TJ to Robert R. Livingston, 3 January 1808, LB.XI.411; Nicholas Biddle, "Eulogium on Thomas Jefferson, delivered before the American Philosophical Society," 253.

3. CB.110–11.

4. On the lands and their extent see M.I.435–46.

5. Francis Calley Gray, quoted in Francis Coleman Rosenberger, ed., *Jefferson Reader*, 55.

6. The staggering number of plants with which Jefferson was familiar can be guessed from the indexes to the *Garden Book* and the *Farm Book* and the lists in NVa.38–43, as well as from Edwin M. Betts and Hazlehurst B. Perkins, *Thomas Jefferson's Flower Garden at Monticello*, 54–58.

ly hints at what actually took place on the farms. By ignoring chronology, it also gives a static picture of the activities, while an important characteristic of Jefferson as a farmer was his constant experimenting with new crops, new breeds of animals, new methods, and new equipment.

For all his record keeping, Jefferson seldom had an overview of his farms as a business. He knew that he was usually in debt, but he blamed this, with some justification, on financial institutions and practices beyond his control. If he had been the small farmer of his economic theory or had stayed out of commerce, he might have been better off. His crops brought fluctuating prices, often much lower than he expected. He paid high interest rates on original loans and on refinancing them later. For decades he laid out money to improve the navigation on the Rivanna River and to construct and maintain mills on it. His own generous expenditures included making good a large note on which a friend defaulted, the financing of his home and later the construction of his house at Poplar Forest, his library, his gardens, and the lavish support of a large family and many guests. In a landscape described as an "Eden of the United States" he faced drought, floods, hailstorms, freezes, and destructive insects.[7]

What income the farms yielded came from the sale of tobacco and wheat. About these two plants Jefferson never modified the feelings expressed in *Notes on the State of Virginia:*

> [Tobacco] is a culture productive of infinite wretchedness. Those employed in it are in a continued state of exertion beyond the powers of nature to support. . . . The cultivation of wheat is the reverse in every circumstance. Besides clothing the earth with herbage, and preserving its fertility, it feeds the laborers plentifully, requires from them only a moderate toil, except in the season of harvest, raises great numbers of animals for food and service, and diffuses plenty and happiness among the whole.[8]

Normally the culture of tobacco so exhausted everything it touched— land, labor, and capital—that when Jefferson wrote of agriculture to his friends, he preferred to avoid speaking of his chief cash crop altogether.[9] He once attempted to disengage himself from tobacco and go

7. TJ to C. D. F. Volney, 9 April 1797, M.III.199. On the Rivanna projects see FB.341–411. The struggle against the Hessian fly, which afflicted his wheat crop, can be traced through nearly three decades of letters in the *Garden Book;* see also BC.XX.445–49, 456–62. The damages of weather may be gauged from correspondence; see, e.g., the index entry "droughts" in the *Farm Book.* Jefferson's financial affairs are summarized in M.VI.506–12.

8. NVa.166, 168.

9. See, e.g., TJ to William Branch Giles, 27 April 1795, F.VII.12.

into wheat but was unsuccessful. At least as much a financial as an agricultural nemesis, tobacco was Jefferson's earliest and most long-standing source of debt, binding him—and most Virginia planters—to British merchants.[10] When the Federalist Congress suspended trade with France in the late 1790s, he protested that this was an attempt "to reduce the tobacco states to passive obedience by poverty." But it doubtless would have satisfied him in the long run if Virginia had been rid of tobacco for good.[11]

No crops approached tobacco and wheat in commercial significance, but corn was required, if disliked, and many other crops were the objects of close attention, including peas (good for both animal and human consumption and for shading the fields during fallow years) and clover (a favorite in the rotation of crops). Jefferson often laid plans for raising cotton, but they were evidently unrealized.

Jefferson thought himself quite poor as a farmer. But he urged agriculture as a science on others and ran Monticello as a combination research station, information center, and agricultural library. His public services as a private farmer are astonishing, and his enthusiasm for agricultural experiments does not appear to have been restrained by costs.[12] Beyond the crops he was accustomed to, he worked to introduce to the United States new plants from abroad, believing that Virginia did not yet grow "all the articles of culture for which nature has fitted our country."[13] Of all the plants he secured from Europe, his greatest hopes lay with olives and with the Piedmont rice of Italy, both of which he obtained for trials in South Carolina. As he explained in a list of his own contributions to the public welfare, "The greatest service which can be rendered any country, is to add an useful plant to its culture, especially, a bread grain; next in value to bread is oil."[14]

---

10. See, e.g., TJ, Answers to Démeunier's Additional Queries, ca. January–February 1786, BC.X.27 (Virginia's debt to British merchants at the end of the Revolution was "near as much as all the rest of the states put together"). His diplomatic service included an intense but failed attempt to alter the terms of international trade in tobacco.

11. TJ to Mary Jefferson Eppes, 17 January 1800, BB.179. On the consequences of tobacco to health and morality see TJ to Benjamin Waterhouse, 9 March 1805, S.I.448–49. Jefferson left only one legacy suggesting any respect for tobacco: a plan for an order of architecture that included a capital of the leaves and flowers of the plant.

12. He claimed that "if in the experiments to introduce . . . new plants, one species in a hundred is found useful and succeeds, the ninety-nine found otherwise are more than paid for." TJ to Samuel Vaughan, Jr., 27 November 1790, BC.XVIII.98. Although he did not say that he expected to pay for the ninety-nine failures himself, that was the effect of his activities.

13. TJ to William Drayton, 6 May 1786, BC.IX.461.

14. TJ, "Services to His Country" (ca. 1800), Pdvr.1289. On the olive tree see TJ to William Drayton, 7 May 1789, BC.XV.101 ("one of the most precious productions of nature").

He relished visits and correspondence with experts from abroad and was honored by election to agricultural societies in England, France, Italy, and Germany.[15] He was proud of the varieties of sheep he acquired for Monticello, was eager to try the latest farm machinery, and publicly disseminated information about his own design for an improved ploughshare.[16] He was also a close student of what may be called agricultural dynamics, calling the atmosphere "the great workshop of nature" because rain and sun regenerated the soil.[17] At the same time, he knew that the sun could bake, and the rain erode, overcultivated fields, so he established systems of fallow rotation, cover crops, manuring, and chemical fertilizer (gypsum) to ensure that the atmosphere was effective at its job.[18] He became a publicist for contour plowing when he saw that on the Virginia hillsides the "horizontal furrows arrested the water at every step."[19] On the basis of an intuitive if inexplicit understanding of ecological relationships he proposed an organic control for the worms that attacked his tobacco plants (turkeys were brought in to eat them), and he noted an ecological succession of plants that, given enough time, might renew even the most severely eroded soils.[20]

To visitors as well as to Jefferson, the setting of Monticello enhanced the appreciation of its agricultural activities. If one looked to the west with the mind's eye, one could see farms beyond the horizon. Across three modest intervening valleys was the spectacular sweep of the Blue Ridge Mountains. According to a French guest, "the enjoyment of this magnificent view" required only "the aid of fancy" to be complete. Fancy, said the duc de la Rochefoucauld-Liancourt,

15. Among the visitors were William Strickland, of the British Board of Agriculture, in 1795 and the duc de la Rochefoucauld-Liancourt, a founder of the French Agricultural Society, who recorded the farming practices at Monticello in 1796. See GB.241–45. Jefferson was in correspondence with John Sinclair, the first president of the Board of Agriculture in London. In France his principal correspondents about plants were the comtesse Noailles de Tessé, a relative of Lafayette's, and André Thouin, superintendent of the National Garden at Paris. Through George Washington, he was in communication with Arthur Young, the leading figure of scientific agriculture in England.

16. Jefferson's ploughshare, the "mouldboard of least resistance," based on a mathematical design, is the subject of many letters. A technical description is given in TJ to John Sinclair, 23 March 1798, 4 Trans. Am. Phil. Soc. 313–22 (1799) (reprinted nearly entire in GB.649–54).

17. TJ to William Strickland, 23 March 1798, GB.263.

18. See FB.188–200.

19. TJ to William A. Burrell, 25 February 1810, LB.XII.365.

20. TJ, "On Tobacco Culture," 1784–86, BC.VII.212; TJ to William Strickland, 23 March 1798, GB.263 (trees spring up providing shade and deciduous leaves; these in turn permit the growth of herbage; the herbage may enable exhausted fields "in a long course of years" to be renewed). Jefferson understood ecological succession in space as well as over time. See TJ to William Drayton, 30 July 1787, BC.XI.649–50 (listing plants en-

must picture to us those plains and mountains such as population and culture will render them in a greater or smaller number of years. The disproportion existing between the cultivated lands and those which are still covered with forests as ancient as the globe, is at present much too great; and even when that shall have been done away, the eye may perhaps further wish to discover a broad river, a great mass of water—destitute of which, the grandest and most extensive prospect is ever destitute of an embellishment requisite to render it completely beautiful.[21]

For political if not aesthetic reasons, Jefferson agreed with this assessment. He, too, saw a disproportion between cultivated and forested land to the west, and he, too, looked beyond the Appalachians to an agricultural republic on the banks of the Mississippi.

Two interrelated issues were involved in the establishment of this republic: which jurisdiction(s) controlled the territory; and how settlers were to secure tracts in it.[22] To Jefferson, the second question was easy to resolve in theory. Between independent settlers who purchased directly from the government and speculators who sold portions of large holdings, there was no choice. Land speculation was a morally offensive and inegalitarian means of distributing land to which all men had a natural right. Jefferson's reasoning with respect to political control was also straightforward:

> Neither the disposition of the people in our western extremity, turbulent and unruly as befits the inhabitants of a mountainous country, nor nature or distance of the country they occupy, nor yet the form of republican government [render] it productive either of their or our happiness that we should remain under one government. Nature [has] pronounced our separation.[23]

But politics did not quickly follow nature. At the end of the Revolution, Virginia's claims to the land that farmers were to settle were undisputed over the territory east and south of the Ohio (current West Virginia and Kentucky) and strong in the territory west and north of the river—the Northwest Territory (today's Ohio, Indiana, Illinois, Michi-

---

countered on crossing the Alps, arranged "according to their different powers of resisting cold").

21. De la Rochefoucauld-Liancourt, *Travels through the United States of North America, in the Years 1795, 1796, 1797,* quoted in Betts and Perkins, *Thomas Jefferson's Flower Garden at Monticello,* 14.

22. A general account is "Virginia and the West," chap. 4 of Peter S. Onuf, *The Origins of the Federal Republic* (Philadelphia, 1983). The documents of cession and an analysis of their evolution are in BC.VI.571–617.

23. TJ, "Outline and preamble of argument on Virginia's claim" (1782), BC.VI.665 (Boyd maintains that this is the rough draft of an article intended for publication).

gan, and Wisconsin). For several reasons, Virginia wished to cede its western territory to the United States, but on its own terms, and the Confederation Congress was not ready. For more than two years after Yorktown, the state's delegates to the Continental Congress worked on the project, but without final success. Only after the formal peace with Britain had been ratified in January 1784 and international boundaries had been established did Congress resolve the issue of the nation's territory. Jefferson, who had recently become a member of the Virginia delegation, prepared the document of cession, and on March 1 the Northwest Territory was accepted by the Congress for the United States.

At the same time, Congress received a report from a committee headed by Jefferson on the temporary government of the new territory (which was expected eventually to include Kentucky and claims of other states to the south). The chief provisions of this plan were that settlers would purchase land directly from the United States (thus ending the claims of land companies to the territory); that new states would eventually be created and admitted into the confederation on an equal footing with existing states (thus ending the possibility of an American colonialism); and (as drafted, but not as accepted by the Congress) that slavery was to be prohibited after 1800. Each of these political ends was founded on a natural right for which Jefferson had argued: a natural right to emigrate, a natural right of self-government, and a natural right not to be a slave.[24]

Jefferson's plans for the western territory included three notable attempts to civilize nature by intellectualizing it: in names for the new states, in setting state boundaries, and in surveying the land. When Congress returned the "Plan of Government for the Western Territory" to committee for revision, among the changes requested was the deletion of the names of the future states. What Jefferson had proposed was a special case of his romance with nature, a nomenclature for states in the west that included Sylvania, Michigania, Illinoia, Assenisipia, Pelisipia, Metropotamia, Polypotamia, and Cherronesus. These names quite deliberately represent nature in the region and are no stranger than words like Philadelphia and Mississippi. But because they were based on little-known Indian words ("Pelisipia" was the upper Ohio) or innovations from the Greek (Polypotamia, the land of many waters, covered the

24. Jefferson's interest in these ideas can be seen in his draft constitution for Virginia of 1776, which looked forward to "free and independent" states to be formed from the state's western territory and would have prohibited the introduction of additional slaves into the state. BC.I.352–53. The Ordinance of 1784 died of desuetude. It was revived, with revisions (including a flat prohibition on slavery), as the Northwest Ordinance of 1787. Jefferson's plan for surveying and disposing of the western territory, discussed below, was not enacted at all, but much of it lived on in the Land Ordinance of 1785.

lower Ohio Valley), and because there were so many of them at once, Congress understandably rejected them.[25]

The proposal for the boundaries of the new states in the western territory was a strictly rational rather than an ecological or romantic approach to nature, and it met with more success. Jefferson suggested a geometrical pattern not very different from what eventuated. Although Congress, in order to reduce the number of states and not be restricted by premature legislation, eliminated the particular limits Jefferson defined, boundaries of the five states that emerged from the Northwest Territory are nearly as straight as is permitted by the waters that surround the territory as a whole.

Jefferson's third plan for civilizing nature in the West was the most rationalistic of all. A plan of survey, it combined his own experience in the field with his sense of scientific order. He proposed to lay out the new territory in a checkerboard pattern, using latitude and longitude as the principal lines. From each intersection of a parallel and a meridian, land was to be marked off in "hundreds," a term of Anglo-Saxon origins but given a new definition: a square of ten geographical miles on a side, divisible into decimal units. Since a geographical mile is the distance of one minute of latitude, somewhat longer than the commonly used statute mile, this proposal, by ignoring not only local topography but also the British system of measurement as well, was tied to universal nature. In the Land Ordinance of 1785 Congress chose "townships" over "hundreds" and insisted on the familiar English miles. But the units were still to be laid off along parallels and meridians, regardless of topography, natural drainage, or ecological considerations. Thus, as Jefferson wished, the western territory contains a permanent, rectangular pattern of roads, fields, and property ownership.[26]

The western lands, however named, divided into states and surveyed, were to be populated by independent farmers, who, practicing republican virtue, would be the most loyal of Americans. Jefferson could have such confidence in westerners because he assumed that nature had provided an Ohio Valley that was in general fertile. In his

25. The names were also removed so that fewer states could be formed in an area that Jefferson had marked out for at eight. Jefferson wanted states of smaller size for republican purposes, but the majority of delegates wanted states of larger size in order to ensure that eastern states would not be outvoted in the Congress by newcomers to the Union. Jefferson complained that this was "reversing the natural order of things." TJ to James Madison, 16 December 1786, BC.X.603. A sketch map of new states for the western territory is reproduced in plate 13.

26. TJ, "Report of a Committee to Establish a Land Office," 30 April 1784, BC.VII.140–48. For a detailed account, see William D. Pattison, *Beginnings of the American Rectangular Land Survey System, 1784–1800*, chaps. 1–4.

mind, that was enough to assure a population of virtuous farmers.[27] But what of the particular vacant lands that Virginia had ceded to the United States? For 180 miles west of what he presumed would be Virginia's western border (a north-south line through the confluence of the Kanawha and Ohio rivers), he himself said there was nothing but "an absolute desert, barren and mountainous, which can never be inhabited."[28] These 180 miles bring a traveler to central Indiana. As to the rest, James Monroe reported to Jefferson after personal inspection that "a great part of the territory is miserably poor [much of it consisting] of extensive plains which have not had from appearances and will not have a single bush on them, for ages."[29] None of this sounded like home, but Jefferson, never visiting the new territories himself, continued to suppose that his own Eden could be replicated in the West.

If nature in the form of fertile territory was to raise up republican farmers, nature in the form of continental geography—the Appalachian barrier and the flow of the Ohio-Mississippi waterway—threatened to undermine the loyalty of those farmers to the eastern states. To prevent any rupture, Jefferson first made a legal pronouncement: any governments established in the West "shall for ever remain a part of this confederacy of the United States of America."[30] Then he proposed to alter nature. If westerners only had convenient geographic and economic access to the East, they would remain tied to it politically. To achieve this tie, Jefferson worked for years on his greatest public-works project, a waterway that would connect the western territory with Virginia and so induce commerce and communication to go across the mountains instead of down the Ohio and the Mississippi.

Jefferson's interest in navigability is recorded in the chapter "Rivers" in *Notes on Virginia,* where he repeatedly encouraged undertaking improvements—on the James, the Shenandoah, the Ohio, and the Great Kanahwa but especially on the Potomac. Whether by removing obstacles from the river, by constructing a canal alongside it, or, most important, by extending its upper reaches to meet the western watersheds of the Ohio and Lake Erie, the improvement of Virginia's most significant river became one of Jefferson's most cherished causes. With a display of

27. Jefferson accepted a sanguine report on the region by the official geographer to the United States, Thomas Hutchins, "A Topographical Description of Virginia . . ." (1778), S.525. See John Hoffmann, "Queries Regarding the Western Rivers; An Unpublished Letter from Thomas Jefferson to the Geographer of the United States," 75 J. Ill. State Hist. Soc. 15–28 (1982).

28. TJ to James Madison, 20 February 1784, BC.VI.548.

29. James Monroe to TJ, 19 January 1786, BC.IX.189.

30. Revised Report of the Committee for the Government of Western Territory, 22 March 1784, BC.VI.608.

apparent objectivity, he remarked that among the three routes by which western goods could reach the Atlantic—down the Mississippi and coastwise across the Gulf of Mexico; across Lake Erie and eventually down the Hudson to New York; or by a connection to the Potomac— the Potomac route was preferable. He agreed that the Mississippi route was valuable, but as between the Hudson and the Potomac he argued strenuously on behalf of the route through Virginia. It required fewer portages, in winter it would be closed less by ice; and for goods from the Ohio Valley it was considerably shorter. As he put it very simply to George Washington, "Nature . . . has declared in favor of the Potomac."[31]

The chief drawback to the Potomac route, according to Jefferson, was that "the Hudson is open and known," while the Potomac still had to be prepared. In fact, however, nature had declared in favor of the Hudson, and only a chauvinistic Virginian whose geographical imagination outran the geographical facts would think otherwise.

Jefferson's arguments for the Potomac are weak if not spurious. He miscalculated the distances until politely corrected by his more nationalist correspondent, Washington.[32] Against the Hudson's being "shut up by the ice three months in the year," Jefferson did not claim that the Potomac was open during that season, only that it led "directly to a warmer climate." He thought that delays caused by freezing on the northern tributaries of the Potomac would be only accidental and short, although the streams were hardly navigable in the first place. As he undoubtedly knew, the nearer the sources of the Potomac approached the upper tributaries of the Ohio, the more inadequate for transportation all the streams became. Increasingly ingenious and expensive engineering would therefore be required to make them satisfactory for commercial use. A geographical visionary, Jefferson proposed the moving of mountains in the service of humanity. But from the moment the Erie Canal opened the Hudson to the West, a year before Jefferson's death, it was far more successful than a Potomac connection could ever

---

31. TJ to George Washington, 15 March 1784, BC.VII.26. This letter and NVa.15–16 are the sources of the discussion in the text. See also TJ to James Madison, 10 July 1785, BC.VIII.280.

32. Reckoning from the mouth of the Cuyahoga River on Lake Erie to New York City by way of the Hudson, and from the same spot to Alexandria, Virginia, he first calculated the two routes as 970 and 430 miles, respectively. When Washington inquired whether the first distance was not too high, Jefferson undertook a "reexamination" of the matter leading to "the detection of an error of 150 miles." George Washington to TJ, 29 March 1784, BC.VII.52; TJ to George Washington, 6 April 1784, BC.VII.83. (The revised figure, 825 miles via the Hudson, appears in NVa.16.) But the new, shorter distance is also inadequate in that it ignores that New York lies directly on the Atlantic, while Alexandria is still 175 miles from the open sea.

hope to be. A transport route from the western territory down the Potomac was one of his fondest dreams. It was also one of his greatest misjudgments of nature.[33]

Jefferson did realize that even if the West were reached by a water route across the mountains, whether the Hudson or the Potomac, the Mississippi River would remain vital for the downstream passage of heavy articles such as timber and flour. It would remain vital, too, for securing the loyalty of western farmers. The establishment of American rights to the Mississippi therefore became one of his most important causes from the time he was governor of Virginia until the Louisiana Purchase, more than twenty years later.

Mississippi rights included both the right of navigating the river to the sea and the right of using a port where goods could be stored and transfered between river transport and ocean vessels, the right of entrepôt. The dispute over these rights began soon after independence, when the Continental Congress sought the aid of Spain in the war against Britain. Virginians at first argued that an allliance was not worth what some northerners proposed, formally confirming to Spain rights over the Mississippi. But when John Jay was sent as agent to Spain (1780–82), the Virginia Assembly, under Jefferson's governorship, reluctantly agreed that downstream navigation could be ceded if it was a bar to a treaty. When nothing came of Jay's mission, the Virginia policy reverted to insisting that no Mississippi rights be given up, even temporarily. This last was always Jefferson's preferred policy.

Over the years Jefferson's strategy respecting the Mississippi took three forms: appeals to Spain's self-interest (principally maintaining peace with the United States); threats of force (normally by westerners, who, he said, were beyond his control); and arguments from the law of nature and nations. While this last hardly provided indisputable support for his case, Jefferson's talent for developing arguments from nature to suit his causes contributed nearly as much to his policy as did political acumen and single-mindedness of purpose.

Soon after his arrival in Paris, Jefferson received from Madison a lengthy guide to American interests in the Mississippi question. Spain, said Madison in language Jefferson could have written himself, "can no

33. The Erie, 360 miles long and completed in 1825, after eight years of work, reached the western territory and was an immediate economic success. Jefferson's route, the C.&O. Canal, 180 miles long and completed in 1850, after twenty-two years of construction and at three times the cost, reached only Cumberland, Maryland (i.e., not the western waters), and was an economic failure. Jefferson's hopes for a water passage across the Rockies are discussed below, in this chapter. For his thoughts on a canal across the Isthmus of Panama, see TJ to M. Le Roy, 13 November 1786, BC.X.529; and correspondence with William Carmichael in 1788.

more finally stop the current of trade down the river than she can that of the river itself." Listing several grounds for believing that Spain would eventually yield to American demands, Madison first pronounced (perhaps to please Jefferson) that "justice and the general rights of mankind" were on the side of the United States. Jefferson soon agreed. Worried about the possibility of Kentucky separating from the confederation if rights to use the river were not secure to the nation, he wrote bluntly to a Virginia neighbor: "The navigation of the Mississippi we must have." When he heard that John Jay, as minister of foreign affairs, continued to entertain the idea that the United States might yield the navigation of the Mississippi for a number of years in return for commercial privileges, he wrote back in vigorous opposition. One of his allies in Congress, Hugh Williamson, of North Carolina, tried to unmake this proposal permanently, introducing a resolution declaring that the United States had a "clear, absolute and unalienable claim" to the free navigation of the Mississippi and that this right was founded on "the great Law of Nature" as well as on treaties. It did not pass.[34]

The next act in the Mississippi drama waited for Jefferson to come on stage as secretary of state. Not long after he entered the cabinet he prepared an outline of his Mississippi policy for use by the American minister to Spain, William Carmichael. A year and a half later he wrote a more detailed statement of policy. The two documents constitute his most considered arguments for American rights to the Mississippi. More telling for versatility than for depth, for advocacy than for analysis, Jefferson's handiwork loses persuasive force by going off in so many directions. But they are the directions of nature. At times nature means justice. At other times it means necessity. Sometimes nature means supposed precedents from the law of nations. Finally it is simply the environment, the physical characteristics of the Mississippi itself.[35]

What, Jefferson asks, is the situation of the western territory when the Mississippi Delta is in the control of Spain? It is, he says, that of a large landlocked nation. It has an obvious waterway out to the world, but the use of it is blocked by the arbitrary and intransigent attitude of another nation. Geographically, this is not a misleading idea, for despite

---

34. James Madison to TJ, 20 August 1784, BC.VII.403 (Boyd suggests that one purpose of Madison's letter was to convince Jefferson that the Mississippi was far more important for American national interests than was a connection between the Potomac and the West); TJ to Archibald Stuart, 25 January 1786, BC.IX.218; TJ to James Madison, 30 January 1787, BC.XI.93; Williamson motion, 14 July 1788, BC.XIX.494.

35. TJ, "Heads of Consideration on the Navigation of the Mississippi for Mr. Carmichael," enclosure with TJ to Carmichael, 2 August 1790, BC.XVII.113–16; TJ, "Report Relative to Negotiations with Spain to secure the free Navigation of the Mississippi, and a port on the same," 18 March 1792, Pdvr.240–56.

the dream of a Potomac connection to the Ohio Valley, the Appalachians constituted a real barrier, and the West could in fact be considered landlocked if settlers could not use the Mississippi. To emphasize his point, Jefferson claimed that the United States held six hundred thousand square miles of habitable territory along the Mississippi and its branches, while Spain had "not the thousandth part of that extent" along the Mississippi south of the American boundary.

In making this argument, Jefferson in effect asks that law follow the environment, that legal rights be conferred because of the dictates of nature as geography. At the mouth of the river Spain is regrettably sovereign. But upstream inhabitants require rights of navigation in order to make use of benefits conferred by nature—the produce of the land and a feasible route to transport it. An "appeal to the law of nature and nations," Jefferson says, shows that "even were the river . . . the exclusive right of Spain, still an innocent passage along it is a natural right in those inhabiting its borders above." This right, Jefferson concedes, would be an "imperfect" one, because its actual working out would depend on accommodations between Spain and the United States. But it would be a natural right nonetheless.[36]

The core of Jefferson's argument for Mississippi rights was not an environmental one, however. It was not even a legal one—that after the Revolution the United States had succeeded to the rights of Mississippi navigation, which Jefferson supposed were confirmed in the treaty between Spain and Great Britain of 1763. It was unabashedly moral: "Our right is built on ground still broader and more unquestionable . . . on the law of nature and nations. If we appeal to this, as we feel it written on the heart of man, what sentiment is written in deeper characters than that the ocean is free to all men, and their rivers to all their inhabitants?" A sentiment written in such deep characters is not easy to prove, especially with respect to rivers. Therefore Jefferson mentioned two examples of presumably relevant natural law.

The first was that Antwerp had claimed against Amsterdam a natural right to the navigation of the river Scheldt. Although the claim had not been successful, it was still, Jefferson said, a valuable assertion "of the natural right of the inhabitants of the upper part of a river to an innocent passage through the country below . . . [tending] to establishing a principle favorable to our right of navigating the Mississippi." A second example came from Roman law, which Jefferson interpreted to have

36. TJ, "Report Relative to Negotiations with Spain," Pdvr.247. If one asks whether inland nations have a general right to reach the sea, it is difficult to accept Jefferson's claim. Natural law does not grant the right to cross another nation's territory by land, no matter how convenient such a crossing might be.

"placed the navigation of their rivers on the footing of nature, as to their own citizens, by declaring them public." But since the Sheldt had not been open for nearly 150 years owing to Amsterdam's military and commercial power, and since the Roman law was domestic only, Jefferson indeed had to retreat to a sentiment written on the heart of man to find a law of nature that supported his position.[37]

When Jefferson turned from navigation on the river ("innocent passage") to entrepôt and deposit at the river's mouth, his natural rights argument took on a different complexion. Entrepôt was a natural right, not because the navigation of the Mississippi was a natural right, that is, not because a basic natural right implies a subsidiary one, but because entrepôt was necessary to make use of the Mississippi regardless of the basis for navigating it:

> It is a principle that the right to a thing gives a right to the means, without which it could not be used, that is to say, that the means follow their end. Thus a right to navigate a river, draws to it [several ancillary rights]. This principle is founded in natural reason, is evidenced by the common sense of mankind, and declared by [writers on natural law].

Even though entrepôt was a natural right, however, since it was to be exercised within Spanish jurisdiction, it required the consent of another sovereign. Jefferson pressed the claim for this right in stages. He began with the request to moor vessels on the river's shore and to land there in case of distress. Next he proposed a right to have pilots and lighthouses within the area in order to decrease the likelihood of distress. Finally, taking into account the "very peculiar circumstances attending the river Mississippi," he held that the United States needed the right of deposit directly, "where warehouses and keepers might be constantly established."[38]

Near the end of his negotiating guidelines, Jefferson reminded his commissioners once again that "Spain does not grant us the navigation of the river. We have an inherent right to it." He therefore hoped that in

37. Pdvr. 246; TJ to Benjamin Harrison, 3 March 1784, BC. VII.6; Pdvr. 248. Jefferson implied that in Roman law the phrase *flumina publica sunt*— "rivers belong to the public"— designated natural law or natural right, but unlike in his Roman arguments elsewhere, he cited no source for the interpretation. Pdvr. 248–49. He also suggested that the American diplomats inquire into the basis of Spanish use of rivers that flowed from Spain through Portugal to the sea in order to determine whether the cause might be helped by "some acknowledgments of this [natural law] principle" by Spain. Pdvr. 246. Among the several later applications of the principle see TJ to Albert Gallatin, 4 July 1807, LB. XI. 257 (Creek Indians may cross from Spanish territory along the Mobile River to their own lands on U.S. soil because "this is exactly what we are claiming of Spain. . . . [D]ifferent nations inhabiting the same river have all a natural right to an innocent passage along it").

38. Pdvr. 247–48.

the treaty to be negotiated nothing would say or imply otherwise. Yet valuing the treaty, that is, the national interest, even more than the abstract principle of nature, he was willing to waive explicit confirmation of the principle if that was necessary to gain Spanish assent. Silence on the point was satisfactory because one could still imagine that Spain had accepted the American claim. But he would not go further and offer any compensation for yielding "what we have a right to, that is to say, the navigation of the river, and the conveniences incident to it of natural right."[39]

Despite these elaborate preparations for a Mississippi treaty, Jefferson's emissaries failed to negotiate one at the time, principally because Spain was not ready for it no matter what the terms. But in October 1795, nearly two years after Jefferson resigned as secretary of state, the countries did sign a treaty. The United States gained the right to navigate the Mississippi to the Gulf of Mexico and the right of entrepôt at New Orleans guaranteed for three years. But such a treaty was inevitably inadequate. Any foreign nation that held territory on the lower Mississippi was, as one of Jefferson's locutions put it, a "natural enemy" of the United States. What the United States needed was not confirmation of the natural rights of passage and deposit but outright ownership of some portion of the lower Mississippi region itself.

Within weeks of his inauguration as president, the occasion for ownership arrived. Jefferson learned, though not with complete certainty, that Spain had ceded to France New Orleans, the Floridas, and the Louisiana Territory. Although he at once recognized that the transfer of Louisiana to France was an "inauspicious circumstance" because France was a far more dangerous neighbor than was Spain, he also knew that it was a stunningly propitious moment to resolve the Mississippi question permanently. Moving quickly, he sent Robert R. Livingston as minister to France and prepared a forceful statement of American policy. As America's ally in the Revolution, he wrote, and because of the aims of her own revolution, France had been a natural friend. As the possessor of New Orleans she had at once become a natural enemy.[40]

As they had been a decade earlier, Jefferson's environmental arguments were reinforced by the imperatives of universal nature. But this time the principles were not sentiments "written on the heart of men." The universal axiom was now a direct principle of physical nature. American enmity "is not a state of things we seek or desire [but] one which [French possession of New Orleans] forces on us as necessarily, as any other cause by the laws of nature, brings on its necessary ef-

39. Pdvr.251, 252.
40. TJ to Robert R. Livingston, 8 April 1802, F.VIII.143–47.

fect. . . . [These consequences are] not controlable by us, but inevitable from the course of things."[41] Nature had taken the form of geographical and political determinism.

What Jefferson predicted came to pass. When the highest Spanish
official at New Orleans temporarily closed the port to American shipping in the fall of 1802 (France then owned the territory, but the Spanish
still controlled it), the crisis was precipitated. Pointing to the extreme
"agitation of the public mind" about suspension of deposit and count-
ing on the financial and strategic exigencies of France in Europe and the
Caribbean to aid his cause, Jefferson prevailed upon James Monroe to
sail for Europe with the "object of purchasing New Orleans and the
Floridas" for the United States.[42]

When Monroe arrived in Paris, Napoleon had already offered Louisiana and New Orleans to the United States through Livingston. Together the two men worked out the terms of sale with the French
minister of the treasury, François Barbé de Marbois, the same man
whose questionnaire over twenty years earlier had elicited from Jefferson the *Notes on the State of Virginia*. Although the president and Congress had not officially authorized the purchase of Louisiana, it is clear
from Jefferson's correspondence that he was prepared to acquire the
entire region. On July 4, as if to declare new independence from Europe, the acquisition of Louisiana and New Orleans was announced in a
Washington newspaper. With it, Jefferson became chief executive of
Western lands for the third time. As governor of Virginia he had had
jurisdiction over Kentucky and the claims of his state west and north of
the Ohio. As secretary of state he was responsible for maintaining
official records of the Northwest Territory. Now he governed land
from the Mississippi to the Rockies.

During the summer of 1803, with the aid of Albert Gallatin, Jefferson prepared a lengthy questionnaire in order to learn from knowledge-
able people what the new territory was really like. He used his collection of Americana at Monticello to prepare "An Examination into the
Boundaries of Louisiana," in which he claimed that Louisiana included
most of western Florida (so that the United States would control both
banks of the Mississippi at New Orleans) and, in the west, a border
along "the highlands encompassing the waters of the Mississippi . . . round the heads of the Missouri and Mississippi." In the fall,
when he called Congress into session earlier than normal in order to
obtain prompt ratification of the Purchase treaty, he remarked on "an
independent outlet for the produce of the western states," on "the

41. Ibid., 145, 146.
42. TJ to James Monroe, 13 January 1803, LB.X.343–45.

fertility of the country, its climate and extent," and on its "ample provision for our posterity." The Senate ratified the treaty on October 20, and a few weeks after that, in a brief "Account of Louisiana," Jefferson explained to Congress as fully as he could what the nation had acquired.[43]

The actual determination of what the new territory held, whether it was a fertile expanse or a great waste, Jefferson placed primarily in the hands of the Lewis and Clark Expedition. This expedition, as political as its purpose was, was also the fruition of a curiosity that went back more than half a century—about the trans-Mississippi west, especially about the upper Missouri River, and most particularly about a passage from there to the "western ocean." By virtue of his age, his position, and perhaps his temperament, Jefferson could not take a journey to the Pacific himself. But he was the initiator and organizer of the Lewis and Clark Expedition and a vicarious companion of the two leaders. It was his culminating enterprise with American nature.[44]

Jefferson's earliest ideas about the West had come from his father and his father's friends who formed the Loyal Company in 1749 to explore and speculate in territory in southwest Virginia. Spurred by accounts of earlier explorations in the West and the maps drawn to represent them, the men of this company also planned an expedition to the Missouri. Their premise was the existence of a Northwest Passage, or something like it. The idea of a Northwest Passage ultimately descended from the European disappointment at discovering the Americas in the first place—an obstacle to direct oceanic communication with the Orient. At first the hope was to discover a water passage through the Western Hemisphere. Failing that, the imagination next settled on an observation of Father Marquette, who in 1673 claimed that only a short portage connected the upper reaches of the Missouri River to the navigable headwaters of another great river, the "River of the West," which flowed down to the "Vermillion Sea."

The "short portage" version of a route to the Orient found support by analogy in the geography of eastern North America. There, the sources of streams flowing west to the Mississippi and of others flowing east towards the Atlantic came very close together at the crest of the Appalachians. The theory was that there should be a similar short portage in the western mountains: North America possessed a "sym-

43. TJ, "An Examination into the Boundaries of Louisiana," 7 September 1803, Pdvr.263; TJ, Third Annual Message, 17 October 1803, Pdvr.402; TJ, "An Account of Louisiana," 14 November 1803, *American State Papers*, Class X, *Miscellaneous*, I.344–56.

44. The discussion in the text draws on John Logan Allen, *Passage through the Garden;* Roy E. Appleman for the U.S. National Park Service, *Lewis and Clark;* and Donald Jackson, *Thomas Jefferson and the Stony Mountains.*

metrical geography." The theory was based on a combination of common knowledge and rationalistic fantasy, that the Mississippi River split the continent in two. The large mass of land on each side of the river contained mountain ranges. These ranges were symmetrically placed, similarly high, and therefore comparably blessed with short portages. This was the theory that had been accepted by the Loyal Company in its unexecuted plan to explore the Missouri. After the Revolution, the next generation of Virginia visionaries, including Jefferson, took the idea up once more.

Near the end of 1783, while he was working on the cession of Virginia's western lands to the United States, Jefferson asked George Rogers Clark whether he would like to lead a party "to search that country [from the Mississippi to California]." He had heard that the British intended to explore the area (he assumed for the purposes of colonizing it) and thought the United States should get there first. Since the prospect of financing an expedition was dim, Clark, though he supported the project, sensibly declined to take it on.[45]

When he embarked for Europe several months later, not only did Jefferson have an actual, if unmounted, expedition in mind but he also had an accelerating scientific curiosity about the upper reaches of the Missouri. The evidence is *Notes on Virginia,* the manuscript for which he carried across the Atlantic. The *Notes* refers to the Missouri River in three of its queries. Since the river lay beyond the borders of Virginia, however, Jefferson felt the need to justify its inclusion in the book. He explained that the river had once been within the state (relying on the abandoned, pre-Revolutionary "sea to sea" claim for Virginia territory); and he remarked that the Missouri opened up "channels of extensive communication" with Virginia, even though these were beyond its jurisdiction.[46] Despite these political and commercial justifications, however, the rather speculative discussion of the Missouri in the *Notes* is almost completely scientific.

What did Jefferson have to say about the river? First, he assumed that the flooding of rivers generally depended on melting snows and that the time of melting depended on latitude. He therefore supposed that because the Missouri flooded later in the spring than did the Mississippi, the source of the Missouri lay further north than that of the Mississippi. Second, he believed that the rapid flow of the Missouri indicated that it came from high mountains. At the same time, he hesitated to associate the cold temperature of the Missouri waters with the altitude rather

45. TJ to George Rogers Clark, 4 December 1783, BC.VI.371; Clark to TJ, 8 February 1784, BC.XV.609.
46. NVa.8.

than the latitude of their origin. One reason for this was that in keeping with the theory of symmetrical geography, he imagined that the Missouri began in mountains that from base to summit were no higher than the Blue Ridge. He attributed the Missouri's flow, therefore, not to the height of the mountains, but to their precipitous descent.[47] Third, Jefferson mentioned, but did not accept, the possibility of an active volcano in the region of the upper Missouri.[48] Finally, he noted that Spanish merchants reported going up the river two thousand miles, and he temptingly remarked that even then the river was not known to its source. He could say only that the Missouri was east of the "mountains which divide the waters of the Mexican Gulf from those of the South Sea" and that on the far side of those mountains was a "river which runs westwardly."[49]

It happened while Jefferson was in Paris that an opportunity arose for discovering the anticipated portage between the Missouri and the unknown River of the West. He proposed that John Ledyard, a romantic American adventurer, undertake a journey across Russia, ship out to the Pacific Northwest, search for the passage, and then work his way by foot back east to the United States. Ledyard, who had explored the South Seas under Captain Cook and knew at first hand the frustrations of seeking a Northwest Passage, eagerly accepted the proposal. But the scheme came to an ignominious conclusion when, far in the interior of Asia, Russian officials deported him back to Europe. Although Ledyard subsequently embarked for Africa, where he died seeking the sources of the Nile, he promised Jefferson that his next adventure would take up the search once more, this time from Kentucky westward.[50]

The next step on the path to the Lewis and Clark Expedition came shortly after Jefferson returned to the United States. In November 1789 the War Department made plans to send an officer disguised as an Indian up the Missouri. This was the east-to-west Ledyard plan, but to be

47. NVa.8–9, 20. Jefferson's only experience in truly high and precipitous mountains—in the Alps—impressed on him the relation between temperature and altitude. But that experience took place after *Notes on Virginia* was in press and probably was not sufficient to alter his belief about the Missouri.

48. NVa.20. The volcanic evidence was "a substance supposed to be pumice" floating in the Mississippi. Jefferson decided that this was an erroneous identification, because no volcano had "ever yet been known at such a distance from the sea."

49. NVa.9, 20, 44. The grip on Jefferson's mind of the Missouri's unknown origin can be seen in the "Dialogue Between my Head and my Heart," composed while he was preparing the *Notes* for publication. The Heart says: "If a drop of balm [to salve any grief the Cosways might suffer] could be found . . . at the remotest sources of the Missouri, I would go thither myself to seek and to bring it." TJ to Maria Cosway, 12 October 1786, BC.X.447.

50. Jefferson's most extensive recollections of Ledyard are TJ, "Meriwether Lewis," 18 August 1813, Pdvr. 909–10. and TJ, Autobiography (1821), KP.70.

undertaken covertly. The scheme was called off a few months later, however, in part because of an anticipated adverse reaction of the Spanish should it be uncovered. Though no concrete evidence exists that Jefferson knew of it, it was concocted by his cabinet colleague Secretary of War Henry Knox, and that he was aware of it is certainly plausible.[51]

Two years later Jefferson returned to his own initiative. In June 1792 he was said to be "much interested" in having a "journey prosecuted up the Missouri," with the South Sea as its goal.[52] By the end of the year an appropriate person had come forward to take on the exploration. It was André Michaux, a far greater scientist than Ledyard and equally intrepid. On behalf of the official sponsor of the exploration, the American Philosophical Society, Jefferson instructed Michaux to "seek for and pursue that route which shall form the shortest and most convenient communication between the higher parts of the Missouri and the Pacific Ocean." Concerned that Michaux might wander from the purpose for which he was being sent, Jefferson repeated the directive to look for the Northwest Passage in five different forms over the twelve paragraphs of the instructions. The concern was well justified, for although the Frenchman carried an introduction from Jefferson correctly identifying him "as a person of botanical and natural pursuits," he was also a political agent for Edmond Genêt, the high-handed French consul in the United States. Michaux soon abandoned the expedition altogether.[53]

Neither Ledyard nor Michaux ever saw the Missouri, but Jefferson conceived of them as predecessors of an expedition that he would eventually sponsor. When he became president, therefore, he was prepared to renew his attempt, this time with a rigor, financing, and support that none of the previous attempts even aspired to. In 1802 the likelihood of British competition in the West added urgency to the task.[54] On foreign policy grounds Jefferson did not mention his plans in

51. See Jackson, *Jefferson and the Stony Mountains*, 84; and Appleman, *Lewis and Clark*, 22.

52. Caspar Wistar to Moses Marshall, 20 June 1792, LC.II.675.

53. TJ to André Michaux, 30 April 1793, LC.II.671 (the instructions are often misdated January 1793); TJ, "The Anas," 5 July 1793, Pdvr.1248. On Michaux (1746–1802) see Donald Culross Peattie, *Green Laurels* (New York, 1936), 201–14. Michaux had been to Persia. He was to be washed ashore on the coast of Europe unconscious, his journals and botanical specimens strapped to his body. Like Ledyard, he ultimately died in Africa on a scientific adventure.

54. In 1801 Alexander Mackenzie, whose transcontinental crossing of Canada in 1793 had been only sparsely recounted at the time, issued a proposal for British dominance of the western fur trade. Jefferson learned of Mackenzie's book, *Voyages from Montreal through the Continent of North America to the Frozen and Pacific Oceans*, early in 1802 and evidently read it that summer. Donald Jackson considers the Lewis and Clark Expedition to be Jefferson's "response to Mackenzie." Jackson, *Jefferson and the Stony Mountains*, chap. 7.

the State of the Union message in December of that year; and when they were communicated to Congress in a confidential message of January 1803, they were embedded in two paragraphs about commerce with the Indians that was to be in the hands of private enterprise. But to open up that commerce required detailed knowledge of the area, and that knowledge could be gathered only by an expedition to the upper Missouri and the Pacific supported by the U.S. government.[55]

Explaining the region to Congress, Jefferson said that the fur country itself was far to the north (in Canada), where it was burdened by an "infinite number of portages and lakes, shut up by ice through a long season." A trade route in that area, therefore, would "bear no competition with that of the Missouri" if the river were once opened to permit "a continued navigation from its source, and possibly with a single portage, from the western ocean." Such an argument had last been broadcast in *Notes on Virginia,* with its list of the advantages of the Potomac over the Hudson. There, too, the preferred route of commerce was a southern one, which had a milder climate, was less subject to freezing, and entailed fewer portages. Avoiding the Virginia orientation of the *Notes,* however, Jefferson now told Congress that when trade from the Missouri country reached the United States, it could proceed eastward by "a choice of channels," which, happily for American politics, included routes through northern states (the Great Lakes and the Hudson), middle states (the Potomac or the James), and southern states (the Tennessee and the Savannah). Having justified a Missouri expedition for purposes of commerce, Jefferson next rationalized it under the Constitution and finally held that Spain (no European country was mentioned by name in the message) would in any case regard the exploration as a "literary pursuit." A few months later the Louisiana Purchase made much of this argument needless.

If his reasons were jumbled, Jefferson easily secured congressional assent and began at once to organize the expedition (in fact he had begun informally much earlier). As commander he chose Meriwether Lewis, born in 1774 on an estate within sight of Monticello and into a family close to Jefferson through both friendship and marriage. Lewis's active interest in trans-Mississippi exploration dated at least to an application, at the age of eighteen, to join the unrealized expedition of the American Philosophical Society under Michaux. In a tribute to him after the explorer's death, Jefferson asserted that Lewis's qualifications were "as if selected and implanted by nature in one body, for [the] express purpose" of leading an expedition to the Pacific. At the time, however,

55. TJ, "Confidential Message to Congress," 18 January 1803, Pdvr.398–401.

Jefferson knew that education was required to supplement nature, and so he arranged for Lewis's technical instruction in the sciences by members of the American Philosophical Society, noting that the captain already possessed "a great mass of accurate observation on all the subjects of nature" he had encountered within the United States.[56]

Lewis chose as his co-commander William Clark, also from an Albemarle County family well known to Jefferson. Devoted to his older brother George Rogers, Clark spent his entire life after the age of fourteen on the frontier, active in the military (where he became friendly with Lewis), traveling in the territories on both sides of the Mississippi, and, on returning from the Pacific, serving as superintendent of Indian affairs and governor of the Missouri Territory. The journals kept by the commanders show Clark, who was several years older than Lewis, to have been the calmer and less complicated of the two men. But they trusted and respected each other completely and by their coinciding and complementary qualities provided the extraordinary leadership required for the success of the Missouri expedition.[57]

While Lewis and Clark were being selected and undergoing training, Jefferson, with the advice of members of his cabinet, prepared a directive for the journey. The "Instructions to Captain Meriwether Lewis" distill a lifetime's concern to discover a Northwest Passage or its equivalent. "The object of your mission," Jefferson wrote,

> is to explore the Missouri river, and such principal stream of it, as by its source and communication with the waters of the Pacific Ocean, whether the Columbia, Oregon, Colorado or any other river, may offer the most direct and practicable water communication across this continent for the purposes of commerce.[58]

To accomplish this object, Jefferson requested the explorers to obtain accurate latitude and longitude marks along the Missouri, "especially at the mouths of rivers, at rapids, at islands, and other places and objects distinguished by such natural marks and characters of a durable kind, as that they may with certainty be recognized hereafter." He requested observations on Indian tribes—their population, territorial extent, languages, customs, occupations, laws, economy, religion—and suggested that Lewis might arrange, for purposes of security, a symmetrical visitation by a group of Indians to the United States while the

56. TJ, "Meriwether Lewis," 18 August 1813, Pdvr.911; TJ to Benjamin Rush, 28 February 1803, F.VIII.219. A standard study is Richard Dillon, *Meriwether Lewis: A Biography* (New York, 1965).

57. On Clark see Jerome O. Steffen, *William Clark: Jeffersonian Man on the Frontier* (Norman, Okla., 1977).

58. TJ, "Instructions to Captain Meriwether Lewis," 20 June 1803, PJ.309.

expedition was under way.[59] He listed "other objects worthy of notice" that the expedition should attend to: soil; plants and animals not known in the eastern United States; minerals; "volcanic appearances"; and climate (with requirements for recording it more suited to a comfortable and fixed location like Monticello than a journey into the wilderness). In keeping with two of his distinctive attitudes towards nature—on the presence of the mammoth and the senselessness of geology—Jefferson asked the explorers to look out for "the remains or accounts" of animals "which may be deemed rare or extinct" but did not ask them to report on the science that was to become the single most important one in the West.[60]

While Lewis and Clark recruited men, gathered supplies, and went into prevoyage training in Illinois, Jefferson presented to Congress and sent to Lewis his official "Account of Louisiana." On the basis of what he wrote about the land adjacent to the Mississippi River itself, it appears that he supplemented his faith in symmetrical geography with a belief that throughout the Louisiana Territory idealized Rivanna Rivers flowed by future Monticellos and that the region even possessed the equivalent of the Natural Bridge. Jefferson's friends from Albemarle were to explore a territory that was western Virginia writ large.[61]

Unfortunately, to their regret and often to their puzzlement, the explorers disproved many of the initial expectations of the expedition. As to the most important goal, they made a claim that requires examination: "We were completely successful and have therefore no hesitation in declaring that such as nature has permitted it we have discovered the best route which does exist across the continent of North America [by way of the Missouri and Columbia rivers]."[62] Confined to the Missouri and Columbia Rivers, the statement implies disappointment; but it holds out the possibility that another expedition, heading in another direction, might yet discover a usable route to the Pacific.[63] At

59. PJ.312. It happened. See TJ to Members of the Osage Nation, 16 July 1804, LB.XVI.409 (visiting "our country and towns toward the sea coast" enables the Indians to acquire "the same knowledge of the country on this side of the Mississippi which we are endeavouring to acquire of that on the other").

60. PJ.311.

61. See "An Account of Louisiana," 346 ("variety of large, rapid streams, calculated for mills and other water-works"; "land yields an abundance of all the necessaries of life, and almost spontaneously"; picturesque heights). Jefferson propounded other ideas about the new territory that were ridiculed at the time but turned out not to be fanciful. He now credited evidence of volcanoes along the upper Missouri (rejected in *Notes on Virginia*) and recounted the story of a great mountain of salt in the area (which may be taken as evidence of the Great Salt Lake).

62. William Clark to [George Rogers Clark?], 23 September 1806, LC.I.326; Meriwether Lewis to [unknown], 29 September 1806, LC.I.336.

63. Jefferson, at least, hoped so. See TJ to Anthony G. Bettay, 18 February 1808, LB.XI.442 (asking for a sketch or account "of the river Platte, of the passage from its head

the same time, lurking in the phrase that the explorers had discovered the best route "such as nature has permitted it" is the recognition that nature had not permitted very much and that a genuinely good route across the continent did not exist. Instead of coming upon a brief portage between the navigable headwaters of two rivers, the explorers had traveled 340 largely miserable miles by land over the snow-covered Rockies.[64]

Jefferson was not eager to recognize this truth. He prepared a report to Congress that in draft form claimed that the expedition had discovered "an important channel of communication with the Pacific." Eventually he gave in to geographic and political reality, revising the phrase to "an interesting communication across our continent." But unlike Lewis and Clark, he did not hold nature accountable for the absence of a Northwest Passage.[65]

Despite his disappointment, Jefferson was justified in saying that "the addition to our knowledge in every department, resulting from this tour . . . has entirely fulfilled my expectations in setting it on foot."[66] This knowledge, in the form of the explorers' notes on flora and fauna, Jefferson expected Lewis to collate, expand, and publish. When Lewis's tragic death in 1809 meant that the scientific results of the journey were never presented as they might have been, at Jefferson's constant urging a two-volume history of the expedition appeared in 1814. To this work Clark contributed a map that, by showing the Rockies as a complex configuration of mountains rather than a single narrow chain, cartographically put to rest the possibility of an easy portage between the eastern and western waters.[67]

---

across the mountains, and of the river Cashecatungo, which you suppose to run into the Pacific").

64. As John Quincy Adams jibed in an anonymously published verse (LC.I. 363):

Good people, listen to my tale,
 'Tis nothing but what true is;
I'll tell you of the mighty deeds
 Achieved by Captain Lewis—
How starting from the Atlantic shore
 By fair and easy motion,
He journied, *all the way by land,*
 Until he met the ocean.

65. Allen, *Passage,* 370; TJ, Sixth Annual Message, 2 December 1806, Pdvr.423.
66. TJ to comte Bernard de Lacépède, 14 July 1808, LB.XII.85.
67. Lewis almost certainly died by suicide. The impress of his character and achievement among his friends is symbolized by the fact that both Jefferson's daughter Martha and William Clark named their sons after the explorer.
The *History of the Expedition Under the Command of Captains Lewis and Clark* (1814) includes very little of the scientific information gathered on the journey. (A map from this volume is reproduced in plate 18.) Lewis's work was not generally available until the

There were other results. Jefferson widely distributed the plants and seeds that Lewis and Clark brought back from the West. Of these, he grew at Monticello Indian corn, varieties of peas and beans, and the snowberry, a shrub. Both Lewis and Clark were honored with genus names of plants they had discovered, and Alexander Wilson named birds after them.[68] The explorers also stamped Jeffersonian names on the land through which they traveled. Where the Missouri divides into its branches at present-day Three Forks, Montana, they named the principal stream the Jefferson and the subordinate ones the Gallatin and the Madison. Where the Jefferson River itself divided into three branches further upstream, they gave the name Jefferson to the middle fork, which they believed had the greatest potential of leading to the passage to the Pacific, and the others they named Wisdom and Philanthropy, "in commemoration of two of those cardinal virtues which have so eminently marked that deservedly celebrated character through life."[69]

The Lewis and Clark Expedition marks the widest compass of Jefferson's life with nature. That life may fittingly close with his most personal encounters: in illness and health, with old age, dying, and death. Jefferson paid the closest attention to health, both his own and that of others. Family deaths surrounded him, as they did so many others of his time. Two of his brothers died in infancy, his father when he was fourteen, two sisters before they were thirty, his wife at the age of thirty-three, four of his six children in infancy, and one of his surviving daughters at the age of twenty-five. Understandably in circumstances as

twentieth century. See Paul Russell Cutright, *A History of the Lewis and Clark Journals* (Norman, Okla., 1976). The maps of the expedition, mainly by Clark, are reproduced and explained in Gary E. Moulton, ed., *Atlas of the Lewis and Clark Expedition* (Lincoln, Nebr., 1983). Most of the original material from the expedition reached Philadelphia, where the explorers' papers went to the American Philosophical Society and the major portion of their surviving botanical specimens went to the Academy of Natural Sciences. Many of the zoological specimens went to Charles Willson Peale for his Museum of Natural History. A painted buffalo robe, sent back from Indian territory, is shown in plate 17. For a summary of the scientific results of the expedition, see John C. Greene, *American Science in the Age of Jefferson*, 195–217.

68. *Lewisia rediviva*, the bitterroot, and *Clarkia pulchella*, a member of the primrose family, were named by Frederick Pursch, a young associate of Benjamin Smith Barton, who himself had named the *Jeffersonia* in 1792. For Clark's crow and Lewis's woodpecker, see Robert Cantwell, *Alexander Wilson: Naturalist and Pioneer* (Philadelphia, 1961), 141, 142.

69. William Clark, Journal entry for 6 August 1805, in John Bakeless, ed., *The Journals of Lewis and Clark* (New York, 1964), 220. The names did not last. The upstream "Jefferson" is now the Beaverhead, and the others are the Big Hole and Ruby rivers. None of the rivers is very navigable. Allen, *Passage*, 289.

unhappy as these, he thought health to be "worth more than learning."[70]

The inadequacies of therapeutic medicine impelled him to practice preventive medicine. He urged walking, for example, as an effective way to maintain one's health. The best of exercise—ball games were distinctly inferior—walking should be reserved for a set time each day, undertaken for two hours and in every weather. Above all, it should be engaged in without thinking, for its object was to relax the mind.[71] The model for walking and a guide to good health generally was the Indian. The Indian diet, Jefferson assumed, provided insurance against certain illnesses. But he was so uncritical of the Indians that he glossed over or held Europeans responsible for the Indians' poor health or short lives, and he never considered that the curative powers of Indian remedies might be related to belief systems that he himself would not have accepted.[72]

Indian medicine, as he understood it, pointed the way to the central tenet of his view of health: the *vis medicatrix naturae,* the healing power of nature.[73] Only insofar as the teaching of nature was accepted were medical theory and treatment warranted. Jefferson was outspoken in his distrust of most remedies, nearly all medical theory, hospitals, and doctors. In view of the alternatives at the time, such an outlook appears sensible. On the one hand was medieval medical theory, with its humors, reliance on the zodiac, and the doctrine of signatures. These were just the sort of superstitions that Jefferson fought against in his battles over "the natural" in other realms of life. On the other hand, modern medical theories and practices often seemed pointless, if not actually harmful. Jefferson's most carefully composed statement on medicine was a condemnation of this alternative and one of his most cogent expositions on the place of nature in human life:

> The utility of medicine goes to the well-defined forms of disease. . . . But the disorders of the animal body, and the symptoms indi-

70. TJ to John Garland Jefferson, 11 June 1790, BC.XVI.482. See also TJ to Thomas Mann Randolph, Jr., 27 August 1786, BC.X.308 (knowledge a "lovely possession" but "health is more so").

71. On walking see TJ to Thomas Mann Randolph, Jr., 27 August 1786, BC.X.308; and TJ to John Banister, Jr., 19 June 1787, BC.XI.477 ("are you a great walker? You know I preach up that kind of exercise"). For his other practices, including a largely vegetarian diet and warding off illness by soaking his feet daily in cold water, see TJ to Dr. Vine Utley, 21 March 1819, LB.XV.187.

72. See TJ to Peter Carr, 19 August 1785, BC.VIII.407 (the Indian versus the "enfeebled white"); TJ to Benjamin Hawkins, 18 February 1803, LB.X.364–65 (concerning gout); and TJ, "Instructions to Captain Lewis," 20 June 1803, PJ.310 (the explorers should ascertain "the diseases prevalent among [the Indians], and remedies they use").

73. The phrase appears in TJ to Benjamin Rush, 6 March 1813, LB.XIII.224.

cating them, are as various as the elements of which the body is composed. The combinations, too, of these symptoms are so infinitely diversified, that many associations of them appear too rarely to establish a definite disease; and to an unknown disease, there cannot be a known remedy. Here then, the judicious, the moral, the humane physician should stop. Having been so often a witness to the salutary efforts which nature makes to re-establish the disordered functions, he should rather trust to their action, than hazard the interruption of that, and a greater derangement of the system, by conjectural experiments on a machine so complicated and so unknown as the human body, and a subject so sacred as human life. . . . [But the adventurous physician] establishes for his guide some fanciful theory of corpuscular attraction, of chemical agency, of mechanical powers, of stimuli, or irritability accumulated or exhausted, or depletion by the lancet and repletion by mercury, or some other ingenious dream, which lets him into all nature's secrets at short hand. . . . The patient, treated on the fashionable theory, sometimes gets well in spite of the medicine. . . . I would wish the young practicioner especially, to have deeply impressed on his mind, the real limits of his art, and that when the state of his patient gets beyond these, his office is to be a watchful, but quiet spectator of the operations of nature, giving them fair play by a well-regulated regimen, and by all the aid they can derive from the excitement of good spirits and hope in the patient.[74]

As to our bodies having apparently numberless symptoms composed of various elements, Jefferson is surely right from an observational point of view. We do have, or are at least capable of complaining about, innumerable bodily ills. But even if this is true, and even though it implies the existence of many unknown diseases, it does not mean that we must be without some relief to commonly described symptoms. Nor does it mean that medical research should cease. Yet Jefferson's humility before nature is impressive, and his views that we should not presume to know "nature's secrets at short hand" and that a physician should be "deeply impressed [with] the real limits of his art" are durable injunctions. It was, indeed, Jefferson himself who was a "quiet spectator of the operations of nature." He was a physician after his own model.

From such an outlook on medicine flowed Jefferson's ungenerous views of doctors in an account of an illness of George Washington. Seriously ailing only days before becoming president, Washington, Jefferson said, "was pronounced by two of the three physicians present to be in the act of death. A successful effort of nature however relieved

74. TJ to Dr. Caspar Wistar, 21 June 1807, F.IX.82–84. For the probable relation between this letter and the theory of the Ideologue physician Georges Cabanis, see Courtney R. Hall, "Jefferson on the Medical Theory and Practice of His Day," 238.

him and us."[75] From this same reasoning sprang his dissatisfaction with hospitals. Except for purposes of surgery, which he accepted as a science, he found them a concentration of harmful speculation about disease. "Nature and kind nursing [at home]," he wrote, "serve a much greater proportion [of people] in our plain way, at smaller expense, and with less abuse." On the basis of similar reasoning, he proposed that the University of Virginia teach "vegetable and chemical pharmacy" through ordinary scientific studies. They would supply all one needed to know about medicine.[76]

Although it might appear that Jefferson should be disposed against medical experiments, or at least torn between experimenting and letting nature take its course, he in fact encouraged medical observation and moderate experimentation. His animus was directed only at medical practice with insufficient scientific support. Most medical theory, he wrote bitingly, "is the charlatanerie of the body as [theology] is of the mind."[77] So much did he value practical results in medicine over even demonstrably correct theory that he could effectually disparage a powerful theory (circulation of the blood) in order to praise a powerful practice (vaccination against smallpox) whose success depended on the theory's validity.[78]

The test was whether the practice worked, and much medicine of his time did not work, regardless of its connection with theory. He blamed a dose of Benjamin Rush's Thunderbolt (a concoction of calomel and jalap) for his failure to recover sooner from a short-term illness in his old age. He found the practice of bleeding patients especially worthless. While he seemed to credit the curative powers of some medicinal springs, his own experience with them was discouraging. The springs were natural enough, but he came to think of them as unscientific and socially contrived remedies for ailments.[79] Rather than specific remedies, even if they derived from nature, he accepted the guidance of Hippocrates and believed in care for the whole body. As he counseled an

75. TJ to William Short, 27 May 1790, BC.XVI.444. Contrast Jefferson's remarks on the dying of Vergennes, the French foreign minister of whom he was scarcely fond: "Nature is struggling to relieve him by a decided gout; she has my sincere prayers to aid her." TJ to C. W. F. Dumas, 9 February 1787, BC.XI.127.

76. NVa.134; TJ, Rockfish Gap Report, August 1818, PJ.343.

77. TJ to Thomas Cooper, 7 October 1814, LB.XIV.200.

78. See TJ to Edward Jenner, 14 May, 1806, LB.XIX.152. Jefferson's interest in vaccination dates at least from his trip to Philadelphia in 1766 for the purpose of having himself inoculated. M.I.99–100. See also the Virginia "Bill concerning Inoculation for Smallpox," 27 December 1777, BC.II.124; and Jefferson's correspondence with Dr. Benjamin Waterhouse, S.I.428–29.

79. On the Thunderbolt see TJ to William Short, 31 October 1819, F.X.143. On bleeding, TJ to Thomas Cooper, 7 October 1814, LB.XIV.200. And on medicinal springs, NVa.34–36; TJ to William Short, 7 April 1787, BC.XI.280; and TJ to Francis W. Eppes, 11 September 1818, BB.426.

ailing friend: "Great confidence may be reposed in the provision nature has made for the restoration of order in your system when it has become deranged; she effects her object by strengthening the whole system, towards which medicine is generally mischievous."[80]

The litany of infant deaths in his family led Jefferson to be especially watchful for the care of his grandchildren. On the birth of his first grandchild, he sent his daughter a book comparing humans to animals and urging, on that account, a natural upbringing for the infant. The book spoke of infancy as "that period in life, when instinct is the only active principle of our Nature, and consequently where the analogy between us and other animals will be found most compleat." When his granddaughter became ill not long before her second birthday, Jefferson beseeched the mother "not to destroy the powers of her stomach with medicine. Nature alone can re-establish infant organs." When the little girl's brother became ill several years later, the advice was the same—to leave "nature free and unembarrassed in her own tendencies to repair what is wrong." Both children recovered.[81]

Indispensable in understanding the body over its course, at the end of life nature relieved the body of its most severe ills by ultimately taking life away. As he grew older, Jefferson's confidence in the underlying goodness of nature enabled him to accept the discomforts of age with graciousness. The approach of death, he said with Epicurean equanimity in his mid-seventies,

> I contemplate with little concern, for indeed in no circumstance has nature been kinder to us, than in the soft gradations by which she prepares us to part willingly with what we are not destined always to retain. First one faculty is withdrawn and then another, sight, hearing, memory, affections, and friends, filched one by one, till we are left among strangers, the mere monument of times, facts, and specimens of antiquity for the observation of the curious.[82]

Jefferson had considered himself an old man years before his death. When at sixty-four he declined to stand for a third term as president (primarily because that violated his republican political theory), he noted that he was "sensible of that decline which advancing years bring

80. TJ to Gideon Granger 24 January 1810, LB.XII.352. For Jefferson as a medical environmentalist on whether to cure individuals or to investigate the causes of disease, see TJ to James Madison, 1 February 1801, F.VII.485 (advising his hypochondriacal friend to seek a change of climate, "even from a better to a worse"); and TJ to William Henry Harrison, 27 February 1803, LB.X.368–69 (on yellow fever and climate).

81. John Gregory, *A Comparative View of the State and Faculties of Man with those of the Animal World* (1766). See BC.XIX.282–83; and TJ to Martha Jefferson Randolph, 6 December 1792, BB.107.

82. TJ to Horatio G. Spafford, 11 May 1819, LB.XV.189.

on" and that he intended "to obey this admonition of nature, and to solicit a retreat from cares too great for the wearied faculties of age." On the same ground he refused a request to help the government during his retirement.[83]

His declining powers reminded him of one of his firmest principles: that "the earth belongs to the living." He was therefore quite content to hand over the tasks of life to a younger generation. As to politics, he said he would "not shrink from the post of duty, had not the decays of nature withdrawn me from the list of combatants. . . . It is a law of nature that the generations of men should give way, one to another."[84] As to education, whose function it was to pass on the truths and values of nature to the young, he noted that he was "employing the slender faculties which time and nature" had spared him to establish the University of Virginia.[85] When he combined politics and education in a plea for state funds for the University of Virginia, his conclusion was the same: "I yield the concerns of the world with cheerfulness to those who are appointed in the order of nature to succeed to them."[86]

In all of this it should be plain that Jefferson did not approach death with Christianity, even religion, in mind. Recalling the Lucretian doctrines he had absorbed when young, he wrote: "As a compensation for faculties departed nature gives me good health, and a perfect resignation to the laws of decay which she has prescribed to all the forms and combinations of matter."[87] In the characteristically resigned prose of his later years he wrote to John Adams: "[After sixty,] with most of us, the powers of life are sensibly on the wane, sight becomes dim, hearing dull, memory constantly enlarging its frightful blank and parting with all we have ever seen or known, spirits evaporate, bodily debility creeps on palsying every limb, and so faculty after faculty quits us, and where then is life?"[88] When death finally came, one had finally "paid his debt to nature."[89]

In March 1826 Jefferson wrote his will. In it he left his plantation and second home, Poplar Forest, to one grandson, Francis Wayles Eppes, the son of his deceased daughter Maria. He left Monticello under the management of another grandson, Thomas Jefferson Randolph, the

83. TJ to the Legislature of Vermont, 10 December 1807, LB.XVI.294; TJ to William Duane, 1 October 1812, F.IX.168.

84. TJ to Spencer Roane, 9 March 1821, F.X.188.

85. TJ to Vachel Worthington and George W. Anderson, 17 June 1819, FBx.247.

86. TJ to Gen. James Breckinridge, 15 February 1821, LB.XV.317–18.

87. TJ to William Duane, 1 October 1812, F.IX.168. Had he not been in good health, Jefferson was rationally prepared to commit suicide (by a preparation of the Jimson weed). TJ to Dr. Samuel Brown, 14 July 1813, LB.XIII.310–11.

88. TJ to John Adams, 1 August 1816, C.II.483–84.

89. The phrase is used in TJ to Phillip Mazzei, 29 December 1813, F.IX.443; and in Martha Jefferson Randolph to TJ, 30 January 1800, BB.182.

oldest son of his daughter Martha, for the benefit of her and her family. He freed several of his slaves. The only person outside the Monticello community who benefited from the will was James Madison, to whom he gave his "gold-mounted walking staff of animal horn, as a token of the cordial and affectionate friendship" that had united them throughout life. Late in April he wrote his last substantive letter on the University of Virginia, detailing the duties of the professor of natural history and plans for a botanical garden near the campus.[90]

Near the end of June, sensing a final weakening of the body, Jefferson sent for his physician, Dr. Robley Dunglison, of the university. During the next days, according to his grandson, who was at his bedside, the dying Jefferson displayed an Epicurean manner, like "that of a person going on a necessary journey—evincing neither satisfaction nor regret." The possibility that the minister of his church was among those in attendance in these last days led him to say only that he would welcome the man "as a kind and good neighbor," implying that he was not interested in the presence of a representative of organized religion. On the evening of July 3, he refused the laudanum that he had taken earlier to relieve his pain. During these same hours he asked, "Is it the Fourth?" and the doctor replied, "It soon will be." Shortly after noon the next day, July 4, 1826, the fiftieth anniversary of the signing of the Declaration of Independence, he died.[91] In a downpour on July 5 he was buried in the family cemetery on the slopes of Monticello.

There was one more touch of nature to come. Among Jefferson's papers was found a memorandum of his wishes for a marker at the gravesite. His directives were introduced by a reiteration, if somewhat oblique, of his pagan and materialist outlook on nature. He began:

> Could the dead feel any interest in monuments or other remembrances of them, when as Anacreon says:
> Ολιγη δε κειςομεςθα
> Κονις, οςτεων λυθεντων
> the following would be to my Manes the most gratifying.[92]

As Jefferson agreed, the dead themselves could not feel any interest in remembrances. Why? Because the dead return to nature. According to

90. Jefferson's will, 16, 17 March 1826, LB.XIX.n.p. (facsimile); TJ to Dr. John Emmet, 27 April 1826, LB.XVI.163–67.

91. The deathbed scenes as recounted by Dunglison and Thomas Jefferson Randolph are in Sarah N. Randolph, *The Domestic Life of Thomas Jefferson* (1871; reprint, New York, 1958), 424–29.

92. Frederick D. Nichols and James A. Bear, Jr., *Monticello*, 69. The original may be found in J. M. Edmonds, ed., *Elegy and Iambus . . . with the Anacreonta*, Loeb edition (Cambridge, Mass., 1961), II.60.

Anacreon: "We will lie here a little dust when our bones have dissolved."[93] However, if the dead could feel an interest in any remembrances, Jefferson continued, he had something in mind that "would be to my Manes the most gratifying." As with the reference to Anacreon, so with the Manes. Jefferson recurred to the beliefs of the ancients about nature, in this case the underworld spirits associated with agricultural life.

And what would be most gratifying? To be known for three accomplishments: the Declaration of Independence, the Virginia Statute for Religious Freedom, and the founding of the University of Virginia. Jefferson died as he lived. Explained through his favorite word, he wished to be known for the proclamation that made America free under the laws of nature, for the statute that permitted worship according to the dictates of nature, and for the institution where his own understandings of nature would be transmitted to posterity.

93. The possibility that the disintegration of the bones was the Christian "corruption of the body" is foreclosed. Anacreon lived in the sixth century B.C. Like most students of the classics at the time, Jefferson was wrong in believing that the poem was by Anacreon himself. Instead, it was composed by a later, unknown writer who was inspired by Anacreon and is therefore known as an Anacreontic. The point of the full poem is most unphilosophic and not in keeping with Jefferson's use of it. Its sentiment is of the variety "Live today, for tomorrow we die," an idea Jefferson himself never expressed and would have considered to be vulgarized Epicureanism.

Chapter VII

CONCLUSIONS AND LEGACIES

NATURE WAS Jefferson's myth for all purposes, a flexible idea that gathered together his deepest beliefs. It was uncritically accepted, pervasively invoked. Nature was the source of all that existed and all that was worthwhile. It was the proper scene of action and contemplation. Nature not only *was* these things, it was the means to them as well. It was the means to the discovery of truth, to understanding the good and the beautiful, and to a life of liberty and prosperity.

Jefferson's God was the creator of nature. Nature itself was thereby invested with divinity. But neither nature nor the divine had anything to do with contemporary doctrines of organized Christianity. Rather, humans, like all else in nature, are complex combinations of Lucretian particles, in our case able to understand the world by use of our Lockean senses. Endowed, in addition, with natural reason and ethics, humans are also capable of recognizing natural ends in political liberty and the appropriateness of a livelihood from agriculture. As a single species, humans are necessarily the same as one another in respect to their distinctively human faculty, moral judgment. Therefore the possession of this judgment and the consequent equality of all human beings is unaffected by unnatural social practices, such as slavery, or the natural division of the social word into public and private realms for men and women. Our moral sense is the basis of a natural social ethic, exemplified best by the life of Jesus. An ethics of personal happiness likewise stems from a consideration of nature but is derived from either the Epicureans or the Stoics. Through an innate sense of beauty, we are enabled to see art in nature directly, as at the Natural Bridge, and to create art from nature, as at Monticello.

Jefferson's political theory, too, is derived from nature. Social beings by nature, humans can successfully establish and maintain civil societies. Nations can live with one another peaceably. A society that respects the natural law of the majority and the natural rights of the minority, that recognizes the rights of the living generation to the earth and an ultimate right to alter the government, assures its members their natural right to pursue happiness. Happiness flourishes best in an economy that is natural both in having the least social or governmental control and in being predominantly agricultural.

This is a world of nature that has many theoretical and practical problems. Jefferson faced very few of them directly. An initial question, and one that can be easily answered, asks whether Jefferson himself was "natural." Except in his conversation, which an informed eulogist said was "as simple and unpretending as nature itself," the answer is "No, he was not 'natural.' "[1] He was, and wished to be, as highly cultivated and civilized as possible. His library and correspondence, his music and architecture, his legal arguments, his scientific inquisitiveness, and his political sophistication all characterize a man deeply and contentedly in the grip of society, not nature. When Jefferson loved nature, it was not as a primitivist. His home was at Monticello, not next to the Natural Bridge. Beyond an attachment to certain practices of American Indians, he found no merit in following the course of people untouched by civilization. On the contrary, his faith lay in progress through technology, individual freedom, and the stages of development expected even of the Indians.

Deficiencies in society caused by ignorance, oppression, or unperfected nature could be corrected by reforms based on natural principles. Such reforms included freedom from clerical control, the establishment of small units of self-government, improved education, and an agricultural economy aided by science. The result was a society in conformity with nature that at the same time fulfilled the potential of human nature.

The tenets of nature that Jefferson held harmonized with leading views of his contemporaries. But the variety of these principles and the intensity with which he held them set him apart from his fellows of the American Enlightenment. It was the raw nature of the New World and the opportunity to create new societies in America that most distinguished the American Enlightenment from the European. It was the blend of the nature of western Virginia—near the frontier and prepared to oppose plantation society with small farms—and the learning of the Scottish Enlightenment that helped most to distinguish Jefferson's outlook from that of Americans elsewhere. The mild environment of Albemarle County suited the cooperative nature taught by the Scottish writers. If all Americans could accept nature as presented in the Decla-

---

1. William Wirt, "Eulogy on Jefferson," LB.XIII.xlviii.

ration of Independence and applaud Jefferson's refutation of the theory that nature degenerated in the New World, it did not follow that all Americans thought Indians were favored by nature; or that virtue lay only in an agricultural life; or that the acquisition of western land was desirable. It did not follow that all were as intently interested in natural science, natural theology and morality, an aesthetics derived from nature and a natural basis for politics, economics, and even medicine. Jefferson's identification with nature is distinctive.

Others recognized this distinctiveness, and Jefferson's affinities with nature often led to disagreement, discomfort, and disparagement. This was true not only in publicly sensitive areas such as religion, where Jefferson's deism conflicted with orthodox Christianity, or in politics, where Republicans tended to argue from nature and Federalists from history. It was also true in private, where Jefferson's devotion to the promptings of nature sometimes set him apart from members of his own circle. No one was intellectually closer to Jefferson than Madison. Yet time and again Madison deliberately avoided or tactfully refuted Jefferson's arguments from nature. Jefferson held the more optimistic view of humanity, according to which harmony was natural to society. Madison believed that it was conflict that was natural and that the only sensible aim was to reduce the harm it might cause. Jefferson inclined towards abstract thought, which encouraged reductionism and resulted in dualisms, whether as part of scientific assumption (the economy of nature) or political speculation (natural enemies and natural friends in international relations). Madison was the more discriminating thinker.[2]

Madison recognized the difference between the two when he generously wrote about "sublime truths . . . seen through the medium of Philosophy" (that is, by Jefferson) that are not yet "visible to the naked eye of the ordinary Politician" (that is, by himself).[3] Instance after instance finds Jefferson the philosophic visionary looking to nature and Madison the realistic politician looking to society. Madison demurred from the doctrine that "the earth belongs to the living" by advancing principles drawn from society. He offered a complex economic and psychological explanation for factions, while Jefferson reduced all differences to politics and referred repeatedly to "two parties by nature." He thought a legislature should regulate interest groups, while Jefferson thought it should enforce natural rights. He pressed American claims to Mississippi navigation without mentioning nature, while Jefferson argued the same cause on the basis of natural rights. Madison penned the

2. A provocative note that lends support to this view is Michael Ross, "Homogeneity and Heterogeneity in Jefferson and Madison."

3. James Madison to TJ, 4 February 1790, Adrienne Koch, ed., *The American Enlightenment*, 449.

Virginia Resolutions without recourse to nature. Jefferson wrote the Kentucky Resolutions with explicit support from natural right. Even in the case of scenery—at the confluence of the Shenandoah and the Potomac—Madison was not impressed with Jefferson's judgment of nature.

Jefferson's attachment to nature was so strong that he was careful not to sully it (or himself) by using it to condemn slavery. His instincts were so ingrained that alleged principles from nature could become the occasion for rhetorical opportunism instead of serious analysis, as when he used nature to strengthen government under the Articles of Confederation and weaken it under the Constitution; or when he held that serving the public was a natural duty but not serving the public was a natural right; or when he replaced a recognized doctrine of natural law in American foreign policy with a new policy that he claimed was closer to the "true" law of nature. His natural right of freedom conflicted with his natural law of self-preservation. His natural law of majority rule clashed with the natural right for minorities. He believed in intervening in nature, as with canal projects, but allowing nature to take its course, as in medicine and economics. His nature ran in many directions, and not surprisingly it sometimes bumped into itself.

Perhaps Jefferson's friends knew something about nature that he did not. When compared with Adams and Madison, Jefferson possessed perhaps the widest range of interests and talents. But he was the least of the three as a philosopher. Adams and Madison may have recognized that nature was uselessly ambiguous, or too simple and too simplifying an idea on which to base arguments about society. They may in fact have thought nature precisely the wrong basis on which to reason. In Jefferson's hands nature took on attributes of divinity. It thereby supplanted some of the most significant explanations and sanctions for social phenomena: history, culture, and human responsibility. To Jefferson, nature was an idea that was so rational that to use it appeared to deny any nonrational features of human communities and at the same time to diminish the distinctive identities of those communities. Thus the argument from nature may have deprived society of both its needs in mystery and its truths in history. Finally, when everything reduces to nature, and without employing more subtlety than Jefferson did, it is impossible to establish priorities in personal or public life.

Despite examples of apparent opportunism and real problems, three pairs of ideas about nature in Jefferson's thought merit independent consideration: free will and determinism, the *is* and the *ought,* and universals versus particulars.

How much choice do human beings have by nature? are we fated, or are we free? On the one hand, Jefferson believed that a society's customs depended largely on its environment, as his own did with regard to slavery. If so, we have little choice of our own. On the other hand, if Jefferson's own life shows anything, it is that he also believed in the efficacy of free will—for himself, for the hundreds of people on whom he showered advice, and for the public policies of the new nation. It is difficult to believe that he thought free will to be mere appearance.

Philosophically Jefferson might have adopted the way out of determinism taken by Lucretius: "When the atoms are travelling straight down through empty space by their own weight, at quite indeterminate times and places they swerve ever so little from their course . . . and so they snap the bonds of fate."[4] To snap the bonds of fate by postulating an unpredictability of this sort may be satisfactory to twentieth-century science, but it does not say much on behalf of free will or express a persuasive moral theory.

Sociologically Jefferson might have claimed that the problem of free will was no problem at all. Since both nature and human nature are good, one hardly needs much choice in order to accomplish nature's goals. We would probably be better off without it. Only if humans were naturally determined with a tilt towards evil—perhaps towards sin, which Jefferson gave no sign of believing in—might it be better for society to hypothesize free will for individuals.

A second problem, which Jefferson also did not recognize, is the distinction between the descriptive and prescriptive properties of nature. Believing that nature could prescribe for man, he moved easily from facts to values, from what he claimed to be true of physical and human nature to the standards he held for the good and the beautiful. He could do this because he believed that humans were endowed with internal, material senses that perceived external, material facts. Certain natural moral or aesthetic facts, having been perceived by the natural senses, automatically became values. The actual process of transformation was no more understood by Jefferson than it has been by his successors. But the doctrines of materialism and sensationism led to such presumed objective conclusions in ethics and aesthetics.

A third problem, and one Jefferson was at least sometimes conscious of, inquires into the difference between universal nature and particular nature. Universal nature speaks to what is permanent and absolute, true at every place and at all times. Particular nature speaks to contingency, nature as the environment or the form a particular society takes. But the universal and particular may be accommodated. Jefferson does this under the idea of progress, which enables a people to move from one

4. *De Rerum Natura* II.216–20.

stage to another, from a nature that is parochial to one that is in greater conformity with universal law. Thus, while natural law may be the same everywhere, the knowledge of it and the capacity to reach it can differ. Universal nature becomes the potential of particular nature.

It is the principles of universal nature, philosophy, that form the great model for Enlightenment thinking, as the English title of Newton's *Principia* (1687) makes clear: *The Mathematical Principles of Natural Philosophy*. But half a century later, the principles of particular nature, history, had their champions, first in natural history with Linnaeus's *Systema Naturae* (1735) and then in civil history with Montesquieu's *Spirit of the Laws* (1748). Although Jefferson's hero among the three was Newton, his inclinations always tended towards investigations in natural history rather than natural philosophy. Nevertheless, the ideal of universal nature persisted for him, and the tension between the two conceptions, especially in his discussions of society and his struggle with natural law, is conspicuous. As he notes when judging slavery in Virginia: "It is difficult to determine on the standard by which the manners of a nation may be tried, whether *catholic,* or *particular*."[5]

For all the theoretic and practical problems imbedded in Jefferson's uses of nature, any critic should consider that the thought of few public figures deserves to be taken as seriously as Jefferson's; that Jefferson's confusions were typical of his time and place; and that on many of the fundamental issues, although we may no longer speak in the language of nature, we are scarcely better off than he was. If Jefferson was uncertain how much of human nature is innate and how much is owing to the environment, so are we. If Jefferson was convinced that humans were by nature peaceful, and was therefore distressed to find us so often at war, that problem has hardly been resolved since. If Jefferson proposed that culture in America varies according to latitude, we are hardly immune from holding that regions of the United States still breed distinctive societies. If Jefferson accepted a single-species explanation for the races of mankind, which we also do, but was uncertain about the "innate" characteristics for red, white, and black races, American society has overcome this scientifically but certainly not socially.

Jefferson's aversion to system and theory in medicine, geology, and chemistry; his concern for knowledge that was useful and drawn from experience rather than from speculation; his outdated conceptions about creation, time, and species—if all of these led him to ignore potentially fruitful areas of inquiry, comparable weaknesses surely afflict us. For all our progress in understanding nature, including (if this is

5. NVa.162.

progress) our largely discarding the word "nature" itself, we may be even worse off than Jefferson. Because developments in understanding nature make it impossible today for single minds to aspire to as much fundamental knowledge as he did, society knows more by individuals knowing less.

In one important area, however, cross-cultural comparison, Jefferson's understanding may in fact be superior to our own, and the reason may be precisely his unwillingness to resolve the universal/particular problem about nature. Legislation, Jefferson said, should in general conform to universal natural law. At the same time, it should be adapted to a community and its environment. This is an ambiguous principle, but it is not impractical. Jefferson did not doubt that America was in the vanguard of nations in its political organization, but he did not believe that other countries could or should have governments exactly like that of the United States. It is difficult to reconcile the doctrines of the Declaration of Independence with this observation from Jefferson in old age: "The qualifications for self-government are not innate. They are the result of habit and long training." But this was the lesson for the French, who "from the natural progress of things must press forward" to liberty but should still be cautious about calling for universal rights. It was true for the Russians, "who are not capable of taking care of themselves," even though the tsar was justified in spreading a "sense of natural rights" throughout the nation.[6] Environmentalism enjoined Jefferson to be a conservative realist in international relations.

Natural rights have returned in the late twentieth century as human rights. But it is an illusion to believe that Jefferson's interlocked assumptions and cast of thought about nature can be recovered whole for the present. American history has often made it convenient and may on occasion have made it necessary to believe that Jefferson's ideas can truly be ours. But with respect to nature this is not so, and this makes it especially difficult to convey his times to our own.[7]

It has been the purpose of this study to recreate Jefferson's world of nature, to begin with his language and then to provide as much coherence as feasible based on that language, all the while pointing to problems raised by the language and its associated thought. The remainder of this chapter has two purposes. The first is to show that even by the time he died Jefferson's understanding of nature had ceased to be

6. TJ to Edward Everett, 27 March 1824, LB.XVI.22; TJ to Richard Price, 8 January 1789, BC.XIV.423; TJ to Joseph Priestley, 29 November 1802, F.VIII.179.

7. This is the guiding assumption, as the title implies, of Daniel J. Boorstin, *The Lost World of Thomas Jefferson*. Gordon S. Wood writes of the "irretrievability and differentness of the eighteenth-century world." *The Creation of the American Republic, 1776–1787,* viii. See, similarly, Drew R. McCoy, *The Elusive Republic*, 7.

that of America.[8] The second is to suggest by a number of examples what America has made of Jeffersonian nature since his time. To appreciate how the nation has either continued Jefferson's views or reacted against them is to appreciate his own stance even better, while enriching an understanding of important elements of the American experience since.[9]

With Jefferson dies an entire mode of discourse that, for all its inconsistencies, had nature at its center, nature used earnestly, optimistically, and for all occasions. Although Americans continued to respond to nature in a patriotic and cultural fashion, Enlightenment ideas and their accompanying language departed from the scene. The most important reason for this was that nature no longer served the political function it had at the time of independence. Indeed it may be said to have become dangerous once a new civil society was established. When the nation was founded, the process of cutting the political bonds with England placed the colonies in a state of nature, or so it may be considered. But once civil society was reestablished, not only was nature no longer needed, it was perhaps even impolitic to mention it. One need only contrast the uses of nature in the Declaration of Independence and Jefferson's First Inaugural to recognize this.

Although the Constitution reflects ideas of natural law in a number of its provisions and is also a "higher law" either by its own terms or by virtue of the sacred place it came to occupy in the minds of Americans, it was not actually "natural law." The Constitution had been accepted, not because it was ordained by nature or because it contained substan-

---

8. In the dozens of well-publicized eulogies pronounced on his death there is a striking absence of Jefferson's language of nature. See, e.g., *A Selection of Eulogies Pronounced in the Several States, in Honor of John Adams and Thomas Jefferson.* While many refer to his interests in natural science or quote passages from his writings that mention nature, it is only the rare one, such as that of William Wirt, that is suffused with the earlier expression. (Wirt did not come upon the subject unannounced: his travel novel of 1803, *The Letters of the British Spy,* may be read as a Jeffersonian tract on nature.)

A periodicization of American history that coincides with Jefferson's passing is evident in national politics by the end of the Virginia dynasty in the presidency and the advent of Jacksonianism. It is demonstrated in culture by Gordon S. Wood, *The Rising Glory of America, 1760–1820* (New York, 1971); and in American science by John C. Greene, *American Science in the Age of Jefferson.* If one looks to Virginia rather than to the nation at large, a cutoff date of the 1820s is warranted, as well. But the reason is more specific, for somewhere between the Missouri Compromise (1820) and Nat Turner's Rebellion (1831), the political division over slavery was irrevocably set, and southern society lost whatever flexibility it may have had under the Jeffersonian dispensation.

9. The task resembles that of Merrill D. Peterson in *The Jefferson Image in the American Mind,* except that the examples selected here refer to nature only and do not require that Jefferson's successors have the man himself in mind, only that their views about nature be reasonably related to his. Peterson's "Guide to Sources," 459–522, has been especially valuable, and his text has been drawn on at a number of places.

tive natural law, but because, following Jefferson's natural law of majority rule, it was what the people had ratified. This is reflected in the early interpretation of the Constitution by the Supreme Court. References to natural law and right soon die out in the justices' opinions, and even the most Jeffersonian justice, William Johnson, changes his mind on the constitutional propriety of natural rights thinking.[10]

Arguments from nature declined near the end of Jefferson's life for cultural reasons as well. The vital European sources of American thought on nature had changed from the days of Jefferson's youth. Material from the Scottish Enlightenment, although part of the college curriculum, meant less to young men in the 1830s than it had to Jefferson in the 1760s. Partly at Jefferson's own suggestion, the classics played a smaller role in education than earlier, reducing the likelihood that either materialist nature or pastoral poetry would contribute as much to the intellectual training of Americans. Freed from European domination, Americans also had less interest in other authorities who relied on nature: Locke, the Physiocrats, the Continental jurists. The European models themselves had changed. Benthamite utilitarianism replaced the natural law of Blackstone. Nineteenth-century organic thought, whether in philosophy, science, or literature, was unquestionably tied to nature. But it had supplanted the more atomistic and classical nature of Lucretius and Newton.

Changes in the political economy also contributed to the end of Jefferson's language of nature. As commerce and industry developed, and despite the continued prominence of agriculture, a decreasing percentage of Americans lived completely rural lives, and the attachment to nature began its transformation from fact into myth and nostalgia. While the myth was originally powerful, in the long run it could not retain its power, even if it could sustain its vocabulary.[11] The post-Jeffersonian changes in the American economy included the rise of the corporation, that "artificial person" which came to dominate commerce and industry and ultimately agriculture itself. As unnatural entities, corporations were free to evolve into what Jefferson so much feared, monopoly. But even if corporations did not become monopolies, they presaged the end of the small economic units that Jefferson

10. John Marshall, Jefferson's powerful and ultimately successful rival as an interpreter of the Constitution, was certainly steeped in the natural law tradition, but he seldom showed it from the bench. For a contrast of Marshall's and Jefferson's understandings of natural rights, see Robert K. Faulkner, *The Jurisprudence of John Marshall*, 172–87. On Johnson see Donald G. Morgan, *Justice William Johnson, the First Dissenter: The Career and Constitutional Philosophy of a Jeffersonian Judge* (Columbia, S.C., 1954), esp. 211–14 and 221–29.

11. On the cultural transformation of the agrarian myth see Thomas Bender, *Toward an Urban Vision*.

believed to be as natural as they were critical for republican virtue.

In the first decades after his death, an artistic movement did perpetuate one aspect of Jeffersonian nature. That was the Hudson River school of painting. The manifesto of this school, Thomas Cole's "Essay on American Scenery" (1836), employs the same aesthetic vocabulary as Jefferson: the sublime, the beautiful, and the picturesque. Like Jefferson, Cole distinguishes America from Europe by the grandeur of its scenery. But there are two crucial differences between the men. First, Cole gives to nature a religious mysticism, a misty romanticism of the supernatural with which Jefferson would have been distinctly uncomfortable. Second, Cole subscribes to a fatalism about the future of American nature that Jefferson did not share. Jefferson did not conceive that the American land might be limited or the nation's scenery destroyed. A decade after Jefferson's death, however, Cole depicted just this fate in a series of five paintings entitled "The Course of Empire."

At the same time, James Fenimore Cooper was reacting to Jefferson's nature in his fiction. In five volumes of the *Leather-Stocking Tales* (1823–41), Cooper expects the scenes of American nature to be both appreciated and (agriculturally) improved in a distinctly Jeffersonian manner; but he is worried that the settlers, from commercial greed or lack of culture, will despoil what nature has provided. He saw as much corruption in the countryside as Jefferson had found in cities. Cooper also undermined Jefferson's view of nature by an ambivalent attitude towards natural law. Cooper's natural law releases men from the artificial codebook law of society. It allows them to live by purer precepts. It is a world in which everyone seems to be ploughman and no one the professor. But the beneficiaries of natural law are not ploughmen, for they become corrupt. Rather it is preagriculturalists like Natty Bumppo who authentically know and value nature. Yet a wilderness hero like Natty, who acts correctly from an innate moral sense, is such a loner in the woods as to be a Jeffersonian impossibility.

The artistic revision, if not rejection, of Jeffersonian nature by Cole and Cooper was matched with a social and political revision at the hands of Andrew Jackson. No one mistook his Hermitage for Monticello. On the contrary, Jackson exploited the reputation of an unlettered man from the forest. He was natural, yes, but without the Jeffersonian accompaniment of culture.[12] Jackson's agricultural values were the same as Jefferson's. But Jacksonian farmers were not very independent—not from the banks, which controlled credit and currency; not from the manufacturers of farm machinery; not from the barges, ships, and

---

12. See, generally, John William Ward, *Andrew Jackson, Symbol for an Age,* in which the first and most important element of Jackson as a symbol is "nature."

railroads that transported their goods to market; and certainly not from themselves as competitors in the production of farm goods for commerce. And as agriculture was failing to become what Jefferson envisioned, industrialism crept, and eventually swept, into the American economy. It came first to small towns, where it preserved at least an ostensible contact with rural America. But it came ultimately to cities, which then began to take on the characteristics of European centers that Jefferson so disliked.

While in culture and society Jefferson's ideas were merely modified, in transcendentalism, America's most distinctive philosophy of nature, they were denounced. Without ever naming Jefferson as an antagonist, the transcendentalists quarreled with all that he stood for regarding nature. They dismissed two of his heroes, Bacon and Locke, and were largely indifferent to Newton. At root the difference was that the transcendentalists were Platonic Idealists, while Jefferson was a Lucretian materialist. Jefferson despised Plato, and the transcendentalists embraced him, for the same reason: in Plato there existed a higher reality than the physical facts of nature.

Jefferson and the transcendentalists agreed, although on opposite grounds, that there was no difference between mind and body. To Jefferson both were material nature. To the transcendentalists they were both spiritual. This led to a perhaps unexpected transcendentalist advantage in science. Because the transcendentalists could find correspondences between natural and spiritual facts, they were receptive to, if not always concretely interested in, scientific speculation, while the fact-minded Jefferson was often a closed-minded scientist. When Jefferson came on information that did not accord with a favored theory, he was likely to challenge the authenticity of the new facts or to insist on a materialist explanation that fit his received rationalistic framework. Since the transcendentalists could accept virtually anything brought to their attention and make some spiritual sense out of it, they, unlike Jefferson, did not quail before theories of geology or hold to premises that barred the acceptance of evolution.

Jefferson's ideas on nature may have been displaced in speculative philosophy in mid-nineteenth-century America, but they were indispensable to the most significant political movement of the era, abolitionism. The natural rights doctrines of the antislavery movement sprang directly from the Declaration of Independence. But because the man who had composed the Declaration had lived, and lived very well, by slavery, the abolitionists (with the canny exception of Frederick Douglass) did not cite Jefferson the person, only the Declaration as a document. Jefferson might have been distraught at the movement, but he would have recognized most of its ideas as his own. At the same time, he would have been dismayed to find that many of his fellow southerners had completely abandoned his own arguments from nature, had discovered a "natural law of slavery," and had converted into dogma his uncertain suggestion that blacks were by nature an intellectually inferior race.

Nothing better demonstrates the ingenuity of the public debate, and with it the degeneration of Jefferson's natural rights arguments, than the interpretation given to the Declaration of Independence in the *Dred Scott* case. In a breathtaking rendition of history and of the meaning of the written word, Chief Justice Taney concluded that it was an "opinion . . . universal in the civilized portion of the white race" that blacks were "beings of an inferior order" and therefore that "if the language [of the Declaration of Independence], as understood in that day, would embrace [the enslaved African race], the conduct of the distinguished men who framed the Declaration of Independence would have been utterly and flagrantly inconsistent with the principles they asserted." Jefferson would have been astonished at the claim that the "general words" of the Declaration did not "embrace the whole human family." It was Taney who had not understood Enlightenment natural rights thinking, not Jefferson who was "incapable of asserting principles" inconsistent with his practices. He was indeed capable of doing that, and it was the torment of his life.

Since Taney was correct about the practices of the founders, the issue in *Dred Scott* was whether the ideas of the Declaration were to be interpreted downward to meet the fact of slavery or whether slavery should be interpreted upward to meet the natural rights ideas of the Declaration. Each side in the case adopted a Jeffersonian view of what was natural, the Court holding that the function of the judiciary was to effectuate the natural right of the majority, and the dissent, recalling that slavery was "contrary to natural right," arguing that constitutional meaning did not remain fixed but should advance towards the natural right of liberty. Neither side alluded to the natural right that the Declaration was specifically written to justify, the right of revolution—silent testimony that the justices knew the issue might be decided outside of constitutional law.

The year after *Dred Scott,* the contest over Jefferson's principles was continued in the Lincoln-Douglas debates. Lincoln argued for the natural principles of equality and liberty, Douglas for the natural principle of the consent of the governed (in the form of "popular sovereignty" for whites). Lincoln, who considered Jefferson "the most distinguished politician of our history," seldom used "nature" or "natural" when speaking of the rights of enslaved Africans. But when he did, he was more outspoken about race and slavery than Jefferson himself: "There is no reason in the world why the negro is not entitled to all the natural rights enumerated in the Declaration of Independence."

But it was not possible for Lincoln to return to the natural rights optimism of the Enlightenment. Over slavery even Jefferson had given up, and it was Lincoln who recalled the words in public: "I will remind Judge Douglas and this audience, that while Mr. Jefferson was the owner of slaves, as undoubtedly he was, in speaking upon this very subject, he used the strong language that 'he trembled for his country when he remembered that God was just.' "[13] Thus later, in his Second Inaugural, Lincoln was following a trace of Jeffersonian thought in looking beyond both society and nature to the "judgments of the Lord" in order to account for the crisis of the Union and the Civil War. Jefferson had claimed that nature had formed the Union. Lincoln realized that nature had failed to preserve it.

In the decades after the Civil War, three related themes in American society recalled a very different element of Jefferson's nature repertoire, the land itself. In agrarianism, the end of the frontier, and the rise of the conservation movement, Jefferson had the opportunity to seem vital once more. Farming was rhapsodized by Lincoln nearly in the master's language:

> No other human occupation opens so wide a field for the profitable and agreeable combination of labor with cultivated thought, as agriculture. I know of nothing so pleasant to the mind, as the discovery of anything which is at once *new* and *valuable*—nothing which so lightens and sweetens toil, as the hopeful pursuit of such discovery. And how vast and how varied a field is agriculture, for such discovery. . . . Every blade of grass is a study; and to produce two, where there was but one, is both a profit and a pleasure.[14]

In a ten-week period in 1862 Lincoln perfected this vision by establishing the Department of Agriculture and signing the Homestead and Land Grant College acts. Under the first, the federal government took on tasks in agricultural science that Jefferson had once attempted to perform virtually single-handedly. Under the second, farmers secured the opportunity—only weakly realized in face of western physiography

13. Lincoln, Speech at Peoria, Illinois, 16 October 1854, in Roy P. Basler, *Collected Works of Abraham Lincoln*, Vol. II (New Brunswick, N.J., 1953), 249; First Debate with Douglas, Ottawa, Illinois, 21 August 1858, Basler, III.16; Reply to Douglas, Galesburg, Illinois, 7 October 1858, Basler, III.220. See also Lincoln, Speech at Springfield, Illinois, 4 October 1854, Basler, II.245 ("What *natural* right requires Kansas and Nebraska to be opened to slavery? Is not slavery universally granted to be, in the abstract, a gross outrage on the law of nature?").

14. Lincoln, Address before the Wisconsin State Agricultural Society, Milwaukee, 30 September 1859, Basler, III. 480.

and the urge to speculate in land—to acquire family-sized freeholds on public domain, thus effectuating the Locke-Jefferson theory that property is the occupancy of nature accompanied by labor. Under the land grant colleges, education was to be open for both future agriculturalists and the natural aristocracy.

Despite these policies and a yeoman myth, American agriculture came to be characterized in the late nineteenth century precisely by what Jefferson feared most. Farmers aimed not at independence but at making a living by bringing their produce to market. Because of transportation charges, credit restrictions, and the wide fluctuation in domestic supply and foreign demand for American crops, they often failed. They then did what their forbears had done: organized politically and appealed to Jefferson's ideas for support. The connections are most pronounced in the careers of two men whose political paths crossed in the 1890s, Henry George and William Jennings Bryan.

The thought of Henry George (1839–97) is so substantially Jeffersonian that to convey it at all is nearly to repeat what has been said about, if not by, Jefferson himself. At its base is a conjunction of natural political rights from the Declaration of Independence and the "economic axiom that all men have equal rights to natural opportunities to land." From this conjunction George reasons that society may rearrange property (land) rights and that the new arrangement should be one of equality. Recognizing that it is not practical to reallocate the land itself, however, George proposes taxing it according to its productivity (potential or actual) and using the proceeds for the common good. This, he asserts, would force people to do with the land what nature intended should be done, namely, raise crops on it. It will effect "a compliance with the 'fundamental natural right to labor the earth,' and our people would once again become, as Jefferson thought they would for centuries remain, virtuous and happy." This has not become the case. George's program has been largely forgotten. It is at once too radical for contemporary Americans, too simplistic for modern economists and the modern economy, and too anachronistic in its invocation of Jefferson and nature for late-twentieth-century ears.[15]

15. Henry George, Jr., "Jefferson and the Land Question" (misquoting, by adding the word "natural" in TJ to James Madison, 28 October 1785, BC.VIII.682. The essay is misattributed to the elder Henry George. Through a comparison of signatures, Anastacio Teodoro, of the New York Public Library, has kindly cleared up the confusion). Merrill Peterson writes that George adopted "Jefferson's faith in the beneficent natural order, his belief in natural economic abundance and in equal access to natural resources, and his firm distrust of concentrated power, economic and political." *Jefferson Image,* 258. For a discussion of the plight of agrarians in an industrial era attempting to recall Jefferson's moral order, see William B. Scott, *In Pursuit of Happiness,* 181–99.

If George was a Jeffersonian economist, William Jennings Bryan was a Jeffersonian politician, and a comparable fate has overtaken him. Unlike George, who would have used his tax on land to eliminate urban poverty, Bryan was an undiluted representative of agrarian, antiurban sentiments. In his "Cross of Gold" speech of 1896 he spoke for "the pioneers away out there, who rear their children near to Nature's heart, where they can mingle their voices with the voices of the birds." Away out there, contact with the soil bred reverence for the Creator. But Bryan's creator was not Jefferson's. He was a fundamentalist Christian, not a deist, and one who transformed Jefferson into a Christ-like figure. The Democratic candidate for president three times, Bryan eventually became the conscientious if unfit successor to Jefferson as secretary of state. After resigning from the cabinet in 1915 he faded as a national political force, along with modern Jeffersonian agrarianism.

At the height of the agrarian movement the other two tides of Jeffersonian nature came in, the frontier thesis and the conservation movement. That all three occurred in the same era is not coincidence. The "end of the frontier" symbolized the end of America's apparently limitless natural resources. The agrarian protest in part, and the conservation movement almost entirely, developed in response to this same perception. To all three movements any subversion of the Jeffersonian assumption about American nature risked a loss of national identity.

Frederick Jackson Turner (1861–1932) is the last intellectual of Jeffersonian nature. Like Jefferson, Turner grew up in an agricultural area near what they both considered the border of "free" land. But while Jefferson had seen a "chosen country, with room enough for our descendants to the hundredth and thousandth generation," Turner, less than a century later (and with a national territory more than four times the size of Jefferson's in 1801), concluded that the room had run out. Prompted to consider what America owed to its frontier heritage, Turner came to the Jeffersonian conclusion that it had contributed individualism and democracy. Both men believed that the crucial characteristics of America were to be explained environmentally, not by ancestry; that the West was the font of American democracy; that the frontier, or nature, represented the absence of dominating social institutions such as feudalism and the church and therefore promoted individual freedom; and that the conditions of nature and the frontier dissolved many of the ties of community and graces of civilization, which had to be won back. Turner concludes that "the frontier has gone, and with its going has closed the first period in American history." It was the period of Jefferson.[16]

16. Frederick Jackson Turner, "The Significance of the Frontier in American History"

While Turner was proclaiming that a period had closed, the conservation movement was working to prolong it. Like the frontier thesis, early traces of the conservation movement may be found in Jefferson. Conservationists could look to Jefferson's acquiring, maintaining, and publicizing the Natural Bridge as a public trust; to his concern for scientific management of the land; to his interest in vanishing (though not extinct) species; and to his real, if unformed, sense of ecological relationships. The gap between Jefferson and the conservationists was nevertheless wide. Deism and Newton had been replaced by transcendentalism and Darwin. Jefferson cared for but knew almost nothing about the West. He was almost deliberately ignorant of geology. He believed in the virtual infinitude of the country's natural resources and so was exempt from having to develop significant public policy about them. Therefore, while the often backward-looking agrarians either overlooked or did not mind these differences and made Jefferson their hero, the conservationists, looking to the future under assumptions, knowledge, and circumstances that Jefferson did not share, did not consider him an important predecessor.

Of the first generation of conservationists the most prominent are the ethnologist and painter of American Indians, George Catlin (1796–1872), and the founder of ecological science in the United States, George Perkins Marsh (1801–82). Like the Hudson River artists, Catlin painted American nature in order to "preserve" it, but instead of accepting its entire disappearance as the cost of progress, he envisioned a national park that would protect at least some live creatures: Indians and buffalo, "joint and original tenants of the soil . . . in all the wild and freshness of their nature's beauty!"[17] Marsh advanced along a very different path. Jefferson had called for studies of "the effect of clearing and culture towards changes of climate."[18] In his rambling, massive *Man and Nature; or, Physical Geography as Modified by Human Action* (1864), Marsh more than carried out this suggestion and laid the basis for the professional study of the interaction of man and nature.

In the early conservation movement Catlin and Marsh were loners. Conservationists in later generations, by astute public relations or asso-

---

(1893), in *The Frontier in American History* (New York, 1920), 38. For a startling literary parallel between Turner and Jefferson, both imagining how civilization emerged from nature, compare Turner, 12, with TJ to William Ludlow, 6 September 1824, LB.XVI.74–75. Richard Hofstadter states that "almost everything Turner says about Jefferson, though most of it is still integral in the American gospel, is either badly nuanced, a misleading half truth, or flatly wrong." *The Progressive Historians: Turner, Beard, Parrington* (New York, 1969), 133.

17. Catlin, *North American Indians,* in *The American Environment,* ed. Roderick Nash, 8, 9.

18. TJ to Lewis E. Beck, 16 July 1824, LB.XVI.72.

ciation with federal agencies, could accomplish actual public policy. The most notable of these are John Wesley Powell, John Muir, and Gifford Pinchot. A natural historian, investigator of the public lands with an eye to their ecological lessons and economic potential, and philosophically minded writer, Powell (1834–1902) was the leading scientist in the U.S. government for a quarter of a century. Shaped by experiences and an intellectual world that set him apart from Jefferson, he also knew the American West. This meant that with extensive field work and a correct approach to geological time, his geology was right and Jefferson's was wrong. It also meant that he was able to demonstrate the impossibility of settling most of the land with small farms, thus shattering an article of Jefferson's geopolitical faith.[19]

John Muir (1838–1914) and Gifford Pinchot (1863–1946), although of different generations, must be paired and then set beside their mutual admirer, Theodore Roosevelt. Muir was a transcendentalist in philosophy, an explorer by temperament, a scientist out of curiosity, and a publicist from necessity. The best-known spokesman on behalf of nature in American history, he was Jeffersonian only in his drive to preserve natural wonders, which he defined very liberally. His efforts led to the founding of the National Park Service. Pinchot, the country's first professionally trained forester, brought the values of the Progressive Era, many of them Jeffersonian, to the cause of nature and was responsible for establishing the U.S. Forest Service. The two men, the spiritual preservationist and the utilitarian conservationist, battled for the attention of Theodore Roosevelt. Roosevelt, the most important "nature president" in American history, accommodated the two drives as best he could (he saved the Grand Canyon from private interests, for instance), but he sided largely with his fellow Progressive, Pinchot.[20]

In the 1920s, a period of little momentum for conservation and, at the end, a devastation for agriculture, a cultural movement with "nature" written all over it formed in Nashville, Tennessee—the Southern Agrarians. Under the name Twelve Southerners, in their book *I'll*

19. For a striking literary contrast between Powell and Jefferson, compare the Natural Bridge passage in *Notes on the State of Virginia* with Powell on the Grand Canyon. NVa.24–25; Powell, *The Exploration of the Colorado River and Its Canyons* (1895), in John Conron, *The American Landscape*, 349–50.

20. A comparison of Roosevelt and Jefferson is instructive. Roosevelt loathed Jeffersonian politics. (Sufficient evidence is supplied merely by the index entries to Roosevelt's *The Winning of the West*.) But he made an exception for the Louisiana Purchase and the Lewis and Clark Expedition and indeed with respect to nature was far more Jeffersonian than he apparently recognized. Both men were self-educated field biologists, and if they are to be believed, both would initially have preferred to devote their lives to natural history. A conservationist in the White House, Roosevelt established the Bureau of Reclamation as well as the U.S. Forest Service. He sponsored an elaborate Conservation Conference and launched a Commission on Country Life. His State of the Union Messages are notable for their lessons on natural resources.

Take My Stand (1930) the Agrarians accomplished a sophisticated re-working and often a perversion of Jefferson's ideas about nature. Much of American society deserved criticism, and the Southerners were distressed by a "progress" that might have distressed Jefferson, too. But their creed, high-toned as it appears, is at heart an apology for a tradition that was outdated, immoral, or both. From the philosophical introduction to the book by John Crowe Ransom, complaining about industrial society's lost "truce with nature" and the failure of religion and the arts to have a "right attitude to nature," through John Gould Fletcher's misapplication of the idea of a natural aristocracy, the Southerners provide an unmatched intellectual example of Jeffersonian nature gone awry.[21]

Within a few years of the Southerners' manifesto, and not many miles from their cultural headquarters, this atavistic perception of Jeffersonian nature was overthrown. The agent of the overthrow was the Tennessee Valley Authority, which laid claim to Jefferson in the direction not of culture but of science and democracy. If TVA could have intellectual heroes, they would be the same as Jefferson's—Bacon, Newton, and Locke—none of whom appealed to the Agrarians. One cannot be certain how Jefferson would have reacted to a project as vast as TVA. But he presumably would have approved of each of its separate aims, for TVA was working out his own vision. Despite his plans for rectilinear boundaries in the western territory, Jefferson would have appreciated TVA's ecologically based jurisdiction, as well as its independence from the national government and its expected responsiveness to local communities. TVA restrained the monopoly powers of private utilities, improved the position of small landholders, engaged in agricultural extension work, soil conservation, and reforestation, and hoped to foster spiritual renewal through its recreation projects. Until its latter-day decline, TVA seemed the complete Jeffersonian project of twentieth-century America.[22]

21. Twelve Southerners, *I'll Take My Stand*, 7, xxv. Many of the essays are haunted by "the Negro problem," one claiming that the Civil War had disrupted the South's "natural course of affairs" (56). The essay by the most truly agrarian among the Twelve, Andrew Nelson Lytle, is an amalgam of racism, anti-industrialism, and selective Jeffersonian theory. Both provocative and illusionary, it even includes a scene enacting the myth of the "sacred fire" passage in *Notes on the State of Virginia* (219). A significant piece historically, because it was later disavowed, is Robert Penn Warren's "The Briar Patch." Although the disavowal took many forms, Warren's *Brother to Dragons*, a poem-dialogue about murder and racism among Jefferson's relatives, is the most notable. If one may infer from its epigraph, Warren accuses Jefferson of failing to follow the creed of Lucretius, which would disperse the "darkness of the mind . . . by the aspect and law of nature" (vii).

22. The heritage of Bacon in TVA appears as a chapter epigraph in David Lilienthal's evangelistic *TVA: Democracy on the March* (New York, 1944): "In order to master Nature,

The Tennessee Valley Authority came into being under Franklin D. Roosevelt, a self-assured Jeffersonian with conservationist credentials second only to those of his Republican cousin. But in the face of the twentieth-century economy and the Depression, New Deal programs suggest the failure rather than the success of Jefferson's understanding of American nature. The Tennessee River basin should have flourished with independent farmers. But many were tenants or sharecroppers, and most were poor. The farmers of the Great Plains should have pursued sound conservation practices cooperatively. But a combination of ignorance, individualism, inadequate financing, and poor weather brought on the Dust Bowl. On the east coast and throughout the far west, migrant labor characterized large segments of agricultural production, creating an un-Jeffersonian class of landless and rootless farm workers.

To this crisis the New Deal brought largely non-Jeffersonian relief in the form of big government programs. As the nation's leading soil conservationist said in a pamphlet comparing Jefferson's times with his own, the reason was that "the problem[s] became too widespread to be solved by the efforts of individuals alone." The Tennessee Basin got TVA. The Great Plains got shelter belts of trees that ultimately gave way to the demands of gigantic agricultural machinery. The far west got irrigation projects that confirmed rather than retarded migrant labor. Agriculture everywhere became implicated in government "support" programs, presided over by Henry A. Wallace, a man whose life and family background were models—scientific, cultural, and political—of Jeffersonian farming.[23]

But if Jeffersonian nature could not return in fact, the Roosevelt administration was at least prepared to display it as symbol. The Jefferson National Forest was established in southwestern Virginia. The nickel that had displayed Catlin's Indian and buffalo was redesigned to show Jefferson and Monticello. The Library of Congress dedicated its Thomas Jefferson Room, decorated with murals dense with the emblems of a rural society (see plate 22). On the bicentennial of Jefferson's

---

we must first obey her" (46). Jefferson is quoted on pp. 26 and 152. For a Jeffersonian vision comparable to Lilienthal's see the Rockfish Gap Report, PJ.336. From the beginning, TVA was criticized as being a sham democracy, its significant decisions determined not by the people but by the experts (a natural aristocracy?). Despite its early conservation policies, TVA's coal-fired plants and the associated strip mining in the region's hills both polluted and ravaged the landscape.

23. Hugh H. Bennett, "Thomas Jefferson, Soil Conservationist," 14. Henry A. Wallace wrote a measured review essay of Jefferson's *Farm Book* when it was published with accompanying documents in the 1950s. 28 Agric. Hist. 133–38 (1954).

birth the Jefferson Memorial was dedicated, and Congress, resolving that Jefferson "throughout his entire career, remained pre-eminently and above all a farmer," established a National Agricultural Jefferson Bicentenary Committee.

Symbolism was nearly all that remained. Jefferson's "nature" receded even further with a changed meaning of environmentalism. In his time, it may be recalled, environmentalism meant that particular nature—climate, latitude, the entire New World—strongly influenced the customs of a people. The reverse—how far a society might change its environment and how far a changed environment might produce a changed society—was of only minor concern. The techniques available to alter nature were limited, and it was often decades before the effects appeared. Only when society's capacity to change nature increased dramatically and observers such as George Perkins Marsh wrote about the cumulative effects of individual mismanagement did environmentalism take on its modern meaning.

The differences between Jefferson's environmentalism and today's are illustrated in the work of Aldo Leopold and Rachel Carson, leading prophets of the modern movement. Leopold (1886–1948) joined the U.S. Forest Service under Gifford Pinchot but veered from Pinchot's doctrine of conservation as "wise use" of natural resources towards a philosophy that did not center on the human use of nature at all. One branch of it led to the designation of "wilderness areas" in the national forests and parks, units large enough to preserve entire ecological systems. A second branch developed a "land ethic," which asks that we attempt to get outside ourselves and recognize "natural rights" to non-human existence. As the heir of the human-centered Renaissance, Jefferson would have been left uncomprehending by such an idea. Leopold had replaced a vertical chain of being, in which humans were at the top, with a many-dimensioned web of relationships in which each element—and entire ecologies—deserved moral consideration.

The contribution to the environmental movement of Rachel Carson (1896–1964) was an intensely practical morality of nature. Her *Silent Spring* (1962), at once technical and poetic, and perhaps the most influential book on nature in twentieth-century America, warned against the use of nonnatural substances, pesticides and herbicides, for agricultural and other purposes. The Environmental Protection Agency, established in the late 1960s, is her legacy.

Although environmentalists were concerned as much with agriculture as with other problems, their work had little effect on the practices of farming in America. It is instructive, therefore, to note the efforts of an agriculturalist who by temperament or timing was not in the movement but who considered himself a twentieth-century Jefferson. The man was Louis Bromfield of Malabar Farm. Bromfield's activities, his vision, and his freely expressed irritations were gripped by the belief that nature establishes a model by which society should live. Since the farmer and the gardener live "nearer to the basic and eternal laws of nature than any other element of society," it is these children of Jefferson who should be the leaders of society. Railing against the corruption of commerce, industry, and the city, Bromfield's message was not nostalgia for the past in the manner of the Southern Agrarians. He admired Jefferson the progressive, whose ideas he saw in scientific farming and the Tennessee Valley Authority. Like Jefferson, he opposed monocropping (his nemesis was cotton); attacked price supports (as Jefferson almost certainly would have); and practiced organic agriculture (Bromfield called it "natural farming").[24]

Although Bromfield is largely forgotten and American agriculture is still predominantly monocropped, corporate, price-supported, and nonorganic, there are forces at work that might shift agriculture at least slightly in a Jeffersonian direction. These include the continuing American belief in the moral superiority of farm life; a cultural critique, exemplified by the essayist, poet, and Kentucky farmer Wendell Berry (b. 1934); the organic farming movement, which battles an establishment of giant farms, land-grant colleges, government agencies, and chemical companies and which has a loose network of organizations and publications (the books and magazines of Rodale Press are the best-known); and the political pressure against government programs that pay farmers not to plant or that purchase products America cannot use and the rest of the world cannot afford.[25]

If most Americans today cannot be virtuous in a Jeffersonian sense because they do not lead economically independent lives in farming, they can still derive values from nature, either accessible in national parks or designed directly into the cities. This has been the work of urban Jeffersonians such as Frederick Law Olmsted and Lewis Mum-

24. Louis Bromfield, *A Few Brass Tacks* (New York, 1946), 8. Bromfield's principal works on agricultural philosophy and practice are *Pleasant Valley* (New York, 1946); *Malabar Farm* (New York, 1948); and *Out of the Earth* (New York, 1950).

25. A poll in 1986 reported 58 percent of the American public agreeing that "farm life is more honest and moral than life in the rest of the country." The *New York Times* said that this showed "an abiding Jeffersonian belief in the nobility of farmers and farm life." 25 February 1986. The Supreme Court has reflected this sentiment in holding that the Amish, mainly because they possess "many of the virtues of Jefferson's ideal of the 'sturdy yeoman,'" deserve exemption from compulsory education. Wisconsin v. Yoder, 406 U.S. 205, 225 (1972).

For Wendell Berry, see *The Unsettling of America;* and *Collected Poems, 1957–1982* (San Francisco, 1985), esp. "The Mad Farmer Manifesto: The First Amendment". For another modern poet strongly but very differently influenced by Jefferson (and by Lucretius as well), see *The Granite Pail: The Selected Poems of Lorine Niedecker* (San Francisco, 1985).

ford. More responsible than any other single figure for democratizing American nature in an urban age was Olmsted (1822–1903), whose grandly imagined parks are a permanent feature of many American cities. Mumford (b. 1895), the country's most durable critic of urban-technological society, has urged a "garden civilization" on the nation. Though this sounds Jeffersonian—a nation of literary agriculturalists in a landscape of miniature Monticellos—Mumford has something else in mind. His garden civilization, rather than dispensing with cities, humanizes them by integrating nature into them. In contrast to Olmsted's large urban parks, which are separated from, though still within, the city, Mumford asks for many small parks and for green space everywhere.[26]

In the National Environmental Policy Act of 1969 several of these streams of modern environmentalism flowed together, as Congress declared it to be "the continuing policy of the Federal Government . . . to create and maintain conditions under which man and nature can exist in productive harmony." About the same time, a constitutional amendment was introduced that in effect would grant Americans a natural right to unspoiled nature.[27] Another segment of the environmental movement proposed a no-growth economy, an idea heretical to most of America and one towards which Jefferson, who assumed that nature would provide for an increasing American population, would have been at least skeptical. Because it violates the premise of unlimited American nature, Jefferson would also have been hard-pressed to make sense of a Wilderness Act that authorizes setting aside immense tracts of the public domain "where man is a visitor but does not remain." Although in France he objected to the aristocracy's keeping lands uncultivated for their own enjoyment, would he accept a democratic decision to do the same in the United States today? Jefferson would have been equally amazed by a law to protect "endangered species," an idea that challenged a world in which plants and animals were immune from extinction.[28]

26. Two other, exceptionally long-lived Jeffersonians who made cause with nature in designing the human habitat are Frank Lloyd Wright and Benton MacKaye. For the organic architecture of Wright (1869–1959), consider the house Fallingwater and his plan for Broadacre City. Benton MacKaye (1879–1975), who served in the Forest Service under Pinchot, worked for TVA, helped found the Wilderness Society with Aldo Leopold, and originated the Appalachian Trail, was also a planner—not of individual buildings, or parks, or even cities, but, if only in concept, of entire regions.

27. House Joint Res. 1321 (90:2, 1968): "The right of the people to clean air, pure water, freedom from excessive and unnecessary noise, and the natural, scenic, historic, and esthetic qualities of their environment shall not be abridged."

28. The application of the Endangered Species Act in the remarkable case of the snail darter ironically demonstrates the continuing relevance of a portion of Jefferson's wider outlook, that nature knows best. In 1966 the Tennessee Valley Authority authorized the construction of a dam that would create a reservoir of more than sixteen thousand acres. A

If modern agriculture, planning, and environmentalism cannot be secure in following Jefferson, what about other fields in which his "nature" roamed? In biology, to which he was devoted, and geology, towards which he was indifferent if not hostile, new ideas have been perhaps more important than the collection of new information. Jefferson did not lack the equipment and methods available to Darwin or to Gregor Mendel, only a mind receptive to the larger truths of evolution and the smaller ones of heredity. In geology, however, methods and measurements unavailable to him were required to accompany a new conception of time and arrive at a theory of plate tectonics to provide a unified explanation for the history and behavior of the earth. As a confirmed Newtonian in physics, Jefferson accepted absolute time and space, solid particles, and a strict sense of causal relations; a non–Newtonian physics would not have been conceivable. But subatomic particles, wave phenomena, and newly discovered forces have made the Lucretian view of all nature as identical particles far too primitive. Materialism still reigns, but it does not rule. In medicine and psychology Jefferson would presumably be gratified by the increased acceptance of the role of the mind in health and healing. Whether this has been prompted by the development of holistic medicine and a distrust of many standard medical practices or by what amounts to the opposite, increased medical research on the relation between disease and emotions, the body and mind are coming together again, as Jefferson believed they should.

That science and technology have outrun Jefferson's world is no surprise, and he expected it. But has society, too? Jefferson's most well-known legacy to America lies in a political theory with roots in natural law and right. Today, however, these roots are also buried deep and seldom visible. The modern right of national self-determination, for instance, though it can be traced to 1776, is no longer justified under natural law. Perhaps a right to sovereign independence has become so thoroughly accepted, so "natural," that there is little need to explain or justify it in political theory at all. Nature won the day and withdrew

---

number of years later, environmentalists obtained an injunction under the Endangered Species Act to halt construction because a small fish, the snail darter, would suffer extinction when the sole stream in which it thrived no longer flowed free. Since the cost of preserving the snail darter was so high—a nearly completed dam costing tens of millions of dollars—and the economic value of the snail darter unquantifiably low, Congress established a committee empowered to decide in extraordinary circumstances whether a species would live or die. The "God Committee," as it is familiarly known, did what was expected and allowed the floodgates of the dam to be closed without regard to the fate of the fish. A few years later, however, the snail darter was found flourishing in streams not far from the dam. Jefferson's faith in the perfection of nature had enjoyed at least a darting victory.

from the field. The right of revolution also is not explained under the dispensation of nature. From the standpoint of American foreign policy, at least, modern revolutions are viewed as conflicts of ideology and power, not as exercises of natural rights.

On the other hand, important features of American foreign policy have been influenced by Jeffersonian thinking about nature. The acquisition of territory in the Spanish-American War is an example. It was defended by some Jeffersonians who claimed that in principle it did not differ from the purchase of Louisiana and was therefore a valuable addition to the United States. It was attacked by others who pointed out that since the Philippines had nothing to do with the settlement of vacant lands or the pursuit of family farming, Jefferson would have opposed the acquisition.[29]

Whether or not American foreign policy has tended towards a Jeffersonian substance, at crucial times it has adopted a Jeffersonian tone, a distinctively moralizing one that stems ultimately from natural rights thinking. In the twentieth century this pattern has been carried out by Woodrow Wilson and others of his bent.[30] The moralism of Wilson, who was born thirty years after Jefferson died and thirty miles west of Monticello, developed not in connection with Enlightenment doctrines of nature but in the context of Protestant Christianity. If the tone of the two presidents is similar, therefore, the intellectual origins are quite different. Wilson's moralism is more evangelical than Jefferson's and exudes a greater sense of righteousness, both self-righteousness and national righteousness. For six years in the 1950s Secretary of State John Foster Dulles carried on a crusade against communism that echoed Wilson's exaggerated version of the Jeffersonian tradition. In contrast to Jefferson's relativistic "natural friend" and "natural enemy" in international affairs, the division of the world to Dulles was absolute as well as Manichean. From natural right and law has descended a view of inter-

29. See the debate between John B. Stanchfield, a prominent New York attorney to whom the Thomas Jefferson Memorial Association gave over the introductory essay in one of its volumes, and William Jennings Bryan. Stanchfield, "The Memory of Thomas Jefferson," LB.XIV.vi–xii; Bryan, "Jeffersonian Principles," 676–77.

30. In an article published four years before Wilson became president, one scholar asserted that the impact of natural law on American foreign relations was slight after Jefferson left office. Jesse S. Reeves, "The Influence of the Law of Nature upon the International Law in the United States." After Wilson's presidency, one of his former students compared the bases of Wilson's and Jefferson's foreign policy, noting the natural law tradition. John Holladay Latané, "Jefferson's Influence on American Foreign Policy." For a man who knew and wrote so much American history and who was Jeffersonian in so many ways, Wilson had very little to say about Jefferson himself, and not all of that favorable. See Wilson, "A Calendar of Great Americans: An Historical Essay" (1894), in *The Papers of Woodrow Wilson,* ed. Arthur Link et al., vol. VIII (Princeton, 1970), 368–80.

national life that is a lasting strain in, and often a strain on, American foreign policy.[31]

The natural rights legacy of Jefferson in international affairs has survived more positively, however, in the modern recourse to human rights. The Universal Declaration of Human Rights of 1948, a document drafted by the United States and reflecting a Western understanding of humanity, makes no reference to nature. But it conspicuously adopts Jeffersonian language in its opening clause on "equal and inalienable rights" and in an article stating that "all human beings are born free and equal in dignity and rights . . . endowed with reason and conscience." Its expatriation clause is Jeffersonian, too, again with "nature" left out: "Everyone has the right to leave any country, including his own."

A specifically American human rights policy was the creation of Jimmy Carter, who was born the year Woodrow Wilson died and shared with Wilson intense religious convictions which he brought to world politics. This was marked at the Camp David negotiations between Egypt and Israel, where the president seemed to pursue not only a diplomatic but also a religious mission, reminiscent of Enlightenment tolerance if not of deism. Carter's human rights policy itself was stated boldly and institutionalized by the creation of a new position in the Department of State. Its ultimate origins in Jeffersonian natural rights are unmistakable.[32]

31. Hans J. Morgenthau explicitly traces to Jefferson the modern American approach to foreign policy, though without precisely blaming him for its results. He holds that Jefferson pursued a realistic foreign policy, even though it was motivated by a moralistic view of the world. Jefferson was saved by his sense of particularistic nature—America's interests and capabilities—which contended with his sense of universalistic nature. By Wilson's time the uneasy balance between these two understandings of nature had disappeared, and moralism not only was enshrined in rhetoric but had become the actual basis for foreign policy decisions. A nonpolitical, universalizing foreign policy, Morgenthau reasons, cannot succeed in a world of particular states. *In Defense of the National Interest: A Critical Examination of American Foreign Policy* (New York, 1951). Morgenthau's critique of moralism was seconded by George F. Kennan, who added legalism as a defect in American diplomacy. Kennan does not explicitly trace modern troubles to the Founders, but it is not difficult to see Jefferson in the background. *American Diplomacy, 1900–1950* (New York, 1951).

32. The moralism in politics that ties Jefferson, Wilson, and Carter together may stem from their common heritage in the Old South. Whether this is viewed as the cultural-political significance of "honor," the importance of religion in the lives of the three men (very different religions), or the burden of slavery and racism, to which they responded quite differently, a "southern explanation" is possible. It is reinforced when one looks to constitutional law, where two of the most ardent Jeffersonians on the Supreme Court since the Civil War, the elder John Marshall Harlan and Hugo L. Black, were also southern moralists. Although the two justices did not speak explicitly of natural rights, their exceptional fervor regarding constitutional rights is in the Jeffersonian tradition. The work of the modern Supreme Court in its explosion of activity about "fundamental

One of the rights that Jefferson unsuccessfully sought to have incorporated into the Bill of Rights was a provision to restrict monopolies. From the battles against the Bank of the United States, through the enactment of antitrust laws, to the present, Americans have sympathized with his complaint. Whether monopolies are established, regulated, or merely condoned by the government, they deny most of society the natural right to pursue individual happiness. One form of monopoly, however, Jefferson reluctantly justified: patents. Patent law may initially seem an unpromising area in which to examine Jefferson's nature updated, but it is in fact an exceptionally rich one.

Inside the realm of patents, and apart from the social effect of monopolies, lie metaphysical problems. Traditionally, patent law distinguished between the work of man, which can be patented, and the work of nature, which cannot. But what is nature? Jefferson's instinct when inspecting devices submitted for patent was to credit the greater part of an invention to nature and therefore to be cautious about issuing patents. In this spirit a justice on the modern Supreme Court has stated that

> patents cannot issue for the discovery of the phenomena of nature. . . . The qualities of [bacteria], like the heat of the sun, electricity, or the qualities of metals, are part of the storehouse of knowledge of all men. They are manifestations of laws of nature, free to all men and reserved exclusively to none. He who discovers a hitherto unknown phenomenon of nature has no claim to a monopoly of it which the law recognizes.

But a concurring opinion rejected this style of analysis just as Adams or Madison might have done if they could have been so blunt with their friend:

> It only confuses the issue to introduce such terms as "the work of nature" and the "laws of nature," for these are vague and malleable terms infected with too much ambiguity and equivocation. Everything that happens may be deemed "the work of nature," and every patentable composite exemplifies in its properties "the laws of nature."[33]

Jeffersonian thinking was not wrong, merely useless.

This was in the 1940s. In 1980 the Supreme Court dealt with a biological science that not only exceeded Jefferson's knowledge but

---

rights" under Chief Justice Warren is another sign that natural rights by a different name are alive in American political thought.

33. Funk Bros. Co. v. Kalo Co., 333 U.S. 127, 130, 134–35 (1948) (opinion for the Court by Justice Douglas and concurrence by Justice Frankfurter).

violated his premises. Recombinant DNA research had created living organisms that were unknown in nature. From Jefferson's standpoint this was a situation as unimaginable as extinction. But the Supreme Court did not hesitate to cite him in support of its conclusion in favor of the patent, affirming that the law is still able to distinguish the works "of nature" from the works of man that have "created nature."[34]

A legal stand on new forms of life necessarily reflects a scientific stand and implies a moral one, as well. If animals can lose their species integrity and be reduced to their chemical compositions, this is either the triumph of materialism or the final overthrow of a chain of being. But Jefferson was never forced to meet the possible incompatibility of his beliefs. It may be that biotechnology was just what Jefferson was involved with, at least with hybrids. But if patentable gene splicing is applied to agriculture, will farmers lose their final shred of independence because they must deal with companies that control the "rights" to valuable plants and animals?

Viewed this way, the patent cases exemplify a contest, if often cooperation, between two large institutions—government and corporations—whose growth since Jefferson's time has ended the possibility of a relatively natural society, if it ever really existed. These institutions have filled the space that in the eighteenth century was considered to be the domain of nature, and hence of individual freedom. It is the expansion of these new institutions, like feudalism and the church before the Enlightenment, that explains why many of Jefferson's ideas about nature and society are no longer easily understood, despite the attempt of some social philosophers to revive them.

When Jefferson looked to nature, he found not only the physical and social space that permitted autonomous individuals. He also found absolute truths in science and society, as well as principles that determined what was proper in religion, ethics, aesthetics, politics, and economics. Like the two kinds of space, these other lessons of nature have largely passed away. New discoveries in science and insights in the philosophy of knowledge have undermined confidence in the nature that we think we do know. Especially with regard to a faith in the certainty of order, today's assumptions in the natural sciences are largely incompatible with those of the eighteenth century, no matter that the search for an orderly universe goes on. The decline is paralleled in the social sciences. When Jefferson asserted that although the majority was to prevail, it had to be reasonable to be right, he identified reason

---

34. According to the Court, because the new form of life was obviously useful, it promoted the "social and economic benefits envisioned by Jefferson." Diamond v. Chakrabarty, 447 U.S. 303, 315 (1980). For other references to Jefferson see 447 U.S. at 308 and 309.

with nature. Nature therefore supplied a standard of social and political truth. The modern democratic view on this is hardly Jeffersonian, asserting instead the relativistic, if not commercial, doctrine that "the best test of truth is the power of the thought to get itself accepted in the competition of the market."[35]

Modern uncertainty in other realms of value can also be related to a decline in the role of nature. The deism of Jefferson's time, according to which religion and nature were one, was short-lived in America. Religious convictions today spring largely from sources other than nature. In ethics the doctrine of J. S. Mill reigns: "Conformity to nature has no connection whatever with right and wrong."[36] The same is true in the arts. Jefferson found an order in nature and said that it lay at the foundation of beauty. This was as much the case for the universal proportions of Palladian architecture as for the particularistic passion of Ossianic verse. But today, when it is not clear that there is an order in nature at all, the arts may deliberately portray nature as disorderly or, acknowledging it to be disorderly, impose a consciously artificial and rigorous order upon it.

We are thus left largely on our own to establish standards that Jefferson said he found in nature. Whether to rely on ourselves means to look to conscience, to established authority, to utility, or to an understanding of society, nature by itself is insufficient. Perhaps only as a symbol for America, in the nation's expanses, its "stupendous scenes," and the dimmest glow from the sacred fire of an agricultural life does nature remain as important to us as it was to Jefferson. With regard to the rest of the world, it is certain that we are no longer "kindly separated by nature and a wide ocean" from turmoil elsewhere.

Jefferson chose nature over its great adversary, history, believing that an understanding of nature would liberate us from a misguided past. The "light of science," he wrote in his last letter, would illumine a "palpable truth" and free us from the "chains [of] ignorance and superstition."[37] The study of history, he would have said, may be indispensable for knowing what to avoid, but the study of nature is required in order to know what to embrace. If the laws of nature, just as the forces of history, seem to bind us down, for Jefferson there was an important difference between them. Nature binds us only to what is true and

35. Justice Holmes dissenting in Abrams v. United States, 250 U.S. 616, 630 (1919). More recently, "Under the First Amendment there is no such thing as a false idea." Gertz v. Welch, 418 U.S. 323, 339–40 (1974). Justice Brandeis, however, apparently retained the earlier view. Citing Jefferson, he wrote that free speech is "indispensable to the discovery and spread of political truth." Whitney v. California, 274 U.S. 357, 375 (1927) (concurring).

36. John Stuart Mill, "Nature," 62.

37. TJ to Roger C. Weightman, 24 June 1826, KP.729.

good. Since this is so, and because nature's laws are eternal, nature also allows us to look with confidence to the future. This is the faith that Jefferson hoped to leave. In retirement he was "still planting trees, to yield their shade and ornament half a century hence. . . . Too old to plant trees for my own gratification, I shall do it for my posterity."[38]

38. TJ to Andrew Ellicott, 24 June 1812, LB.XIX.185; TJ to Constantine Samuel Rafinesque, 9 October 1822, GB.604.

ACKNOWLEDGMENTS

Two paths have led to this study, one in the Appalachians, the other in the academy. The first is set in Jefferson's western country. It is marked by visits to West Virginia in the 1940s, summers and travels in the Blue Ridge Mountains of North Carolina in the 1950s, and since then as much time in the Shenandoah Valley of Virginia as a life of teaching elsewhere has permitted. The second began in the Swarthmore College Honors Program, with its unmatched freedom to learn. It has continued at Clark College (Atlanta), Princeton University, and Lake Forest College, especially in a course entitled "Nature in American Life."

Among my Appalachian guides have been Pauline Golladay Clem of Paw Paw, West Virginia, Mr. and Mrs. Ira W. Bolick of Blowing Rock, North Carolina, and William A. and Dorothy P. Good of New Market, Virginia. My wider landscape has been enriched by John and Gena Milenković Fine, Miriam S. Harris, Vivian W. Henderson, Sylvia Miller, Roy Mottahedeh, J. Roland Pennock, Joseph J. Senturia, and Reinhart W. Wettmann.

More directly, this study has benefited from critical readings of the entire manuscript by Thomas L. Miller and Arthur Zilversmit and advice from Joyce Appleby, John M. Hoffmann, David Hollinger, Charles D. Louch, William Moskoff, and David H. Porter. I appreciate a fellowship at the Newberry Library. At Lake Forest College I am grateful for a sabbatical year, the assistance of Arthur H. Miller, Jr., and the staff of the college library, and the encouragement of my companions in learning, both faculty and students.

SELECT BIBLIOGRAPHY

BIBLIOGRAPHIES

Huddleston, Eugene L. *Thomas Jefferson: A Reference Guide.* Boston, 1982.
Malone, Dumas. *Jefferson and His Time.* 6 vols. Boston, 1948–81. Bibliography
  at end of each volume.
Peterson, Merrill D. *The Jefferson Image in the American Mind.* New York, 1960.
  Pp. 459–522.
———. *Thomas Jefferson and the New Nation: A Biography.* New York, 1970. Pp.
  1011–47.
Shuffelton, Frank. *Thomas Jefferson: A Comprehensive, Annotated Bibliography of
  Writings about Him (1826–1980).* New York, 1983.

PRIMARY SOURCES

Betts, Edwin M., ed. "The Correspondence between Constantine Samuel
  Rafinesque and Thomas Jefferson." 87 Proc. Am. Phil. Soc. 368–80 (1944).
———. *Thomas Jefferson's Farm Book.* Charlottesville, 1976 (orig. 1953).
———. *Thomas Jefferson's Garden Book, 1766–1824.* Philadelphia, 1944.
Betts, Edwin M., and James Adam Bear, Jr., eds. *The Family Letters of Thomas
  Jefferson.* Columbia, Mo., 1966.
Boyd, Julian P., and Charles T. Cullen, eds. *The Papers of Thomas Jefferson.* 21
  vols. to date. Vols. 1–20 edited by Boyd; vol. 21 edited by Cullen. Princeton,
  1950–.
Cappon, Lester J., ed. *The Adams-Jefferson Letters: The Complete Correspondence
  between Thomas Jefferson and Abigail and John Adams.* 2 vols. Chapel Hill, 1959.
Chinard, Gilbert, ed. *The Commonplace Book of Thomas Jefferson: A Repertory of
  His Ideas on Government.* Baltimore, 1926.
———. *Correspondence of Jefferson and du Pont de Nemours, with an Introduction on
  Jefferson and the Physiocrats.* Baltimore, 1931.
———. *The Letters of Lafayette and Jefferson.* Baltimore, 1929.
———. *The Literary Bible of Thomas Jefferson: His Commonplace Book of Philoso-
  phers and Poets.* Baltimore, 1928.
Davis, Richard Beale, ed. *Correspondence of Thomas Jefferson and Francis Walker
  Gilmer, 1814–1826.* Columbia, S.C., 1946.
Foley, John P., ed. *The Jefferson Cyclopedia: A Comprehensive Collection of the*

Views of Thomas Jefferson, Classified and Arranged in Alphabetical Order under Nine Thousand Titles. New York, 1900.

Ford, Paul Leicester, ed. *The Writings of Thomas Jefferson.* 10 vols. New York, 1892–99.

Ford, Washington Chauncey, ed. *Thomas Jefferson Correspondence, Printed from the Originals in the Collections of William K. Bixby.* Boston, 1916.

Jackson, Donald, ed. *Letters of the Lewis and Clark Expedition with Related Documents, 1783–1854.* 2d ed. 2 vols. Urbana, 1978.

Jefferson, Thomas. "A Memoir on the Discovery of Certain Bones of a Quadruped of the Clawed Kind in the Western Parts of Virginia." 4 Trans. Am. Phil. Soc. 246–60 (1799).

———. *Notes on the State of Virginia.* Edited by William Peden. Chapel Hill, 1954.

Koch, Adrienne, and William Peden, eds. *The Life and Selected Writings of Thomas Jefferson.* New York, 1944.

Lipscomb, Andrew A., and Albert Ellery Bergh, eds. *The Writings of Thomas Jefferson.* Memorial Edition. 20 vols. Washington, D.C., 1904.

Padover, Saul K., ed. *The Complete Jefferson; Containing His Major Writings, Published and Unpublished, Except His Letters.* New York, 1943.

Peterson, Merrill D., ed. *The Portable Thomas Jefferson.* New York, 1975.

———. *Thomas Jefferson: Writings.* New York, 1984.

Sowerby, E. Millicent, comp. *Catalogue of the Library of Thomas Jefferson.* 5 vols. Washington, D.C., 1952–59.

SECONDARY SOURCES

Adair, Douglass Greybill. "The Intellectual Origins of Jeffersonian Democracy: Republicanism, the Class Struggle, and the Virtuous Farmer." Ph.D. diss., Yale University, 1943.

Adams, William Howard. *Jefferson's Monticello.* New York, 1983.

———, ed. *The Eye of Thomas Jefferson.* Washington, D.C., 1976.

———. *Jefferson and the Arts: An Extended View.* Washington, D.C., 1976.

Aldridge, Alfred Owen. *Benjamin Franklin and Nature's God.* Durham, 1967.

Allen, John Logan. *Passage through the Garden: Lewis and Clark and the Image of the American Northwest.* Urbana, 1975.

Appleby, Joyce. *Capitalism and a New Social Order: The Republican Vision of the 1790's.* New York, 1984.

———. "Commercial Farming and the 'Agrarian Myth' in the Early Republic." 68 J. Am. Hist. 833–49 (1982).

———. "What Is Still American in the Political Philosophy of Thomas Jefferson?" 39 Wm. & M. Qtly. 287–309 (1982).

Appleman, Roy E., for the U.S. National Park Service. *Lewis and Clark: Historic Places Associated with Their Transcontinental Exploration (1804–1806).* Washington, D.C., 1975.

Bailyn, Bernard. "Political Experience and Enlightenment Ideas in Eighteenth-Century America." 67 Am. Hist. Rev. 339–51 (1962).

Barker, Ernest. "Natural Law and the American Revolution." In *Traditions of Civility,* 263–355. Cambridge, 1948.

Baumer, Franklin L. *Modern European Thought: Continuity and Change in Ideas, 1600–1950.* New York, 1977.

Bean, W. G. "Anti-Jeffersonianism in the Ante-Bellum South." 12 N.C. Hist. Rev. 103–24 (1935).

Becker, Carl L. *The Declaration of Independence: A Study in the History of Political Ideas*. New York, 1922.

Bender, Thomas. *Toward an Urban Vision: Ideas and Institutions in Nineteenth-Century America*. Lexington, Ky., 1975.

Bennett, Hugh H. "Thomas Jefferson, Soil Conservationist." U.S. Department of Agriculture Soil Conservation Service, Miscellaneous Publication No. 548. April 1944.

Benson, Randolph. *Thomas Jefferson as Social Scientist*. Rutherford, N.J., 1971.

Berman, Eleanor Davidson. *Thomas Jefferson among the Arts: An Essay in Early American Esthetics*. New York, 1947.

Berry, Wendell. *The Unsettling of America: Culture and Agriculture*. San Francisco, 1977.

Bestor, Arthur. "Thomas Jefferson and the Freedom of Books." In Bestor, ed., *Three Presidents and Their Books*, 1–44. Urbana, 1955.

Betts, Edwin M., and Hazlehurst B. Perkins. *Thomas Jefferson's Flower Garden at Monticello*. 2d ed. Charlottesville, 1971.

Biddle, Nicholas. "Eulogium on Thomas Jefferson, delivered before the American Philosophical Society, on the eleventh day of April 1827." In Rosenberger, *Jefferson Reader*, 251–59.

Bidney, David. "The Idea of the Savage in North American Ethnohistory." 15 J. Hist. Ideas 322–27 (1954).

Blum, John Morton. *Woodrow Wilson and the Politics of Morality*. Boston, 1956.

Boorstin, Daniel J. *The Lost World of Thomas Jefferson*. New York, 1948.

———. *The Mysterious Science of the Law*. Cambridge, Mass., 1941.

Boyd, Julian P. "The Megalonyx, the Megatherium, and Thomas Jefferson's Lapse of Memory." 102 Proc. Am. Phil. Soc. 420–35 (1958).

Brodie, Fawn. *Thomas Jefferson, an Intimate History*. New York, 1974.

Brown, Stuart Gerry. "The Mind of Thomas Jefferson." 73 Ethics 79–99 (1963).

Browne, Charles A. "Thomas Jefferson and the Scientific Trends of His Time." 8 Chronica Botanica 363–426 (1944). Reprinted in Cohen, *Jefferson and the Sciences*.

Bryan, William Jennings. "Jeffersonian Principles." 168 No. Am. Rev. 670–78 (1899).

Bryant, William Cullen, ed. *Picturesque America*. 1872.

Bryson, Gladys. *Man and Society: The Scottish Inquiry of the Eighteenth Century*. Princeton, 1945.

Bush, Clive. *The Dream of Reason: American Consciousness and Cultural Achievement from Independence to the Civil War*. New York, 1978.

Caldwell, John Edwards. *A Tour through Part of Virginia, in the Summer of 1808*. Edited by William M. E. Rachal. Richmond, 1951.

Caldwell, Lynton K. "The Jurisprudence of Thomas Jefferson." 18 Ind. Law. J. 193–213 (1943).

Calvino, Italo. *The Baron in the Trees*. New York, 1959.

Campbell, R. H., and Andrew S. Skinner. *The Origins and Nature of the Scottish Enlightenment*. Edinburgh, 1982.

Cardwell, Guy A. "Jefferson Renounced: Natural Rights in the Old South." 58 Yale Rev. 388–407 (1969).

Cassirer, Ernst. *The Philosophy of the Enlightenment*. Boston, 1955.

Chastellux, marquis de. *Travels in North America, 1780, 1781, and 1782*. Edited and translated by Howard C. Rice, Jr. 2 vols. Chapel Hill, 1963.

Chateaubriand, François René. *Atala*. Translated by Irving Putter. Berkeley, 1952 (orig. 1801).

Chinard, Gilbert. "Eighteenth Century Theories on America as a Human Habitat." 91 Proc. Am. Phil. Soc. 27–57 (1947).

———. "Jefferson among the Philosophers." 53 Ethics 255–68 (1943).

———. "Jefferson and the American Philosophical Society." 87 Proc. Am. Phil. Soc. 263–76 (1943).

———. *Thomas Jefferson, the Apostle of Americanism*. Boston, 1933.

Clark, Harry Hayden. "The Influence of Science on American Ideas, from 1775 to 1809." 35 Trans. Wisc. Ac. Science, Arts, & Letters 305–49 (1944).

Clay, Diskin. *Lucretius and Epicurus*. Ithaca, 1984.

Clive, John, and Bernard Bailyn. "England's Cultural Provinces: Scotland and America." 11 Wm. & M. Qtly. 200–213 (1954).

Cohen, I. Bernard, ed. *Thomas Jefferson and the Sciences*. New York, 1980.

Cohen, Lester H. *The Revolutionary Histories: Contemporary Narratives of the American Revolution*. Ithaca, 1980.

Cohen, William. "Thomas Jefferson and the Problem of Slavery." 56 J. Am. Hist. 503–26 (1969).

Colbourn, H. Trevor. *The Lamp of Experience: Whig History and the Intellectual Origins of the American Revolution*. Chapel Hill, 1965.

Commager, Henry Steele. *The Empire of Reason: How Europe Imagined and America Realized the Enlightenment*. New York, 1977.

———. *Jefferson, Nationalism, and the Enlightenment*. New York, 1975.

Commager, Henry Steele, and Elmo Giordanetti. *Was America a Mistake? An Eighteenth-Century Controversy*. Columbia, S.C., 1968.

Conron, John. *The American Landscape: A Critical Anthology of Prose and Poetry*. New York, 1974.

Creese, Walter L. "Jefferson's Charlottesville." In *The Crowning of the American Landscape: Eight Great Spaces and Their Buildings*, 9–42. Princeton, 1985.

Curti, Merle. *Human Nature in American Thought: A History*. Madison, 1980.

Cuthbert, Norma B. "Poplar Forest: Jefferson's Legacy to His Grandson." 6 Huntington Libr. Qtly. 333–56 (1943).

Darwin, Erasmus. *The Temple of Nature; or, The Origin of Society. A Poem, with Philosophical Notes*. 1804.

Davis, David Brion. *The Problem of Slavery in Western Culture*. Ithaca, 1966.

Davis, Richard Beale. *Intellectual Life in Jefferson's Virginia, 1790–1830*. Chapel Hill, 1964.

Diggins, John P. "Slavery, Race, and Equality: Jefferson and the Pathos of the Enlightenment." 28 Am. Qtly. 208–28 (1976).

Dorfman, Joseph. "The Economic Philosophy of Thomas Jefferson." 55 Pol. Sci. Qtly. 98–121 (1940).

Dumbauld, Edward. *Thomas Jefferson, American Tourist*. Norman, Okla., 1946.

———. *Thomas Jefferson and the Law*. Norman, Okla., 1978.

Eisinger, Chester E. "The Influence of Natural Rights and Physiocratic Doctrines on American Agrarian Thought during the Revolutionary Period." 21 Agric. Hist. 12–23 (1947).

Ellis, Richard E. "The Political Economy of Thomas Jefferson." In Weymouth, *Thomas Jefferson*, 81–95.

Eubanks, Seaford Williams. "A Vocabulary Study of Thomas Jefferson's Notes on Virginia." M.A. thesis, University of Missouri, 1940.

Everett, Edward. "Address Delivered at Charlestown, August 1, 1826, in Commemoration of John Adams and Thomas Jefferson." In *Orations and Speeches on Various Occasions*, 122–40. 1836. Reprint. 1972.

Faulkner, Robert K. *The Jurisprudence of John Marshall*. Princeton, 1968.

Foner, Philip S., ed. *We, the Other People: Alternative Declarations of Independence by Labor Groups, Farmers, Women's Rights Advocates, Socialists, and Blacks, 1829–1975*. Urbana, 1976.

Foucault, Michel. *The Order of Things: An Archeology of the Human Sciences*. New York, 1970.

Ganter, Herbert L. "William Small, Jefferson's Beloved Teacher." 4 Wm. & M. Qtly. 505–11 (1947).

Gay, Peter. *The Enlightenment: An Interpretation*. 2 vols. New York, 1966–69.

———, ed. *The Enlightenment: A Comprehensive Anthology*. New York, 1973.

George, Henry, Jr. "Jefferson and the Land Question." In Lipscomb and Bergh, *Writings of Thomas Jefferson*, 16: i–xiv.

Gerbi, Antonello. *The Dispute of the New World: The History of a Polemic, 1750–1900*. Translated by Jeremy Moyle. Pittsburgh, 1973.

Gillispie, Charles Coulston. *The Edge of Objectivity: An Essay in the History of Scientific Ideas*. Princeton, 1960.

———. *Genesis and Geology, a Study in the Relations of Scientific Thought, Natural Theology, and Social Opinion in Great Britain, 1790–1850*. Cambridge, Mass., 1951.

Goetzmann, William. "Savage Enough to Prefer Woods: The Cosmopolite and the West." In Weymouth, *Thomas Jefferson*, 107–40.

Grampp, William D. "A Re-examination of Jeffersonian Economics." 12 Sthn. Ec. J. 263–82 (1946). Reprinted in Peterson, *Thomas Jefferson: A Profile*, 135–63.

Greene, John C. "The American Debate on the Negro's Place in Nature, 1780–1815." 15 J. Hist. Ideas 384–96 (1964).

———. *American Science in the Age of Jefferson*. Ames, Iowa, 1984.

———. *The Death of Adam: Evolution and Its Impact on Western Thought*. Ames, Iowa, 1959.

———. "Objectives and Methods in Intellectual History." 44 Miss. Valley Hist. Rev. 58–74 (1957).

Griswold, A. Whitney. *Farming and Democracy*. New Haven, 1948.

Hall, Courtney R. "Jefferson on the Medical Theory and Practice of His Day." 31 Bull. Hist. Med. 235–45 (1957).

Hamowy, Ronald. "Jefferson and the Scottish Enlightenment: A Critique of Garry Wills's *Inventing America: Jefferson's Declaration of Independence*." 36 Wm. & M. Qtly. 503–23 (1979).

Hindle, Brooke. *The Pursuit of Science in Revolutionary America, 1735–1789*. Chapel Hill, 1956.

Huth, Hans. *Nature and the American: Three Centuries of Changing Attitudes*. Lincoln, 1957.

Jackson, Donald. *Thomas Jefferson and the Stony Mountains: Exploring the West from Monticello*. Urbana, 1980.

Jones, Howard Mumford. *The Pursuit of Happiness*. Cambridge, Mass., 1953.

Jordan, Winthrop D. *White over Black: American Attitudes toward the Negro, 1550–1812*. Chapel Hill, 1968.

Kallen, Horace. "The Arts and Thomas Jefferson." 53 Ethics 269–83 (1943).
Klein, Jacob. "On the Nature of Nature." 3 Indep. J. Phil. 101–9 (1979).
Koch, Adrienne. *Jefferson and Madison: The Great Collaboration*. New York, 1950.
———. *The Philosophy of Thomas Jefferson*. New York, 1943.
———. *Power, Morals, and the Founding Fathers: Essays in the Interpretation of the American Enlightenment*. Ithaca, 1961.
———, ed. *The American Enlightenment*. New York, 1965.
Latané, John Holladay. "Jefferson's Influence on American Foreign Policy." 17 Alumni Bull. Univ. Va. 245–69 (1924).
Lehmann, Karl. *Thomas Jefferson: American Humanist*. New York, 1947.
Leiss, William. *The Domination of Nature*. New York, 1972.
Levy, Leonard. *Jefferson and Civil Liberties: The Darker Side*. Cambridge, Mass., 1963.
Lewis, C. S. *Studies in Words*. 2d ed. Cambridge, 1967.
Lovejoy, Arthur O. *The Great Chain of Being: A Study in the History of an Idea*. Cambridge, Mass., 1936.
———. " 'Nature' as Aesthetic Norm." In *Essays in the History of Ideas*, 69–77. Baltimore, 1948.
———. "Some Meanings of Nature." In *A Documentary History of Primitivism and Related Ideas*, edited by Lovejoy et al., 447–56. Baltimore, 1935.
Lucretius. *De Rerum Natura*. Translated by Palmer Bovie under the title *Lucretius: On the Nature of Things*. New York, 1974.
McCoy, Drew R. *The Elusive Republic: Political Economy in Jeffersonian America*. Chapel Hill, 1980.
Malone, Dumas. *Jefferson and His Time*. 6 vols. Boston, 1948–81.
Marsh, George Perkins. *Man and Nature; or, Physical Geography as Modified by Human Action*. Edited by David Lowenthal. Cambridge, Mass., 1965.
Martin, Edwin T. *Thomas Jefferson: Scientist*. New York, 1952.
Marx, Leo. *The Machine in the Garden: Technology and the Pastoral Idea in America*. New York, 1964.
Matthews, Richard K. *The Radical Politics of Thomas Jefferson*. Lawrence, Kans., 1984.
May, Henry F. *The Enlightenment in America*. New York, 1976.
Meek, Ronald L. *Social Science and the Ignoble Savage*. Cambridge, 1976.
Meyer, Donald H. *Democratic Enlightenment*. New York. 1976.
Mill, John Stuart. "Nature." In *Three Essays on Religion*, 3–65. New York, 1884 (orig. 1873).
Miller, August C., Jr. "Jefferson as Agriculturist." 16 Agric. Hist. 65–78 (1942).
Miller, John Chester. *The Wolf by the Ears: Thomas Jefferson and Slavery*. New York, 1977.
Miller, Perry, ed. *The Transcendentalists: An Anthology*. Cambridge, Mass., 1950.
Miller, Ralph N. "American Nationalism as a Theory of Nature." 12 Wm. & M. Qtly. 74–95 (1955).
Mitchell, Lee Clark. *Witnesses to a Vanishing America: The Nineteenth Century Response*. Princeton, 1981.
Mitchill, Samuel L. *A Discourse on the Character and Services of Thomas Jefferson, more especially as a promoter of Natural and Physical Science, delivered before the New-York Lyceum of Natural History, October 11, 1826*. New York, 1826.

Mumford, Lewis. "The Universalism of Thomas Jefferson." In *The South in American Architecture,* 43–78. New York, 1941.

Nash, Roderick. *Wilderness and the American Mind.* New Haven, 1967.

———, ed. *The American Environment: Readings in the History of Conservation.* Reading, Mass., 1968.

Nichols, Frederick D., and James A. Bear, Jr. *Monticello.* Monticello, Va., 1967.

Nichols, Frederick D., and Ralph E. Griswold. *Thomas Jefferson, Landscape Architect.* Charlottesville, 1978.

Novak, Barbara. *Nature and Culture: American Landscape and Painting, 1825–1875.* New York, 1980.

Pattison, Willlam D. *Beginnings of the American Rectangular Land Survey System, 1784–1800.* Chicago, 1957.

Peterson, Merrill D. *The Jefferson Image in the American Mind.* New York, 1960.

———. "Jefferson, The West and the Enlightenment Vision." 70 Wisc. Mag. Hist. 270–80 (1987).

———. *John Adams and Thomas Jefferson: A Revolutionary Dialogue.* Athens, Ga., 1976.

———. *Thomas Jefferson and the New Nation: A Biography.* New York, 1970.

———. "Thomas Jefferson's *Notes on the State of Virginia.*" 7 Studies in Eighteenth-Century Culture 49–72 (1978).

———, ed. *Thomas Jefferson: A Profile.* 1967.

———. *Thomas Jefferson: A Reference Biography.* New York, 1986.

Pole, J. R. "Enlightenment and the Politics of American Nature." In *The Enlightenment in National Context,* edited by Roy Porter and Mikuláš Teich, 192–214. Cambridge, 1981.

Porter, Charlotte M. *The Eagle's Nest: Natural History and American Ideas, 1812–1842.* University, Ala., 1986.

Potter, David M. *People of Plenty: Economic Abundance and the American Character.* Chicago, 1954.

Reeds, Chester A. *The Natural Bridge of Virginia and Its Environs.* New York, 1927.

Reeves, Jesse S. "The Influence of the Law of Nature upon International Law in the United States." 3 Am. J. Internat. Law 547–61 (1909).

Rice, Howard C., Jr. "Jefferson's Gift of Fossils to the Museum of Natural History in Paris." 95 Proc. Am. Phil. Soc. 597–627 (1951).

Rolston, Holmes, III. "Can and Ought We to Follow Nature," 1 Environmental Ethics 7–28 (1979).

Rosenberger, Francis Coleman, ed. *Jefferson Reader.* New York, 1953.

Ross, Michael. "Homogeneity and Heterogeneity in Jefferson and Madison." 13 Internat. Rev. Hist. & Pol. Sci. 47–50 (1976).

Scott, William B. *In Pursuit of Happiness: American Conceptions of Property from the Seventeenth to the Twentieth Century.* Bloomington, Ind., 1977.

Sears, Louis Martin. "Jefferson and the Laws of Nations." 13 Am. Pol. Sci. Rev. 379–99 (1919).

A Selection of Eulogies Pronounced in the Several States, in Honor of John Adams and Thomas Jefferson. 1826.

Sellers, Charles Coleman. *Mr. Peale's Museum: Charles Willson Peale and the First Popular Museum of Natural History and Art.* New York, 1980.

Sheehan, Bernard W. *Seeds of Extinction: Jeffersonian Philanthropy and the American Indian.* Chapel Hill, 1973.

Smith, Frank E. *The Politics of Conservation*. New York, 1966.

Smith, Henry Nash. *Virgin Land: The American West as Symbol and Myth.* Cambridge, Mass., 1950.

Smith, Samuel Harrison. *Memoirs of the Life, Character, and Writings of Thomas Jefferson, delivered before the Columbian Institute of Washington.* 1827.

Spurlin, Paul Merrill. *The French Enlightenment in America: Essays on the Times of the Founding Fathers.* Athens, Ga., 1984.

Staum, Martin S. *Cabanis: Enlightenment and Medical Philosophy in the French Revolution.* Princeton, 1980.

Stearns, Raymond Phineas. *Science in the British Colonies of America.* Urbana, 1970.

Stuart, Reginald C. *The Half-way Pacifist: Thomas Jefferson's View of War.* Toronto, 1978.

Tate, Thad W. "The Social Contract in America, 1774–1787: Revolutionary Theory as a Conservative Instrument." 22 Wm. & M. Qtly. 375–91 (1965).

Tompkins, Edmund P., and J. Lee Davis. *The Natural Bridge and Its Historical Surroundings.* Natural Bridge, Va., 1939.

Tucker, David. "Jefferson's *Notes on the State of Virginia.*" Ph.D. diss., Claremont Graduate School, 1981.

Twelve Southerners. *I'll Take My Stand: The South and the Agrarian Tradition.* New York, 1930.

Udall, Stewart L. *The Quiet Crisis.* New York, 1963.

Von Eckardt, Ursula M. *The Pursuit of Happiness in the Democratic Creed: An Analysis of Political Ethics.* New York, 1959.

Ward, John William. *Andrew Jackson, Symbol for an Age.* New York, 1953.

Warren, Robert Penn. *Brother to Dragons: A Tale in Verse and Voices.* New York, 1953.

Weyant, Robert G. "Helvétius and Jefferson: Studies in Human Nature and Government in the Eighteenth Century." 9 J. Hist. Behav. Sci. 29–41 (1973).

Weymouth, Lally, ed. *Thomas Jefferson: The Man, His World, His Influence.* New York, 1973.

White, Morton. *The Philosophy of the American Revolution.* New York, 1978.

Willey, Basil. *The Eighteenth-Century Background: Studies on the Idea of Nature in the Thought of the Period.* New York, 1940.

Williams, Raymond. *Keywords: A Vocabulary of Culture and Society.* New York, 1976.

Wills, Garry. *Inventing America: Jefferson's Declaration of Independence.* Garden City, N.Y., 1978.

Wiltse, Charles M. "Thomas Jefferson on the Law of Nations." 29 Am. J. Internat. Law 66–81 (1935).

Wirt, William. *The Letters of the British Spy.* Chapel Hill, 1970 (orig. 1803).

Wood, Gordon S. *The Creation of the American Republic, 1776–1787.* Chapel Hill, 1969.

INDEX